PREHISTORIC JOURNEYS

PREHISTORIC JOURNEYS

edited by

Vicki Cummings and Robert Johnston

OXBOW BOOKS

First published in the United Kingdom in 2007. Reprinted in 2021 by
OXBOW BOOKS
The Old Music Hall, 106–108 Cowley Road, Oxford OX4 1JE

and in the United States by
OXBOW BOOKS
1950 Lawrence Road, Havertown, PA 19083

Paperback Edition: ISBN 978-1-84217-250-6

A CIP record for this book is available from the British Library

For a complete list of Oxbow titles, please contact:

UNITED KINGDOM
Oxbow Books
Telephone (01865) 241249, Fax (01865) 794449
Email: oxbow@oxbowbooks.com
www.oxbowbooks.com

UNITED STATES OF AMERICA
Oxbow Books
Telephone (610) 853 9131, Fax (610) 853 9146
Email: queries@casemateacademic.com
www.casemateacademic.com/oxbow

Oxbow Books is part of the Casemate Group

Cover design by: Anna Badcock and Robert Johnston

Contents

List of contibutors

ADRIAN CHADWICK
Archaeological Services WYAS
PO Box 30
Nepshaw Lane South
Morley
Leeds
LS27 0UG

VICKI CUMMINGS
School of Natural Resources
University of Central Lancashire
Preston
PR1 2HE

DUNCAN GARROW
Institute of Archaeology
34–36 Beaumont Street
Oxford
OX1 2PG

ROBERT JOHNSTON
Department of Archaeology
University of Sheffield
West Street
Sheffield
S10 2TN

THOMAS KADOR
UCD School of Archaeology
Newman Building
University College Dublin
Belfield,
Dublin 4
Ireland

GORDON NOBLE
Department of Archaeology
University of Glasgow
The Gregory Building
Lilybank Gardens
Glasgow
G12 8QQ

ULLA ODGAARD
National Museum of Denmark
Frederiksholms Kanal 12
DK-1220 København K
Denmark

BRONWEN PRICE
School of History and Archaeology
Cardiff University
Colum Drive
Cardiff
CF10 3EU

FELIX RIEDE
Department of Archaeology
University of Cambridge
Downing Street
Cambridge
CB2 3QY

JOHN ROBERTS
Department of Archaeology
University of Cambridge
Downing Street
Cambridge
CB2 3QY

Gary Robinson
Department of History, Welsh History and Archaeology
University of Wales, Bangor
Bangor
Gwynedd
LL57 2DG

Peter Robinson
16 Larne Avenue
Stretford
Manchester
M32 8DT

Eileen Wilkes
Archaeology and Historic Environment Group
Bournemouth University
Talbot Campus
Poole
Dorset
BH12 5BB

1 Leaving Place: an introduction to prehistoric journeys

Vicki Cummings and Robert Johnston

> 'The act of travelling from one place to another: an excursion (exploration, pilgrimage, quest, ramble, tour, trip, voyage etc.) or to travel.'

The experience of a place begins after a journey; travel is the 'means to an end'. This perspective has long dominated archaeological approaches to the journeys that people undertook during prehistory. Yet, leaving and arriving at places marks the beginning and end of a journey, and the time that passes in between departure and arrival is frequently no less important or memorable than experiences at the destination. Indeed, journeys may not have a certain destination, or the expected end may never be reached. These premises form the basis for this collection of papers, with each of the contributors considering the implications and challenges of studying what it meant to be 'on the move' at different times in prehistory.

Journeys in prehistoric archaeology

Ideas of journeys and travel are integral to many traditions of interpreting the prehistoric archaeological record. The narratives that we have long accepted, challenged or which we expect to develop currency in the future rely on journeys and travel as mechanisms for change, the transformation of identity, and the enculturation of the landscape. Despite the accepted importance of travel, very few archaeologists have dealt explicitly with journeys as events or places in their own right, nor are there many attempts to consider the conceptual issues attendant to an archaeology of journeys.

Given this relative lack of theorising and centring of journeys in archaeological narratives, it is ironic that journeys were frequently the frame through which the majority of early archaeological fieldwork was conducted. Sir Richard Colt Hoare, Thomas Pennant and William Stukeley, for example, all took to horseback and visited, described and mapped antiquities in the countryside throughout Britain and Ireland (Piggott 1950). Their 'methods' can be paralleled in the travels of men and women from western Europe throughout the classical world, the Middle East, Africa and the Americas (e.g. Layard's investigation of the Assyrian civilisation; the 'western' discovery of Great Zimbabwe and Stephens and Catherwood in central America: cf. Bahn 1996). The journey may have figured as a narrative device to structure their descriptions, but, with few exceptions, the writings of these early explorers, antiquarians and archaeologists were concerned with the stopping off points on their travels and their destinations. Perhaps this was not dissimilar to the accounts written by the elite of eighteenth century Europe portraying their experiences on the Grand Tour: '[s]kimming across the surface of the country, they would alight, here and there, to admire the view' (Ingold 2004, 322).

The primacy of the destination remained into archaeology's age of synthesis and grand narrative. The processes of migration and invasion that have come to dominate our caricatures of culture-historical archaeology were fundamentally about movements of peoples from one region to another, and journeys to new homelands (e.g. Piggott 1954). A perspective that is at odds with many realities of the diaspora experience, where disjointedness and feelings of being out-of-place may be more prevalent than any sense of arrival (Bender 2001; Clifford 1997). European prehistory as written in the 1930s, 40s and 50s did not conceive of travel solely in terms of mass migration or invasion. Cultural and technological diffusion was equally reliant on the movement of individuals, whether as traders, itinerant craftsmen or ritual specialists, with the routes that people were supposed to have followed across land and sea being mapped out with surprising assuredness (e.g. Fox 1932; Gresham and Irvine 1963).

The ultimate disembodiment of journeys was to be found, since the 1960s, in processual and ecological perspectives, where universal patterns of mobility were devised and travel remained destination and task oriented. This work also signalled a change in scale, with greater focus on movement around sites (Rowley-Conwy 1983) or the journeys undertaken within quite tightly defined settlement systems (Binford 1980). Ironically, one of the key elements of processualism was the ethnoarchaeological study of living populations who frequently included mobile hunter-gatherers for whom being on-the-move was a key part of their lives (e.g. Lee and Devore 1968).

A paradigm derived from the natural sciences may have contributed to a reduction in the overall awareness of prehistorians towards the social and cultural aspects of mobility and travel. But scientific analyses, more broadly, began to make a significant contribution to our understanding of the distances over which objects and people travelled. The petrological analysis of polished stone axes in Britain, for instance, demonstrated that many of these artefacts had been deposited considerable distances, sometimes hundreds of miles, from their source (Clough and Cummins 1979; cf. Rohl and Needham 1998). Yet, a simple equivalence between the journeys of objects and specific individuals was rarely accepted, and it was instead necessary to devise complex models of exchange and technological diffusion and innovation to explain the movement of objects, styles and ideas from one region to another.

This sense of rootedness is being lost as the direct analysis of human bone over recent years has shown, albeit still equivocally, that individuals in prehistory did travel considerable distances during their lives (e.g. Fitzpatrick 2002). This return to an acceptance that individuals and human populations may have considered various scales of mobility and travel to be a part of their way of life, rather than an exceptional experience, has also found support in more theoretical work (e.g. Kristiansen and Larsson 2006; Whittle 1997). The change in emphasis from roots to routes is complemented by phenomenological approaches to landscape, which have found their clearest expression in British and northern European archaeology. The broader landscape setting of sites is now considered a fundamental part of the experience and engagement with places (Cummings and Whittle 2004), but so is the act of moving through the landscape (e.g. Edmonds 1999; Ingold 2000, 219; Tilley 1994, 29–30). Journeys, however they are defined, have a part to play in structuring the landscape and people's experiences of places.

Journeys and landscape archaeology

We are of the opinion, and this seems to be implicit in the approaches taken by each of the contributors, that it is not problematic that the term 'journey' can have a diffuse meaning and be employed in different ways dependent on context: from long distance and exceptional travel, to routine and familiar trips. Indeed, if we are to avoid the trap of mapping a modern experience of travel onto the past, then it is imperative that journeys are defined in terms of their historical context.

Yet, this approach is in itself not an argument for the concept of journeys having a role in social analysis, nor does it necessarily preclude the possibility that there are universal qualities to how and why people undertake journeys. A stronger case can be made if we consider that journeying involves people in an engagement with the landscape, where landscape is defined as the culturally mediated world that individuals experience in and beyond places. Indeed, many of the recent attempts to theorise landscape within archaeology have explicitly discussed how movement is an essential element in the way the world is experienced and given meaning (e.g. Bender 2001; Chadwick 2004; Tilley 1994).

We should, then, position our 'prehistory of journeys' within this, albeit broad, constituency of contemporary landscape archaeology. Journeys are, therefore, a means of describing the ways in which people travel, explore, colonise, socialise, determine and affirm ownership, communicate, map and name, leave and arrive at places, and so forth. These are socially meaningful and historically constituted practices that respond to and transform their cultural context. They are embodied experiences, real and mythical, that constitute a person's identity and condition their relationships with other people.

In isolation, such statements are trite and somewhat general, and so it is mainly in the specificity of accounts about particular journeys that we get a sense of how journeying demands an open and dynamic definition, contingent upon society, history and culture. Grounded in this way, an archaeology of journeys that is situated within landscape archaeology is not tied to a rigid agenda nor, importantly, is it free from debate. The contributions to this volume provide just such a variety of interpretative case studies, and in the summary which follows we have attempted to draw out issues of consensus and debate.

Themes in the prehistory of journeys

The papers are organised into groups according to their perspectives on single or related issues: colonisation and journeys into unfamiliar landscapes, artefacts and the feasibility of reconstructing journeys archaeologically, monuments as the focus for and embodiment of journeys, ritual journeys and the formation of landscapes (imagined and real), interpreting the relationship between ceremonial sites and trackways, and the ways in which travel across sea and land is structured by the material and animal world. This thematic order corresponds with a rough (given the geographical scope of the papers, including contributions on Greenland and Egypt) chronological sequence, starting in the late Palaeolithic and working through to the Iron Age and Romano-British period.

Journeys into unfamiliar landscapes

Felix Riede begins by looking at the issue of journeying into new, unknown landscapes in his consideration of the late Palaeolithic settlement of southern Scandinavia. He argues that we have no ethnographic parallels we can draw on which may inform our understanding of this process, and that our present-day experiences of travel are also of limited value. Instead, we are left with only a few archaeological remains from the period. Riede suggests that by examining three key types of data – the tools used, materials cached and settlement patterns – we can actually begin to get at the types of journeys that people took, on occasions into uncharted landscapes. Interestingly, he argues that the types of journeys taken by early hunter-gatherer groups influenced the material culture they used. Furthermore, non-pedestrian transport (i.e. boats) would have been absolutely key in enabling successful inroads into unsettled areas. Riede evokes the epic qualities of the journeys that formed these first encounters with the landscapes of southern Scandinavia; journeys that may have become creation myths for later generations.

Ulla Odgaard's contribution considers another extreme environment, this time in western Greenland. She draws together archaeological, historical and ethnographic evidence to discuss the now-abandoned region of Angujaartorfiup Nunaa, which is best understood as 'a landscape of journeys'. Her focus is the Thule culture, a group of hunter-gatherers who occupied Greenland from around AD 1200. In the summer months, family groups headed inland in order to hunt caribou. The routes that they followed were long-established networks of places linked together by cairns and other, more subtle, waymarkers. The latter enabled Odgaard and her colleagues to retrace routes and relocate a spectrum of places. At one level, the landscapes they surveyed 'made sense' because they were able to follow the routes that Thule hunters had taken on their travels inland. That empathy was later tempered by finding features and places with which they were not familiar and whose meaning could not be understood.

There is a obvious link between travel and the exploration or colonisation of unfamiliar landscapes. For Riede, unfamiliarity with a landscape was a challenge that people had to overcome during the late Palaeolithic, and it is a barrier to archaeologists understanding what journeys meant during this period. For Odgaard, the journeys which had at first seemed familiar and predictable, became more foreign when particular waymarkers no longer made sense. In both cases, the authors consider the value of drawing on comparative, ethnographic evidence. Even if analogy currently has a rather uneasy place within archaeological discourse, it is clear that it represents a rich source of inspiration for how people travel and the cultural role of journeys (Coleman and Eade 2004; Helms 1988). Since it is clear that there are genuine problems in identifying and interpreting journeys archaeologically (see below), ethnographic parallels offer a way of responding to these problems, and making the unfamiliar seem more familiar.

Journeys and material culture

Thomas Kador's contribution continues the theme of hunter-gatherer landscapes, and returns to the issue of how stone artefacts might provide a means of reconstructing the scales and meanings of journeys. In a series of case studies from Mesolithic Ireland he examines the contexts of stone tools found both considerable distances from and very close to the raw material sources from which they derived, and suggests some of the ways in which these objects could have made the journeys from source to deposition. Kador emphasises the physical engagement of people with the world while making journeys, which he sees as contrasting with approaches that focus on the places at either end of a journey. The resulting interpretations demonstrate the varied geographic scales at which journeys might serve to imbue objects with cultural significance.

In the first of a series of papers on the Neolithic, Duncan Garrow carries on from Thomas Kador by again considering the role of material culture in reconstructing journeys. Yet for Garrow, it is the places at either end of the journey that should form the focus for interpretation as these are where archaeological signatures were formed. He derives this conclusion from a study of two early Neolithic sites situated 17km apart in south-eastern England, and comprising very similar assemblages of material culture – all of it recovered from clusters of small pits. It is reasonable to suppose, Garrow argues, that the similarities in the ways these places were occupied resulted from the fact that the same people used and travelled between them. Inspired by recent work in experiential archaeology, Garrow walked between the sites to see if he could begin to get at what such a journey might have meant during the Neolithic. The experience was not fulfilling: 'paths have been lost from memory, grown over, ploughed away'. Instead, he returned to the assemblages of pottery from the pits, where he was able to recognise a series of temporally discrete occupations. The time between clusters of pits being dug was the duration that people spent away from the site: the journey.

One of the issues raised by these two papers, and within the volume as a whole, is whether or not it is realistic to claim that we can identify past journeys in the archaeological record. Thomas Kador suggests that once we know the raw material source from which artefacts originated, then we can begin to speculate on the journeys that those objects may have taken to the location of their final deposition. Yet, the journeys that Kador reconstructs are embodied in the cultural meanings of the artefacts, rather than being clearly defined routeways. In attempting to find the physical expression of journeys in the landscape, Duncan Garrow is able to challenge this more literal interpretation of the archaeological record of a journey. While we may be left with the archaeology 'at either end', we can never know the actual journeys taken. Even if we could find the routes taken, the landscape has changed so much since prehistory, along with the cultural conditions of knowledge, that we would struggle to find meaning in what we saw.

Travelling to monuments

Vicki Cummings considers a different set of material evidence from the early Neolithic: the chambered tombs of western Britain. Previous approaches to these monuments have primarily considered the landscape settings of the sites. However, she suggests that approaches to these monuments may have been of equal significance. She argues that although journeying was a part of everyday Neolithic life, some journeys took on a special significance because they were associated with ritualised activity. She considers the symbolic importance of journeys associated with the construction and use of megalithic architecture and suggests that megaliths embody a set of different journeys within their fabric. Furthermore, objects that had themselves taken long journeys (either physically or transformatively) were being deliberately deposited in megaliths. In this way, chambered tombs may have been understood as the embodiment of a number of places and journeys. The actual megalith, and the view from it, then, may only have been half the story: the journeys involved in creating it being as important to the people involved.

Gordon Noble's paper also considers the relationship between journeys and Neolithic monuments. The subjects of his paper are the later Neolithic monument complexes of Scotland, which are defined by the exceptional numbers of monuments found in close proximity with one another and the presence of 'exotic' architectural forms such as causewayed enclosures, henges and cursuses. Not only are the monuments themselves exotic, but other forms of material culture found in these areas are also rather special, notably including stone axes and rock art. He supports the case made for similar complexes in other regions of Britain that the complexes are located on major routeways, particularly at points between 'regions' and close to routes which would enable people to avoid treacherous or extended journeys. Rather than placing exchange and trade at the forefront of his explanation for this spatial juxtaposition of monuments and paths, as earlier commentators have done, he argues that the complexes emerge as the result of interaction between communities, sometimes over quite wide geographical areas. Since these complexes are at key points along routeways, people may have used these places for generations, before eventually marking them with architectural forms.

These two papers raise issues regarding the motivations for people undertaking journeys. The papers in the volume as a whole suggest that there may have been a range of reasons why people undertook journeys. None of the authors consider journeying to be something that simply needs to be done, a means to an end. Instead, the reason to move is considered a key element of social and cultural identity. Cummings discusses the idea of journeying being a part of the engagement with ritualised landscapes, while Noble suggests there was a dialectic between routeways, routine and ritualised places. Whether journeys took people into new uncharted landscapes, or across familiar occupied waters, journeying was clearly not just a part of the search for food. There were many social and spiritual reasons for people to move about. Motivations for journeying may have been explicit – the desire to undergo life-changing circumstances – or implicit – an unexpressed desire to be on the move. Nevertheless, it is clear that the motivations for people to move were varied in both space and time and that the motivations for journey almost certainly differed from society to society, as well as within society.

Distant and local

The next paper moves further afield by considering journeying in an ancient Egyptian context, and is the first of three contributions to explore the archaeology of formalised, sacred journeys. Peter Robinson uses theories of cognitive mapping to re-evaluate the origin and role of Middle Kingdom coffin texts. The texts served as guides, located inside the coffins of the deceased, to navigate along prescribed routes within the landscape of the afterlife. These 'cognitive maps' were not directly experienced worlds, but their form still drew upon elements of people's experiences of their landscape, including familiar geographic forms: paths, regions and nodal points. It is the journeys that living people took to far off lands, and the stories that they brought back with them, that informed the imagined landscapes of myth and legend.

Bronwen Price's paper returns us to the British Isles but remains with the theme of sacred journeys. In her consideration of the stone axe quarry and associated monumental structures at Graig Lwyd in north Wales, Price argues that axes were the outcome of a series of socially transformative journeys taken to the stone source rather than being the primary motivation for people's travel to the site. She suggests that Graig Lwyd began as a significant node in the landscape, tied to local mythology, a dangerous and mythical place at the end of the earth. Over time, people began making journeys to the site, perhaps as part of initiation ceremonies or as acts of pilgrimage. Axes were produced at the culmination of these journeys, turning the event into an enduring memory for the community. Over time, the routes taken to Graig Lwyd became formalised as monuments were constructed and thresholds within the landscape were controlled. Price finds inspiration for her interpretation in ethnographies of pilgrimage and initiation rites, where formalised and sacred journeys engender liminal spaces within which transformations of social identity are possible.

John Roberts' contribution deals with the same area of north Wales as Price, yet he identifies a number of tensions between 'local' and 'distant' in accounts of the Neolithic and Bronze Age trackways leading to the quarry and monuments at Graig Lwyd. These accounts, he argues, emphasise a linear, destination-oriented form of travel at the expense of other types of movement around the landscape. This sense of travelling through landscapes contributes to areas such as Graig Lywd being perceived as distant and marginal to everyday life. This too is anachronistic, as it ignores the evidence for people clearing these landscapes of trees and using the land for pasture. Roberts presents an alternative model for the development of the landscape around Graig Lwyd, in which he pays closer attention to the evidence for how the landscape was occupied and on the changing relationship between people and land. The monuments, which feature so prominently in accounts of prehistoric trackways, do not, he argues, merely conform to a linear distribution. They, instead, form clusters analogous to separate grazing areas or 'stints'. In our obsession with moving through these landscapes, we have forgotten that most prehistoric journeys were about moving around.

Robinson, Price and Roberts each demonstrate, though in different ways, how journeys were fundamentally about defining and transforming social identity. The ways in which people moved through the landscape, the reasons for travel, and the transformative effect of particular journeys all served to condition personhood and wider corporate identities. While this may be manifest through formal events, such as rites of passage, journeys were also personal experiences that conditioned an individual's perception of 'here' and 'elsewhere' (Minh-ha 1994; Slavin 2003). Crucially, the ways in which archaeologists choose to characterise journeys is contingent upon the intellectual frameworks within which they work and their perceptions of how and why people travelled.

Landscapes and seascapes

Various contributors to the volume discuss the role that water-borne journeys play in structuring people's perception of the landscape, and in the paper by Gary Robinson this is taken at its most literal as he incorporates the results of fieldwork completed from the perspective of the sea. With a case study set in the Isles of Scilly, Robinson examines the location of the late Neolithic entrance graves. He argues that, just like landscape, a seascape is filled with a whole series of named places, mythologies, biographies and patterns of movement. In the case of Scilly, there is considerable evidence for people moving around by sea in prehistory, and Robinson suggests that the entrance graves were located in order to be seen from key points on the sea, specifically defining the means of safe passage into and between natural harbours. Tombs were considered to be meaningful landmarks because of their ancestral associations and the potential this symbolism may have played in guiding travel. The resulting 'genealogy of the seascape' was therefore integral to a system of wayfinding.

A maritime perspective is also offered in Eileen Wilkes' contribution on journeys around the English south coast during the Iron Age. She begins with the point, also made by Robinson, that seascapes are as textured and structured as landscapes, before going on to explore how these structuring conditions might be studied in order to identify the locations of desirable ports on the south coast. Wilkes describes the distinctive journey towards one of the key maritime nodes, Poole Harbour. Local landmarks and the characteristics of the channels in these tidal waters were fundamental constraints on how the harbour was approached. Perhaps most significantly, the journey culminated with a pair of timber and stone-built 'moles'; substantial jetty-like platforms that controlled access into the harbour area. These seem to have been deliberately monumental structures, making a visual statement about arriving into Poole Harbour at journey's end. Thus, movements through seascapes could be as controlled and orchestrated as those through the landscape.

Adrian Chadwick's paper also considers the ways in which journeys are structured by nonhuman agencies, but here he turns his attention to trackways across the landscape and the roles that animals play in conditioning human movement. In his study of the significance of journeying and trackways in the English north Midlands during the Iron Age and Romano-British period, he argues that people and domesticated animals were in part defined in terms of their relationships with one another. Human lives and animal lives were inextricably linked, not just in practical terms but symbolically as well. Drawing on the archaeological evidence, Chadwick evokes a series of 'everyday' journeys undertaken by people and animals. He suggests that trackways were particularly significant for creating connections between people, places, memories and traditions. They were not just bound into practices of everyday life, but were also conduits for power, the social movements of people and ritual activity. Furthermore, the trackways referenced earlier constructions and histories of use of these landscapes, tying the present into the past. Chadwick creates a view of the landscape during the Iron Age and Romano-British periods which was not about exploitation, but part of a process of creating geographies and defining identities (of people, animals and communities).

These papers return us to the challenge of 'reconstructing' journeys archaeologically. Yet, unlike artefacts, the landscape seems to form a more tangible means of defining journeys. It has a duality whereby it both structures and is structured by travel. In Gary Robinson's paper, there were material conditions that structured movement through the islands, setting in place proscribed channels for journeys to take. These patterns of movement went on to determine where monuments were sited, and presumably also contributed to their cultural meaning. As Wilkes and Chadwick make clear, successful inhabitation of the landscape, or seascape, also required knowledge and skills derived from long experience and the ability to respond to the historical context of previous journeys. What is key, then, is not location (i.e. sets of place) but historical knowledge of movements through the landscape. It is history and knowledge that makes journeys significant, not the journey in an abstracted sense.

Destinations

The circular path that characterises the ways in which ideas and approaches in prehistoric studies return into currency after many years may itself be served by a metaphor of a journey without a clear destination or expected completion. We did not set out with a clear definition of 'journey', and as we have outlined there is no clear consensus amongst the different authors about journeying. What is clear is that travel was a fundamental part of life in prehistory, not just as a means of getting around, but a key aspect of identity and being-in-the-world. Journeys are of intrinsic importance, rather than being a 'means to an end'.

Acknowledgements

This volume is the result of a session held at the Theoretical Archaeology Group conference in Glasgow in 2004, and we would like to thank all the speakers at the original session and the conference organisers who made it such a success. Many of the contributors to this publication spoke at the original session, but there are a few additional papers. All the authors have been both patient and helpful throughout the editorial process. Vicki would like to thank the Leverhulme Trust and the University of Central Lancashire for their support while the volume was in production. Bob acknowledges a debt to the two seminar groups of masters students that have taken the 'Journeys and Landscape' module at the University of Sheffield for sharing and debating their ideas and research so openly.

Bibliography

Bahn, P.G. (ed.) 1996. *Cambridge illustrated history: archaeology.* Cambridge: Cambridge University Press.

Bender, B. 2001. Landscapes on-the-move. *Journal of Social Archaeology* 1(1), 75–89.

Binford, L. 1980. Willow smoke and dogs' tails: hunter-gatherer settlement systems and archaeological site formation. *American Antiquity* 45, 4–20.

Chadwick A.M. (ed.) 2004. *Stories from the landscape: archaeologies of inhabitation.* Oxford: Archaeopress.

Clifford, J. 1997. *Routes, travel and translation in the late twentieth century.* Cambridge, MA: Harvard University Press.

Clough, T. and Cummins, W. (eds) 1979. *Stone axe studies.* London: Council for British Archaeology.

Coleman, S. and Eade, J. (eds) 2004. *Reframing pilgrimage: cultures in motion.* London: Routledge.

Cummings, V. and Whittle, A. 2004. *Places of special virtue: megaliths in the Neolithic landscapes of Wales.* Oxford: Oxbow.

Edmonds, M. 1999. *Ancestral geographies of the Neolithic: landscapes, monuments, and memory.* London: Routledge.

Fitzpatrick, A. 2002. 'The Amesbury Archer': a well furnished Early Bronze Age burial in southern England. *Antiquity* 76, 629–30.

Fox, C. 1932. *The personality of Britain.* Cardiff: National Museum of Wales.

Gresham, C.A. and Irvine, C.H. 1963. Prehistoric routes across North Wales. *Antiquity* 37, 54–58.

Helms, M.W. 1988. *Ulysees' sail: an ethnographic odyssey of power, knowledge and geographical distance.* Princeton: Princeton University Press.

Ingold, T. 2000. *The perception of the environment: essays in livelihood, dwelling and skill.*. London: Routledge.

Ingold, T. 2004. Culture on the ground: the world perceived through the feet. *Journal of Material Culture* 9(3), 315–40.

Kristiansen, K. and Larsson, T.F. 2006. *The rise of Bronze Age society: travels, transmissions and transformations.* Cambridge: Cambridge University Press.

Lee, R. and DeVore, I. (eds) 1968. *Man the hunter.* New York: Aldine.

Minh-ha, T.T. 1994. Other than myself/my other self. In G. Robertson, M. Mash, L. Tickner, J. Bird, B. Curtis and T. Putnam (eds), *Travellers' tales: narratives of home and displacement*, 9–26. London: Routledge.

Piggott, S. 1950. *William Stukeley.* Oxford: Clarendon.

Piggott, S. 1954. *The Neolithic cultures of the British Isles*. Cambridge: Cambridge University Press.

Rohl, B. and Needham, S. 1998. *The circulation of metalwork in the British Bronze Age: the application of lead isotope analysis*. London: British Museum Press.

Rowley-Conwy, P. 1983. Sedentary hunters: the Ertebølle example. In. G. Bailey (ed.), *Hunter-gatherer economy in prehistory: a European perspective*, 111–126. Cambridge: Cambridge University Press.

Slavin. S. 2003. Walking as spiritual practice: the pilgrimage to Santiago de Compostela. *Body and Society* 9(3), 1–18.

Tilley, C. 1994. *A phenomenology of landscape: places, paths and monuments*. Oxford: Berg.

Whittle, A. 1997. Moving on and moving around: Neolithic settlement mobility. In P. Topping (ed.), *Neolithic Landscapes*, 14–22. Oxford: Oxbow.

2 'Stretched thin, like butter on too much bread...': some thoughts about journeying in the unfamiliar landscapes of late Palaeolithic Southern Scandinavia

Felix Riede

'After only a short walk we have reached the foot of the great Ahrensburg moraine; across coarse scree we make our way upwards. A few more steps and we will reach the top. But then we freeze in our steps – what a sight! "The Homeland of Death", exclaims Ule and everyone stares silently. Far away on the horizon lies the ice, the edge of the glacial mass, which stretches into the distance towards midnight.' Rust (1962, 87, my translation).

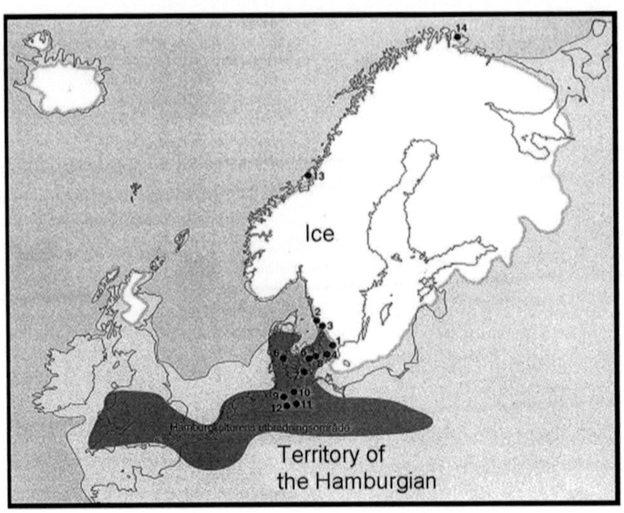

Fig. 2.1. Burenhult's (1999, 164) map of the Hamburgian. The shaded area represents the territory of the Late Palaeolithic groups of the Late Glacial, i.e. the Hamburgian sensu lato *(including, for example, the English Creswellian). The glacier's edge at the time of Hamburgian settlement would have been at the southern edge of the Swedish highlands, far from sites such as Stellmoor and Ahrensburg, as Bokelmann (1979) had argued, but not at all very far from sites such as Vängamossen or Molleröd (Andersson* et al. *2004; Larsson 1993; 1994; 1996a). It is likely that the Hamburgian groups were strongly aware of the awesome presence of the inland ice.*

Prelude: journeying in unfamiliar landscapes

This is how Alfred Rust, excavator of the famous Late Palaeolithic sites in the Ahrensburg Tunnel-valley, described the scene when his Hamburgian family caught sight of the great Scandinavian glacier on their journey northwards. Ironically, the same passage was used by Klaus Bokelmann (1979) who magisterially reviewed the geological and archaeological evidence known at the time and argued cogently that the first settlers of southern Scandinavia (encompassing modern-day northern Germany, Denmark and Scania) never actually saw the glaciers, which had long retreated into the Swedish highlands.

However, new archaeological evidence has since caught up with this situation and very early sites, belonging to the first phase of colonisation, traditionally referred to as the Hamburgian period, are now known not only from Denmark but also from Scania (Larsson 1993; 1994; 1996). Current maps thus show a site distribution virtually bordering the main glacier (Burenhult 1999; Fig. 2.1). Yet, the question is not really whether the Hamburgians ever saw glaciers or not. It remains a fact that as the Pleistocene came to a fitful end, Late Palaeolithic groups moved into a landscape that had only very recently seen tremendous geological violence; a landscape in which plant and animal communities had not had time to colonise; a landscape that was still dotted with dead-ice lakes, with bogs and swamps; a landscape that was inundated annually by vast amounts of glacial melt-water; a landscape in which icebergs were still common in the open sea as well as in lakes. In short, this was not a hospitable landscape, but a dangerous and *unfamiliar* landscape (Rockman and Steele 2003).

This paper investigates how, through a diachronic comparative analysis of the Late Pleistocene cultures of southern Scandinavia and by using some inspirations from the ethnographic and ethnohistoric record of the High Arctic, we can begin to investigate journeying in the unfamiliar landscapes of the Late Palaeolithic.

Introduction: one caveat, two challenges

This paper must necessarily begin with a caveat. In a recent paper entitled *Culture on the ground: the world perceived through the feet*, Tim Ingold (2004) reminds us that the very notion of 'travelling', of 'journeying', is intimately connected to the rise of an urban boot-clad bourgeoisie for whom travel on foot had ceased to be a daily necessity. Hunter-gatherers famously 'move around a lot' (Lee and DeVore 1968, 11; but see Panter-Brick *et al.* 2001 and Rowley-Conwy 2001), but whether moving because one *likes to* or moving because one *has to* is bound to have a significant impact on the attitudes towards travel and journeying. It thus has to be recognised that 'journeying' amongst hunter-gatherer groups in general, and more specifically in highly mobile Late Palaeolithic groups, cannot be understood in the contemporary Western sense without severe reservations.

Nevertheless, even after accounting for potential environmental and economic factors, the human colonisation of, in the first instance, the world beyond Africa, and later the rapid post-glacial reclaiming of previously glaciated regions, remains one of the most interesting riddles of prehistory. In fact, as Clive Gamble (1993) has pointed out, constant colonisations of this sort seem to be a feature of the biological and cultural make-up of both modern humans and ancestral hominids. Climatic factors alone cannot explain why people today live in landscapes for which they are, by their biological endowment, inherently unsuited. It follows that cultural aspects have played a major role in the numerous colonisation episodes that mark human prehistory. Because we have no documented cases of colonising hunter-gatherers, it is the archaeological record that primarily informs us about this critical feature of human life. The first challenge is to tease apart ecological from economic and cultural facets of the colonisation process, and to integrate them into one explanatory framework that allows us to speak meaningfully about 'journeying' in deep prehistory (Riede 2005).

The second challenge stems from the absence of any modern analogues for the territorial expansion of hunter-gather groups. The vast majority of contemporary foraging groups have either been in contact with non-foragers for a long time, have been marginalised in the wake of political developments or indeed have only recently adopted a hunting and gathering lifestyle (Layton 2001; Shrire 1980). Therefore, we must be extremely careful when applying ethnographic material to the period in question, constantly being aware of the fact that we are dealing with a behaviour that has most definitely not been observed in any living populations. It is an ethnographic truism that hunter-gatherers are experts when it comes to environmental knowledge of all kinds. However, this kind of knowledge has to be acquired in the first place, a process that probably takes many generations. With the colonisation of Late Pleistocene southern Scandinavia, we must practically assume the opposite scenario: these groups move into unfamiliar landscapes, where the lack of landscape knowledge severely constrains movement and economic activities. Journeying commonly implies a destination, somewhere or someone to go to. In the Late Palaeolithic of southern Scandinavia this was not always the case. In this 'life without...neighbours' (Åkerlund 2002, 43), neither an enculturated landscape (Barrett 1999) nor interaction partners existed, creating a very particular context for the journeys to be examined (Knutsson 2005).

The *process* of colonisation, and the changing attitudes and modes of journeying, are here best addressed using the notion of 'landscape learning' (Meltzer 2002; 2003). This presents a useful analytical nexus as it emphasises culturally contingent properties of a given landscape. An environment is perceived by humans in terms of 'affordances' (Ingold 1986, 2), which will always be a sub-set of all potentially useable properties of the environment. The perception of these affordances is historically and culturally contingent, and can thus lead to rather dissimilar perceptions of a given landscape among different cultural groups. With human action constrained by these perceptions, they can also be expected to leave tangible material signatures and it is these that are examined in this paper.

The paper is divided into three parts. In the first part I briefly introduce the three archaeological cultures that will be compared; Fischer (1991; 1996) essentially considers all three to be colonising societies. Then, I present a suite of archaeological data that can be used to highlight critical differences in the forms of mobility and the modes of transport in these cultures. In the second part, I will investigate how the archaeological evidence can be used to argue for different attitudes towards, and outcomes of, the journeys undertaken by Late Palaeolithic foraging groups. It will be argued that the Hamburgian journey ultimately had a tragic end, resulting in the extinction of this group. The later groups are compared against this, and it will be argued that the observable differences in mobility and landscape use reflect a different attitude towards journeying. Rather more mundanely, these differences also contributed to the relative cultural and biological success of these groups even in the face of the severe climatic downturn of the Younger Dryas. It is argued that this shift in mobility – its cultural position as well as its execution – was engendered by the emergence of non-pedestrian means of transport. Finally, the third part concludes the paper with a general discussion of the symbolic representation of landscape knowledge in the context of the Late Palaeolithic of southern Scandinavia in the light of ethno-archaeological information from Greenland.

The late Palaeolithic of Southern Scandinavia, 13,500–10,000 BC

As the last Ice Age drew to a close, c. 18,000 years ago, plant and animal communities began to move northwards again; an ecological succession that is now well documented both in the geological, faunal and floral record (Huntley and Birks 1983; Lowe and Walker 1997), as well as genetically (for animals: Hewitt 1999; for plants: Petit *et al.* 2002; for people: Forster 2004). The general thrust of this re-colonisation was north-western, and with evident typological connections to the middle phases of the western European (i.e. French and Belgian) Magdalenian, the earliest colonisers of the Great European Plain ultimately derived from the surviving populations of south-western France and northern Spain.

Although it remains unclear how exactly the different archaeological cultures or techno-complexes are related, both culturally and biologically (Gramsch 2004), the general cultural succession in southern Scandinavia is *Hamburgian sensu strictu*, *Hamburgian-Havelte*, *Bromme* (contemporary with the peripheral and not further considered Federmesser), and *Ahrensburgian* (Andersson *et al.* 2004; Eriksen 2002; Fig. 2.2). It has been argued that the Ahrensburgian is characterised by an increasing diversification of artefact forms and a further spread northwards into the areas of northern Scandinavia at the beginning of the Holocene (Burenhult 1999; Schmitt 1999; Taute 1968).

Technologically the three cultures differ substantially in their blade production technique, contingent on varying methods of core handling and hammer application (Fig. 2.3). Typologically, the Hamburgian is characterised by shouldered points, long blade scrapers, often with fine lateral retouch, burins of different kinds, usually on blades, Zinken (*becs*), and combination tools (e.g. a scraper at one end and burin at the other: Tromnau 1975). The Bromme culture is typologically impoverished, showing only large tanged points, scrapers and burins (Fischer 1985; Jensen 1999; Madsen 1992). With the Ahrensburgian, the shift towards a more varied tool kit is initiated. Small tanged points, various scrapers and burins as well as an increasing variety of quasi-microlithic tools and organic tools appear (Andersson *et al.* 2004; Clausen 2004), particularly in those assemblages thought to be of later date (Taute 1968).

These differences in tool manufacture and morphology cannot readily be related to changes in adaptive regimes or weapon delivery systems (Fischer *et al.* 1984). Rather, we must seek explanations contingent on the cultural trajectories of the groups as well as their larger technological systems. That is to say, we must look – 'harsh light, soft focus' – towards mobility and the overall 'way of life' in order to explain these differences. Through such an explanation we will gain useful insights into the ways in which Late Palaeolithic journeys in these cultures were organised. 'Tacking' (Gamble 1999, 5) from the fine-grained to the coarse-grained evidence and back again, we can use both the gesture-by-gesture record of flint-knapping episodes and the various hierarchies of settlement organisation and raw material economy as evidence for the preparation and execution, and by inference, the attitudes and outcomes, of these journeys.

Late Palaeolithic journeys: some evidence

Although thinking about prehistoric journeys is a novel approach in archaeology, the evidence marshalled here in support of some journeying scenarios is, in fact, very traditional. They are the three staples of Stone Age archaeology: (1) raw material economy, (2) caching, and (3) settlement patterns at the micro- and macro-scale. Summarily presented in Table 2.1, I will address each category in turn and show, first, how they are intimately linked through the nexus of mobility and, secondly, how 'mobility' can be addressed in terms of journeying.

Years BC	Chronozones	Southwest Germany	Thuringian Basin	South Scandinavia
10,000				
	Dryas III	(Fürsteiner)	Find hiatus	Ahrenburgian
11,000				
	Alleröd	Late Palaeolithic		Bromme Federmesser
12,000	Dryas II		Magdalenian Sensu lato	Hamburgian
	Bölling	Magdalenian Sensu lato		
13,000				
	Dryas I			
14,000				

Fig. 2.2. A broad culture-historical overview (from Eriksen 1996, 10). Of particular interest here is the scheme (shaded grey) on the right for southern Scandinavia as well as the climatic succession on the left. Note that Federmesser presence in Scandinavia is slight and interesting, but not further considered here.

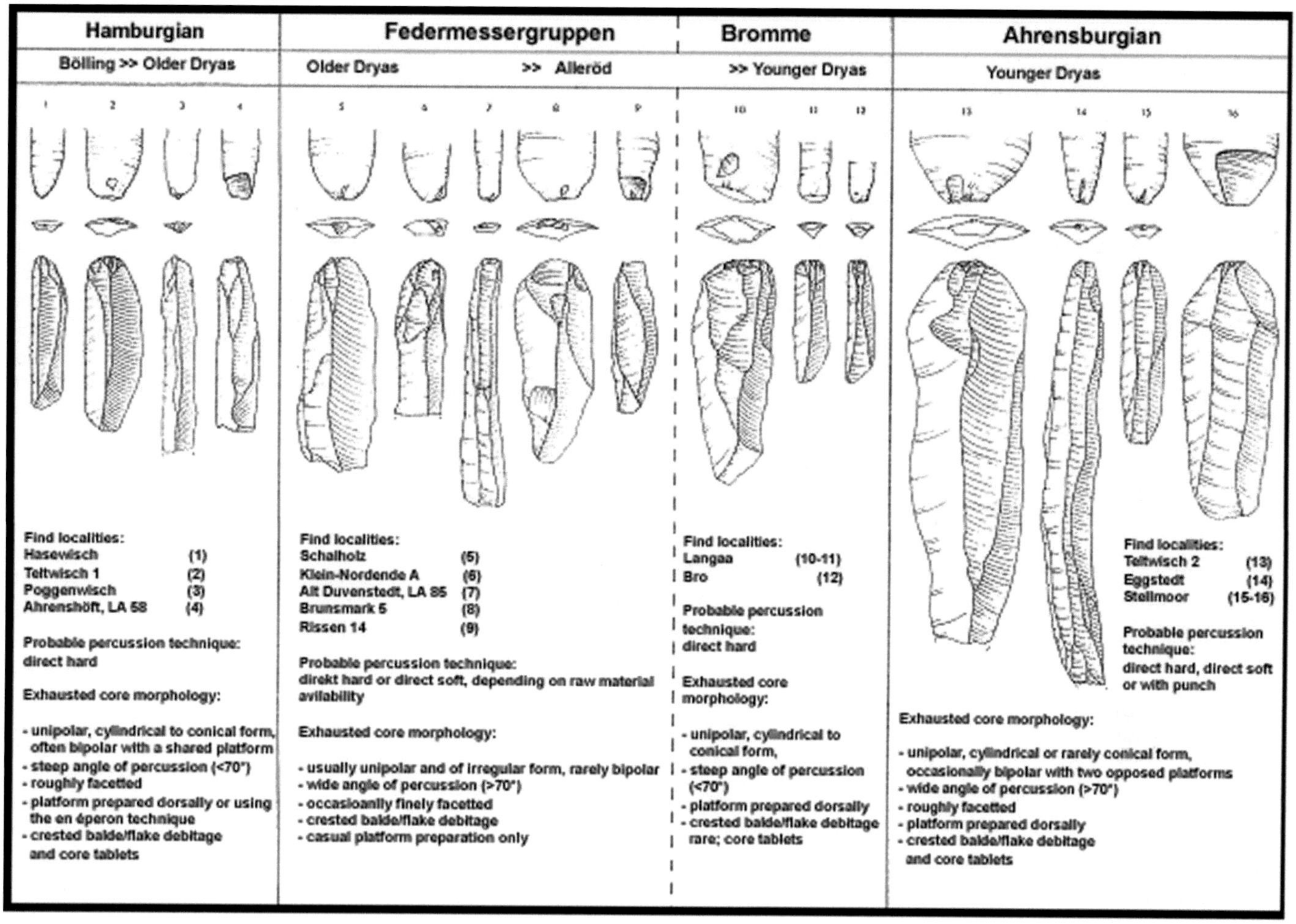

Fig. 2.3. The fundamental technological characteristics of the Late Glacial cultures occurring in southern Scandinavia (after Hartz 1987, 27).

Raw material economy

The raw material economy of the Hamburgians is doubtlessly amongst the most refined and most stringent of the entire Palaeolithic period. Tightly standardised blades, which make up the blanks for the vast majority of tools, are produced in a precise and controlled manner. The blades themselves are very light and thin; soft-hammer percussion is used throughout the reduction process and generally only high-quality raw material is selected and, interestingly (discussed below), a large number of combination tools are produced (Madsen 1992).

The differences with the succeeding Bromme culture are most striking in tool morphology, but in fact are also found in the method of manufacture (exclusively hard-hammer) and the raw material selection, which shifted to the abundant locally available moraine flint. This was often of very high quality, but could also be rather ill-suited to tool production (Madsen 1993; Petersen 1993). Tool size increased in all dimensions.

With the Ahrensburgian, the raw material strategies seemingly revert to a pattern more akin to that of the Hamburgian. Morphologically the tools are clearly distinct, but blank manufacture again becomes more standardised, now with a double-pronged trend towards both much smaller as well as very large blades. The size of the formal tools is generally reduced; raw material selectivity appears higher and becomes, in some regions, locally distinct (Taute 1968).

Experiments with the arrowheads from these three cultures have indicated that they are functionally identical and that differences in morphology cannot readily be related to changes in weapon delivery systems (Fischer *et al.* 1984). Assuming that the functional differences in all these tools are negligible, what stands out as most striking is the difference in overall *weight* of the tool kit. A preliminary analysis of the volumetric qualities of 2031 artefacts (points, scrapers and burins; a 'weight index' is calculated with length, width and thickness) from the Hamburgian, Federmesser, Bromme and Ahrensburgian has revealed that the Bromme tool-kit weighs in significantly higher in all respects and that Ahrensburgian tools are bulkier than Hamburgian tools (with the exception of the points; Table 2.2). Assuming that it was primarily these

Across = Period Down = Evidence	Hamburgian	Bromme	Ahrensburgian
Lithic Economy	*Extremely efficient; light, multi-purpose tools; some important and mostly high-quality raw material*	*Wasteful; large and chunky tools; local raw material*	*Efficient; in part very large sturdy blades produced but also small, very slim ones; later, raw material regionalisation*
Caching	*Present (Flint)*	*Absent*	*Present (Meat)*
Settlement System	*Linear (South – North across ecological zones)*	*Radial (West – East within ecological zones)*	*Linear (South – North across ecological zones)*

Table 2.1. The three staples of Stone Age archaeology

Typological Assessment	Tool Type	N	Minimum	Maximum	Mean
Hamburgian	Point	108	540	26180	2811.66
	Scraper	313	40	60528	8180.36
	Burin	275	729	80352	10401.05
Federmesser	Point	50	434	14950	3280.08
	Scraper	298	840	46784	9524.18
	Burin	119	897	57816	9499.72
Bromme	Point	176	1476	102960	12237.84
	Scraper	464	1600	180320	16300.43
	Burin	373	1650	117925	20105.82
Ahrensburgian	Point	108	272	9576	1801.44
	Scraper	179	880	107793	12097.42
	Burin	79	98	46144	11598.61

Table 2.2. Descriptive statistics: weight and bulk. 'Weight index' (length × width × thickness) for three formal tools types of the Late Glacial, based on a sample of more than two thousand complete tools from the four cultural groups (N=2031). This is to be understood as a heuristic calculation supporting the significance of tool weight and bulk with regards to mobility, particular long-distance mobility as evidenced by the colonising cultures of the Late Glacial (see Kuhn 1994 for a similar approach).

formal tool types that were transported from site to site, overall size and weight should reflect mobility to some degree. The striking difference highlights the economical orientation of the Hamburgian tool-kit, or, in other words, the strictures that extreme mobility put on what people were able to transport as part of their personal gear.

Seen from this perspective, the high frequency of combination tools in Hamburgian assemblages also begins to make sense. Whilst using combination tools is actually quite risky (if you break one end, you probably lose both tools), it represents one solution to the problem of limited personal transport capacity. Overall, the interpretation of these emerging patterns in raw material economy are interpreted to reflect the extreme mobility of the Hamburgian groups (also see below) in the absence of non-pedestrian transport. Bromme mobility was greatly reduced, perhaps primarily due to environmental factors – the Bromme falls into the warmer and moister Allerød phase during which extreme seasonal mobility had perhaps not only become unnecessary, but indeed quite difficult – whilst Ahrensburgian mobility approached that of the earlier Hamburgian groups. However, the greater bulk of the Ahrensburgian tool-kit is the result of an increasing component of very large tools, the so-called 'giant blades' (Barton 1986; 1998) and, eventually, axe-like implements (Fischer 1978a; 1978b; Sørensen and Sternke 2004). It is argued here that it was the emergence of non-pedestrian transport, such as boats or sleighs, that led to the weight-related bimodality in the Ahrensburgian tool-kit: light tools for personal use taken along during short-distance on-foot travel and large implements were site-specific and only transported during aided travel.

Caching

Overall, the evidence for caching in the Late Palaeolithic is very slim. For groups operating in an unfamiliar landscape, however, it is a highly significant practice (Meltzer 2002; 2003) and it is found quite commonly in other colonising contexts such as Paleoindian North America (Kelly and Todd 1988) and the Arctic (Fitzhugh 2004). Both lithic resources as well as food can be cached, and both practices create significant places in the landscapes as well as modifying the very fundamental ecological parameters of that landscape. The significance of storage, both in a physical (Rowley-Conwy and Zvelebil 1989) as well as in a cognitive sense (Renfrew and Scarre 1998), has been extensively discussed. Interestingly, a landscape learning perspective would suggest that caching reflects not some ingenious logistical strategy, but rather a *lack* of information about the parameters of the very same landscape that is to be travelled through (Hazelwood and Steele 2003; Kelly 2003; Kelly and Todd 1988; Riede 2005).

The strongest evidence for caching comes from the Hamburgian site of Teltwisch 1 (Tromnau 1975; 1984b), where a small pit set aside from the main concentration of finds contained a total of 651 pieces of flint. Of these, 40 were blades (5/%), 651 flakes (93.4%), one Zinken (0.1%), two retouched flakes (0.3%), one scraper (0.1%) and two broken pieces of retouched tools (0.3%). The excavator maintains that there was no organic material in the cache and that all flint pieces had been struck from only three or four cores (which presumably would have exhausted them quite thoroughly). Whilst Tromnau (1975) generally excludes a 'ritual' function for this cache, I would maintain that there need not be an opposition between it being viewed as functional and it having been ritually deposited. The practice of caching would have imbued a place with great ecological significance as a major concentration of semi-processed lithic raw material as well as possibly being associated with the naming of a locale (Gustafsson 1998; Tolan-Smith 2003). However, inspection of the flint material from this cache in early 2005 by the author casts doubt on its identity as a true cache. While there are many refitting sequences, true blades are rare and the overall impression is one of discarded knapping debris rather than deliberately deposited flint valuables.

It is interesting to note that the Hamburgian sites in northern Germany are large when compared to any finds accumulations further to the north (e.g. Sølbjerg 2, Jels 1 and 2), and that they are situated south of the area reached by the last glaciations. The Hamburgian groups thus had launching platforms for their journeys in a landscape that was already quite mature and, most importantly, differed little from the vast plains to the south. The sites in the Ahrensburg Tunnelvalley are thus the northernmost outposts of Hamburgian landscape familiarity – beyond that lay a, relatively at least, *terra incognita.* The immaculate tool economy as well as the possible Teltwisch 1 cache represent the 'gearing-up' for journeying into this pristine landscape.

A further indicator for the length of, and attitude towards, the journeys Hamburgian groups undertook is the relative completeness of refitting series at sites such as Sølbjerg 2. The majority of tools at the site were produced elsewhere, while the tools made at Sølbjerg were themselves taken away (Johansen 2000). Provisions were clearly made, perhaps indicating lengthy journeys and a limited knowledge about flint resource occurrence *en route.*

Caches from the Bromme culture are unknown (a possible but enigmatic exception: Ommels Hoved on Ærø; Holm 1972), and it is only in the Ahrensburgian that caching behaviour can again be observed. However, here we are dealing with meat caches rather than flint caches (at Meiendorf and Stellmoor: Grønnow 1985; but see Bratlund 1991). This is informative in two ways. The absence of flint caches can be seen to reflect both the ability to transport greater quantities of flint due to the availability of non-pedestrian transport (coupled with the general tendency towards smaller tools), as well as a shift towards a larger organic component in the Hamburgian tool-kit: wooden arrows, bone and antler harpoons as well as other antler tools are frequently recorded from that period (Clausen 2004; Jensen 1999; Rust 1943). Yet, the fact that meat was cached does reflect the increase of mobility in the Ahrensburgian phase vis-à-vis the Bromme. While it remains somewhat unclear whether we are dealing with separate, perhaps specialised groups exploiting smaller territories or whether Ahrensburgian territoriality had in fact increased (Kindgren 2002; Schmitt 1994; 1995; 1999), the re-emergence of caching suggests that (a) the environment was perceived as risky and unstable, and (b) there was an intention to return to the same locale.

So, whereas patterns in raw material economy provide glimpses of the actual travelling part of a Late Palaeolithic journey – *Was it very long? Why was it undertaken? What was taken along?* – caches reflect how these journeys were connected by nodes in the landscape. Both repeatedly occupied sites as well as cache localities would have provided traditional stopping points and way-markers. The last part of this section will examine whether we can reconstruct some of the routes taken and how far they fit the picture that has been emerging so far.

Settlement pattern

Based on ethnography, hunter-gatherer societies have been broadly divided into two groups from an economic, a social and a technological point of view: Binford's (1980) logistical and residential groups, Woodburn's (1982) immediate and delayed return societies and Bleed's (1986) expedient and curated tool categories. There is no one-to-one correspondence between these categories, but a relatively tight overlap. A given society that follows a residential mobility strategy, also usually exhibits patterns of delayed return and manufactures a significant proportion of curated tools and *vice versa.* Although tremendously stimulating to hunter-gatherer research (Bettinger 2001), they might be somewhat restrictive if applied to scenarios of primary colonisations.

Beaton's (1991) attempt to adapt this dual classification for migration situations – with transient explorers opposed to estate settlers – further continued this rather rigid opposition. Whilst this model explores the interesting issue of linearity of settlement vectors (i.e. with sites organised along natural corridors and across ecological zones like beads on a string) in colonising scenarios, Kelly (2003) has pointed out that it not only lacks unequivocal empirical support in the archaeological record, but that it is also unsupportable from a theoretical point of view. He (Kelly 1983; 1992; 2003; Kelly and Todd 1988) instead proposes that it might be feasible for colonising hunter-gatherers to integrate the strategies of residential and logistic mobility, of delayed and immediate return economies and the associated tool-making. Kelly concludes that it would indeed be advantageous for such groups to pursue a habit of linear residentially-mobile settlement along natural corridors that offer resources of transferable familiarity, particularly coastlines or rivers (Kelly 2003).

The southern Scandinavian evidence seems to support this model reasonably well. Linear mobility is evident, with the routes following closely that of the reindeer (Fig. 2.4; Petersen and Johansen 1993; 1996), which in turn followed the main river valleys. These river valleys would have afforded the easiest and least dangerous routes, both for pedestrian travellers as well as for those with watercraft. Again, a comparative perspective yields interesting contrasts. The Hamburgian settlement first clusters in the areas of the old moraines in northern Germany and southern Jutland, and sites are lined up along the river valleys. In contrast, the highest density of Bromme sites is found in the previously glaciated area. Mobility seems reduced and more radial, rather than strictly linear. With the Ahrensburgian, there was a return to linear mobility patterns, coupled with an overall extension of the total 'territory' (the area of occurrence of unambiguously Ahrensburgian artefacts). Finds also occur in maritime environs, such as south-western Norway and western Sweden (Eriksen 2002).

Thus, the journeys of Hamburgian and Ahrensburgian groups followed roughly similar routes if perhaps with different means of transport, whereas the Bromme people had a rather more restricted horizon of travel. Recovery biases might skew the picture, but it seems that Hamburgian journeys were quite strictly limited to the river valleys as a result of their high mobility, but also their conservative economic and social structure. Specialising in reindeer, these groups were forced to follow their preferred prey ever further north, stretching to the maximum their social networks and their ability to keep up with the animals. The double-pronged thesis of this paper then, emerging from the review of the

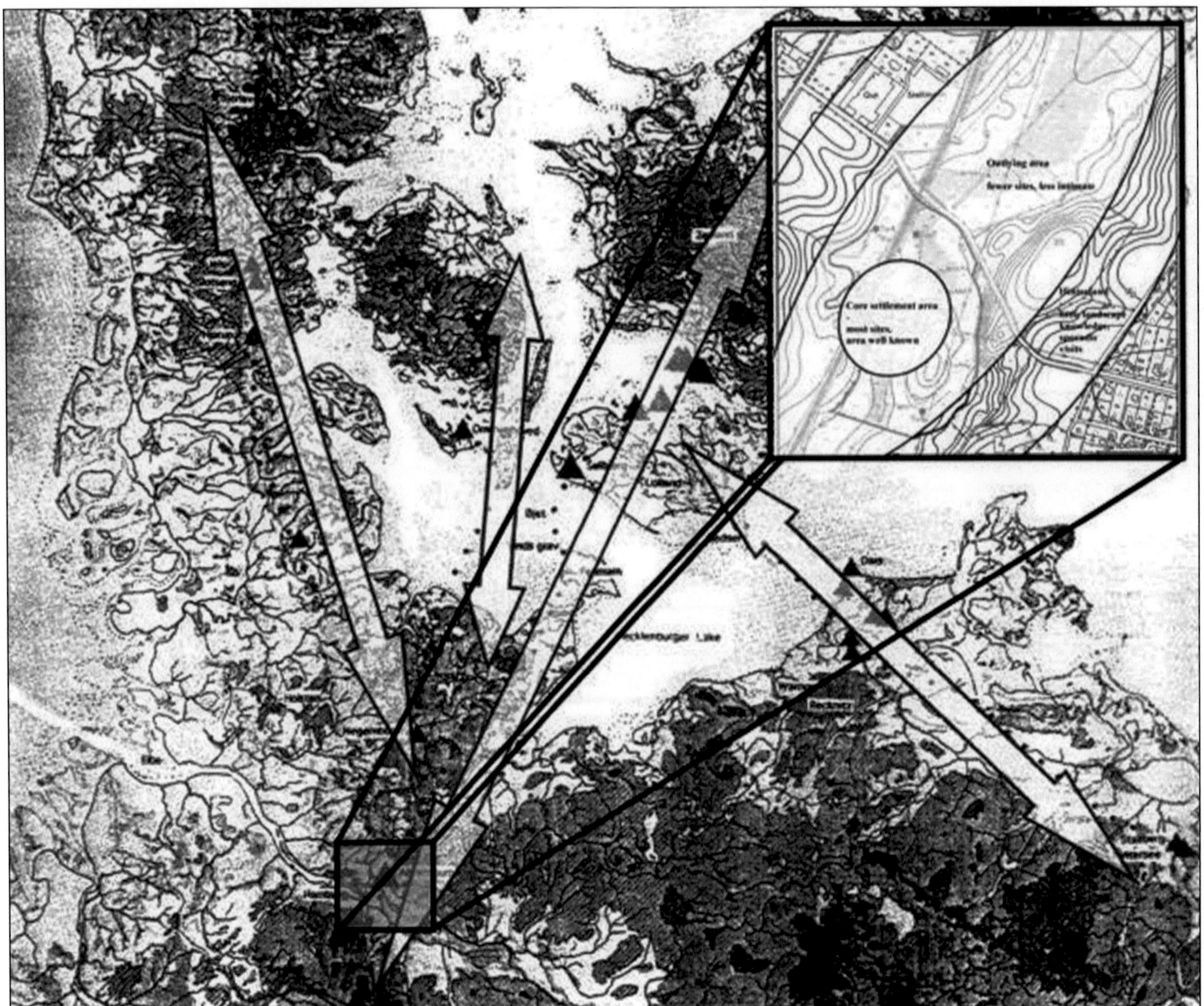

Fig. 2.4. Hamburgian and Ahrensburgian trajectories of movement and travel routes ('settlement vectors'). Based on site distribution and bathymetric maps Petersen and Johansen (1993; 1996) have been able to reconstruct the most likely travel routes of the Late Glacial hunting groups. The inset map is a similar attempt at the micro-scale: Tromnau's (1975) work and later surveys by Bokelmann (1996) in the Ahrensburg Tunnelvalley have demonstrated that the distribution of sites is not only linear but also limited to certain repeatedly visited locales even though many other suitable camping spots would have been available (see also Riede 2005).

evidence above and elaborated on in the concluding section below, is that (1) Hamburgian settlement – and with that their journeying – was extremely linear for both ecological as well as cultural reasons and collapsed at the onset of the Older Dryas climatic down-turn; and (2) Ahrensburgian settlement pattern and journeying returned to a similar linearity, but was far more successful due to the availability of waterborne transport (discussed in greater detail below), allowing them to travel farther and to respond more flexibly to the severe climate of the Younger Dryas. Finally, it will be argued that whilst ethnographic analogies can allow us to speculate about such things as legends and way-markers that accompanied and facilitated journeying in the Late Palaeolithic, they can also restrict our imagination unduly when it comes to interpreting the archaeological record.

Discussion and conclusion: the wet and the wild – Late Palaeolithic journeys on foot and by boat

Ethnographic and archaeological fieldwork among the Inuit of Greenland has demonstrated that journeys in an arctic environment are highly organised and channelled by natural as much as by artificial landscape features (Gripp 1941/1942; Pasda 2004; see also Odgaard, this volume). The distribution of sites indicates linear trajectories of movement, with repeatedly visited sites making up the nodes that connect different paths (Pasda 2004). What can be taken away from this is that Late Palaeolithic journeys were probably also organised along convenient and familiar landscape types and features, and that the landscape, once explored, enculturated and known, was named and modified, albeit minimally, with way signs and symbols (Pasda 2004; see also Barrett 1999 and Odgaard, this volume). Yet, it becomes equally obvious that an uncritical comparison with arctic societies is not warranted. The archaeological signatures of Inuit sites differ markedly from that of Late Palaeolithic ones: very few artefacts and a lasting settlement architecture against a large amount of artefact waste and practically no architecture. This again might highlight that a combined residential/logistic strategy, as proposed by Kelly and Todd (1988), might be more likely for colonising hunter-gatherers.

In a similar vein, there has often been discussion on whether or not Late Palaeolithic groups practised herd following (Bahn 1977; 1982; Burch 1972; Burch and Blehr 1991; Gordon 1990; Gordon 2003; Narr 1968; Sturdy 1975; White 1989; see Baales 1996 for a good summary). This is usually rejected on ethnographic grounds, assuming instead that a logistically organised interception tactic was employed (Burch 1972; Bokelmann 1979). Yet, freeing ourselves from the constraints of the ethnographic perspectives, one should also consider the following scenario: the Hamburgian groups were made up of people who chose not to give up their ancestral early Magdalenian way of life even when the climate in southern France made specialised reindeer hunting somewhat difficult. Many groups adopted a more mixed economy (Eriksen 1996), whereas some – the ancestors of the Hamburgian – instead shifted their territories northwards along with the reindeer herds, through the Paris Basin (Rozoy 1998; Schmider 1982; 1987), the Low Countries (De Bie and Vermeersch 1998) into northern Germany and so onwards into Denmark and Sweden (Burenhult 1999; Clausen 1998; Johansen 2000). It is tentatively proposed here that Hamburgian groups did indeed practise an extreme form of herd following, and that this was part of the initial impetus for why they quickly migrated so far north and, ultimately, why this culture collapsed at the onset of the Older Dryas.

The Hamburgian way of life was closely organised, with a precise and tightly constrained lithic reduction strategy (Madsen 1992), a rather fixed schema of hunting tactics and site selection (Bokelmann 1991) and a conservative mobility that took them along the linear trajectories of the relatively familiar river valley corridors, and rarely beyond. As Madsen (1992, 128, my emphasis) points out, the Hamburgian had 'a more complex technology, *perfectly fitted to having scarcer and perhaps more distant and varied lithic resources*' despite the great abundance of easily collected flint in southern Scandinavia (Petersen 1993; Madsen 1993). The reason, therefore, why the Hamburgian culture fits uncomfortably into the dual classification of hunter-gatherers into complex and simple (see above and Keeley 1991) is because we have no analogues for this kind of social organisation. In some respects, such as knowledge about reindeer behaviour and biology, tool manufacturing skills, and knowledge of raw materials, it would have been extremely complex, yet in others, such as mobility strategies, hunting tactics and social organisation, it would have been relatively simple and indeed much closer to immediate return societies. This, however, would have been largely contingent on the extreme mobility necessitated by the herd-following lifestyle – a factor that has long been thought to have a major impact on forager social organisation (Lee and DeVore 1968).

Given that no adequate ethnographic analogies exist for reconstructing Hamburgian settlement dynamics, it will be even more challenging to think about Hamburgian journeys. Their landscape would have been vast, stark and beautiful, but also unfamiliar and extremely dangerous (Gustafsson 1998; Mandryk 1993; 2003). Moving was part and parcel of everyday life, occasionally through

Table 2.3. (adapted from McGrail 1987, 158).

Activity	Tools & Techniques	Earliest Evidence	Evidence from the Ahrensburgian
1. Skin Animals	*Knives & Scrapers*	*Middle Palaeolithic*	*Scrapers are the most common tool type, usually made on blades, some possibly hafted*
2. Bindings and Frame Material	*Cutting Tools*	*Upper Palaeolithic*	*See Rust's (1937) 'Riemenschneider', a composite tool for cutting strips of skin*
3. Make Framework	*Woven Basketry, Lashing, Pegging, Nailing*	*Upper Palaeolithic*	*See Clausen (2004), Ellmers (1980) and Tromnau (1984a; 1987) for microscopic and macroscopic arguments for boat frame constructions involving antler tines*
4. Cover Frame	*Lashing*	*Upper Palaeolithic*	*See Taute (1968) for needles/awls from Ahrensburgian contexts*

landscapes that no human being had yet seen, named or travelled in, a pristine environment re-claimed by these 'pioneers in deglaciated landscapes' (Fischer 1991, 100), operating at the 'border of human habitat' (Fischer 1996, 157). Journeys were undertaken daily, weekly, monthly, annually, following the reindeer year in, year out. Ultimately, these journeys were tragic.

It might thus seem surprising that later Ahrensburgian groups thrived, even expanded, during the extremely harsh Younger Dryas cold phase. Yet, Stewart (1968) noted nearly four decades ago that non-pedestrian transport was one of the most significant factors in the development of social complexity in foraging societies. Whilst direct evidence of watercraft is still not forthcoming from Ahrensburgian contexts, a recent microscopic analysis of tools traditionally referred to as 'antler axes' shows that the wear patterns do not support this intuitive interpretation (Clausen 2004). It is interesting to note that 25 years ago it was claimed that at least some of these antler instruments might have been part of skin boat constructions (Ellmers 1980), and that Ahrensburgian settlement pattern is also consistent with hunting from boats (Tromnau 1984a; 1987). Furthermore, it can be added that many hunting lesions from the mass-kill sites of Stellmoor and Ahrensburg also indicate hunting from boats (Bratlund 1996), and that all the technological requirements needed to make skin boats were beyond doubt present in the Ahrensburgian culture (Table 2.3).

However, beyond increased hunting proficiency (due, in part, to 'inventions' such as the use of dogs and bow-and-arrow technology: Bokelmann 1991; Bratlund 1996), watercraft would have facilitated a major change in the organisation of, and attitude towards, travel. The Canadian Arctic provides a most interesting parallel: raw material patterns followed a similar trajectory to the one sketched here, but it has also been noted that once watercraft had been introduced, long-distance movements became less contingent on raw material necessities and rather more motivated by kin ties, trade, and politics (Fitzhugh 2004). The expanded territory of the Ahrensburgian, now including very diverse eco-zones, might actually imply that some groups began to specialise in, for example, hunting of marine mammals in order to trade their harvest with more southerly groups (Kindgren 2002; Schmitt 1999). Ahrensburgian groups had the advantage of moving in a landscape more mature than that of the Hamburgians by nearly one thousand years, but the freedom with which they operated in the harsh Younger Dryas environment indicates a greater confidence with regards travel. If indeed journeys, by individuals and groups, had become integrated into complex socio-political strategies, these journeys would also have had a very different quality to those undertaken by the Hamburgians.

Investigating journeys in the Late Palaeolithic of southern Scandinavia remains elusive. Nevertheless, the archaeological record provides us with a plethora of evidence. Lithic reduction strategies inform us how people geared up for their journeys, caching and the absence of it yields insights into the cautionary measures with which people tried to insure themselves against catastrophic outcomes of their journeys, and settlement patterns give clues as to which paths were actually taken. It has been argued that journeys in the context of the colonisation of pristine landscapes cannot be usefully understood in the modern sense of the word, neither with respect to Western society nor with regards to foraging populations. Moving is, for hunter-gatherers, a way of life and not separate at all from the rest of their existence. Nevertheless, some hunter-gathers are more mobile than others, and many types of archaeological remains can provide insights into how people prepared for their journeys, where they went, how they got there and why. Here, some steps have been taken towards addressing these issues in the Late Palaeolithic of southern Scandinavia.

Acknowledgements

This paper was inspired by the session on 'Prehistoric Journeys' organised by Vicki Cummings and Bob Johnston at TAG 2004 in Glasgow. I had a 'Guten TAG' (sorry, Dave) – thanks! The title for this paper was borrowed from Bilbo Baggins, in J.R.R. Tolkien's *Lord of the Rings*.

Bibliography

Andersson, M., Karsten, P., Knarrström, B. and Svensson, M. 2004. *Stone Age Scania. Significant places dug and read by contract archaeology*. Lund: Riksantikvarieämbetet.

Baales, M. 1996. *Umwelt und Jagdökonomie der Ahrensburger Rentierjäger im Mittelgebirge*. Bonn: Habelt.

Bahn, P. 1977. Seasonal migration in south-west France during the Late Glacial period. *Journal of Archaeological Science* 4, 245–57.

Bahn, P. 1982. Inter-site and inter-regional links during the Upper Palaeolithic: the Pyrenean evidence. *Oxford Journal of Archaeology* 1, 247–68.

Barrett, J.C. 1999. Chronologies of landscape. In P. Ucko and R. Layton (eds), *The archaeology and anthropology of landscape: shaping your landscape*, 21–30. London: Routledge.

Barton, R.N.E. 1986. Experiments with long blades from Sproughton, near Ipswich, Suffolk. In D. Roe (ed.), *Studies in the Upper Palaeolithic of Britain and northwest Europe*, 129–41. Oxford: British Archaeological Reports International Series 296.

Barton, R.N.E. 1998. Long blade technology and the question of British late Pleistocene /early Holocene lithic assemblages. In F. Healy, N. Ashton and P. Pettitt (eds), *Stone Age archaeology. Essays in honour of John Wymer. Lithic Studies Society Occasional Paper 6*, 158–64. Oxford: Oxbow.

Beaton, J.M. 1991. Colonizing continents: some problems from Australia and the Americas. In T.D. Dillehay and D.M. Meltzer (eds), *The first Americans: search and research*, 209–30. Boca Raton: CRC Press.

Bettinger, R.L. 2001. Holocene hunter-gatherers. In G.M. Feinman and T.D. Price (eds), *Archaeology at the millennium: a sourcebook*, 137–95. New York: Kluwer/Plenum Publishers.

Binford, L.R. 1980. Willow smoke and dogs' tails: hunter gatherer settlement systems and archaeological site formation. *American Antiquity* 45, 4–20.

Bleed, P. 1986. The optimal design of hunting weapons: maintainability or reliability. *American Antiquity* 51, 737–47.

Bokelmann, K. 1979. Rentierjäger am Gletscherrand in Schleswig-Holstein? Ein Diskussionsbeitrag zur Erforschung der Hamburger Kultur. *Offa* 36, 12–22.

Bokelmann, K. 1991. Some new thoughts on old data on humans and reindeer in the Ahrensburg Tunnelvalley in Schleswig-Holstein, Germany. In R.N.E. Barton, A.J. Roberts and D. Roe (eds), *The late-Glacial in north-west Europe*, 72–81. London: Council for British Archaeology, Report No. 77.

Bokelmann, K. 1996. Ahrensburg, Kr. Stormarn. Baggersondagen bei Vierbergen im Ahrens-burger Tunneltal. *Offa* 53, 372.

Bratlund, B. 1991. Die spätglazialen 'Opfertiere' von Meiendorf und Stellmoor, Kreis Stormarn. *Offa* 48, 41–73.

Bratlund, B. 1996. Hunting strategies in the late Glacial of northern Europe: a survey of the faunal evidence. *Journal of World Prehistory* 19, 1–48.

Burch, E.S., Jr. 1972. The caribou/wild reindeer as a human resource. *American Antiquity* 37, 339–68.

Burch, E.S., Jr., and O. Blehr 1991. Herd following reconsidered. *Current Anthropology* 32, 439–45.

Burenhult, G. (ed.) 1999. *Arkeologi i Norden*. Stockholm: Natur och Kultur.

Clausen, I. 1998. Neue Untersuchungen an späteiszeitlichen Fundplätzen der Hamburger Kultur bei Ahrenshöft, Kr. Nordfriesland. Ein Vorbericht. *Archäologische Nachrichten aus Schleswig-Holstein* 8, 8–49.

Clausen, I. 2004. The reindeer antler axe of the Allerød period from Klappholz LA 63, Kreis Schleswig-Flensburg / Germany. Is it a relic of the Federmesser, Bromme or Ahrensburg culture?. In Th. Terberger and B.V. Eriksen (eds), *Hunters in a changing world*, 141–64. Rahden, Westfalen: Verlag Marie Leidorf GmbH.

De Bie, M. and Vermeersch, P.M. 1998. Pleistocene-Holocene transition in Benelux. *Quaternary International* 49/50, 29–43.

Ellmers, D. 1980. Ein Fellboot-Fragment der Ahrensbuger Kultur aus Husum, Schleswig-Holstein?. *Offa* 37, 19–24.

Eriksen, B.V. 1996. Regional variation in late Pleistocene subsistence strategies. Southern Scandinavian reindeer hunters in a European context. In L. Larsson (ed.), *The earliest settlement of Scandinavia and its relationship with neighbouring areas*, 7–21. Lund: Acta Archaeologica Lundensia Series IN 8°, No. 24.

Eriksen, B.V. 2002. Reconsidering the geochronological framework of late Glacial hunter-gatherer colonization of southern Scandinavia. In B.V. Eriksen and B. Bratlund (eds), *Recent studies in the final Palaeolithic of the European plain*, 25–42. Højbjerg: Jutland Archaeological Society.

Fischer, A. 1978a. På sporet af overgangen mellem palæolitikum og mesolitikum i Sydskandinavien. *Hikuin* 4, 27–50.

Fischer, A. 1978b. Bonderup-bopladsen. Det mangelnde led mellem dansk pæleolitikum og mesolitikum? *Antikvariske Studier* 5, 87–103.

Fischer, A. 1985. Late Palaeolithic finds. In K. Kristiansen (ed.), *Archaeological formation processes. The representativity of archaeological remains from Danish prehistory*, 81–88. Copenhagen: Nationalmuseet.

Fischer, A. 1991. Pioneers in deglaciated landscapes. In R.N.E. Barton, A.J. Roberts and D. Roe (eds), *The late-Glacial in north-west Europe*, 100–121. London: Council for British Archaeology, Report No. 77.

Fischer, A. 1996. At the border of human habitat. The late Palaeolithic and early Mesolithic in Scandinavia. In L. Larsson (ed.), *The earliest settlement of Scandinavia and its relationship with neighbouring areas*, 157–76. Lund: Acta Archaeologica Lundensia Series IN 8°, No. 24.

Fischer, A., Hansen, P.V. and Rasmussen, P. 1984. Macro and micro wear traces on lithic projectile points. *Journal of Danish Archaeology* 3, 19–46.

Fitzhugh, B. 2004. Colonizing the Kodiak archipelago: trends in raw material use and lithic technologies at the Tanginak spring site. *Arctic Anthropology* 41, 14–40.

Forster, P. 2004. Ice ages and the mitochondrial DNA chronology of human dispersals: a review. *Philosophical Transactions of the Royal Society of London, Series B* 359, 255–64.

Gamble, C. 1993. *Timewalkers. The prehistory of global colonization*. Stroud: Sutton.

Gamble, C. 1999. *The Palaeolithic societies of Europe*. Cambridge: Cambridge University Press.

Gordon, B.C. 1990. More on the herd-following hypothesis. *Current Anthropology* 31, 399–400.

Gordon, B.C. 2003. The enigma of the far northeastern European Mesolithic: reindeer herd followers or semi-sedentary hunters?. In L. Larsson, H. Kindgren, K. Knutsson, D. Loeffler and A. Åkerlund (eds), *Mesolithic on the move*, 115–18. Oxford: Oxbow.

Gramsch, B. 2004. From the late Palaeolithic to the early Mesolithic in north-eastern Germany. In Th. Terberger and B.V. Eriksen (eds), *Hunters in a changing world*, 183–202. Rahden, Westfalen: Verlag Marie Leidorf GmbH.

Gripp, K. 1941/2. Grönländische Rentierjäger. *Offa* 6/7, 40–51.

Grønnow, B. 1985. Meiendorf and Stellmoor revisited. An analysis of late Palaeolithic reindeer exploitation. *Acta Archaeologica* 56, 131–66.

Gustafsson, P. 1998. The earliest Stone Age occupation of eastern middle Sweden. *Current Swedish Archaeology* 6, 47–62.

Hartz, S. 1987. Neue spätpaläolithische Fundplätze bei Ahrenshöft, Kreis Nordfriesland. *Offa* 44, 5–52.

Hazelwood, L. and Steele, J. 2003. Colonizing new landscapes: archaeological detectability of the first phase. In M. Rockman and J. Steele (eds), *Colonization of unfamiliar landscapes: the archaeology of adaptation*, 203–221. London: Routledge.

Hewitt, G. 1999. Post-glacial re-colonization of European biota. *Biological Journal of the Linnean Society* 68, 87–112.

Holm, J. 1972. Istidsjægere på Æro. *Fysnke Minder* 1972, 5–16.

Huntley, B. and Birks, H.J.B. 1983. *An atlas of past and present pollen maps for Europe: 0–13,000 years ago*. Cambridge: Cambridge University Press.

Ingold, T. 1986. *The appropriation of nature. Essays on human ecology and social relations*. Manchester: Manchester University Press.

Ingold, T. 2004. Culture on the ground: the world perceived through the feet. *Journal of Material Culture* 9, 315–40.

Jensen, J. 1999. *Danmarks Oltid. Stenalder, 13.000–2.000 f.Kr.*. Copenhagen: Gyldendal.

Johansen, L. 2000. The late Palaeolithic in Denmark. In B. Valentin, P. Bodu and M. Christensen. (eds), *L'Europe centrale et septentrionale au Tardiglaciaire. Mémoires du Musée de Préhisoire d'Ile-de-France no 7, Nemours*, 19–54. Paris: APRAIF.

Keeley, L.H. 1991. Ethnographic models for late Glacial hunter-gatherers. In N. Barton, A.J. Roberts and D. Roe (eds), *The late-Glacial in north-west Europe*, 179–92. London: Council for British Archaeology, Report No. 77.

Kelly, R.L. 1983. Hunter-gatherer mobility strategies. *Journal of Anthropological Research* 39, 277–306.

Kelly, R.L. 1992. Mobility/sedentism: concepts, archaeological measures, and effects. *Annual Review of Anthropology* 21, 43–66.

Kelly, R.L. 2003. Colonization of new land by hunter-gatherers: expectations and implications based on ethnographic data. In M. Rockman and J. Steele (eds), *Colonization of unfamiliar landscapes: the archaeology of adaptation*, 44–58. London: Routledge.

Kelly, R.L. and Todd, L.C. 1988. Coming into a country: early Paleoindian hunting and mobility. *American Antiquity* 53, 231–44.

Kindgren, H. 2002. Tosskärr. Stenkyrka 94 revisited. In B.V. Eriksen and B. Bratlund (eds), *Recent studies in the final Palaeolithic of the European plain*, 49–60. Højbjerg: Jutland Archaeological Society.

Knutsson, H. (ed.) 2005. *Pioneer settlements and colonization processes in the Barents region*. Vuollerim: Vuollerim 6000år.

Kuhn, S.L. 1994. A formal approach to the design and

assembly of mobile toolkits. *American Antiquity* 59, 426–42.

Larsson, L. 1993. Neue Siedlungsfunde der Späteiszeit im Südlichen Schweden. *Archäologisches Korrespondenzblatt*, 23, 275–83.

Larsson, L. 1994. The earliest settlement in southern Sweden. Late Palaeolithic settlement remains at Finjasjön, in the north of Scania. *Current Swedish Archaeology* 2, 159–77.

Larsson, L. 1996. The colonization of southern Sweden during the deglaciation. In L. Larsson (ed.), *The earliest settlement of Scandinavia and its relationship with neighbouring areas*, 141–56. Lund: Acta Archaeologica Lundensia Series IN 8°, No. 24.

Layton, R. 2001. Hunter-gatherers, their neighbours and the nation state. In C. Panter-Brick, R. Layton and P. Rowley-Conwy (eds), *Hunter-gatherers. An interdisciplinary perspective*, 292–321. Cambridge: Cambridge University Press.

Lee, R.B. and DeVore, I. 1968. Problems in the study of hunters and gatherers. In R. B. Lee and I. DeVore (eds), *Man the hunter*, 3–12. Chicago: Aldine.

Lowe, J. J. and Walker, M. J. C. 1997. *Reconstructing Quaternary environments*. London: Longman.

Madsen, B. 1992. Hamburgkulturens flintteknologi i Jels (The Hamburgian flint technology at Jels). In J. Holm and F. Rieck (eds), *Istidsjægere ved Jelssøerne*, 93–132. Haderslev: Skrifter fra Museumsrådet for Sønderjyllands Amt 5.

Madsen, B. 1993. Flint – extraction, manufacture and distribution. In S. Hvaas and B. Storgaard (eds), *Digging into the past. 25 years of archaeology in Denmark*, 126–9. Højbjerg: Jutland Archaeological Society.

Mandryk, C.A.S. 1993. Hunter-gatherer social costs and the nonviability of submarginal environments. *Journal of Anthropological Research* 49, 39–71.

Mandryk, C.A.S. 2003. Foreword. In M. Rockman and J. Steele (eds), *Colonization of unfamiliar landscapes: the archaeology of adaptation*, xiii–xv. London: Routledge.

McGrail, S. 1987. *Ancient boats in N. W. Europe: the archaeology of water transport to AD 1500*. Harlow: Longman.

Meltzer, D.J. 2002. What do you do when no one's been there before? Thoughts on the exploration and colonization of new lands. In N. Jablonski (ed.), *The first Americans: the Pleistocene colonization of the New World*, 27–58. Golden Gate Park: University of California Press.

Meltzer, D.J. 2003. Lessons in landscape learning. In M. Rockman and J. Steele (eds), *Colonization of unfamiliar landscapes: the archaeology of adaptation*, 222–41. London: Routledge.

Narr, K.J. 1968. *Studien zur älteren und mitleren Steinzeit der Niederen Lande*. Bonn: Habelt.

Panter-Brick, C., Layton, R. and Rowley-Conwy, P. 2001. Lines of enquiry. In C. Panter-Brick, R. Layton and P. Rowley-Conwy (eds), *Hunter-gatherers. An interdisciplinary perspective*, 1–11. Cambridge: Cambridge University Press.

Pasda, C. 2004. *Hotel Grønland. Human use of caves and rockshelters in West Greenland*. Oxford: British Archaeological Reports International Series 1309.

Petersen, P.V. 1993. *Flint fra Danmarks Oltid*. Copenhagen: Gyldendal.

Petersen, P.V. and Johansen, L. 1993 Sølbjerg I – an Ahrensburgian site on a reindeer migration route through eastern Denmark. *Journal of Danish Archaeology* 10, 20–37.

Petersen, P.V. and Johansen, L. 1996. Tracking late Glacial reindeer hunters in eastern Denmark. In L. Larsson (ed.), *The earliest settlement of Scandinavia and its relationship with neighbouring areas*, 75–88. Lund: Acta Archaeologica Lundensia Series IN 8°, No. 24.

Petit, R.J., Brewer, S., Bordács, S., Burg, K., Cheddadi, R., Coart, E., Cottrell, J., Csaikl, U.M., van Dam, B., Deans, J.D., Espinel, S., Fineschi, S., Finkeldey, R., Glaz, I., Goicoechea, P.G., Jensen, J.S., König, A.O., Lowe, A.J., Madsen, S.F., Mátyás, G., Munro, R.C., Popescu, F., Slade, D., Tabbener, H., de Vries, S.G.M., Ziegenhagen, B., de Beaulieu, J.-L. and Kremer, A. 2002. Chloroplast DNA variation in European white oaks. Phylogeography and patterns of diversity based on data from over 2600 populations. *Forest Ecology and Management* 156, 5–26.

Renfrew, C. and Scarre, C. (eds) 1998. *Cognition and material culture: the archaeology of symbolic storage*. Cambridge: McDonald Institute Monographs.

Riede, F. 2005. 'To boldly go where no (hu-)man has gone before' – some thoughts on the pioneer colonisation of pristine landscapes. *Archaeological Review from Cambridge* 20, 20–38.

Rockman, M. and Steele, J. (eds) 2003. *Colonization of unfamiliar landscapes: the archaeology of adaptation*. London: Routledge.

Rowley-Conwy, P. 2001. Time, change and the archaeology of hunter-gatherers: how original is the 'original affluent society'? In C. Panter-Brick, R. Layton and P. Rowley-Conwy (eds), *Hunter-gatherers. An interdisciplinary perspective*, 39–72. Cambridge: Cambridge University Press.

Rowley-Conwy, P. and Zvelebil, M. 1989. Saving it for later: storage by prehistoric hunter-gatherers in Europe. In P. Halstead and J. O'Shea (eds), *Bad year economics*, 40–56. Cambridge: Cambridge University Press.

Rozoy, J.G. 1998. The (re-)population of northern France between 13,000 and 8,000 BP. *Quaternary International* 49/59, 69–86.

Rust, A. 1943. *Die Alt- und Mittelsteinzeitlichen Funde von Stellmoor*. Neumünster: Wachholtz Verlag.

Rust, A. 1962. *Vor 20,000 Jahren. Rentierjäger der Eiszeit*. Neumünster: Wachholtz Verlag.

Schmider, B. 1982. The Magdalenian culture of the Paris River-Basin and its relationship to the Nordic cultures of the late Old Stone Age. *World Archaeology* 14, 259–69.

Schmider, B. 1987. Environment and culture in the Seine Basin during the Late Glacial period. In J.M. Burdukiewicz and M. Kobusiewicz (eds), *Late Glacial in central Europe. Culture and environment*, 11–24. Krakow: Prace Komisji Archeologicznej No. 5.

Schmitt, L. 1994. The Hensbacka: a subsistence strategy of continental hunter-gatherers, or an adaptation at the

Pleistocene-Holocene boundary? *Oxford Journal of Archaeology* 13, 245–63.

Schmitt, L. 1995. The west Swedish Hensbacka: a maritime adaptation or a seasonal expression of the north-central European Ahrensburgian? In A. Fischer (ed.), *Man and sea in the Mesolithic*, 161–70. Oxford: Oxbow.

Schmitt, L. 1999. Comparative points and relative thoughts: the relationship between the Ahrensburgian and Hensbacka assemblages. *Oxford Journal of Archaeology* 18, 327–37.

Shrire, C. 1980. An enquiry into the evolutionary status and apparent identity of San hunter-gatherers. *Human Ecology* 8, 9–32.

Stewart, J.H. 1968. Causal factors and processes in the evolution of pre-farming societies. In R.B. Lee and I. DeVore (eds), *Man the hunter*, 321–34. Chicago: Aldine.

Sturdy, D.A. 1975. Some reindeer economies in prehistoric Europe. In E.S. Higgs (ed.), *Palaeoeconomy. Papers in economic prehistory 2*, 55–95. Cambridge: Cambridge University Press.

Sørensen, M. and Sternke, F. 2004. Nørregård VI – Lateglacial hunters in transition. In Th. Terberger and B.V. Eriksen (eds), *Hunters in a changing world*, 85–112. Rahden, Westfalen: Verlag Marie Leidorf GmbH.

Taute, W. 1968. *Die Stielspitzen-Gruppen im nördlichen Mitteleuropa. Ein Beitrag zur Kenntnis der späten Altsteinzeit.* Köln: Böhlau Verlag.

Tolan-Smith, C. 2003. The social context of landscape learning and the late glacial-early postglacial recolonization of the British Isles. In M. Rockman and J. Steele (eds), *Colonization of unfamiliar landscapes: the archaeology of adaptation*, 116–29. London: Routledge.

Tromnau, G. 1975. *Neue Ausgrabungen im Ahrensburger Tunneltal. Ein Beitrag zur Erforschung des Jungpaläolithikums im Nordwesteuropäischen Flachland.* Neumünster: Karl Wachholtz Verlag.

Tromnau, G. 1984a. Rentierjagd während des Spätpaläolothikums von Booten aus?. *Hammaburg N.F.* 6, 29–38.

Tromnau, G. 1984b. Siedlungsmuster Hamburger Kultur. Beispiel Teltwisch 1 (Ahrensbuger Tunneltal). In H. Berke, J. Hahn, C.-J. Kind (eds), *Jungpaläolithische Siedlungsstrukturen in Europa*, 235–9. Tübingen: Archaeologica Venatoria.

Tromnau, G. 1987. Late Palaeolithic reindeer-hunting and the use of boats. In J. M. Burdukiewicz and M. Kobusiewicz (eds), *Late Glacial in central Europe. Culture and environment*, 95–106. Krakow: Prace Komisji Archeologicznej Nr.5.

White, R. 1989. Husbandry and herd control in the Upper Palaeolithic: A critical review of the evidence. *Current Anthropology* 30, 609–32.

Woodburn, J. 1982. Egalitarian societies. *Man* 17, 431–51.

Åkerlund, A. 2002. Life without close neighbours. Some reflections on the first peopling of east Central Sweden. In B.V. Eriksen and B. Bratlund (eds), *Recent studies in the Final Palaeolithic of the European plain*, 43–48. Højbjerg: Jutland Archaeological Society.

3 On the trail of the Caribou hunters: archaeological surveys in Western Greenland

Ulla Odgaard

Introduction

In Western Greenland, just south of the polar circle and the long fjord Kangerlussuaq (Søndre Strømfjord), lies a now abandoned landscape – Angujaartorfiup Nunaa – sheltered by ice-caps (Fig. 3.1). In this area there is a long hunting tradition in a practically intact and fossilised landscape, where the archaeological remains are so well preserved you can almost feel the presence of the hunters of the Thule culture (from *c.* 1200 AD). They lived on the coast most of the year, but used to make a yearly, long and strenuous journey to get to this inland area and spend

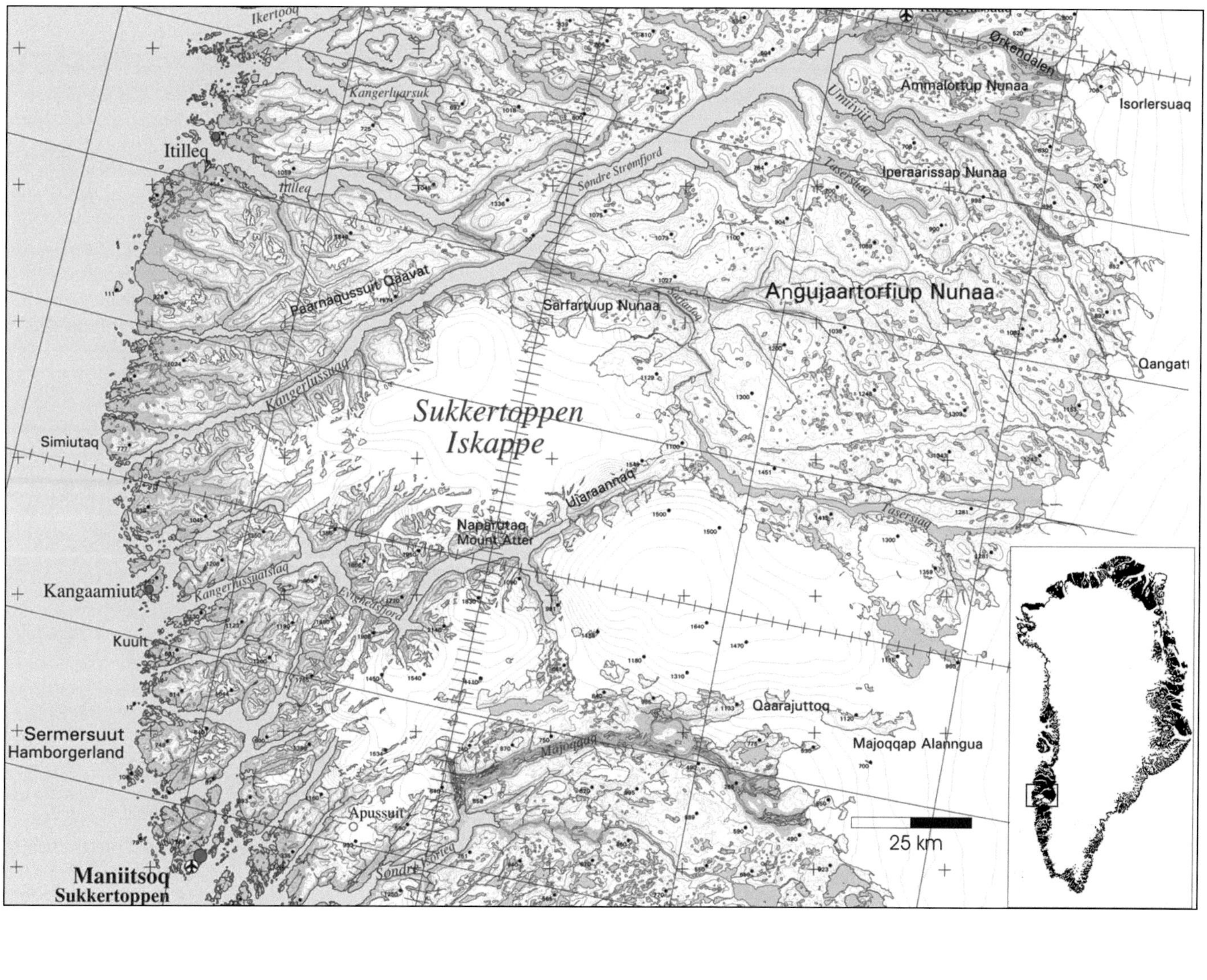

Fig. 3.1. The Maniitsoq area in Western Greenland

the summer hunting caribou. The hunters of the Thule culture were direct ancestors of modern Inuit, and in several cases it has been possible to interpret archaeological structures with the help of the existing ethnographic and ethno-historic source material describing life in this area (Grønnow 1986; Grønnow *et al.* 1983).

The economy of the Thule culture was primarily based on marine resources, and their mode of transportation was designed for journeys on the sea and through fjords: kayak and umiak in summer and dog-sledge during the winter. Most of Greenland is covered by inland ice with a rather narrow strip of ice-free land around it. There are, however, a few areas in Greenland where it is possible to write of an 'inland', where transportation had to be by foot.

The Thule culture has its origin in Alaska around 1000 AD, from where it spread eastwards; it reached northern Greenland in the twelfth century AD. During the following three centuries this expansive culture colonised most of Greenland, which was then occupied only by the Norse in the south-westernmost part of the country (Gulløv 1997; 2004). Older archaeological traces derive from the Palaeo-Eskimos (2500 BC–1000 AD), who belonged to a Stone Age tradition. They were not directly related to the Inuit and it seems that they had left Greenland, except for the Thule-area, when the Inuit arrived (Gulløv 2004).

In Greenland, the tradition of going hunting at a summer camp is still upheld by some families, but modern life requires more equipment, and travelling is difficult and time consuming in Angujaartorfiup Nunaa. The consequence is that for the last 40–50 years hunters have primarily used the areas near the coasts of the 150km long Søndre Strømfjord, where access is possible by motorboat, while the inland is left with only traces of former summer life.

The project

Previous research was carried out in a geographically and topographically more accessible area, at Aasivissuit north of the Søndre Strømfjord, where an interdisciplinary team (archaeology, ethnology and zoo-archaeology) investigated caribou hunting methods and processing of game on the basis of excavations in the midden area of a hunting camp (Grønnow *et al.* 1983). This work was succeeded by mapping and survey south of Søndre Strømfjord in the Paradise Valley, which drew attention to the hunting grounds in Angujaartorfiup Nunaa as a potential area for future research (Grønnow 1986).

In 2001 the project 'Coastal, fjord and inland dwellers: settlement patterns in central west Greenland' was implemented by SILA – The Greenland Research Centre at the National Museum of Denmark. The fieldwork was carried out by an international team of archaeologists (from Denmark, Germany, Norway and Greenland) in collaboration with the National Museum of Greenland.

During three field seasons (2001–2003), we have concentrated on undertaking reconnaissance in the highland areas of Angujaartorfiup Nunaa, a region where no archaeological surveys had previously taken place (Gabriel *et al.* 2002; Odgaard and Knudsen 2005; Odgaard *et al.* 2003).

In 2003 fieldwork was supplemented by ethno-archaeological investigations in a camp of modern caribou hunters in Angujaatorfik, at the Søndre Strømfjord. During her work on a thesis on traditional knowledge about caribou hunting in Angujaartorfiup Nunaa, Pauline Knudsen interviewed the few surviving people who used to go hunting inland from the early 1900s to the 1950s (Knudsen 2001). One of these women still has a camp in Angujaartorfik, where she demonstrated how the caribou meat was cut and dried in the traditional way (Odgaard and Knudsen 2005).

Historical sources

Prior to our first encounter with the landscape we had some preconceived ideas about human presence and use of the area. At the request of H.J. Rink, who collected Greenland legends, Aron of Kangeq and Jens Kreutzmann, both nineteenth century hunters but also painters, made watercolours and drawings to illustrate myths and legends. Aron illustrated, for example, the legend of the poor girl who, after escaping from a grave where her parents-in-law buried her alive with her dead husband, crawled on her knees all the way from Tasersiaq in the south, over the high plain of Angujaartorfiup Nunaa, to the coast of Søndre Strømfjord (Fig. 3.2). Both Aron and Kreutzmann participated in hunting in Angujaartorfiup Nunaa, and both have left a number of watercolours and drawings showing in some cases identifiable sites and landscapes (Fig. 3.3). In addition to these sources we have ethnographic information about traditional Greenland life dating from 1950, when many old men and women from all the districts in west Greenland answered questionnaires designed by the ethnographer Kaj Birket-Smith of the National Museum of Denmark (Grønnow 1986).

The use of maps

Among the historical information is a map produced by Jens Kreutzmann in 1863 (Fig. 3.4). At that time, geographical maps of the coast existed but the inland was not yet mapped. Kreutzmann's map shows the area from the Søndre Strømfjord in the north,

Fig. 3.2. Aron's watercolour of the poor girl who had to crawl on her knees over the high plain (from Thisted 1997)

Fig. 3.3. The assembly camp in Angujaartorfik, with skin tents, umiaks and people, as Aron saw it in the mid nineteenth century (from Thisted 1997)

southwards to include Maniitsoq, and from the outermost islands at the west coast to the inland ice – an area of about 200km across. It was drawn with ink on paper sized 25 x 39cm. There are, of course, inaccuracies when comparing Kreutzmann's map with the modern geographical map, but the overall picture is quite precise. Kreutzmann had a tent house in the area, and he drew the land he had walked and which had been described to him by other hunters. On the map he noted information such as 'people from Sarfannguit visit this area' and 'usually nobody comes here in this area'. Kreutzmann noted 270 place names, indicated on the map with numbers. He also noted camps and routes from the coast to the inner part of the area in Angujaartorfiup Nunaa; it is possible to identify three different locations on the coast of Søndre Strømfjord from where these inland journeys began (Fig. 3.5).

Most of the lakes, rivers and sites have descriptive names or names related to use: for example Kangerlussuaq – 'big fjord', Tasersuaq – 'big lake', Angujaartorfik – 'the place where they catch up on each other', Umiivii – 'place where the umiaks are landed', Eqalummiut – 'the trout fishers camp'. Others have names related to legends and myths: Tasersiaq – 'the acquired lake' and Qivittoq Nunaa – 'land of the mountain-wanderers'. The latter refers to outcasts or people who for psychological reasons were hiding in the wilderness to escape society. They became mythical and acquired the frightening characteristics of ghosts because it was unknown whether they were dead or alive (Guldberg Mikkelsen 1998).

Nutall (1992) refers to the Greenlandic landscape as a 'memoryscape', where points in the local area are thought about and remembered with reference to specific events and experiences (Nutall 1992).

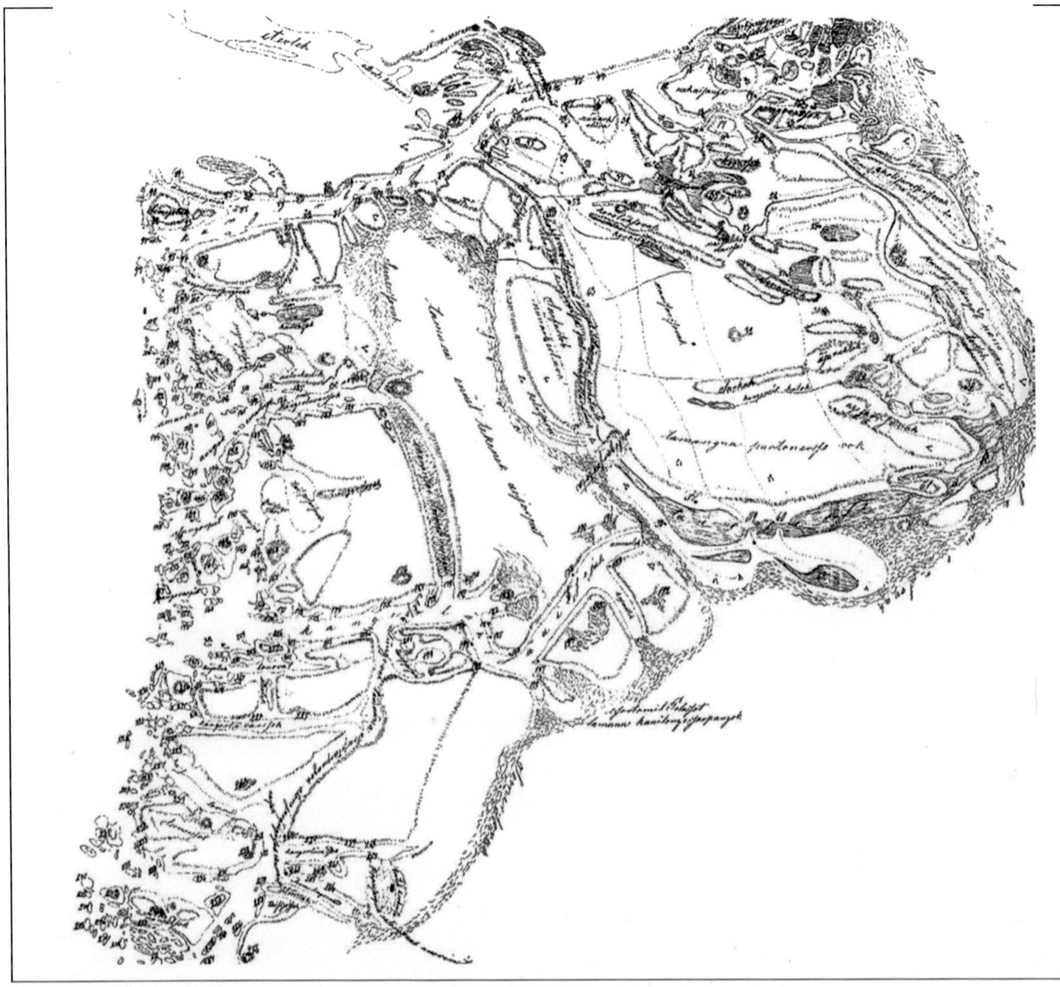

Fig. 3.4. The map of the Maniitsoq area drawn by Jens Kreutzmann in 1863 (from Meldgaard 1982)

Jens Kreutzmann was able to turn his own knowledge and experience of the landscape into a geographical map that makes sense to us in the modern world. According to Whitridge (2004), the Inuit possessed technical practices that reified space in a manner hardly distinguishable from Western scientific spatialities. A traditional Inuit map was not portable; instead it consisted of schematic representations of major topographic features drawn in outline or sculpted in relief in snow or sand. They were typically created as visual aids when providing travel directions, and were accompanied by detailed descriptions of such things as wind and sea conditions, landmarks, available resources, travel routes, travel times, and the all important place names: 'The map and the recitation of place names together traced a path through a hybrid socionatural landscape, a simultaneously real and imaginary geography' (Whitridge 2004, 223).

Most modern Greenlanders navigate using scientific geographical maps, but during interviews of six people, who spent the summers in the inland of Angujaartorfiup Nunaa 'in the old days', only one of them was able to point out his own camps and routes on a modern geographical map (Knudsen 2001). Petersen (1986) referred to the same problem in connection to his own interviews of older hunters from another area. Also Nuttall (1992) records from his fieldwork in north-west Greenland that 'most older hunters I interviewed had difficulty relating to sheet maps' (Nuttall 1992, 49). As demonstrated above, this does not mean that traditional hunters were not able to communicate locations and routes. On the contrary, scientific maps were considered inaccurate compared with a hunter's memory of the places they chart, and the place names that are recorded on the maps are often wrong (Nuttall 1992, 49).

The landscape and the approaches

Angujaartorfiup Nunaa is a topographically isolated area of approximately 17,000km^2, surrounded by the Søndre Strømfjord to the north and three ice caps to the west, south and east. The central part of the area is a high plain (1000–1300m Above Mean Sea Level) with mountain peaks up to 1500m and many rivers and lakes. The climate this far inland is

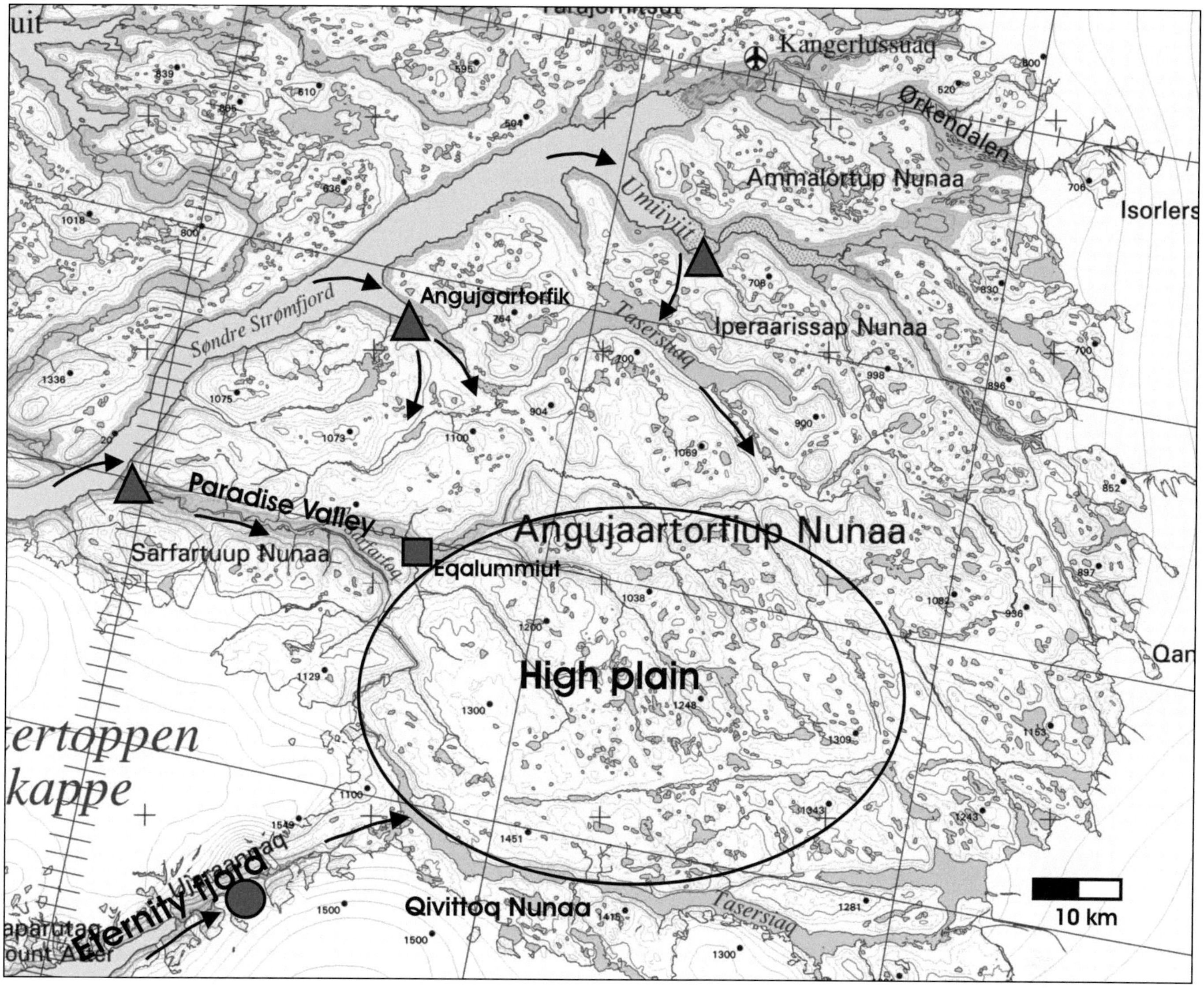

Fig. 3.5. Map of Angujaartorfiup Nunaa: ▲ *= approaches according to Kreutzmann,* ● *= possible earlier approach,* ■ *= the base camp Eqalummiut*

'arctic desert', with very cold winters and temperatures of below -30 °C, but with usually fairly dry and sunny summers.

At the northernmost approach location, 'Umiiviit' (Fig. 3.5), the umiaks were carried up to Lake Tasersuaq. It was said to be an exhausting job lasting for a whole day, but rewarding since it made it possible to continue further inland by boat (Petersen 1992). To get to the highland and the attractive hunting grounds, the journey had to continue by foot.

At the other approaches the umiaks were left, and families would walk inland from the fjord in the north, and some families would walk as far as the huge, 90km long, glacial lake Tasersiaq to the south (Fig. 3.6). At the eastern end, the lake is bounded by the ice cap expulsing ice into the lake; at the western end it runs out in a violent river system. To cross this ice-cold, dangerous lake the historical sources describe that some would bring their kayaks, carrying them up in the mountains, over the high plain and this far inland. Two kayaks tied together could serve as a 'ferry' for people and gear across the lake (Fig. 3.7)(Petersen 1992). In historical times this has been the only way to get to this area, but ancient tales tell of a time when it was possible to get easier access, and even bring umiaks, to the Tasersiaq lake (Thisted 1999). This shorter route went from the south-west through the Eternity Fjord (Fig. 3.5), whose inner part is blocked by glaciers and now impassable. This information is likely to be true, reminding us that the impression of an intact environment is mistaken. The ice caps appear solid at first glance, but the glaciers are constantly moving, covering areas today that earlier were exposed and inhabitable.

The terrain is rocky and in most places difficult to walk over. Our leather boots got heavily worn and damaged from the sharp-edged rocks. The skin kamiks (sealskin boots) of the Thule hunters must have needed constant repairing, and some of the

Fig. 3.6. Settlement on the northern bank of Tasersiaq. Antlers are lying inside a dwelling structure.

Fig. 3.7. Aron's watercolour showing people crossing Tasersiaq in kayaks (from Thisted 1997)

historical sources do mention that hunting teams had to include people who were able to repair the kamiks (Nellemann 1969/70).

The principal game was the caribou, which migrate inland where they calve in June in the areas close to the ice. They stay inland until autumn, when they again migrate out to spend the winter in sheltered coastal valleys. Other game in the area were arctic hare, arctic fox, and waterfowl (Grønnow *et al.* 1983). Today the dominant animal is the musk ox, which was imported in the 1960s from north-eastern Greenland.

The fieldwork

The principal method used during our archaeological fieldwork was to walk – mostly in two teams of two or three persons – with our gear and provisions for one week in backpacks. A helicopter put us down at one spot from where we would walk to an appointed place. Here the helicopter would come back with new supplies after a week, sometimes also lifting us over large rivers or moving us to another area. Every field season during the archaeological survey we walked a couple of hundred kilometres, mapping the sites on our way with GPS. Every site and structure has been photo documented and described, and selected structures have been measured and sketched.

Our first move in 2001 was to go by helicopter deep into the area on the rugged and harsh high plain. To be left there in a totally deserted, and to us unknown, area was a shocking experience. But the shock was rather quickly overcome when we found the first traces of earlier human presence. In the following days we moved around by foot and found more signs of human activity, and so the landscape became more and more 'familiar' to us. This deserted, mountainous area turned out to be filled with structures that were not put there for us. But their presence changed the landscape from a wilderness to a cultural landscape.

Camp-systems

During the three field seasons we found more than 300 sites, varying in size from just a single archaeological structure to a base camp with many structures. The structures are tent houses, tent rings, hunter's beds, rock shelters, graves, caches, cairns, fox-traps, shooting blinds and hunting drive-systems (for the location of sites see Fig. 3.8). The various types of dwelling structures were used on different types of journeys:

(1) *Tent houses* consist of low stone and/or turf walls over which the tent was raised. There is usually only one room inside the tent house, with a low 'sleeping platform' at the rear (Fig. 3.9). From the survey it is possible to distinguish at least five types of tent houses (Odgaard *et al.* in prep.).
(2) *Tent rings* are the rings of rocks that anchored the skin (and later canvas) tents.
(3) *Hunters' beds* are rectangular or oval stone frames consisting of a single course or two courses of large stones (Fig. 3.10). The sizes vary, but in general they measure between 1.5 x 2m and 2 x 4m. The function of hunters' beds is known from historic and ethnographic sources: the frame was filled with heather (if available) and covered with caribou skins to make a warm mat on which hunters, lying side by side, could stay overnight (Grønnow 1986, 72).
(4) *Rock shelters* can be recognised by traces of human activity such as fireplaces, artefacts, and broken marrowbones, which are often found in natural cavities under cliffs or large boulders. In some cases, the shelter is improved by means of a small stone wall built in front of the cavity (Fig. 3.11) (Grønnow 1986; see also Pasda 2004).

These structures were used at different stages of

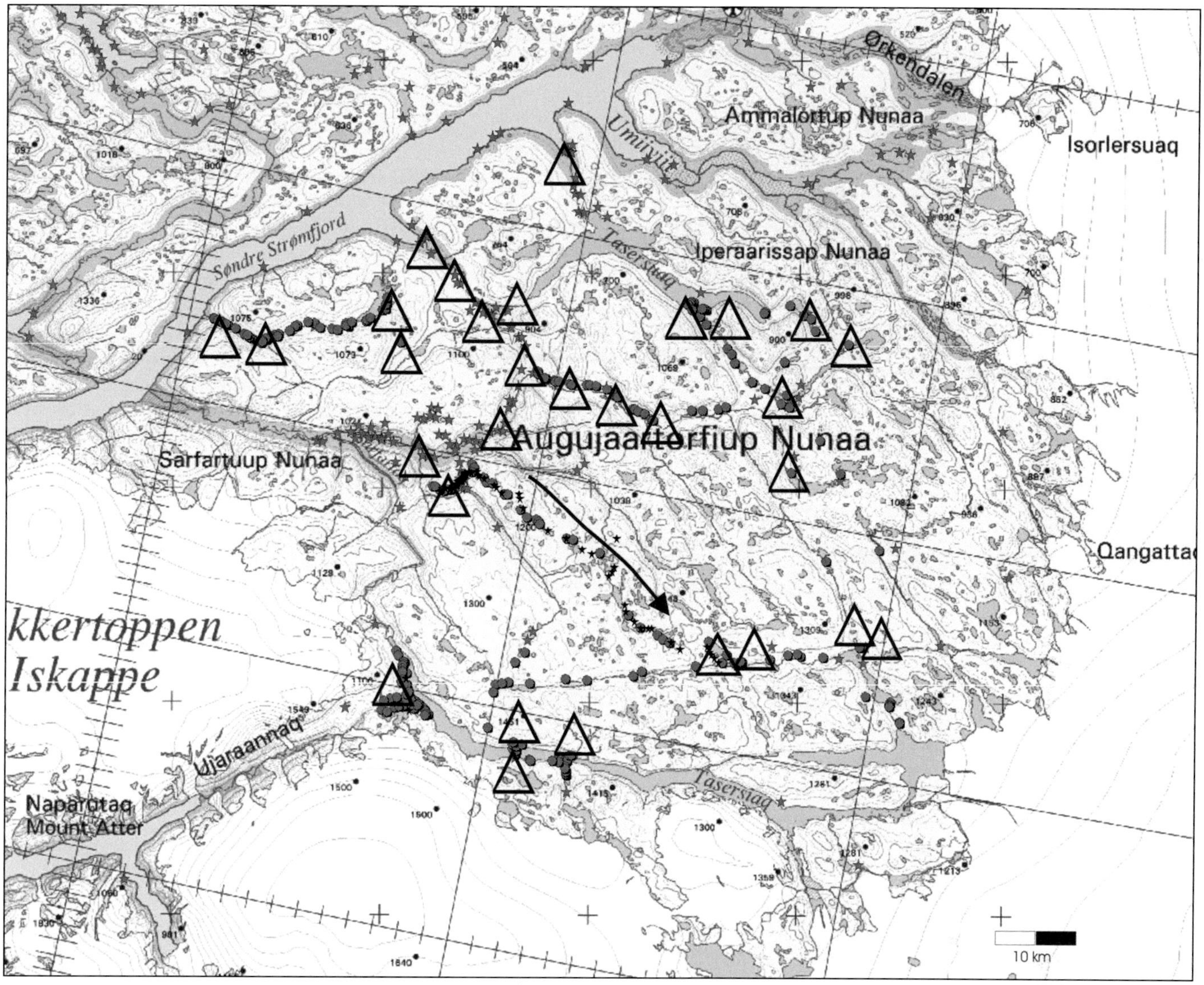

Fig. 3.8. ★ *= surveys prior to the project,* ● *= the project's records,* △ *= location of basecamps;* ★ *= cairns (only a few of the many hundreds are marked). The arrow shows the 'cairn-route' across the high plain*

the journey inland. Grønnow (1986) deduced five different camp types based on ethnographic records:

(1) *Assembly camps* by the fjord, where family groups coming from the settlements at the coast stored their umiaks before they proceeded to the different hunting areas. They met here again after the hunting season, and before they started the long journey back to the coastal winter settlements.
(2) *Travelling camps*, used as sleeping and resting places along the route inland to the main caribou hunting area.
(3) *Primary base camps*, inhabited by families or segments of families during the entire caribou-hunting season.
(4) *Overnight camps*, used by hunting groups during hunting expeditions from the primary base camp.

Fig. 3.12 is a graphic representation of a camp-system in a fictitious summer caribou hunt based on the above classification of the camps (Danholm *et al.* 1991).

Tents are found at assembly camps and travelling camps, when people were on their way to or from the base camps and transporting their tent with them. Base camps can be defined by primarily the presence of tent houses, where the family would stay for the summer. The tent house is the marker of the base camp but other types of structures, such as caches, graves, traps and also tents, can also be present. Hunter's beds and rock shelters were used on hunting trips from the base camp. When applying this model

Fig. 3.9. Tenthouse, seen from the rear

Fig. 3.10. Two hunters' beds: one to the right in the foreground, another one a little further away

Fig. 3.11. Rock shelter

for the locations of the sites, a web of former journeys and territoriality appears (Pasda 2004).

There is also evidence that hunters used the area long before the Thule culture. It has long been known that the Stone Age cultures of Greenland – the Palaeo-Eskimos – have left many sites at the coast of Søndre Strømfjord. It was, however, a new discovery when Grønnow *et al.* (1983) found Palaeo-Eskimo traces inland. Excavations of the soil behind some of the shooting blinds revealed chalcedony flakes and pieces of gun flints, indicating that the blinds were used in Palaeo-Eskimo as well as Neo-Eskimo times (Grønnow 1986, 64). The Palaeo-Eskimo dwelling was the tent, and the present project documented a few Palaeo-Eskimo inland sites with tent-rings that are much less visible than the Thule structures. A targeted effort with the employment of test excavations is necessary to unveil the Stone Age use of the inland.

Route markers

One kind of structure that we cannot relate to the ethno-historical sources of the area is the 'head-cairn' used as a route-marker. The ethno-history does not describe any human-made route markings. The routes are described as related to rivers, passes, lakes and other spots in the landscape (Petersen 1992), but what we encountered on our walks was that rocks had been deliberately arranged to catch the eye. For example, single rocks were placed on top of boulders marking the locations of structures such as hunters' beds, rock-shelters or meat-caches, while routes across the landscape were marked with head-cairns.

It was a phenomenon we observed during the first year of survey, and we tested it during the second year by following a row of route-markers. We started out at the southern side of the large base-camp 'Eqalummiut', where we knew, from Jens Kreutzmann's map and historical sources, that hunters used to travel south across the high plain. We succeeded in following a route of about 50km by walking from one cairn to the next (see Fig. 3.8). The head-cairns were often one smaller rock on top of a larger boulder in a different colour (Fig. 3.13), or the small rock had a distinct angular shape attracting our attention. On our way we found hunters' beds, rock-shelters and shooting blinds, which would have been very difficult to locate in the rocky and expansive terrain if we had not been directed by the cairns. In some areas there were many markers, in other areas only a few. But we were never in doubt which way to go, except sometimes when we lost the trail. In these (two) cases there were no more markers and no other kinds of structures, but when we found our way back to the trail, sites began to appear again.

It is remarkable that the historical sources do not mention these markers. In one instance we tried to follow a route described by an older woman – another of Knudsen's informants – who used to walk this route in the 1930s and 1940s. Confronted with the question of whether there were cairns marking the route, she answered in the negative, and her description was purely related to the natural landscape. When we followed the route it turned out there were cairns that were impossible to overlook. When presented with photos of cairns, the woman confirmed to have seen them, but she did not relate any significance to them (P. Knudsen, *pers comm.*).

Although cairns, in the form of well-build cone-shaped stone-structures, are often found as landmarks along the coast in many places in Greenland, route marking with rocks inland is no longer used or part of historical memory. However, this phenomenon is well known from the history of the Canadian Inuit, where the cairns are known as 'inuksuk', meaning 'that which acts in the capacity of a human'. According to Hallendy (2000) some of these inuksuit 'have been carefully arranged in sequences stretching great distances, marking out a particular route across an area complicated by hills, rivers and lakes'. This is an exact description of our experience.

Spirit of the place

While walking on the trails of the caribou hunters, the landscape with its traces of former hunting life started to make so much sense to us we could nearly predict where the locations of sites on our way would be found. We almost imagined that we understood the prehistoric hunters and were sharing the experience of the landscape with them in an empathic way (Fig. 3.14). However, this illusion was destroyed by another type of structure that the historical sources had not prepared us to meet. These were 'arrangements' of rocks, for example on an eye-catching, huge, square, natural rock with an anthropoid rock standing in a small 'chamber' of four other rocks (Fig. 3.15). This arrangement is located in an otherwise desolate, inhospitable area of the landscape north of the last mountain range to be crossed before reaching the glacial meltwater lake 'Tasersiaq'. Another rather similar arrangement was located when we were following the 'cairn-route', and on this trail we found that other anthropoid or zoomorphic rocks had been arranged to catch the eye. These structures did not immediately make sense and we have had to consider explanations other than the purely functional.

The historical sources were written after the arrival of the Christian mission to Greenland, and we only encounter the previous religious ideology in tales and legends. One account of a caribou hunt, taking place in the mid eighteenth century, describes how, since no animals were met, the hunters carried out 'old hunting magic' whereupon the caribou appeared. The description of the magic ritual is only fragmentary, but it implied the manufacture of a caribou representation and the recitation of a magic formula. When the hunters returned to their base camp with their game, it turned out that the Divine (Christian) Providence had discovered this offence and through the appearance of two angels warned against it being repeated (Lidegaard 1986).

These hunters lived in a time of ideological change: the missionaries preached Christianity and a number of people were already baptised. But magic could still be applied when hunting far inland, apparently with success. We must acknowledge that the earlier hunters' perception of the landscape differed totally from the landscape we experienced. It is, however, possible to get an idea of what these people experienced. Some of the historical legends provide insights into a landscape with creatures other than game animals. It is told that prior to the arrival of the Christian mission people lived in the realm of the 'angakoks' (Inuit shamans). The land was not only inhabited by real human beings, the Inuit, but also by a vast number of different spiritual creatures. The relationship to these 'others' was usually strained and most of the old stories describe a conflict, with 'non-humans' robbing and often mistreating a human being. Inuit lived at the coast, while 'the others' lived both out on the other side of the outermost islands and further inland. Therefore, strange things could happen when people went too far out on the open sea, just as it was perceived as dangerous when in the summer Inuit went inland (Thisted 1997, 20).

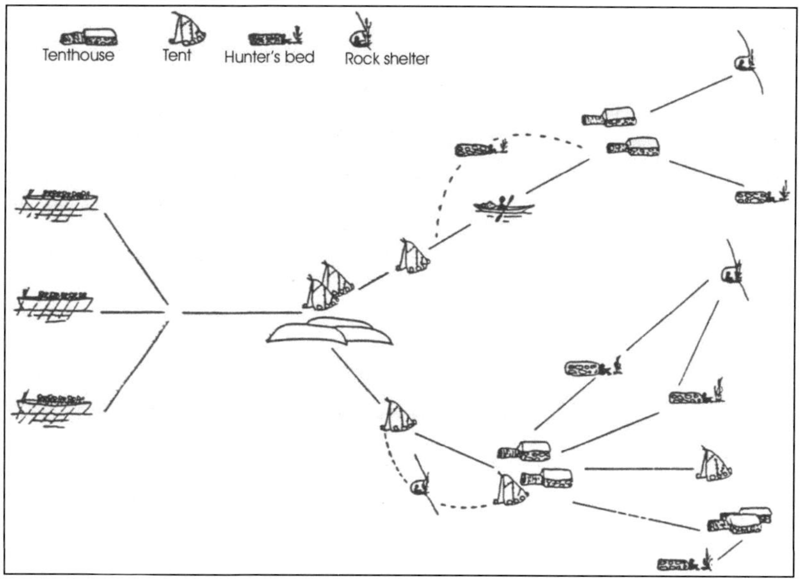

Fig. 3.12. Model of a fictional summer hunt (Danholm et al. *1991)*

Fig. 3.13. Head-cairn: white rock on top of black boulder

Fig. 3.14. Members of the team taking a break in a hunters' bed build in conjunction with some boulders

Is it possible that this shamanistic worldview can explain the strange rock arrangements?

From Inuit in Canada a possibly similar phenomenon is known. Some inuksuks are formally grouped to define a specific place or to form a circle, which, at least in traditional times, was a place of power that demanded respect. Others were single upright stones where people left offerings in the hope of receiving protection from helpful spirits (Hallendy 2000). This phenomenon transcends the Inuit culture. In northern Scandinavia the Saami people, who were reindeer hunters and later reindeer herders, venerated strangely formed rocks. These stones are usually known as 'seite' and are thought to be connected with spirits or gods. In one of the oldest records, from the Lule Lappmark in Sweden, they are described as 'stone gods which the Saami find in the mountains or at lakes having either the likeness of men or animals; these stones they raise on mountains or in crevices or along rivers and lakes where in olden days they have heard some ghostly disturbances' (Rheen 1897, 39 quoted in Hultkrantz 1994). It is also said that a seite 'exercises power over all animals….so that they can give good luck (to the hunter) to catch them' (Rheen 1897, 39 quoted in Hultkrantz 1994). Maybe the Greenlandic anthropoid cairns had similar functions as representations of spirits that could protect and/or offer success in hunting. Birket-Smith (1924), who conducted expeditions to Inuit areas, including Greenland, mentions that he noticed a belief in 'the spirit of the place': 'From of old the Greenlanders look upon several places as dangerous to pass, unless they sacrifice to the spirit of the place. It is by no means valuable things, which are required. The spirit is content with a bit of blubber or an empty match-box' (Birket-Smith 1924, 219).

It seems that when on a journey to the inland, which was filled with hostile spirits, there could be good reasons for making offerings and/or reciting magic formulas to appease these powers. We can conclude from analogy that structures similar to our stone arrangements were known as representations of spirits or gods that could protect and provide luck in hunting. It is even possible that we can get close to the core of the Greenland cairn phenomenon when recalling Hultkrantz's conclusion: 'It is obvious that the seite was supposed to be the master of the place, or district. As such, it was also seen as the master of all game that lived within its jurisdiction. This is a good illustration of the intermingling of the principle of territorialism and the principle of animalism, as the seite functions as master of both place and game' (Hultkrantz 1994, 362). So the rock arrangements possibly constituted a way of gaining contact with the spirits of the landscape and also served as a territorial marker. But their presence also meant that 'places' were created, which again can refer to the Inuit way of navigating a landscape by following a route of named places.

Reasons for journeys

But why did the caribou hunters and their families risk going on the long journey, at first by umiak from the settlements on the outer coast, and then by foot through strenuous terrain carrying heavy loads of gear and dried caribou meat when returning? One of Knudsen's informants had ten children and was often pregnant during the travel, when she carried the youngest child on top of her pack. Her husband carried the next youngest child on his pack, while the rest of the children had to walk, which demanded much persuasion and encouragement

Fig. 3.15. Arrangement of rocks

along the way (Knudsen 2001). They could have chosen to stay at the coast, which some people actually did, subsisting from sealing and fishing all through the summer. The obvious answer is that they wanted the caribou skins, preferred for clothes and for sleeping, and also the tasty caribou meat that was dried and brought back for winter supply. But social factors were just as important. The journey meant opportunities to visit friends and relatives along the way. At the assembly camp, Angujaartorfik, people would stay for some time to enjoy each other's company and celebrate the successful hunting season before going back to their respective camps at the coast (Knudsen 2001; Petersen 1992).

Aporta (2004) concludes, from the Oral History Project at Igloolik, Canada, that even though subsistence plays an important role in residence and mobility patterns, both ethnographic literature and interviews with contemporary elders, suggest a much larger set of reasons for travelling. These include love of change, trading, visiting relatives, geographic curiosity, exploration and social pressure: 'Travelling for the Inuit is not a transitional activity of going from point A to point B. Life happens while travelling. Other travellers are met, children are born, and hunting, fishing and other subsistence activities are performed' (Aporta 2004, 13).

Conclusion and perspectives

The landscape of Angujaartorfiup Nunaa is best understood as a landscape of journeys, where many of the archaeological features are directly related to travelling and movement. It is still possible to walk on the trails of the caribou hunters and see the same landscape as they did. But through time the journeys on these trails have been through different realms, seen from different perspectives, ideologies and ethics.

One of the strengths of this project is the possibility of combining the archaeology with the ethno-history in a contextual study of the dynamics and change of human use of the area. The project still has objectives to pursue that will involve further fieldwork and excavation at selected sites. At this stage, when only a few test-excavations and C-14 samples have been made, it is possible to see the journeys as an overall web (Pasda 2004), which should however not be understood as static. The central resource, the caribou, was unstable, with dramatic population fluctuations and hunting strategies that changed through time (Grønnow 1986; Grønnow *et al.* 1983). The peak of the hunting in the early eighteenth century, which can be connected to communal drive-hunts as documented by the Aassivissuit excavation north of Søndre Strømfjord (Grønnow 1986; Grønnow *et al.* 1983), could also be traced in our test excavations, showing the changing hunting strategy of the Neo-Eskimo Thule culture (Odgaard *et al.* in prep.). Angujaartorfiup Nunaa was, in historical times, inhabited usually from July to September, when people from the coast used the area. The situation at the coast was never static for the Inuit, who from the thirteenth to the sixteenth centuries colonised all of Greenland. From the beginning of the eighteenth century, European whalers and missionaries at the west coast of Greenland provided opportunities for trade, causing a new change in occupation patterns and dwelling design. They also introduced epidemic diseases that spread and decimated the population, destroying some of the former social structures (Gulløv 1997; 2004). The sites of Angujaartorfiup Nunaa must be interpreted in relation to these factors. Another perspective is that the Thule people were not the first to make Angujaartorfiup Nunaa their hunting grounds. When they arrived, the Palaeo-Eskimos (2500 BC–1000 AD) had left the area, but they had also left behind a cultural landscape furnished with traces of their camps and hunting structures. These two hunting cultures were extremely different with regards economy, technology and social organisation, and the possibility of comparing their strategies of colonisation and exploration of the landscape adds time-depth and new perspectives to this project.

Bibliography

Aporta, C. 2004. Routes, trails and tracks: trail breaking among the Inuit of Igloolik. *Inuit Studies* 28, 9–38.

Birket-Smith, K. 1924. *Ethnography of the Egedesminde District, with aspects of the general culture of West Greenland. Meddelelser om Grønland*, bind LXVI. Copenhagen. Kommissionen for ledelsen af de geologiske og geografiske undersøgelser i Grønland.

Danholm, B., Ravn, L. and Sørensen, L 1991. Neoeskimoiske indfaldsveje og bopladsplaceringer. In Pind, J., Grønnow, B., Ipsen, J., Odgaard, U. and Schilling, H. (eds) *Aasivissuit. Bopladser og rensdyrjagt i det vestgrønlandske indland.* . 43–58. , University of Copenhagen.

Gabriel, M., Grønnow, B., Odgaard, U., Pasda, C. and Pasda, K. 2002. Bosættelsesmønstre i det Centrale Vestgrønland – Rapport om undersøgelserne i Angujaartorfiup Nunaa, Maniitsoq Kommune, sommeren 2001. *Sila-Feltrapport 4*, Nationalmuseet København. Field report on file at the National Museum of Denmark.

Grønnow, B. 1986. Archaeological investigations of West Greenland caribou hunting. *Arctic Anthropology* 23, 57–80.

Grønnow, B., Meldgaard, M. and Nielsen, J. 1983. *Aasivissuit: The Great Summer Camp: archaeological, ethnographical and zooarchaeological studies of a caribou-hunting site in West Greenland.* Copenhagen: Meddelelser om Grønland, Man and Society 5.

Guldberg Mikkelsen, H. 1998. Polarcirklens dæmon. *Tidsskriftet Grønland* 3, 107–111.

Gulløv, H.C. 1997. *From middle ages to colonial times: archaeological and ethnohistorical studies of the Thule culture in south west Greenland 1300–1800 AD.* Copenhagen: Meddelelser om Grønland, Man and Society 23.

Gulløv, H.C. (ed.) 2004. *Grønlands forhistorie.* Copenhagen, Gyldendal.

Hallendy, N. 2000. *Inuksuit: silent messengers of the Arctic.* University of Washington.

Hultkrantz, Å. 1994. Religion and environment among the Saami: an ecological study. In T. Irimoto and T. Yamada (eds), *Circumpolar religion and ecology: an anthropology of the north*, 347–74. University of Tokyo Press.

Knudsen, P. 2001. *Rekonstruktion af brugen af Angujaartorfiup Nunaa I 1900-tallet, baseret på 6 interviews.* University of Nuuk. Greenland: Unpulished B.A. thesis.

Lidegaard, M. 1986: Profeterne i Evighedsfjorden. Habakuk og Maria Magdalena. *Tidsskriftet Grønland* 6–7, 177–244.

Meldgaard, J. 1982. *Aron.* Copenhagen: The National Museum of Denmark.

Nellemann, G. 1969/70. Caribou hunting in West Greenland. *Folk* 11–12, 133–53.

Nuttall, M. 1992. *Arctic homeland: kinship, community and development in northwest Greenland.* Toronto: University of Toronto.

Odgaard, U., Grønnow, B., Gabriel, M., Pasda, C., Pasda, K. and Damm, C. 2003. Bosættelsesmønstre i det Centrale Vestgrønland – Rapport om undersøgelserne i Angujaartorfiup Nunaa, Maniitsoq Kommune, sommeren 2002. *SILA-Feltrapport 12.* Field report on file at the National Museum of Denmark.

Odgaard, U. (ed.), Grønnow, B., Knudsen, P., Pasda, C. and Pasda, K. In prep. *Landscape of the caribou hunters.*

Odgaard, U. and Knudsen, P 2005. Bosættelsesmønstre i det centrale Vestgrønland. Rapport om undersøgelserne i Angujaartorfiup Nunaa, Maniitsoq Kommune, sommeren 2003. *SILA – Feltrapport 20.* Field report on file at the National Museum of Denmark.

Pasda, C. 2004. *Hotel Grønland: human use of caves and rock shelters in West Greenland.* Oxford: British Archaeological Reports International Series 1309.

Petersen, H.C. 1986. Recording the utilization of land and sea resources in Greenland. *Arctic Anthropology* 23, 259–69.

Petersen, H.C. 1992. *Ataraaq. Aaqqissuisut: Nunat Aqqinik Aalajangiisartut.* Nuuk, Grønlands Stednavnenævn.

Thisted, K. 1997. *Jens Kreutzmann: Fortællinger og akvareller.* Nuuk, Atuakkiorfik.

Thisted, K. 1999. *Således skriver jeg, Aron. Samlede fortællinger og illustrationer af Aron fra Kangeq (1822–1869).* Nuuk Atuakkiorfik.

Whitridge, P. 2004. Landscapes, houses, bodies, things: 'place' and the archaeology of Inuit imaginaries. *Journal of Archaeological Method and Theory* 11, 213–50.

4 Stone age motion pictures: an object's perspective from early prehistoric Ireland

Thomas Kador

Preview

Archaeologists have long been struggling to find an appropriate unit and scale of analysis to approach people's journeys. Since, with some notable exceptions, prehistoric paths and tracks themselves tend not to survive, the focus has generally remained on the common units of archaeological investigation, such as site, landscape and artefact. Narratives of people's journeys are then usually constructed around these units. The general rationale would appear to be that the fact that a particular place was visited is a reflection of the importance of this place. Similarly materials and objects which have evidently been moved for a considerable distance are thought to have had high value, standing and significance – and this is the reason why they were moved. The possibility that people's movements could actually have served to bestow meaning and significance onto a certain place or object is rarely considered. Yet, just as objects may be transported and places visited because they are already significant, both places and objects may equally take on significance because they form, or have formed, part of people's journeys. That mobility in itself has been an important consideration in early prehistory can be seen in the way people structured their social landscapes as well as in terms of the artefacts they utilised. The majority of the latter are inherently mobile and hence it would seem obvious that their potential mobility must have been meaningful and represents an important aspect of the role these objects played in people's lives; in producing mobile artefacts people had journeys on their mind.

In this paper I will suggest that the relationship between people, places and materials is much more reflexive and interactive than most of the general narratives would allow for, as they tend to 'freeze-frame' one single aspect of this relationship. Based on case studies from early prehistoric Ireland, I will discuss the importance of individual journeys and how they may have related to people's social lives, with the aim of presenting a more flexible approach capable of following people and objects on their journeys.

Towards a mobile perspective

Most current – and indeed past – archaeological studies of prehistory involving mobility tend to take the path of 'freeze-framing' individual aspects of human movement. For example, they investigate the resource base and its location(s), material culture or the distribution of artefacts and/or settlements across the landscape. As all these approaches strive towards a static view (of mobility) – that is they focus on either one or another end of the spectrum, but never the actual journeys connecting them – they cannot capture the mobile and flexible nature of the subject. The subject of human movement should of course be the moving person, and if we want to gain an understanding of the motivations behind people's movements in prehistory as well as of what the experience of their journeys may have meant to them we need to engage directly with the physicality of their journeys. Such an intimate approach – one that replaces the 'top-down' bird's eye perspective of the data set and instils a human one in its stead – transforms us from by-standing onlookers into participating 'spect-actors' (see Boal 1992) who take an active role in the production of an archaeological understanding. In relation to movement this means treating walking not just 'as a way of getting about, but equally as a way of getting to know the environment, primarily by way of contact through the feet, but also thanks to the sights and sounds that the movement affords' (Ingold 2001, 240). This allows us to assume a truly mobile perspective of people's journeys. It is this moving and constantly changing perspective of the world, in line with Bachelard's (1964, 11) notion of the 'muscular consciousness' – engaging not only the visual but all the senses – which I have termed 'motion pictures'. Such motion pictures would thus allow us to move away from the dominance of the static and visual in relation to interpretive accounts of people's activities across the landscape and towards a more holistic and mobile view of their engagements.

The main problem facing prehistorians in this regard would appear to be that of linking the available evidence with actual journeys that took place in the past. At the centre of this paper are a number of short practical case studies, based on events from early prehistoric Ireland, which have helped me to think about people's movements in different ways to those commonly pursued. There are of course also several important theoretical issues relating to the questions that arise from the approach adopted here. Rather than treating these separately from the evidence I hope to integrate their discussion directly into that of the practical examples. Before we can begin considering these examples, however, we need to address the question of our ability to discuss people's journeys in the past in a meaningful manner. The difficulty with this is the often rather limited range of available evidence. This is especially the case in relation to an early prehistoric data set where we frequently have to content ourselves with a body of evidence made up entirely of lithic artefacts.

Making lithics move

It would appear that the low-key nature of early prehistoric material from western Europe has contributed to a certain pessimism among archaeologists in relation to their ability to discuss people's activities beyond the strictly functional domain, focusing primarily on material procurement and subsistence economy. Consequently, human movement in early prehistoric contexts has often been treated implicitly and, in line with the general tone of the accounts, has been portrayed as a largely 'embedded' practice: a means to an end or necessary evil, designed to get people, food and other resources from one place to another. Therefore there was little apparent need for a more intimate treatment of the subject beyond these functions. This view, however, contrasts markedly with the many ethnographic studies from around the world that offer insights into movement as a socially and spiritually meaningful activity and a motor frequently driving social change (e.g. Blu 1996). Given the longstanding and strong relationship linking ethnography and prehistory this major disjoint between the two disciplines, when it comes to mobility, seems rather surprising. However, part of the reason for this two-tier treatment of human movement may lie in a perception that journeys are quite hard to detect archaeologically, and researchers did not see themselves in a position to produce detailed accounts of early prehistoric journeys grounded in solid archaeological evidence.

Yet perhaps we have actually been too cautious and overestimated the extent of the difficulties involved. I have already mentioned that much of early prehistoric evidence comprises worked stone artefacts commonly known as lithics. The vast corpus of objects collated under this broad heading – apart from being made of stone – shares one major attribute: their potential mobility. It would appear fairly safe to suggest that most blades, flakes and other objects that make up early prehistoric stone tool assemblages have been designed to be carried around and thus were produced with mobility as a central concern on their makers' minds. Moreover, in many cases these lithics were removed at least some distance from their original source and their site of production. Therefore it should not take a great theoretical leap to accept that journeys are at the forefront of the life history of most prehistoric lithic artefacts. Once we know their find location we can begin to, at least, speculate about the particular journeys these objects may have been part of and can thus adopt an object's perspective of these journeys. This is what I will attempt over the following pages, but beforehand I must add a word of caution. It would be beyond the scope of this paper to provide a detailed account of the specific journeys people undertook or may have undertaken in relation to the case studies presented. Rather, I wish to illustrate the range of possibilities for investigating the varied types and scales of movements underlying the often fairly inconspicuous material available for early prehistoric research.

Tales of three journeys

Import, export and transit at Bay Farm

The first example takes us to the later Mesolithic site at Bay Farm, Carnlough, County Antrim, where excavations yielded some 29,000 lithics (Figs 4.1 and 4.2). One large flake made from decarbonated chert was found among these, representing the only chert object from the entire excavation (Woodman and Johnson 1996, 156). In contrast to the abundance of flint, mainly in the form of beach pebbles available very close to the site, chert is not found locally, and thus the object must have been brought from some distance. Its most likely source is located in the Irish midland region of north-west Leinster, some 70 to 150km to the south-west (Woodman and Johnston 1991–92, 136). Since it is unlikely that chert could have been carried north from its source naturally through glacial activity, the flake must have found its way to Bay Farm 'by human means' (Woodman and Johnston 1991–92, 134–6). The object was uncovered in a pit within a lens of particularly black soil, packed in with a great quantity of knapped flint and overlying a rather large number of hammer stones (Fig. 4.3; Woodman and Johnson 1996, 156). From this we may infer that this large

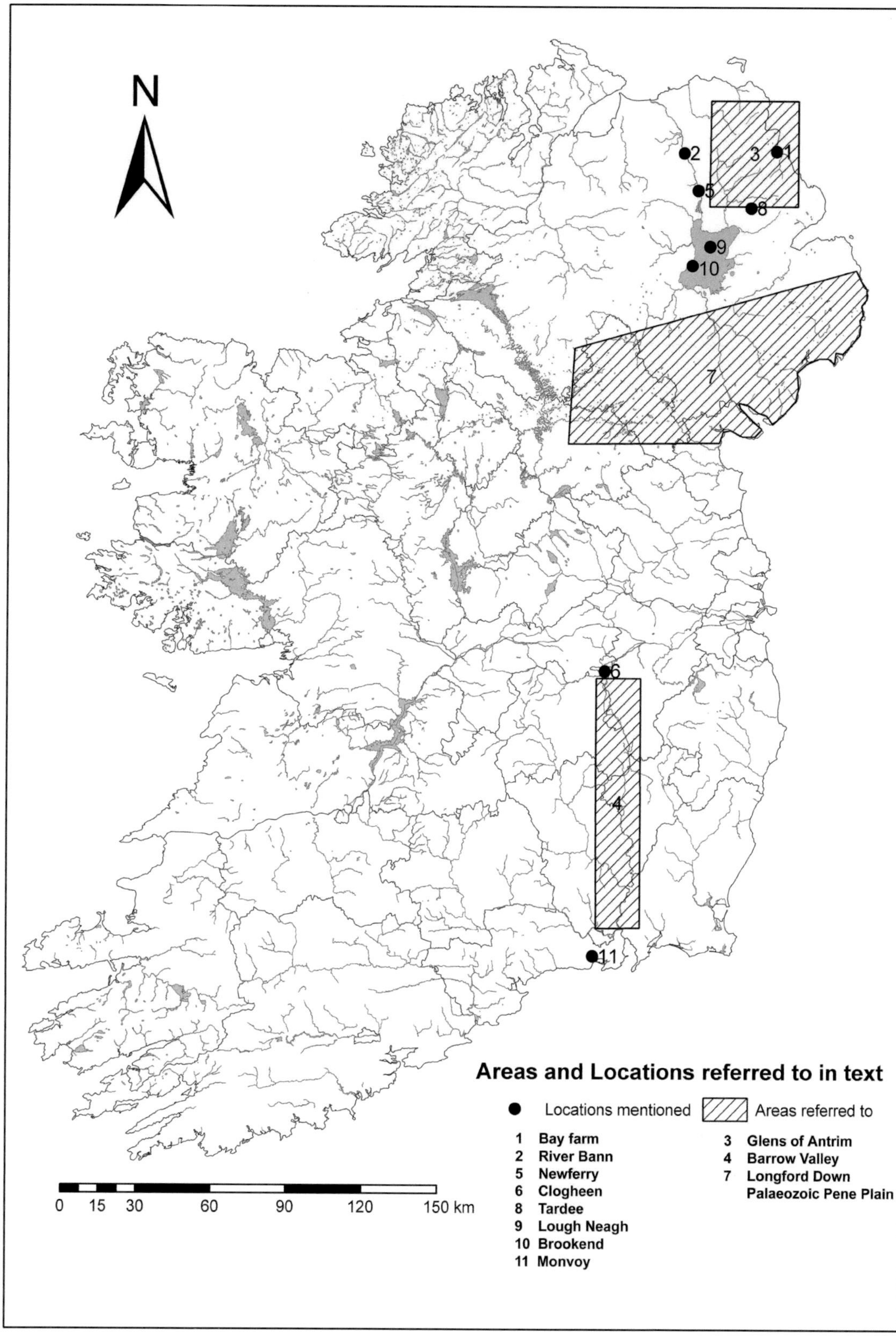

Fig. 4.1. Locations and areas mentioned in the text

chert flake was not lost or discarded carelessly but intentionally placed in the pit in the form of a deposit. Recently this has been interpreted to 'indicate…concern with the process of stone working' expressed through 'acts that give form to the relationships, material and otherwise, entangled' in this process (Warren 2006, 8). 'Acts such as the procurement of resources, the construction of

Fig. 4.2. View from the early prehistoric location at Bay Farm, County Antrim

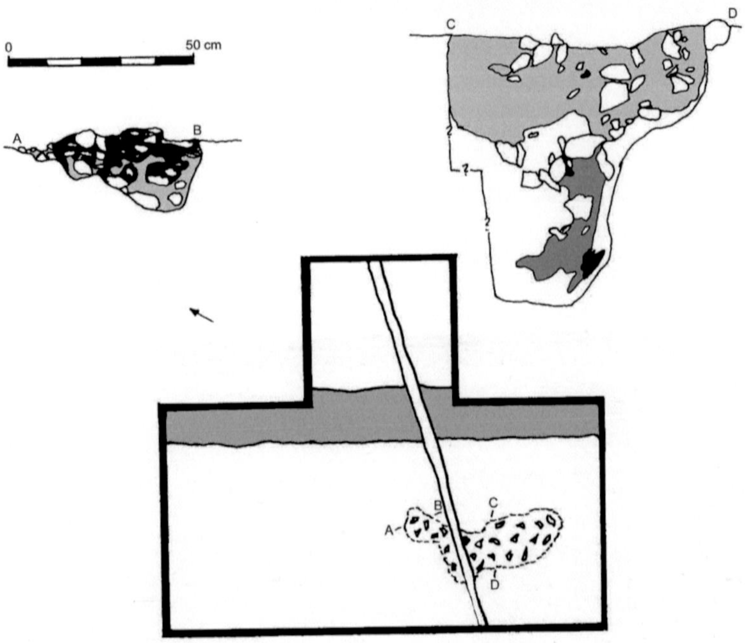

Fig. 4.3. Pit at Bay Farm (Feature F1) containing a large decarbonated chert flake (based on Woodman and Johnson 1996)

artefacts, or the deposition of debris formed the fabric of people's lives' (Warren 2006, 3) and 'the skills underpinning these practices can be produced and reproduced only in communities' (Hind 2004, 43). Without doubt many of the practices and relationships borne out on the chert flake were tied up with, and maintained, through people's movements. This becomes apparent through further considering what we can say about the object's biography.

If we accept that the most likely place of origin of this chert flake is to be found at a distance of at least 70km, but could be as much as twice as far (see above), it becomes obvious that, like the object's deposition, this journey did not take place haphazardly or accidentally. Instead, it would seem probable that it reached its place of deposition through a rather complex network of movement and communication. From both its archaeological context and the considerable distance this artefact had travelled, and therefore the care that must have been taken of it on such a journey, we can deduce that the object held considerable significance to the people who came into contact with it. Similar points have been made about polished stone axe heads moved and exchanged across large parts of north-west Europe (Bradley and Edmonds 1993). Interestingly, from a functional point of view, chert is clearly not superior in terms of knapping properties and durability to the large nodular flint that is so abundant at Carnlough beach very close to the Bay Farm site. Hence if the object was viewed as being important, it appears unlikely that this was due to functional considerations. Instead, I would like to suggest that its significance may have had much more to do with the journey it had taken part in before reaching Bay Farm. This requires some elaboration.

The transportation of stone tools appears to have been a quite frequent occurrence in Mesolithic north-east Ireland, particularly during the later parts of the period (*c.* 6000–4000BC). The Bann Valley, some 50km inland from Bay Farm (Fig. 4.1), has produced vast quantities of flint objects, predominantly of the later stages of reduction (Costa *et al.* 2005, 28; Woodman 1987, 144). Yet the closest sources of the stone are to be found along the east Antrim coast, at locations such as Carnlough (near Bay Farm), Glenarm and Ballygalley. This suggests that there must have been regular movement of people and material from the coast, across the Antrim Plateau and into the Bann Valley (Griffith and Woodman 1987; Woodman 1987, 144). Furthermore, thousands of ground stone axe heads of baked mudstone were unearthed in the Bann Valley, many from Mesolithic contexts. This means they were found 'at least 50 miles [*c.* 80km] from the nearest potential geological source', the Longford-Down Palaeozoic Peneplain (Woodman and Johnston 1991–92, 136). The western region of this north midland plain also represents one of the richest source areas for chert in Ireland and corresponds to the most probable area of origin for the chert flake found at Bay Farm (Woodman and Johnston 1991–92, 136). Since there is no evidence from Bay Farm suggesting 'direct contact' with the midlands – other than this one object – the chert flake could represent evidence for a more complex scenario involving movements of people and objects between all three regions: the Antrim coast, the Bann Valley and the Longford-Down Palaeozoic Peneplain (Fig. 4.1). On the one hand, people engaged in frequent journeys between the Peneplain and the Bann Valley – as indicated by the movement of large numbers of baked mudstone axes as well as by the presence of several decarbonated chert flakes at Newferry, an early prehistoric site on the River Bann (Woodman 1987, 144; Woodman and Johnston 1991/92, 135; Fig. 4.1). On the other hand, the transportation of large amounts of flint artefacts, found at many sites along the River Bann, suggests frequent contacts between the east Antrim coast and the Bann Valley. It seems that the locations on the Bann, at which artefacts from different parts of the country were found, represent an interface area for movements to the south as well as the east: 'Each place is part of a network that connects places together in a chain, and the links on either side depend for their connection on the one in the middle' (Morphy 1995, 186). Thus I would propose that it is possible that the decarbonated chert flake, which found its way into a pit at Bay Farm, had originated at a source in the Irish midland region and travelled to east Antrim via the Bann Valley; in total a journey of at least 120–150km. Whether the flake moved with a person or between people (Hind 1998) is difficult to ascertain, though it would seem more likely that it was initially brought into the Bann Valley along with other chert and mudstone objects of southern origin known from locations such as Newferry (Woodman and Anderson 1990, 382; Woodman and Johnston 1991–92), and then made its way to the Antrim coast as part of another journey or journeys, perhaps in exchange for an object made of east Antrim flint. This considerable journey and the knowledge of its distant origin (e.g. Bradley and Edmonds 1993, 178; Helms 1988, 68) may have earned this object a significant position among the people at Bay Farm, which is reflected in the care that was shown in its deposition.

Similarly the people who took part in the journeys may have moved beyond their own community's sphere and could thus have brought with them knowledge, stories and new ideas along with the objects; in turn their movements may have granted them political power and influence (Helms 1988, 18). If such contacts between communities from different regions were of an elaborate and regular nature so that they could be described as exchange networks, it would suggest a more complex social organisation than the general views of communities of the sixth and fifth millennia BC (cf. Cooney and Grogan 1999, 24; Kimball 2000, 42). The literature about this period is dominated by ideas of logistical versus embedded strategies for the procurement of raw materials and other resources during the 'exploitation of annual territories' (e.g. Woodman *et al.* 1999). This can be opposed with an account of people following paths, tracks and trails along watercourses and across upland plateaux as they submit to collective rhythms, and engaged in carrying 'forward the processes of social life' (Bourdieu 1977, 162–3; Ingold 1993, 157). A more detailed discussion of people's movements in relation to this case study would exceed the scope of this particular paper. However, elsewhere (Kador 2003; 2005) I have dealt with specific movements of people in early prehistoric north-east Ireland more directly and in greater detail.

A long journey south

The next snapshot leads us further south to County Kildare and the northern catchment of the River Barrow (Fig. 4.1), a river that provided one of the main north-south communication routes until quite recent times (e.g. Lucey 1998, 100; O'Sullivan 2001). Here a flake of banded rhyolite was found on the site of a medieval monastic settlement in Clogheen townland (Rynne 1983–84; Fig. 4.4). The flake in question would appear to be a diagnostic example of a large leaf-shaped butt-trimmed form or 'Bann flake' (Fig. 4.5), known only from the latest phases

Fig. 4.4. Later Mesolithic find location at the early medieval enclosure at Clogheen, County Kildare

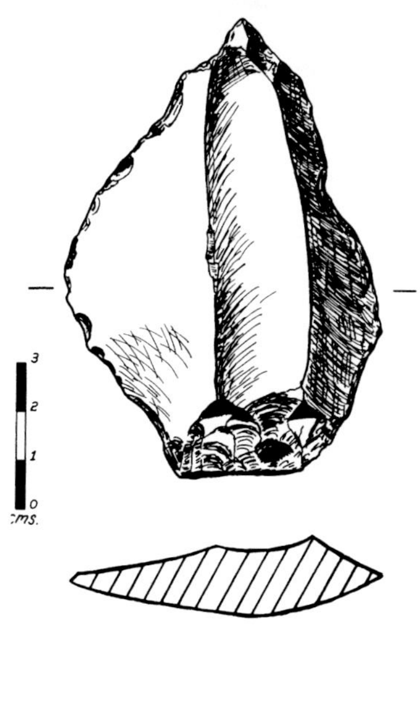

Fig. 4.5. Later Mesolithic (butt trimmed) flow banded rhyolite flake from Clogheen, County Kildare (reproduced from Rynne 1983–84)

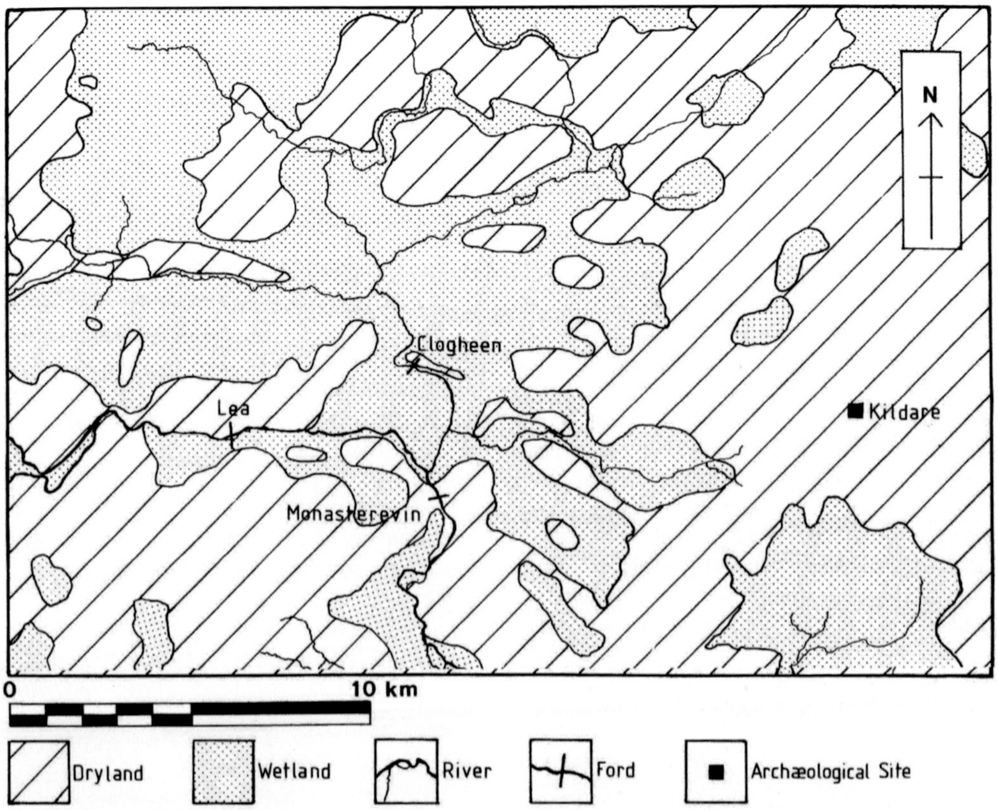

Fig. 4.6. Environment around Clogheen, County Kildare showing rivers, wetland, dryland areas and fording points (based on O'Donovan 1994)

of Irish later Mesolithic contexts (Anderson and Johnson 1993, 87; Woodman and Anderson 1990, 378–9). An intensive programme of research between 1990 and 1992 has demonstrated that the broader region of the Barrow Valley has seen extensive activity during early prehistory (Ramsden *et al.* 1995; Zvelebil *et al.* 1996). Arguably the most interesting aspect of this particular find is that, like the decarbonated chert flake in our first example, the material used for the manufacture of the flake was evidently not available locally.

Superficial geological examination at NUI Galway suggested that the object is made from flow-banded rhyolite probably originating in the Tardee area of County Antrim (Rynne 1983–84, 329) – a region containing disused quarry sites for this rare igneous rock (EHSNI 2003). At this point it is important to mention that the geological provenance of the object has recently been questioned (Woodman 1987, 142), yet until geochemical analysis can confirm or deny the independent findings of the two leading geologists at NUI Galway who examined the object we must assume their assessments to be correct. Clogheen and Tardee are some 200km apart 'as the crow flies'. Thus no matter how the artefact reached Clogheen it would have taken considerable effort to bring it there, and a journey of several days if not weeks, provided that we assume the movement occurred as part of a deliberate effort to transport it from one place to the other. It would perhaps seem more likely that, similar to the decarbonated chert flake form Bay Farm, the Clogheen flake indicates a more elaborate and complex process involving movement within a social network, probably incorporating a number of actors and several stops along its way. Interestingly, however, rhyolite is a rather uncommon stone for tools in prehistoric Ireland and its use usually tends to be rather localised in or near those areas were it occurs naturally (e.g. Green and Zvelebil 1990, 69–70; Woodman 1987, 144). Although the object was a stray find, and we therefore do not have a secure context for it, simply by the virtue of what we know of its life history it would seem reasonable to suggest that this artefact was equally seen and treated as significant. The object 'is dark brownish in colour, with lighter coloured bands and a rather oily appearance' (Rynne 1983–84, 329). Given this strikingly different colour and texture compared to the grey to black cherts and cream or beige flints commonly found in the Barrow Valley area, it must have been obvious to people that the object had travelled a considerable distance.

The graveyard and medieval enclosure at which the flake was discovered is situated on a terrace forming a dryland island, known as St. John's Island, jutting out into the Black River, a tributary to the Barrow. It is also the site of an ancient fording place (O'Donovan 1994, 7; Fig. 4.6). While it is hard to ascertain that this ford had been frequented during early prehistoric times, a number of polished and ground stone axe heads have been dredged from the riverbed at this point, further suggesting early prehistoric activity at this location (information courtesy of the Irish Stone Axe Project). Moreover, the large number of prehistoric stone objects recovered from similar locations throughout the Barrow Valley and elsewhere in Ireland (Mahr 1937; O'Donovan 1994) would suggest that these places represented significant foci of activity from prehistoric times onwards. The choice of locations such as Clogheen emphasises the importance of waterways in terms of their potential for communication on the river, as well as movement along its banks (see Spikins 1996, 88), and the significance of fording points used during overland journeys. The importance of travel along waterways is also emphasised if we consider the object's likely place of origin at Tardee, County Antrim. This hilly upland area is situated just a few kilometres northeast from the northern shore of Lough Neagh, Ireland's largest lake, and spectacular views overlooking the Lough can be gained from many of the slopes and summits within the area (Fig. 4.1). This brings the Lough and its potential role for early prehistoric travel into the picture. As outlined in the first example, the mudstone axes found in the Bann Valley and perhaps the chert flake excavated at Bay Farm came from the Palaeozoic Pene Plain, which is located to the south of the Lough. Thus it raises the question of how significant Lough Neagh was for people's journeys north and south, up and down the country, during early prehistory. Fredengren (2002, 119–20) has explored the question of movement along water bodies – both rivers and lakes – in the Irish midland region throughout prehistory, and the bulk of her arguments could certainly be extended to large water bodies elsewhere in Ireland. The significance of Lough Neagh for early prehistoric travel is further underscored by the find of part of a possible logboat of Mesolithic date (5490–5246 cal BC: UB-4066) at Brookend, County Tyrone, on the Lough's western shore (Figs 4.1 and 4.7), which is the only example of a vessel known from Ireland dating to before 4000BC (Fry 2000, 116).

It would seem in journeying through early prehistoric Ireland people exploited various means of travel and engaged in movements at many different scales. This is emphasised by the above examples which have focused on two small and highly mobile stone objects and their potential journeys across land and water, covering considerable distances. With the help of these examples I have aimed to illustrate how we can build a narrative about the journeys of objects but also of the people who travelled with them, quite literally from the ground up.

If we zoom out and consider the bigger picture, it transpires that rather than representing exceptional cases it would in fact appear that these examples form part of a more general pattern, particularly with Irish later Mesolithic artefact finds. Time and again fieldwork programmes and excavations have revealed a small percentage of 'non-local' materials among assemblages dominated by 'local' stone (e.g. Ramsden *et al.* 1995; Woodman 1987, 144; Woodman *et al.* 1999; Zvelebil *et al.* 1996, 23). The commonsense explanation sometimes offered for this – seeing it as the introduction of superior materials from further afield to supplement the rather poor local assemblages, perhaps for carrying out specific tasks – does not stand up to scrutiny. Frequently the materials moved are actually inferior in terms of knapping properties and durability to the locally available ones, and the two examples presented above are a case in point. Functional motivations relating to raw material procurement would therefore not appear to have been the main motivation behind people's movements between different areas. Perhaps it is more likely that the lithics are merely the only – or the most commonly – surviving evidence of movements having taken place (Cooney and Grogan 1999, 24), and are thus where our investigations have to start. Moreover, as Paton has pointed out: 'artefacts can be foremost symbols communicating coded information' and '[b]eyond this [they] may have little or no value' (Paton 1994, 174). Therefore the actual motivations behind the journeys have probably all but disappeared from the record together with less durable materials and many of the less tangible aspects that would also have travelled along with and between people, such as songs, stories and ritual knowledge (Helms 1988, 68). Having said that, evidence for the care that was shown to such objects in their use, movement and deposition (see above and Kador forthcoming) allows us to conclude that non-local objects might have been viewed in a somewhat different or special light. Could it thus be that rather

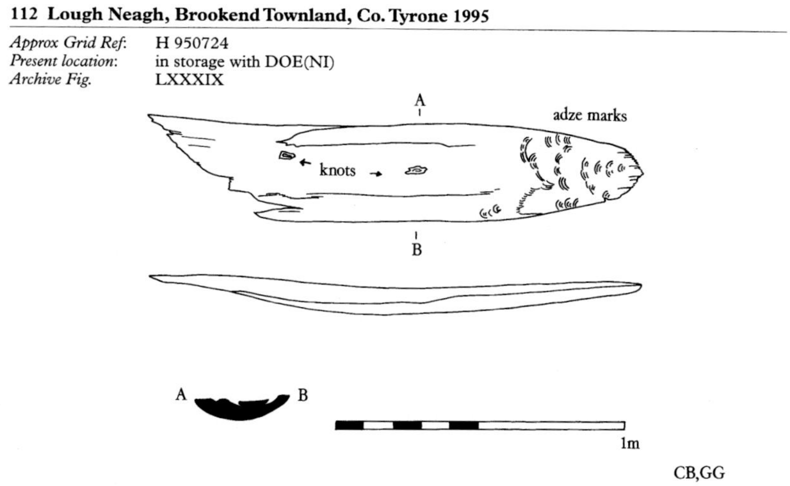

Fig. 4.7. Part of a possible Mesolithic log boat from Lough Neagh, Brookend townland, County Tyrone (reproduced from Fry 2000; original drawing by Cormack Bourke and Gillian Greer)

Fig. 4.8. Early prehistoric rhyolite quarry at Monvoy near Tramore, County Waterford; view north and south from top of the outcrop

than being brought in because they were important or valuable – for example due to their superior quality or striking appearance – the objects attained increased significance because of their distant origin (Bradley and Edmonds 1993, 178; Helms 1988, 69); a fact that would have been quite obvious to people at the time? Such objects may have been kept in circulation longer than normal, and their special meaning could have been granted to them because they had travelled for a significant distance and thus epitomised someone's journey: perhaps a relative, a member of the local community, an ancestor or a legendary traveller from a distant area. Consequently they would have attracted a wealth of traditions and myths associated with their origin, production, meaning and movements (Warren forthcoming). Alternatively they may have been looked upon as tokens for contacts, relationships and social networks with people and groups in quite distant regions. Ethnography tells us that the most important aspect of exchange systems may in fact be the 'maintaining of social links and communicating information about matters such as land and resource ownership' (Paton 1994, 176).

No paths lead to Monvoy?

The final example will take us to the other end of the spectrum. While the objects in the first two instances had both been moved considerable distances from their source, on this occasion we shall remain focused on a source location of raw material in the form of a quarry site. Excavations at the prehistoric rhyolite quarry at Monvoy near Tramore, County Waterford, by the Ballylough Archaeological Project have yielded some 30,000 artefacts (Figs 4.1 and 4.8), including diagnostic later Mesolithic and Neolithic forms. Similar to Bay Farm – a location where lithic raw material (i.e. large flint nodules and pebbles) was readily available at the nearby beach, and perhaps as expected from a quarry location, the artefacts mainly represent the early stages of the lithic reduction process (Green and Zvelebil 1990, 70). Yet what is most striking is that the concentration of these artefacts decreases dramatically within a short distance from the quarry face: 'indicating a rapid drop-off away from the main area of activity around the outcrop' (Green and Zvelebil 1990, 69). In fact, within the first 100m from the outcrop the 'density of finds drops from thousands per square metre to double digits or even single figures' (Green and Zvelebil 1990, 70, fig. 14). Beyond a core area of some 3km away from the source, rhyolite artefact finds become 'extremely rare' (Green and Zvelebil 1990, 70; Zvelebil *et al.* 1987, 18–22). While other examples of prehistoric quarries with limited distribution and dominated by finds close to the source are known from Ireland, such as the Neolithic porphyry quarry on Lambay Island (Cooney 2004, 196), none display such an extremely small radius of distribution and dramatic decline in density.

The excavators offered two explanations for this. The first one suggests that rhyolite might have been specifically quarried for export outside of the region (Green and Zvelebil 1990, 70). However, in contrast to locations such as Bay Farm where this has also been suggested (see above), no corresponding location has yet been identified further afield to which the quarried artefacts may have been moved. The second explanation proposes that flint was generally the preferred material for artefact manufacture, and rhyolite was only used in close vicinity to its natural source as it was so much more readily available (Green and Zvelebil 1990, 70). Yet as we have seen in the second example – that of the Clogheen flake – a rhyolite object of similar properties to the material from Monvoy was evidently moved for a considerable distance. It is also hard to see how the perceived accessibility of materials should change so dramatically within such a short distance, as there is no apparent major source of flint within the wider region other than small riverine and beach pebbles. Besides, the quality of this local pebble flint is very poor, especially for producing the large blades and flakes typical of later Mesolithic assemblages (Green and Zvelebil 1990, 70). In addition, neither of the two explanations offered by the excavators accounts for the virtually complete exclusion of objects made from raw materials other than rhyolite from the area around the quarry.

It would thus seem obvious that the use and distribution of rhyolite quarried at Monvoy and the absence of other stone tools from the area around the quarry cannot be understood in purely functional terms, based entirely on a concern with procuring the best lithic raw material available. Perhaps there were strong cultural or spiritual reasons for the way stone from this quarry was used and circulated, and access to the quarry itself may have been restricted. An ethnographic example from northern Australia demonstrates how access to quarries can be highly regulated, and tied to conventions of knowledge and meaning associated with quarrying and its products (Paton 1994, 178). Only certain members of the community were entitled to 'hit the rock' and others to give permission to do so. At the same time, access to other rock sources may have been left relatively open: 'The nature of restriction of access to resources is thus closely bound up with the idea of responsibility for…creation myths, associated with the resource and not necessarily with its scarcity and abundance' (Paton 1994, 178).

The find circumstances from the Monvoy quarry could be explained, as the excavators suggest, largely as a result of preservation and material visibility. That is, rhyolite was exploited only incidentally and over a long period of time by local groups (Green and Zvelebil 1990, 70), leading to such a small concentration of objects away from the immediate source area that they were not recovered using rather coarse field surveying strategies. However, given the dramatic drop off in material, the near complete absence of rhyolite objects from beyond a very confined area, and the equally total exclusion of other worked materials from the rhyolite rich area, it would appear that factors other than taphonomy alone must be responsible for this peculiar distribution pattern. As I have suggested above, these may have included the meanings associated with the material, the practice of working it (e.g. Warren forthcoming) and the restriction of access to its source (e.g. Paton 1994, 178). It seems inconceivable that people who frequented this location and quarried for stone there did not travel beyond 3km in any direction during the course of their daily movements, especially in the light of evidence from elsewhere in Ireland – as outlined above – suggesting frequent and far reaching contacts between various regions of the island. At the same time we should not forget about the movements that would have taken place within a 3km radius of the quarry, for which we do have some evidence. A multi scalar approach may help us here. As we have seen, artefact density is extremely high within the immediate surroundings of the quarry face and movements here appear to have been quite unrestricted and without clear directionality, although a marked drop off in material concentration can already be noted after some 60m from the outcrop. Beyond this core area, finds of rhyolite continue to decline rapidly in all directions, and only occasional finds have been noted at distances greater than 3km from the quarry. While there is no obvious directionality to the drop off it appears that rhyolite occurs somewhat more frequently in areas close to the shoreline, both south-east and south-west from the source, as well as to the west in general (Zvelebil *et al.* 1987, 21). Hence, just as we could suggest that access to the source may have been restricted, it seems equally plausible that the movement of the material from there was confined to particular routes. It is the identification of these routes that will help us to bring people's journeys to life. Although we currently have little evidence for these journeys the discovery of even a small number of objects, as illustrated in the first two examples above, could change this dramatically.

Moving beyond the general

I have presented these three examples with the aim of demonstrating how we can employ early prehistoric evidence, particularly in the form of lithics, to access the journeys they were part of and which preceded their 'deposition'. The most promising approach here would appear to be adopting a personal and intimate viewpoint of human movement and build our narratives from the bottom up. In the absence of more direct evidence for past people's movements, such as actual tracks or fossilised footprints, this means assuming an object's perspective. This brings us back to the notion of 'motion pictures', the muscular, aural, olfactory and visual impression the world affords us – constantly transforming and reconfiguring itself – as we move through it.

However, within the confines of this paper I have not been able to go into sufficient detail to do justice to the small scale and intimate experiences such a perspective would grant us. Instead, my main objective has been to merely highlight the range of possibilities open to archaeologists when discussing people's journeys from the earlier parts of prehistory. Exploring these possibilities also forms a central aspect of my ongoing research, and elsewhere I have attempted a closer, more direct engagement with both the evidence and people's movements through a combination of landscape surveying and a number of GIS-based techniques (Kador 2003; 2005).

At the onset of this paper I also remarked on the implicit and generic way in which mobility in prehistory has been treated. The debate of population movement versus exchange systems (Rynne 1983–84, 330; Woodman and Johnston 1991–92, 137), commonly offered to discuss the movement of artefacts, introduces an unhelpful dichotomy and focuses on too grand a scale to get even close to the dimension at which human movement actually takes place. Similarly the opposition of mobile and sedentary lifestyle, so dominant in relation to the earlier parts of prehistory, is rather misleading. People, whether 'sedentary hunter gatherers' or 'mobile farmers', were constantly on the move and apparently keen to keep in contact (e.g. Kelly 1992, 60). Yet if we only strive for the most general scale possible and look for 'ultimate causation' (Cartwright 2001, 7) to explain the evidence we inevitably fail to recognise and appreciate the very subtle, fine grained and highly varied nature of people's movements. Regardless of whether the journeys in question were daily and habitual trips, over land, off shore, more long ranging seasonal movements, or occasional travels for spiritual, political or personal reasons, engaging with the evidence also means acknowledging its often coincidental and circumstantial nature. Yet this aspect frequently seems to go missing in our constant drive to explain and generalise rather than observe and understand. No matter what the exact nature of the movement of the artefacts discussed here – whether they moved with a person or between people (Hind 1998; 2000) or most likely partook in both types of movement – they represent evidence for contacts and communication between people and communities in areas close together and far apart. Finally I hope to have demonstrated the possibility that even finds of single artefacts – with or without known context – can serve as useful sources of evidence and, since the objects concerned are highly portable, adopting a 'mobile perspective' of analysis can be especially helpful to discuss such finds in a meaningful manner. Though we may not know much about the people who engaged in the journeys manifest in these objects, discussing the journeys themselves, based on what the objects and the locations they have passed through on these journeys reveal, may shed some light on the people behind them and perhaps also enable us to start viewing their daily lives and activities in a fresh, more intimate manner.

Acknowledgements

I would like to acknowledge the funding for my research provided by the Irish Research Council for the Humanities and Social Sciences (IRCHSS) under the Government of Ireland Scholarship Scheme and the support of the UCD Humanities Institute of Ireland (HII). I am also indebted to Professor Marek Zvelebil for his helpfulness and assistance in relation to the material from the Ballylough Archaeological Project, Professor Peter Woodman for comments on the case studies I used in this contribution and Graeme Warren for reading a previous version of this paper and his undying support and encouragement. Thanks must also go to Mel Giles and Dan Hind for their kindness in assisting my work with the Ballylough collections in Sheffield, and to Malcolm Fry and Professor Etienne Rynne for their kind permission to reproduce images from their publications. Finally, I would also like to thank Vicki Cummings and Bob Johnston for having organised the conference session at which this paper was first presented, for having invited my contribution and for their helpful comments on previous versions of this paper.

Bibliography

Anderson, E. and Johnson, G. 1993. A refitting and use-wear analysis of a later Mesolithic flint assemblage from Bay Farm, County Antrim. *Archaeomaterials* 7, 83–100.

Bachelard, G. 1964. *The poetics of space.* (translated by M. Jolas) Boston: Beacon Press.

Blu, K.I.1996. Where do you stay at? Home place and community among the Lumbee. In S. Field and K.H. Basso (eds), *Senses of place*, 197–227. Santa Fe,New Mexico: School of American Research.

Boal, A. 1992. *Games for actors and non-actors.* London: Routledge.

Bourdieu, P. 1977. *Outline of a theory of practice.* Cambridge: Cambridge University Press.

Bradley, R. and Edmonds, M. 1993. *Interpreting the axe trade: production and exchange in Neolithic Britain.* Cambridge: Cambridge University Press.

Cartwright, J.H. 2001. *Evolutionary explanations of human behaviour.* London: Routledge.

Cooney, G. 2004. Neolithic stone axe quarries and production sites in Scotland and Ireland. In I.A. Shepherd and G.J. Barclay (eds), *Scotland in ancient Europe: the Neolithic and Early Bronze Age of Scotland in their European context*, 191–201. Edinburgh: Society of Antiquaries of Scotland.

Cooney, G. and Grogan, E. 1999. *Irish prehistory: a social perspective.* Dublin: Wordwell.

Costa, L.J., Sternke, F. and Woodman, P.C. 2005. Microlith to macrolith: the reasons behind the transformation of production in the Irish Mesolithic. *Antiquity* 79, 19–33.

EHSNI 2003. Disused quarry at Sandy Braes, County Antrim. Website of the Environment and Heritage Service of Northern Ireland, http://www.ehsni.gov.uk; accessed May 2005.

Fredengren, C. 2002. *Crannogs: a study of people's interaction with lakes, with particular reference to Lough Gara in the north-west of Ireland.* Dublin: Wordwell.

Fry, M.F. 2000. *Coití: logboats from Northern Ireland.* Belfast: Northern Ireland Archaeological Monographs No. 4.

Green, S.W. and Zvelebil, M. 1990. The Mesolithic colonization and agricultural transition of south-east Ireland. *Proceedings of the Prehistoric Society* 56, 57–88.

Griffith, D. and Woodman, P.C. 1987. Cretaceous chert sourcing in N.E. Ireland: preliminary results. In G. Sieveking and M.H. Newcomer (eds), *The human uses of flint and chert: proceedings of the fourth International flint symposium*, 249–52. Cambridge: Cambridge University Press.

Helms, M.W. 1988. *Ulysses' sail: an ethnographic odyssey of power, knowledge, and geographical distance.* Princeton: Princeton University Press.

Hind, D. 1998. Chert use in the Mesolithic of Northern England. *Assemblage: the Sheffield Graduate Journal of Archaeology* 4; http://www.shef.ac.uk/assem/4/, accessed 28/03/2003.

Hind, D. 2000. *Landscape and technology in the Peak District of Derbyshire: the fifth and fourth millennia BC.* Unpublished PhD thesis, Department of Archaeology, University of Sheffield.

Hind, D. 2004. Where many paths meet: towards an integrated theory of landscape and technology. In A.M. Chadwick (ed.) *Stories from the landscape: archaeologies of inhabitation.* 35–51. Oxford: Archaeopress, BAR International Series 1238.

Ingold, T. 1993. The temporality of landscape. *World Archaeology* 25, 152–74.

Ingold, T. 2001. Evolving skill. In H. Rose and S. Rose (eds), *Alas poor Darwin: arguments against evolutionary psychology*, 225–46. London: Vintage.

Kador, T. 2003. *Moving off the beaten track: mobility as a way of understanding the Mesolithic in northeast Ireland.* Unpublished MA thesis, Department of Archaeology, University College Dublin.

Kador, T. 2005. Reopening old trails – rethinking mobility: a study of the Mesolithic in northeast Ireland. In D. Hoffmann, J. Mills and A. Cochrane (eds), *Elements of being: mentalities, identities and movements.* 107–21. Oxford: Archaeopress, British Archaeological Report International Series 1437.

Kador, T. forthcoming. Moving perceptions: movement, mobility and the material dimension. In P.C. Woodman, S. McCartan, G. Warren and R. Schulting (eds), *Proceedings of the 7th international Conference on the Mesolithic in Europe.* Oxford, Oxbow.

Kelly, R.L. 1992. Mobility/sedentism: concepts, archaeological measures and effects. *Annual Review of Anthropology* 21, 43–66.

Kimball, M.J.2000. Variation and context: ecology and social evolution in Ireland's Later Mesolithic. In G.J.A. Desmond, M. McCarthy, J. Sheehan and E. Shee Twohig (eds), *New agendas in Irish prehistory: papers in commemoration of Liz Anderson.* 31–47. Bray, Co. Wicklow: Wordwell,.

Lucey, J.1998. The Barrow, the Nore and the Suir. In C. Moriarty (ed.) *Studies of Irish rivers and lakes.* 99–117. Dublin: Marine Institute.

Mahr, A. 1937. New aspects and problems in Irish prehistory. *Proceedings of the Prehistoric Society* 3, 264–436.

Morphy, H. 1995. Landscape and the reproduction of the ancestral past. In E. Hirsch and M. O'Hanlon (eds), *The anthropology of landscape: perspectives on place and space*, 184–209. Oxford: Oxford University Press.

O'Donovan, E. 1994. *The finds from the river Barrow and its tributaries.* Unpublished MA thesis, Department of Archaeology, University College Dublin.

O'Sullivan, T.F. 2001. *Goodly Barrow: a voyage on an Irish river.* Dublin: Lilliput.

Paton, R. 1994. Speaking through stones: a study from northern Australia. *World Archaeology* 26, 172–84.

Ramsden, P., Zvelebil, M., Macklin, M.G. and Passmore, D.G. 1995. Stone age settlement in south-eastern Ireland. *Current Anthropology* 36, 330–32.

Rynne, E. 1983–84. An Antrim Bann flake from near Monasterevin. *Journal of the Kildare Archaeological Society* 16, 328–30.

Spikins, P. 1996. Rivers, boundaries and change: a hypothesis of challenging settlement patterns in the Mesolithic of Northern England. In T. Pollard and A. Morisson (eds), *The early prehistory of Scotland*, 89–107. Edinburgh: University of Edinburgh Press.

Warren, G.M. 2006. Technology. In C. Conneller and G.M. Warren (eds), *Reconstructing the Mesolithic: key debates in Britain and Ireland.* London: Tempus.

Warren, G.M. forthcoming. The archaeology of the Mesolithic in eastern Scotland: deconstructing culture, constructing identity. In K. Pedersen and C. Waddington (eds), *The Late Palaeolithic and Mesolithic of the North Sea Basin and Littoral.* Oxford: Oxbow Books.

Woodman, P.C. 1987. The impact of resource availability on lithic industrial traditions in prehistoric Ireland. In P. Rowley-Conwy, M. Zvelebil and H.P. Blankholm (eds), *The Mesolithic in north-west Europe: recent trends*, 138–49. Sheffield: University of Sheffield, Department of Archaeology and Prehistory.

Woodman, P.C. and Anderson E. 1990. The Irish later Mesolithic: a partial picture. In P.M. Vermeersch and P. Van Peer (eds), *Contributions to the Mesolithic in Europe,* 377–87. Leuven: Leuven University Press.

Woodman, P.C., Anderson, E. and Finlay, N. 1999. *Excavations at Ferriter's Cove 1983 – 1995: last foragers first farmers in the Dingle Peninsula.* Dublin: Wordwell.

Woodman, P.C. and Johnson, G. 1996. Excavations at Bay Farm 1, Carnlough, Co. Antrim, and the study of the 'Larnian' technology. *Proceedings of the Royal Irish Academy* 96, 137–235.

Woodman, P.C. and Johnston, I. 1991–92. A petrological examination of some Mesolithic stone artefacts. *Ulster Journal of Archaeology* 54/55, 134–7.

Zvelebil, M., Macklin, M.G., Passmore, D.G. and Ramsden, P. 1996. Alluvial archaeology in the Barrow valley, southeast Ireland: the 'Riverford culture' re-visited. *The Journal of Irish Archaeology* 7, 13–40.

Zvelebil, M., Moore, J. and Henson, D. 1987. Regional survey and the analysis of lithic scatters: a case study from southeast Ireland. In P. Rowley-Conwy, M. Zvelebil and H.P. Blankholm (eds), *The Mesolithic in north-west Europe: recent trends*, 9–32. Sheffield: Department of Archaeology and Prehistory.

5 'It's 17km as the crow flies ...': Neolithic journeys seen through the material at either end

Duncan Garrow

Introduction

This paper is concerned with the 'archaeological signature' of Neolithic journeys. It discusses whether it is actually possible to identify prehistoric journeys *archaeologically* in the spaces where they occurred, or if we are actually better off looking for them in the material found at either end. As well as describing a recent journey made between two sites, a number of related themes are considered: the potential that phenomenological methods have to offer away from upstanding monuments, the archaeological visibility of impermanent settlement during the Neolithic, and the possibility of identifying separate places, occupied by the same people, at that time.

Fig. 5.1. A pit cluster at Hurst Fen (Clark et al. *1960, Plate XXII)*

Fig. 5.2. A pit cluster at Kilverstone

Sites at either end of a journey? Kilverstone and Hurst Fen

My interest in the possibility of journeying between sites in the Neolithic came about as a result of encountering material from two specific places: Hurst Fen in Suffolk (Clark *et al.* 1960) and Kilverstone in Norfolk (Garrow *et al.* 2005; Garrow *et al.* 2006). Despite being dug almost fifty years apart, the two sites are connected in many different ways. For a start, although on either side of a county boundary, they are actually only 17km away from each other, as the crow flies; a reasonable journey on foot, but one which it's perfectly possible to make in a day. The two sites are also linked as a result of being made up solely of pits in very large numbers: 200 at Hurst Fen and 226 at Kilverstone. The pits on each were closely comparable, in terms of how they were grouped together (Figs 5.1 and 5.2), their size and the way they had been filled. Perhaps most importantly of all, the material recovered from both sites was also extremely similar. The comparison is most easily made through the pottery (Figs 5.3 and 5.4): in terms of their forms, sizes, rim types, decorations and temper, the pots from either site were essentially interchangeable; and, importantly, were more comparable with each other than with other 'Mildenhall' assemblages in the region (such as those from the causewayed enclosure at Etton (Kinnes 1998) and the pits at Spong Hill (Healy 1988); see Knight (2006) for a more detailed comparison of these assemblages).

What we have with Kilverstone and Hurst Fen, then, are two sites, 17km apart, with similar densities, of similar pits, containing very similar material culture. Clearly, there is no way of *knowing* whether the same people actually did visit both sites, digging

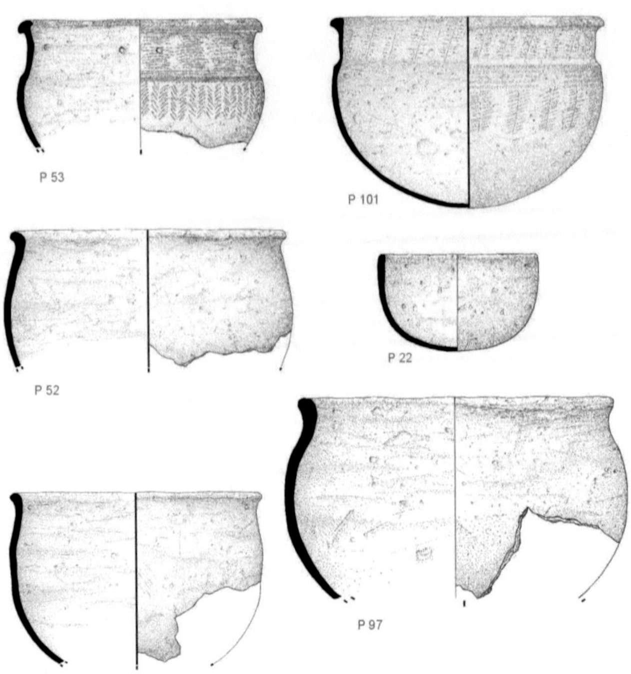

Figs 5.3. (top) and 5.4. (bottom) Pots from Hurst Fen (Clark et al. *1960, Plate XXIII) and Kilverstone (drawings by M. Brudenell)*

the pits on each. But the fact that they are *so* comparable raises the possibility that they might have done.

A prehistoric journey? Kilverstone to Hurst Fen

Due to the material, spatial and temporal proximity of the two sites, I had always thought about walking between them. The fact that a TAG session on prehistoric journeys (on which this publication is based) was being organised finally spurred me into action. I decided to see whether actually making the journey between the two sites would change the way I saw their relationship. I also liked the idea that, by making that walk, I would in some ways be adding to a 'tradition' of archaeological walking (part performance, part archaeology) – Chris Tilley's exploration of the Dorset cursus, of course (Tilley 1994; see also Johnston 1999), Mike Brookes and Mike Pearson's 'The First Five Miles …/Rhyfel y Sais Bach…' project in Ceredigion (Pearson and Shanks 2001, 142–6), and even Richard Long's walks on Dartmoor and elsewhere (e.g. Long *et al.* 1991; see also Renfrew 2003, 26–39).

From a more directly archaeological point of view, I wanted to find out whether it is actually possible to 'do' phenomenology in the agricultural landscapes of East Anglia. Other archaeological journeys have usually been guided, to an extent, by archaeology: Tilley had cropmark ditches and long barrows, Brookes and Pearson the fields constructed during the period they were revisiting. In making the walk between Kilverstone and Hurst Fen, on the other hand, there was nothing from the earlier Neolithic to act as a guide (other than tangentially related find spots from the counties' sites and monuments records).

> *So, early one Sunday morning in late September, I set off from Kilverstone with three friends. It was interesting to see the site again after a gap of two years. The houses had not yet been built, and you could still see many of the pits we had dug, marked out in the sandy soil by new growths of broom. It was hard to decide upon a route. We initially tried to follow the River Thet south out of Thetford, but there was no path along the river bank and the nettles were high. Instead, we headed through suburbia, negotiating cul de sacs and unofficial 'paths' through back gardens. The ford at the medieval Nun's Bridges represented the first sites and monuments record find spot (a polished axe), so I stopped to take a photo – neatly tended verges, elegant swans, people feeding the ducks. Soon, we were making our way across the open heathland of the Brecks. It wasn't long before we crossed the county border into Suffolk – overgrown hedgerows, MOD 'Danger – Keep Out' signs, an American couple looking for 'projectile points' in a field. We ate lunch*

under a chestnut tree, close to the second find spot (another polished axe), then moved on – through gates, across roads, past pig farms, onion fields and tractors ploughing. The third find spot (a leaf-shaped arrowhead this time) took a while in coming – large machine-cut dykes, a man on a bike monitoring cygnets, a nice cup of tea. It was actually a long day's walk. While it might be 17km as the crow flies, our route following footpaths and skirting around planted fields had taken us closer to 30km. We made it to Hurst Fen just as the sun was setting – lush grass, pink clouds, weary legs.

Throughout the walk (Figs 5.5 to 5.10), it has to be said it was hard to imagine being back in the Neolithic: farming methods involved tractors and elaborate water sprinkling systems, crops were row upon row of onions, and the only monument we saw was a twenty-metre high column dedicated to those who gave their lives in the First World War. Even when we spotted some deer tracks (something which could well have been seen in the Neolithic), alongside them was a touch of modernity (in the form of bike tracks) to bring us back to the present with a bump. All of these artefacts made the point very clearly – we were separated from the earlier Neolithic, and the pits at either end of our journey, by five and a half thousand years.[1]

Approaches which use experiences in the present to inform understanding of the past have been criticised, often quite rightly, for imposing a uniform,

Figs 5.5–5.7. (left-hand column, top to bottom): Walking across the Breckland; lunch under a chestnut tree; deer (and bike) tracks

Figs 5.8–5.10. (right-hand column, top to bottom): Farming; crops; monument

static or gendered subjectivity on that past (Brück 2001; Thomas 2000). Phenomenology has, however, usually encouraged archaeologists to engage with *archaeology*: to visit upstanding monuments, to consider the views, and think about how it feels to be there. As a result, those experiences can inform interpretive practice in the present at least. In our case, though, as with most prehistoric journeys (which would not, helpfully, have been defined by earth-cut ditches and banks, etc.), there really was no archaeology in between the two sites through which we could make that journey *archaeological*. There was little to connect us with the past, other than our imaginations. By the same token, if no photographs had been taken, there would be no material record, no archaeological signature, of *our* journey. We didn't drop any litter, we left little trace.

Impermanent settlement?

In order to approach the issue of journeying in the Neolithic in a more archaeological way, I will turn now to a number of sites where archaeological signatures *do* persist, where material has actually transcended those five and a half thousand years. I will consider whether or not those sites *were* impermanent settlements, whether journeys between them did actually take place; and, if so, whether that impermanence, those journeys, are visible archaeologically.

Some years ago now, the concept of permanent Neolithic settlement was called into question (e.g. Thomas 1991). It has since been argued by many that, while they took on domesticated plants and animals and pottery, the indigenous population of Britain maintained a relatively transient way of life. The foundations on which this argument has been built are a valuable deconstruction of the concept of the Neolithic as a period of farming and settling down (e.g. Thomas 1993), and a lack of convincing houses (Darvill 1996; Thomas 1996). Over the past five years or so, however, this picture of an impermanent, journeying Neolithic has had to be qualified to an extent. In addition to the impressive buildings known about for a long time in Orkney and Shetland, more and more have been found in Ireland (e.g. Grogan 2002), and occasionally other places as well (e.g. Oxford Archaeological Unit 2000). Some have criticised what has been termed the 'consensus' view, suggesting that in order to incorporate significant variability we need to address the issue of Neolithic settlement at a regional, not a national, level (Barclay 2000; Cooney 1997; 2001). I would like to respond to that suggestion now, considering impermanent settlement in East Anglia in a bit more detail.

Very few convincing earlier Neolithic structures

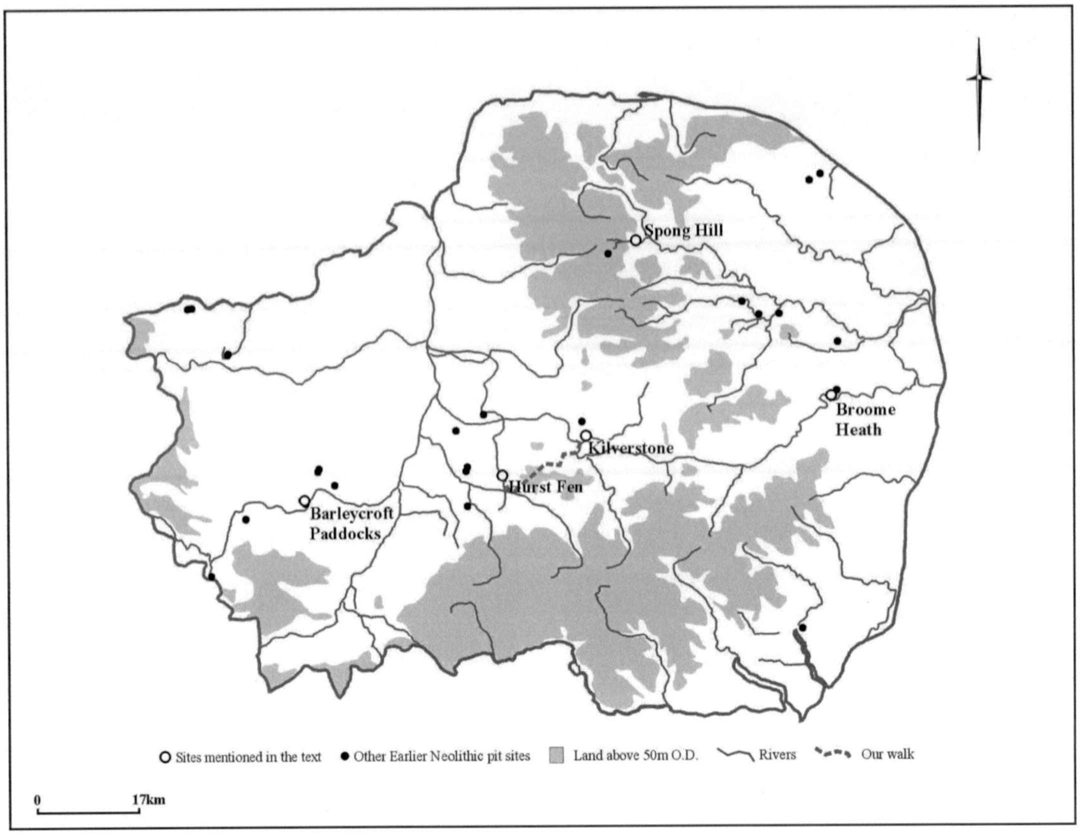

Fig. 5.11. Earlier Neolithic pit sites in Norfolk, Suffolk and Cambridgeshire

have been identified in the region (Darvill 1996; Garrow 2006). Sites made up solely of pits, however, are found in large numbers across the whole of East Anglia[2] (Fig. 5.11). These are sometimes associated with monuments, but can often be isolated, away from other contemporary features. They vary massively in scale, ranging from single features or small clusters, to dozens and even hundreds of pits. These are places where people in the earlier Neolithic *made* their mark, where they *did* leave an archaeological signature. It does seem likely that, if they were living a relatively mobile way of life (e.g. Whittle 1997), people would have travelled between these sites. The landscape may well have been textured with pathways, clearings and small fields (e.g. Edmonds 1997). What our walk made very clear, however, is that the journeys between these places would not have left an archaeological signature – at least, one that *persists* for us to work with. Those paths have been lost from memory, grown over, ploughed away.

Pits have often been thought of as fairly ephemeral things, matching the supposedly ephemeral character of Neolithic occupation. Certainly, when you are dealing with one or two in a vast landscape, it is easy to understand why. However, on sites like Kilverstone and Hurst Fen, and others with large numbers of pits (e.g. Broome Heath (Wainwright 1972), Spong Hill (Healy 1988), and Barleycroft Farm (Evans and Knight 1997) to name just three), 'ephemeral' does not seem quite the right word.

It is difficult to estimate the kinds of occupation with which these sites were associated through the pits themselves; of course, if you wanted to, it would be perfectly possible to dig two hundred of them very quickly. The material within the pits, however, does afford some insight into the character of occupation in these places. One way of approaching the issue of how long sites were occupied is to consider the number of vessels represented on each: the number of pots that had been broken while people were there. When discussing artefacts in pit contexts, it is important to be cautious. A substantial amount of work within prehistoric archaeology in Britain over the past couple of decades has served to problematise 'the archaeological record', reminding us that, often, specific things were deposited in particular places for very particular reasons (e.g. Hill 1995; Richards and Thomas 1984). However, given the fact that there was no clear evidence that pots had been deliberately smashed, or any artefacts brought specially to the sites for deposition, it seems reasonable to stick with the idea that the material within the pits was indeed 'created' (i.e. pots broken, flint working waste produced, etc.) during the course of occupation at the site where it was deposited. If so, as long as we stop short of using quantities as a *direct* measure,[3] the number of vessels represented can be a reasonable way of thinking through the amount of time those sites were occupied.

Material signatures

The largest number of vessels recovered within the pits on any one site was approximately 300, at Hurst Fen. Broome Heath produced 272 different vessels, Kilverstone 151, Spong Hill 118 (estimates of vessel numbers were not available for Barleycroft Paddocks). These are large numbers, and if, as seems to have been the case, the pots were broken during the course of everyday life on those sites, we must be dealing with substantial durations or intensities of occupation. It is also interesting to note that on these five sites there was evidence of cereal cultivation as well.[4] Of course, the cereals *need* not have been grown *at* the sites, but it is certainly possible that they were. While cereals do not necessarily require year-round attention (Gibson 2003, 140; Jones 2000, 83; Thomas 1999, 25), they do imply that people were committed to being in those places, at least for a while, at certain times of the year.

At first glance, it might seem that, despite the absence of convincing structures, the evidence is beginning to point towards permanent occupation at these sites. On closer inspection, however, strong patterns within the material contradict such an interpretation.

At Kilverstone, the majority of the pits were grouped into spatially discrete clusters. Many of these were relatively well defined (the pits within them spaced closely together, and separated from the next cluster by several metres), but others were more diffuse; there were also a few 'isolated' pits which did not fall clearly within any particular grouping. During post-excavation analysis, a substantial amount of time was spent investigating re-fits. A particular emphasis was placed on establishing links *between* pits, seeing where parts of the same pot, or the same flint knapping sequence, had ended up in *separate* features (Beadsmoore 2006; Knight 2006). The patterning which emerged was that, while there were numerous re-fits between pits in the same cluster, there were none which extended between pits in *different* clusters. The spatial separation of clusters was echoed by a material separation (Fig. 5.12).

At Hurst Fen, because the site is so dense, clusters are slightly less visible. However, towards the edges, groups of pits very much like those at Kilverstone can be made out. If the limited number of re-fits that Clark identified in his report are plotted (he only described them for two clusters; Clark *et al.* 1960, 244), a very similar picture emerges (Fig. 5.13): sherds from the same vessel connecting pits within

Fig. 5.12. Kilverstone, Area E. Flint and pottery connections (flint in grey, pottery in black)

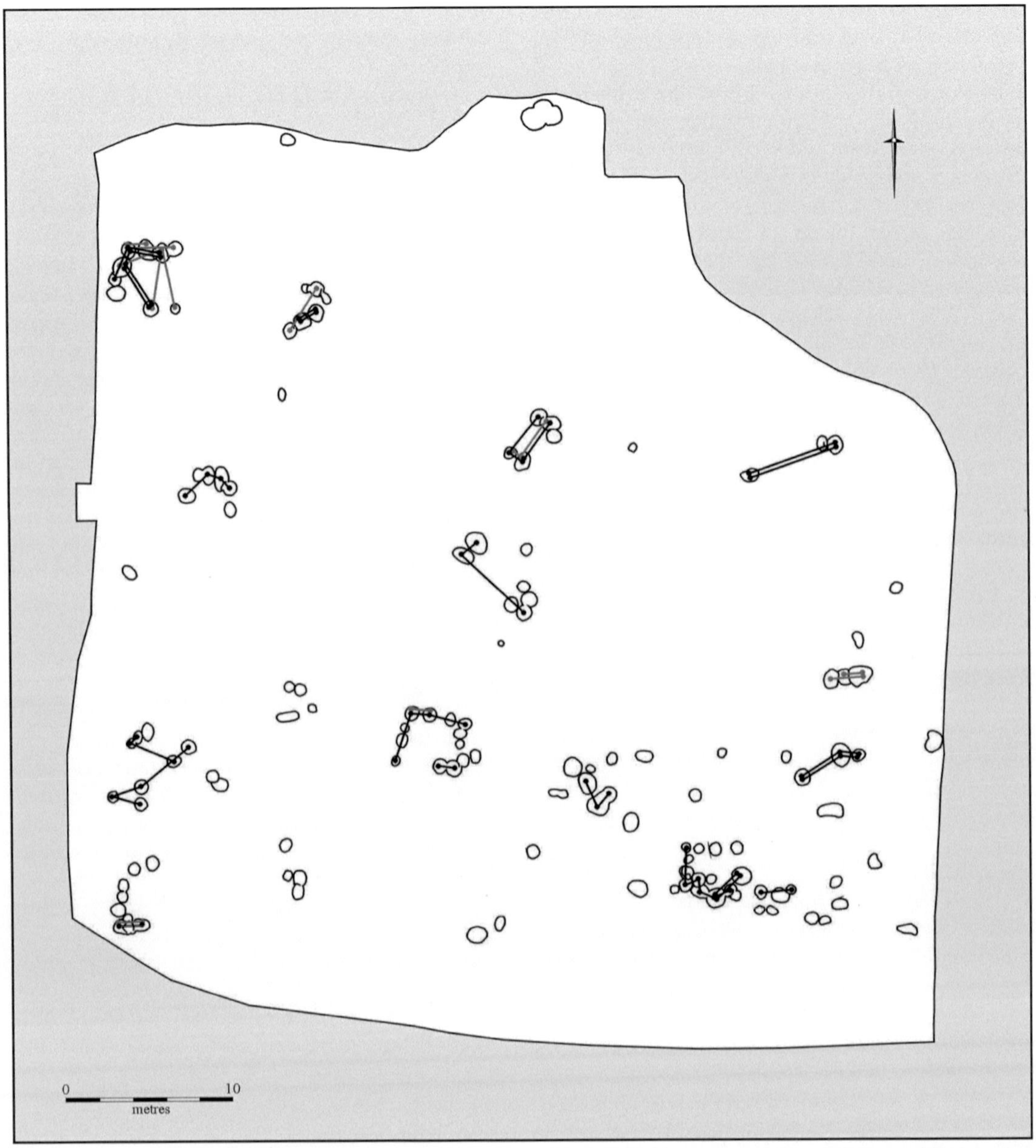

each cluster, but not those in separate clusters. At Spong Hill, although the image is slightly less striking because the clusters are so much further apart, the same is true (Fig. 5.14). At Barleycroft, although the pits came in pairs rather than clusters, the pattern is repeated: those in each pair are linked (this time by shared fabric types rather than direct re-fits), but those in separate pairs are not (Fig. 5.15). Information about vessel locations was not available for Broome Heath.

On all of these earlier Neolithic pit sites, then, finds assemblages exist not at the level of the site, or at the level of the pit, but at the level of the cluster (or pair): one set of pots in one cluster, another set of pots in another, but no links between them. While a number of different explanations of this patterning are possible (see Garrow *et al.* 2006 for a full discussion), it is difficult to imagine why, if we *are* talking about continuity of settlement, there should be such clear discontinuities in terms of the material deposited. If we accept that these patterns relate to, or correspond with, past practice, it therefore follows that there must have been similar gaps, disjunctions, in that as well. Consequently, the most likely explanation is that we are in fact dealing with repeated, but not continuous, occupation. Each cluster of pits represents a period of time when that place came into focus – people were there, 'creating' broken pots and knapping debris, leaving their archaeological signature. The fact that there were material and spatial gaps between the clusters implies that there may well have been temporal gaps which

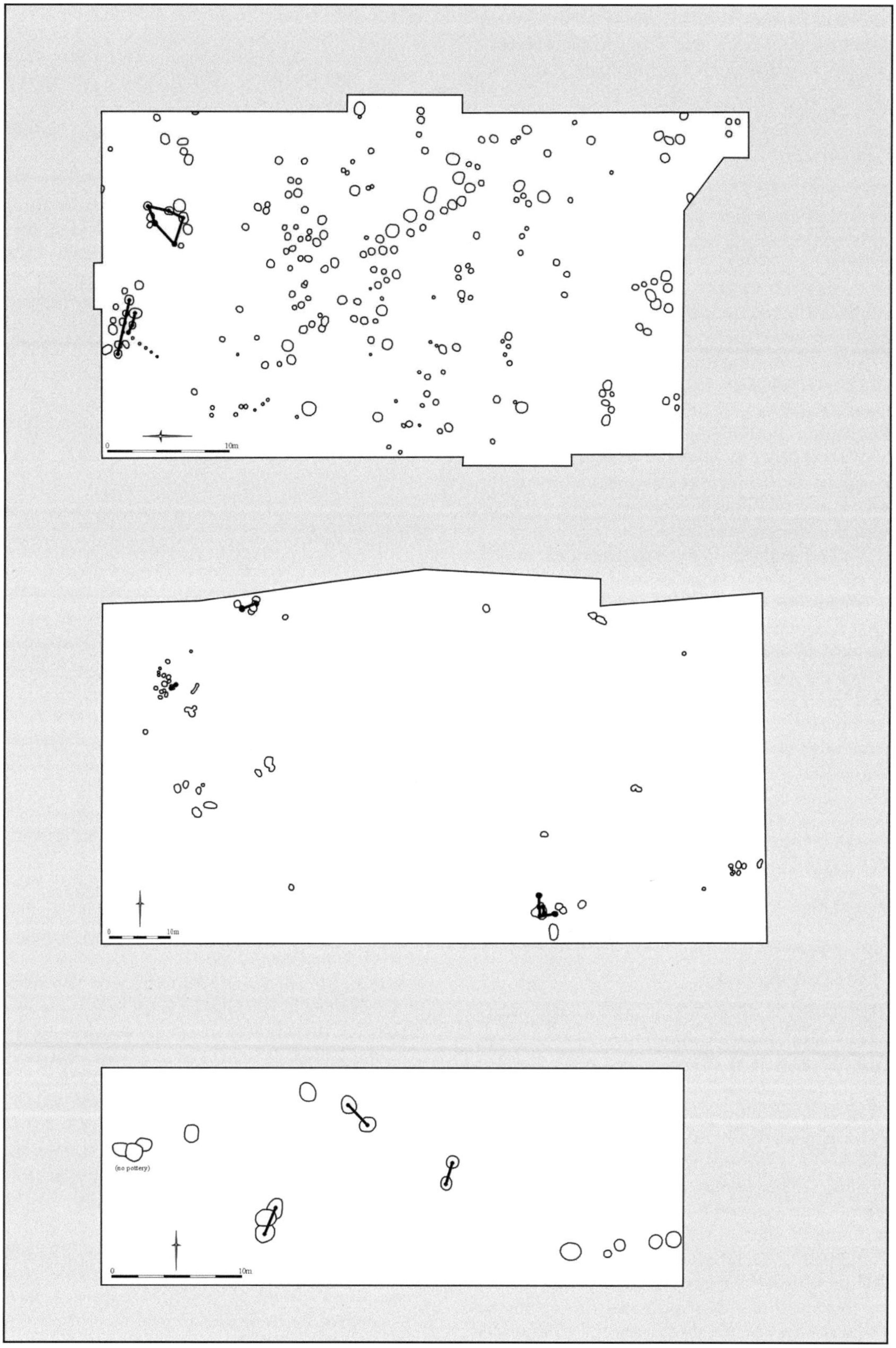

Figs 5.13–5.15. Pottery connections at Hurst Fen (after Clark et al. *1960, Plate XXVI); Spong Hill (after Healy 1988, fig. 5; only pits containing EN pottery are shown); Barleycroft Paddocks (after Evans and Knight 1997, fig. 16)*

separated them as well. The spaces in between represent the periods of time when people were away: *they* are the archaeological signatures of journeys.

Conclusion

This paper has explored the archaeological signatures of earlier Neolithic journeys. It began with two extremely similar sites, in terms of the features which had been dug and the material deposited within those features. As a result of their comparability, the *possibility* that people may actually have journeyed between them was raised. The process of making that journey in the present emphasised the fact that most prehistoric journeys would not have left an archaeological signature. During our phenomenological experiment, we had little to connect us with the past other than our imaginations. We had no real traces of the past to follow, and ourselves left no persistent trace. Our walk was not archaeological.

Subsequently, the point was made that, in order to understand prehistoric journeys archaeologically, it is necessary to focus on places where archaeological signatures *were* made. The quantities of material found on larger pit sites in East Anglia during the earlier Neolithic suggest that they must have been associated with substantial amounts of occupation overall. By examining the spatial patterning of that material, it proved possible to argue that settlement was impermanent. Discontinuities of material suggested discontinuities of occupation. These prehistoric journeys were visible – as gaps (spatial and material) between clusters – in the places which, ironically, were where they ended or began.

Acknowledgements

I would like to thank Chantal Conneller, Anwen Cooper and Thomas Yarrow for making the journey with me; Emma Beadsmoore and Mark Knight – the post-ex analysis and interpretation of Kilverstone was entirely a joint project; Anwen Cooper, Mark Knight, Lesley McFadyen, David Robinson and Thomas Yarrow for their comments on the original TAG presentation and subsequent text; and Vicki Cummings and Bob Johnston for inviting me to publish this paper, and for their editorial comments. I would also like to acknowledge the AHRC whose PhD funding enabled much of the research within this paper; and the Prehistoric Society, who very kindly allowed me to reproduce the images from Hurst Fen in Figs 5.1 and 5.3.

Notes

1 The pits at Kilverstone were radiocarbon dated to c. 3650–3400 BC (see Garrow *et al.* 2005 for the full range of dates).
2 East Anglia is taken here as Norfolk, Suffolk and Cambridgeshire
3 The intention here is not to generalise about pot breakage rates. Studies which have tried to do so cross-culturally (e.g. Arnold 1985, 152–5; Rice 1987, 303) have failed to reach a consensus. More importantly, it seems unwise to ignore the importance of context in relation to the uses, and therefore breakages, of pots.
4 Direct evidence in the form of charred seeds at Kilverstone, Spong Hill and Barleycroft Paddocks; indirect evidence in the form of quernstones and seed impressions in pottery at Hurst Fen and Broome Heath.

Bibliography

Arnold, D. 1985. *Ceramic theory and cultural process*. Cambridge: Cambridge University Press.

Barclay, G. 2000. Between Orkney and Wessex: the search for the regional Neolithics of Britain. In A. Ritchie (ed.) *Neolithic Orkney in its European context*, 275–85. Cambridge: McDonald Institute.

Beadsmoore, E. 2006. The Earlier Neolithic flint. In D. Garrow, S. Lucy and D. Gibson, *Excavations at Kilverstone, Norfolk: an episodic landscape history*. Cambridge: East Anglian Archaeology 113.

Brück, J. 2001. Monuments, power and personhood in the British Neolithic. *Journal of the Royal Anthropological Institute* 7, 649–67.

Clark, J.G.D., Higgs, E. and Longworth, I. 1960. Excavations at the Neolithic site at Hurst Fen, Mildenhall, Suffolk (1954, 1957 and 1958). *Proceedings of the Prehistoric Society* 26, 202–45.

Cooney, G. 1997. Images of settlement and the landscape in the Neolithic. In P. Topping (ed.), *Neolithic landscapes*, 23–31. Oxford: Oxbow.

Cooney, G. 2001. Bringing contemporary baggage to Neolithic landscapes. In B. Bender and M. Winer (eds), *Contested landscapes: movement, exile and place*, 165–80. Oxford: Berg.

Darvill, T. 1996. Neolithic buildings in England, Wales and the Isle of Man. In T. Darvill and J. Thomas (eds), *Neolithic houses in northwest Europe and beyond*, 77–112. Oxford: Oxbow.

Edmonds, M. 1997. Taskscape, technology and tradition. *Analecta Praehistorica Leidensia* 29, 99–110.

Evans, C. and Knight, M. 1997. *The Barleycroft Paddocks excavations, Cambridgeshire*. Unpublished Cambridge Archaeological Unit Report No. 218.

Garrow, D. 2006. *Pits, settlement and deposition during the Neolithic and Early Bronze Age in East Anglia*. British

Archaeological Reports British Series No. 414. Oxford: John and Erica Hedges.

Garrow, D., Beadsmoore, E. and Knight, M. 2005. Pit clusters and the temporality of occupation: an earlier Neolithic site at Kilverstone, Thetford, Norfolk. *Proceedings of the Prehistoric Society* 71, 139–157.

Garrow, D., Lucy, S. and Gibson, D. 2006. *Excavations at Kilverstone, Norfolk: an episodic landscape history.* Cambridge: East Anglian Archaeology 113.

Gibson, A. 2003. What do we mean by Neolithic settlement? Some approaches, 10 years on. In I. Armit, E. Murphy, E. Nelis and D. Simpson (eds), *Neolithic settlement in Ireland and Western Britain*, 136–45. Oxford: Oxbow.

Grogan, E. 2002. Neolithic houses in Ireland: a broader perspective. *Antiquity* 76, 517–25.

Healy, F. 1988. *The Anglo-Saxon cemetery at Spong Hill, North Elmham, Part VI: occupation during the seventh to second millennia BC.* Norwich: East Anglian Archaeology 39.

Hill, J.D. 1995. *Ritual and rubbish in the Iron Age of Wessex.* Oxford: British Archaeological Report British Series 242.

Johnston, R. 1999. An empty path? Processions, memories and the Dorset cursus. In A. Barclay and J. Harding (eds), *Pathway and ceremonies. The cursus monuments of Britain and Ireland.* 39–48. Oxford: Oxbow.

Jones, G. 2000. Evaluating the importance of cultivation and collecting in Neolithic Britain. In A. Fairbairn (ed.), *Plants in Neolithic Britain and beyond*, 79–84. Oxford: Oxbow.

Kinnes, I. 1998. The pottery. In F. Pryor, *Etton – excavations of a Neolithic causewayed enclosure near Maxey, Cambridgeshire 1982–7.* London: English Heritage Archaeological Report 18.

Knight, M. 2006. The Mildenhall pottery. In D. Garrow, S. Lucy and D. Gibson, *Excavations at Kilverstone, Norfolk: an episodic landscape history.* Cambridge: East Anglian Archaeology 113.

Long, R., Cork, R. and Fulton, H. 1991. *Richard Long: walking in circles.* London: George Braziller.

Oxford Archaeological Unit 2000. White Horse Stone – a Neolithic longhouse. *Current Archaeology* 168, 450–53.

Pearson, M. and Shanks, M. 2001. *Theatre/archaeology.* London: Routledge.

Renfrew, C. 2003. *Figuring it out.* London: Thames and Hudson.

Rice, P. 1987. *Pottery analysis: a sourcebook.* Chicago/London: Chicago University Press.

Richards, C. and Thomas, J. 1984. Ritual activity and structured deposition in Later Neolithic Wessex. In R. Bradley and J. Gardiner (eds), *Neolithic Studies: a review of some current research*, 189–218. Oxford: British Archaeological Reports British Series 133.

Thomas, J. 1991. *Rethinking the Neolithic.* Cambridge: Cambridge University Press.

Thomas, J. 1993. Discourse, totalization and 'The Neolithic'. In C. Tilley (ed.), *Interpretative archaeology*, 357–94. Oxford: Berg.

Thomas, J. 1996. Neolithic houses in mainland Britain and beyond – a sceptical view. In T. Darvill and J. Thomas (eds), *Neolithic houses in northwest Europe and beyond*, 1–12. Oxford: Oxbow.

Thomas, J. 1999. *Understanding the Neolithic.* London: Routledge.

Thomas, J. 2000. Reconfiguring the social, reconfiguring the material. In M. Schiffer (ed.), *Social theory in archaeology*, 143–55. Salt Lake City: University of Utah Press.

Tilley, C. 1994. *A phenomenology of landscape: places, paths and monuments.* Oxford: Berg.

Wainwright, G. 1972. The excavation of a Neolithic settlement on Broome Heath, Ditchingham, Norfolk. *Proceedings of the Prehistoric Society* 38, 1–97.

Whittle, A. 1997. Moving on and moving around: Neolithic settlement mobility. In P. Topping (ed.), *Neolithic landscapes*, 15–22. Oxford: Oxbow.

6 Megalithic journeys: moving around the monumental landscapes of Neolithic western Britain

Vicki Cummings

Introduction

For many years Neolithic scholars have considered the evidence for movement and mobility in Neolithic Britain. Many different types of evidence have been evoked, from the movements of material culture such as axes, to the presence (or absence) of permanent settlement. These considerations of the movements of people around the landscape, for the most part, are tied to essentially economic and domestic worlds. To complement this, movement and journeying has been explored in ritual terms through the study of monumental landscapes. In this paper I will explore the possible journeys to and movements around early Neolithic chambered tombs. I will argue that the ritual and domestic were not separated out into different realms, and that a consideration of the different journeys involved in the construction and use of these sites may add another dimension to how we understand and interpret them.

Neolithic journeys: mobility and movement

I want to begin by considering the issue of mobility in the Neolithic, then move on to consider the potential significance and meanings of journeys and journeying. For many years there was an implicit assumption that people in the Neolithic were sedentary, linked to the idea that they were fully-fledged farmers living in houses. After decades of searching for supporting evidence, it is now clear that while the Neolithic saw the widespread introduction and adoption of domesticated animals, in particular cattle, there is still very limited evidence for cereal cultivation (Fairbairn 2000; Schulting 2004; Schulting and Richards 2002). If cereal cultivation did take place it was almost certainly in the form of garden-like plots, which need not have been tended all year round (e.g. Whittle 2003). Houses have now been found in Ireland and eastern and northern Scotland (Armit *et al.* 2003; Barclay *et al.* 2002; Richards 2003), but whether these were all permanently occupied farmsteads remains to be seen (e.g. Cross 2003). For the rest of Britain there is very little evidence of houses or permanent settlements, suggesting that people were, for the most part, mobile.

Although it is clear that people were not sedentary in Neolithic Britain, the exact nature of the settlement pattern remains difficult to pin down. Recently, Whittle (1997) has discussed the different types of mobility that we might envisage for the Neolithic. These include 'residential' or 'circulating' mobility, which may have involved people moving between a series of short-stay camps, some visited repeatedly, as part of a round of the landscape, or 'radiating' mobility where people lived in more centralised base camps which were occupied on a seasonal basis with outlying camps for herding, hunting and cultivation. He argued that communities may well have altered their mobility patterns regularly, changing to whatever suited them most. The evidence seems to show therefore, that people were mobile, to a greater or lesser extent, and the way in which they moved may well have changed over time.

While such a consideration of mobility is important, it remains difficult to document it in the archaeological record. The distances people may have covered annually or over the course of a lifetime remains unclear. Other strands of evidence, however, offer possible clues. The long distance movement of Neolithic material culture is well documented, with some objects found far from their sources: the jadeite axes recovered from early Neolithic contexts in Britain, 500km from their origin in the Alps (e.g. Coles and Coles 1986); stone axes distributed considerable distances from their original quarries (Bradley and Edmonds 1993; Clough and Cummins 1979; 1988; Cooney and

Mandal 1998); and lithics made from Grimes Graves flint, Arran pitchstone and Antrim flint transported many kilometres from the source of the raw material (Barber *et al.* 1999; Cooney 2000). Likewise, pottery was also moved around the landscape, clearly evidenced by the assemblage from Windmill Hill, which included vessels from as far away as Cornwall (Whittle *et al.* 1999). However, although this demonstrates that objects were moved across wide parts of the landscape, the mechanisms for the movement and subsequent deposition of these objects is inconclusive (see Kador and Price this volume). Portable artefacts such as axes and pots may well have been exchanged between neighbouring communities, which does not help us in understanding the movement patterns of people. However, the recent development of strontium isotope analysis may enable us to get a better sense of the movements of individual people. The analysis of skeletal remains from a series of LBK sites on the continent demonstrates that some people were not born and raised locally, but moved into the area (Bentley forthcoming; Bentley *et al.* 2003; Price *et al.* 2001). An intriguing insight into the British evidence (albeit from the Early Bronze Age) showed that the 'Amesbury Archer' had travelled to Wessex from central Europe (Fitzpatrick 2002).

At present, we can only speculate as to the types of movements people may have made in the Neolithic. It seems clear that most people were mobile, and there remains the exciting possibility that people may have moved considerable distances over the course of their lives. I now want to turn to the nature of journeying itself, in particular why people move around.

Past and present journeys

Ethnography offers us some interesting insights into how people perceive mobility and journeying. Much has been written about movement in relation to hunter-gatherers, and although people in the Neolithic had domesticates, analogies with hunting and gathering communities can still be considered relevant. Just like people in the Neolithic, modern hunter-gatherers famously 'move around a lot' (Lee and Devore 1968, 11), but this is rarely because they have used up all the resources in an area. There are many reasons that groups move. The ethnographic record indicates that groups frequently move for social reasons. An oft-cited reason for moving is social tension: instead of resorting to arguing or fighting, individuals or families will move away (Kelly 1995, 148). They may go and join another group or simply have some time apart from their group. Journeys are also undertaken for other reasons, the death of a family member being one good reason to move on. There may also be a desire to visit other people, and this is often tied into broader exchange networks (Kelly 1995, 148). The trade and exchange of objects is an extremely important part of modern hunter-gatherer lifeways, as may also have been the case for people in the Neolithic. This is well documented in the ethnographic record, from the vast literature on the Melanesian kula exchange (Leach and Leach 1983; Malinowski 1922; Ray 2004) to the gathering together of objects for potlatch (Spencer and Jennings 1977). Interestingly, people move considerable distances to trade and exchange not just in order to gain material objects or prestige. In the Ju/'hoansi Bushmen's *hxaro* exchange network, all gifts must be passed on, so that no single individual ever gains more material culture than anyone else (Biesele and Royal-/O/OO 1999; Kelly 1995, 188). This is an example of exchange being a 'levelling' mechanism, and it is documented amongst other groups (e.g. Gregory 1994). The case in point is that people are willing to move considerable distances in order to engage in trade and exchange of objects and gifts, and this is not necessarily in order to gain wealth or personal prestige. People also undertake journeys for more spiritual reasons, for example, in order to attend ritual festivals or visit shamans. The mobility ethos is also well documented amongst modern hunter-gatherer groups, where moving around is actually highly valued in society. Some groups choose to continue moving around, even when they could have become sedentary. And amongst groups who were until recently mobile hunter-gatherers but have been forced to settle down, people express a strong desire to move and state it is one of things they miss most about a foraging existence (Kelly 1995, 152–3).

Journeys amongst non-western societies, then, are undertaken not only as part of economic practices, but also for other social and spiritual reasons. Moving around seems to be a fundamental part of social identity. By analogy, we can see these ideas as being relevant for understanding Neolithic movements. Furthermore, if journeying was embedded within a cosmological understanding of the world, no journey was value-free. So in the Neolithic there may not have been such a thing as a 'mundane' journey, a value-free and purely economic process. Even the quick journey to collect water from a stream in the morning may well have held a whole series of ritual and symbolic connotations. It is more likely that physical journeys and journeying in the Neolithic, even those that were part of everyday social practice, were intimately connected to cosmology and ideology, the wider meanings embedded in the landscape, and the materiality of the substances which people engaged with. Journeying then, would have been highly significant and symbolic, a critical part of reinforcing and reworking ideologies and belief systems.

Yet if all journeys, from short walks to collect

water to longer movements across landscapes, were significant and symbolic, we are left with a rather amorphous, generic and non-specific understanding of past movements. However, while I would argue that all journeys were embedded in the dominant cosmology and broader understandings of place, space and substance, some journeys were *more directly* concerned with ritual and spiritual matters than others, and as such may have had a stronger resonance in people's minds. It is these 'special' and 'ritual' journeys that are of most relevance to this paper, which considers the importance of journeying in relation to monumental architecture. This emphasis on movement directly connected to overt ritual practice is one way we might tease out differences between longer journeys to specific locations such as monuments and shorter, more everyday journeys.

Previous approaches to monuments and landscape

A consideration of journeying in relation to monuments is not new. There is a growing literature on the movement around and experience of Neolithic monuments, particularly in relation to later Neolithic sites. At monuments such as Avebury and Stonehenge there are clearly marked out routeways and approaches to each monument in the form of avenues, and as such it has been possible to discuss how moving along these avenues reveals different parts of the monument and the surrounding landscape (e.g. Barrett 1994; Cleal *et al.* 1995; Pollard and Reynolds 2002; Watson 2001a). The experience of engaging with and moving along cursus monuments has also been discussed, leading to the interpretation of them as conduits for funnelling movement and controlling people's experiences of the landscape (e.g. Brophy 1999; 2000; Tilley 1994; but also see Johnston 1999). Even at monumental complexes, such as Thornborough, North Yorkshire, where a series of henges are located in close proximity, it is possible to speculate about movements from one site to the next (e.g. Harding 2000; 2003; and see Noble this volume). Journeying has also been considered in relation to the large-scale movement of stones across the landscape, such as those utilised at Avebury and Stonehenge (Gillings and Pollard 1999; and papers in Cunliffe and Renfrew 1997). At these sites, the origin of the stones used to construct each monument is known, and most famously in the case of the Stonehenge bluestones, the route over which the stones were moved has been postulated and the journeys re-enacted.

It is fair to say that while monuments with clearly defined approaches have been discussed in terms of movements around and between sites, there has been less consideration of journeys to and from early Neolithic chambered tombs. There is now a considerable literature on the landscape settings of these sites, in particular what was visible *from* the site, but little has been said about what it may have been like, or what it might have meant, to move *around* these landscapes (but see Fraser 2004 on Arran). This is hardly surprising as there are no defined avenues leading to these sites, so the approach in each case is more speculative. In some areas, such as Orkney, there have been suggestions that the approach to chambered tombs may have been from the occupation areas below the monuments, as at Cuween and Quanterness (Richards 2003). Here it is possible to suggest that people may have walked uphill towards the monuments, which on approach would appear skylined on the horizon (Cummings and Pannett 2005). While this suggestion may be valid for Orkney, it would be unwise to impose it universally. The lack of settlement evidence from most parts of Britain further complicates that particular approach, and even when occupation evidence has been located close to monuments, there is the problem of temporality: were occupations contemporary with the monuments? Thus, for the most part, journeying to and from early Neolithic chambered tombs has been little considered, with the focus more often on the monument itself.

A quick introduction to the sites

There is a discrete distribution of early Neolithic chambered tombs in western Britain (Fig. 6.1). In west Wales and Cornwall, the majority of sites are dolmens, similar to their Irish counterparts and consisting of a simple chamber topped with a massive capstone. The chamber deposits are frequently disturbed, but excavations have produced early Neolithic pottery and human bone. There is also a tradition of long cairn construction in western Britain, the dominant form being the 'Clyde' monument (Henshall 1972). These sites are found in western Scotland, with similar outliers on the Isle of Man and in north Wales. These sites usually have chambers divided into compartments, large forecourt areas and a long cairn. Finds from these sites include human bone, pottery and lithics from the chambers with additional evidence of activity in the forecourt.

Building megaliths

To start off with, I want to discuss the construction process itself, which involved a number of journeys, all of which may have contributed to the meaning and significance of the megalith and had resonances within the domestic sphere. Building a megalith

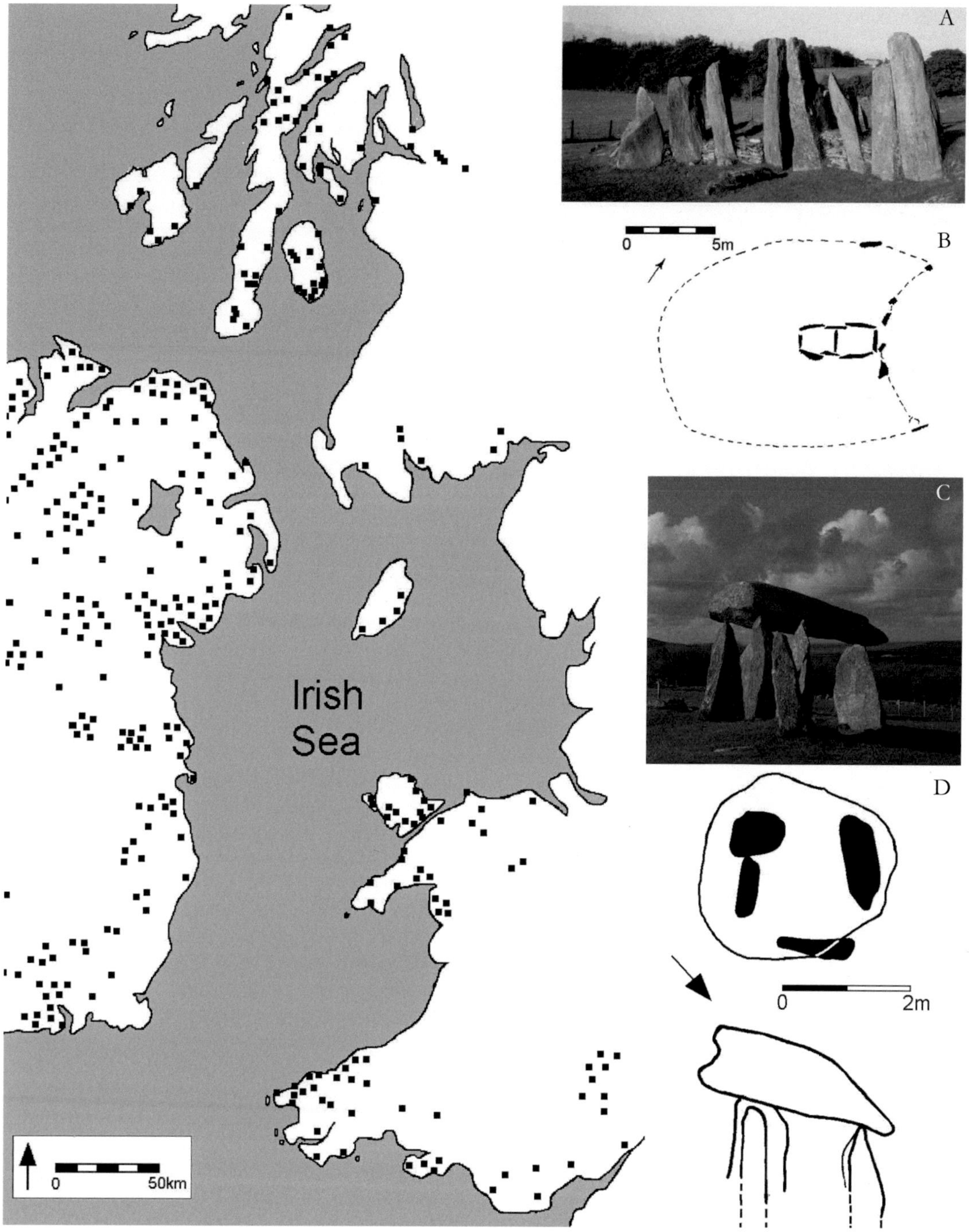

Fig. 6.1. Map of the distribution of chambered tombs in western Britain and eastern Ireland. Examples of Clyde cairns; A, Cairnholy I; B, Achnagoul II (after Henshall 1972). Examples of dolmens: C, Pentre Ifan; D, Carreg Coetan (after Barker 1992)

would have required bringing people together. We can only guess at the kinds of distances that people may have had to travel in order to meet up for the construction of a site, but it would have involved travelling. These journeys would not only have been for the building of a megalith, but also to plan the build. Colin Richards (2004) has written about the amount of effort required prior to any actual construction work on a monument. The process would need to be planned, a suitable location found for the site and stones selected to make up the chamber (Gillings and Pollard 1999). Rope would need to be made, trees turned into rollers and antler picks collected. Food would need to be hoarded or saved for the actual event, as a large workforce would almost certainly require feeding in exchange for labour. For what may have been years prior to the construction of a megalith, people may have been looking after animals with the explicit aim of keeping them for a feast during monument construction. It seems hard to imagine that this knowledge and planning would have no impact on the meanings and significances attached to these animals, nor the journeys that they and their herders may have undertaken (see Chadwick this volume). This is one of many points where the economic and 'ritual' may have been indistinguishable.

The various journeys that people and things may have undergone prior to a single stone being erected may all have added to the overall biography of each place. None of these journeys were purely economic, all were embedded within underlying cosmologies and planned futures, each monument then being a constant renegotiation between people, places, materialities and biographies (McFadyen 2002; 2003). The actual construction of a site may well have been perceived as a social gathering, with the journey to the construction site one of excitement and anticipation, and perhaps also anxiety and fear. Richards has also argued that there was considerable risk investing so much time and energy into megalithic construction, which, if it went wrong, could have dire consequences for those involved (Richards 2004).

Once people had travelled to the location of a site, a series of smaller journeys would have been made, some repeatedly and repetitively over perhaps quite long periods of time. For example, the stones that were used to construct the cairns would have been collected together and moved, then carefully positioned within the cairn (McFadyen 2003). It has been suggested that the capstones of some dolmens were actually excavated and lifted up on the spot to create a chamber (Cummings and Whittle 2004; Lynch 1975; Whittle 2004). At a number of the chambered tombs in western Britain, however, there is evidence that some of the stones used were not local. For example, at Carreg Samson in south-west Wales, the site is constructed from two different lithologies, one of which is likely to have come from some distance away (Cummings 2002b). Even at early Neolithic sites then, chosen stones would have been moved considerable distances across the landscape. The process and effort involved in moving these stones would have been quite an event, again adding to the biography of the monument. We may be looking at days of dragging a stone across the landscape and all the procedures surrounding that literally monumental undertaking. If we envisage stones as active agents in their own right, the journey of a particular stone may have been analogous to the journey of a deceased person on their way to their final resting place.

The construction process, then, involved many journeys: the journeys of people planning and building a megalith, the tending and moving of animals kept for the feast, the movement of stones as they were transported longer or shorter distances. These journeys, and the process of construction, may have been as important as the finished product (cf. Barrett 1994; McFadyen 2003). Furthermore, this process was not static and embedded in only one place in the landscape, but included journeys to and from a number of places. In many ways then megaliths are the embodiment of different locales and many journeys at a single point in space and time. The significance of these monumental places was also not solely within the realms of the 'ritual' but embedded within many different types of 'domestic' and economic practices and journeys.

Visiting megaliths

So far I have talked about a whole series of different journeys which may have been a crucial part of the social biography and broader significance of megalithic constructions. It has only been possible to consider these journeys in rather general terms. But once a megalith was constructed, its physical form existed at one point in the landscape, a point which could be repeatedly visited and accessed, and a point which survives in the archaeological record. Elsewhere I have argued that the precise location chosen in the landscape for the construction of the monuments of western Britain was of significance, with builders choosing locales that had views of a range of different landscape features, particularly the mountains and the sea (Cummings 2002a; 2004; Cummings and Whittle 2004; Cummings forthcoming; Fowler and Cummings 2003). While I maintain that the views from megaliths were of particular significance, I would also suggest that the ways in which these sites may have been approached was also important. We will, of course, never be able to unequivocally demonstrate the direction from which megaliths were approached, even assuming that there was a single 'correct' way of approaching these sites in the past. There are further complications including changes to the landscape since the Neolithic, not only in terms of modern development but also vegetation cover, the presence of paths and trackways (Tilley 1994) and so on (see Garrow this volume). Approaches to sites may also have changed within the course of a year or over the use-life of the site. Nevertheless, the presence of a megalith gives us a starting point from which we may make some suggestions.

It has been noted that a number of megaliths in western Britain were constructed alongside or close to rivers (Cummings forthcoming; Cummings and Whittle 2004). Although we can never be certain, the journey to and from these megaliths may well have been alongside, or even in boats along, the river. Many parts of the early Neolithic landscape would have been wooded, and access through these landscapes would have been facilitated by the presence of rivers, either by walking alongside them, or by floating along them. The movement of people along a river may have been a crucial part of the experience and engagement with these riverine megaliths. It has been suggested by many authors that water and rivers seem to hold a special place in a Neolithic economy of substances, being associated with rebirth, renewal, cleansing and transformation (Bradley 2000; Fowler and Cummings 2003; Richards 1996; Thomas 1998a). It has even been suggested that rivers could be considered pre-cursors to linear Neolithic monuments such as cursuses and avenues (Brophy 1999; 2000; Thomas 1998b). Furthermore, increasing numbers of Neolithic human remains have been recovered from rivers, in particular the Trent and Thames, which may suggest that rivers also played an important role in the deposition of the dead (Fowler and Cummings 2003; Thomas 2003). Rivers, then, may well have represented other journeys taken by both the living and the dead and they may have been an important part of the journey to and from some megaliths.

While the experience of moving along a river may have added to the significance of a site, and channelled encounters with each site in a specific way, not all rivers in Neolithic Britain had megaliths constructed along them. However, the vast majority of sites in western Britain *are* positioned in relation to the sea. This relationship is particularly striking in western Scotland, where megaliths cluster around the Clyde waterways as well as the extensions of the Clyde, Loch Fyne and Loch Awe (see Fig. 6.2), but many sites in west Wales are also positioned near to the sea (Cummings and Whittle 2004; Tilley 1994). In the past I have discussed the visual impact of the sea when actually engaging with a megalith. However, it would be intriguing if the sea also played a crucial role in the approach to the megaliths of western Britain (also see G. Robinson this volume). While visiting the megaliths of western Scotland I was struck by the relationship between the sea and megaliths. Sites are repeatedly located so that they would be easily accessible by boat: they were close to a natural harbour or landing place and located just a short uphill walk from the shore. Access to these sites overland, as is the case today, would have been much more problematic. In many cases, when a megalith was approached from any direction but the sea, it was quite difficult to find. Megaliths were invisible until one was quite close by and there were often no distinctive features in the landscape which might indicate where the megalith was situated. In contrast, when I approached some of the megaliths from the coast, they were much easier to locate. They were frequently visible from the sea, skylined on the horizon, and it was also notable that there were distinctive coastal features at the point where one would walk uphill towards the megalith, almost marking out the position of the megalith in the landscape. At these sites, then, it is possible to suggest that some people at least may have journeyed by boat in order to reach a site (G. Robinson this volume). A short but steep walk followed, marking out the final part of the journey by being quite strenuous. On reaching the megalith itself, participants would then be able to see the wider landscape within which the monument was placed.

Fig. 6.2. Clyde monuments located in relation to water-ways

Some megaliths cluster together, and there is a sense that these sites may have been designed to be visited in a prescribed order. A good example of this is the group of sites along Loch Fyne, which could have been visited one after the other by boat, each monument being just a short uphill walk from the water. This may also have been the case with the four monuments found at the north-west tip of the Isle of Bute. From the south, the first site encountered is Glecknabae, only a short distance from the shore and at the point where there are distinctive quartz outcrops. Next is Carnbaan, which involves a longer and steeper uphill walk following a stream. Only a short distance again by sea is Michael's Grave, again close to the shore and finally Glenvoidean, uphill from Michael's Grave.

What might journeying to a megalith by boat have meant? Just as with rivers, it is possible to suggest that the sea may have been a highly potent substance in the Neolithic. Journeying across the sea in order to reach a megalith may have been key in the experience of each site, referencing the symbolic properties of water. The sea is also a liminal place, and the inter-tidal zone an interface between the land and the sea (Scarre 2002). It is a place for other journeys, journeys to lands across the Irish Sea. These are journeys we know people were taking, evidenced in the movements of raw materials such as Antrim flint and polished stone axes. The sea may also have been intimately connected with the journeys taken by the dead. The persistent reference of the sea at chambered tombs in western Britain may be due to the close metaphorical connection between the dead and the sea. This may be one of the reasons why people were eating fewer marine resources in the Neolithic (Fowler and Cummings 2003; Thomas 2003). The sea may also have been connected with origins, particularly of the Neolithic and monumentality. A sea journey then may have stood for the origins of what it was to be Neolithic, both in terms of material culture and social identity. The visit to a megalith may have been preceded by a rather special journey. These movements on water may themselves have held a whole series of connotations, related to other boat journeys.

The journey to a megalith, then, may have been a fundamental part of the experience and meaning of the site. The landscapes encountered while moving to and from a site may well have been as important as the landscapes visible from the site itself (an interesting contrast with site-based landscape studies: e.g. Cummings and Whittle 2004), and the careful orchestration of the journey to and from a site may have been created so that things (views, landscape features, built features) were presented to participants in a particular way. The fact that approaches to and from megaliths were not formalised in stone does not rule out the possibility that there were formalised approaches. This could be done by cutting down thin swathes of trees around those megaliths which were in wooded environments (Cummings and Whittle 2003), or simply by maintaining pathways through the landscape (Tilley 1994). Knowledge of specific approaches could also have been passed on. None of these would leave an archaeological signature.

Activity at megaliths

People undertook journeys in order to build and use megaliths. The stones used in the construction of megaliths also undertook journeys. The final aspect of the evidence for journeying I wish to discuss comprises the deposits found within megaliths. At the most simplistic level, megaliths frequently have deposits of materials that have travelled considerable distances. In western Scotland, for example, many of the excavated sites have produced deposits of Arran pitchstone (Henshall 1972). For everywhere but Arran itself, this distinctive shiny stone would have had to have been transported over land and sea. The deposition of pitchstone at megaliths quite probably relates in part to a referencing of the Isle of Arran; a reference which also seems to have been visually important at many sites. I would argue that Arran held a particular place in landscape mythology in the early Neolithic, linked in part to its visually impressive profile, and associated myths and legends (Cummings forthcoming). However, the meaning of Arran pitchstone may also have come from the journey it has taken before being deposited. Again, the journeys involved in communities obtaining pitchstone may not have been either exclusively 'ritual' or 'domestic' but entwined in both everyday practice and more spiritual matters. Occasionally even more exotic objects were deposited in megaliths. At Cairnholy I in south-west Scotland, for example, a flake of a jadeite axe was found (Piggott and Powell 1949), an object which had undertaken a very long journey from the Alps, with parts of this journey almost certainly embedded in the social biography of the object itself.

While it is easy to see the physical journeys undertaken by objects deposited in megaliths, it is also relevant that other deposits undertook a different type of journey. It has been suggested that chambered tombs were places of transformation, where the dead underwent a series of transformations or journeys from living to dead to ancestor (e.g. Bradley 1993). These journeys may have involved the defleshing of the deceased, quickly in the form of a cremation or more slowly through deposition or excarnation. It is also notable that burnt material is ubiquitously found at megaliths in western Britain, representative perhaps of the transformative journeys that these megaliths signify. It is not only the megalith itself then that embodies a diverse set of journeys, but the deposits made within megaliths also refer to a whole series of journeys as well, actual physical journeys of people and things as well as transformative journeys, of personhood and substance (Fowler 2003).

Discussion

Journeying and moving around the landscape was clearly a part of everyday Neolithic social practice. So why might referencing journeys have been important and significant in relation to early Neolithic monuments? I have already discussed the possibility that megaliths were essentially the embodiment of a set of journeys, so that each megalith represented in material form a number of important movements around the landscape. This may have been not only the journeys of the architects, the builders of the site, for whom the process of construction may well have been as significant as the finished product. Megaliths may also have represented the 'original' journey of the first people, perhaps those who brought over a new material culture and a new social identity from mainland Europe, or if we imagine considerable continuity with the past, the founding ancestors embedded deep within a creation mythology. There were also the journeys of both the living and the dead, the people who visited, used and were deposited in the megaliths. And if we envisage the stones used to construct these megaliths as active social beings in the Neolithic world, the journeys that they took to their final resting place in the landscape adds to the overall biography of the monument. In short, journeys were a fundamental part of the creation and use of these sites, and cannot be ignored when thinking about their significance.

The embodiment of journeying at megaliths, and the journeys to megaliths, may also have worked at other levels too. Here we can draw some inspiration from landscape ethnography. Basso (1984), for example, discusses how various myths and moral tales are embedded within Native American landscapes – to move around and engage with the landscape is to be reminded of one's own moral place in the world. Journeys also form an important part of ritual life: journeys to particular places to seek meetings with other worlds and other beings. We could envisage very similar engagements with the landscape in the Neolithic, the movement to and from megaliths being an encounter with mythical places in the landscape (Cummings and Whittle 2004). To move to and from a megalith may have been to engage with a narrative or sets of stories. It has also been suggested that megaliths, like similar locales in Native American landscapes, were places where people took journeys to other worlds. The possible use of narcotics at megaliths, the acoustic properties of the sites and the presence of rock art all hint at megaliths being the starting place for spiritual and otherworldly journeys (Dronfield 1995a; 1995b; Sherratt 1991; Watson 2001b).

Journeying is a fundamental part of people's being-in-the-world and social identity. Moving and journeying, which these megaliths embody, may well have been a mode of dwelling that Neolithic people chose to follow. Monuments, then, may have embodied in physical form a set of journeys, some of stone and objects, some of people, some metaphorical or transformative, and others mythical. But what is clear is that movements to, from and around these sites were of fundamental importance. Some journeys were connected with more 'economic' concerns while others were more tightly focussed on ritual practice, but all contributed to the meaning and significance of these sites.

Conclusion

In this paper I have suggested that journeys may have been an important part of the construction, use and meaning of megaliths. In a very general sense I have highlighted some of the possible ways we can think about the importance of journeying in relation to these megaliths. However, there is clearly more work to be done. A closer consideration of engagements with the landscape, not just at the monument itself but also moving around the landscape and between monuments, is needed. Furthermore, moving across landscapes should not be restricted to the land but also be considered by boat along rivers or on the sea (see G. Robinson this volume). It is possible that evidence exists that might further refine our understandings of specific movements through the landscape. Strontium isotope analysis offers one way of considering the different origins of the people whose remains were deposited at megaliths. The excavation of chambered tombs has, so far, focussed on the site itself, and a wider excavation area may reveal more formalised approaches to the site (perhaps in timber). Whether or not we are ever able to really get to grips with the kind of journeys people undertook in the early Neolithic, what is crucial is that journeying was significant. I have argued here that it was important and embedded within a broader understanding and engagement with the world, even at the everyday level. It may have come more sharply into focus during special journeys, journeys concerned with the dead, building architecture or particular ritual practices. To travel, to move, to journey through the landscape would have been a highly evocative and physical experience

Acknowledgements

My own specific journeys around the megaliths of the western Irish Sea have benefited enormously from help and discussion from many people: Chris Fowler; Robert Johnston; Amelia Pannett and Alasdair Whittle. The Board of Celtic Studies, The Leverhulme Trust and the British Academy all provided financial assistance for visiting the megaliths of western Britain. I am very grateful for useful comments on this paper from Lesley McFadyen and Robert Johnston.

Bibliography

Armit, I., Murphy, E., Nelis, E. and Simpson, D. (eds) 2003. *Neolithic settlement in Ireland and western Britain.* Oxford: Oxbow.

Barber, M., Field, D. and Topping, P. 1999. *The Neolithic flint mines of England.* Stroud: Tempus.

Barclay, G., Brophy, K. and MacGregor, G. 2002. A Neolithic building at Claish Farm, near Callander, Stirling Council, Scotland, UK. *Antiquity* 76, 23–4.

Barker, C. 1992. *The chambered tombs of south-west Wales*. Oxford: Oxbow.

Barrett, J. 1994. *Fragments from antiquity*. London: Blackwell.

Basso, K.H. 1984. 'Stalking with stories': names, places and moral narratives among the Western Apache. In E. Bruner (ed.), *Text, play and the story: the reconstruction of self and society*, 19–55. Washington: American Ethnological Society.

Bentley, R.A. forthcoming. *Tracing early Neolithic human mobility with strontium and oxygen isotopes: evidence from south-west Germany.* In A. Whittle and V. Cummings (eds), *Going over: the Mesolithic/Neolithic transition in north-west Europe*. London: British Academy.

Bentley, R.A., Chikhi, L. and Price, T.D. 2003. The Neolithic transition in Europe: comparing broad scale genetic and local scale isotopic evidence. *Antiquity* 77, 63–6.

Biesele, M. and Royal-/O/OO, K. 1999. The Ju/'hoansi of Botswana and Namibia. In R. Lee and R. Daly (eds), *The Cambridge encyclopedia of hunters and gatherers*, 205–209. Cambridge: Cambridge University Press.

Bradley, R. 1993. *Altering the earth*. Edinburgh: Society of Antiquaries of Scotland Monograph.

Bradley, R. 2000. *The archaeology of natural places*. London: Routledge.

Bradley, R. and Edmonds, M. 1993. *Interpreting the axe trade*. Cambridge: Cambridge University Press.

Brophy, K. 1999. Seeing the cursus as a symbolic river. *British Archaeology* 44, 6–7.

Brophy, K. 2000. Water coincidence? Cursus monuments and rivers. In A. Ritchie (ed.), *Neolithic Orkney in its European context,* 59–70. Cambridge: The McDonald Institute for Archaeological Research.

Cleal, R., Walker, K. and Montague, R. 1995. *Stonehenge in its landscape: twentieth-century excavations*. London: English Heritage.

Clough, T. and Cummins, W. (eds) 1979. *Stone axe studies*. London: Council for British Archaeology.

Clough, T. and Cummins, W. (eds) 1988. *Stone axe studies: volume two*. London: Council for British Archaeology.

Coles, B. and Coles, J. 1986. *Sweet Track to Glastonbury: the Somerset Levels in prehistory.* London: Thames and Hudson.

Cooney, G. 2000. *Landscapes of Neolithic Ireland.* London: Routledge.

Cooney, G. and Mandal, S. 1998. *The Irish stone axe project.* Bray: Wordwell.

Cross, S. 2003. Irish Neolithic settlement architecture – a reappraisal. In I. Armit, E. Murphy, E. Nelis and D. Simpson (eds), *Neolithic settlement in Ireland and western Britain*, 195–202. Oxford: Oxbow.

Cummings, V. 2002a. Between mountains and sea: a reconsideration of the monuments of south-west Scotland. *Proceedings of the Prehistoric Society* 68, 125–46.

Cummings, V. 2002b. Experiencing texture and touch in the British Neolithic. *Oxford Journal of Archaeology* 21, 249–61.

Cummings, V. 2004. Connecting the mountains and sea: the monuments of the eastern Irish Sea zone. In V. Cummings and C. Fowler (eds) *The Neolithic of the Irish Sea: materiality and traditions of practice*, 29–36. Oxford: Oxbow.

Cummings, V. forthcoming. From midden to megalith? The Mesolithic/Neolithic transition in western Britain. In A. Whittle and V. Cummings (eds), *Going over: the Mesolithic/Neolithic transition in north-west Europe.* London: British Academy.

Cummings, V. and Pannett, A. 2005. Island views: the settings of the chambered cairns of southern Orkney. In V. Cummings and A. Pannett (eds), *Set in stone: current research on Neolithic monumentality in Scotland.* Oxford: Oxbow.

Cummings, V. and Whittle, A. 2003. Tombs with a view: landscape, monuments and trees. *Antiquity* 77, 255–66.

Cummings, V. and Whittle, A. 2004. *Places of special virtue: megaliths in the Neolithic landscapes of Wales.* Oxford: Oxbow.

Cunliffe, B. and Renfrew, C. (eds) 1997. *Science and Stonehenge.* Oxford: Oxford University Press.

Dronfield, J. 1995a. Migraine, light and hallucinogens: the neurocognitive basis of Irish megalithic art. *Oxford Journal of Archaeology* 14, 261–75.

Dronfield, J. 1995b. Subjective vision and the source of Irish megalithic art. *Antiquity* 69, 539–49.

Fairbairn, A. (ed.) 2000. *Plants in Neolithic Britain and beyond.* Oxford: Oxbow.

Fitzpatrick, A. 2002. 'The Amesbury Archer': a well furnished Early Bronze Age burial in southern England. *Antiquity* 76, 629–30.

Fowler, C. 2003. Rates of (ex)change: decay and growth, memory and the transformation of the dead in early Neolithic southern Britain. In H. Williams (ed.), *Archaeologies of remembrance: death and memory in past societies*, 45–64. London: Kluwer Academic Press.

Fowler, C. and Cummings, V. 2003. Places of transformation: building monuments from water and stone in the Neolithic of the Irish Sea. *Journal of the Royal Anthropological Institute 9*, 1–21.

Fraser, S. 2004. Metaphorical journeys: landscape, monuments and the body in a Scottish Neolithic. *Proceedings of the Prehistoric Society* 70, 129–51.

Gillings, M. and Pollard, J. 1999. Non-portable stone artefacts and contexts of meaning: the tale of Grey Wether (www.museums.ncl.ac.uk/Avebury/stone4.htm). *World Archaeology* 31:2, 179–93.

Gregory, C. 1994. Exchange and reciprocity. In T. Ingold (ed.), *Companion encyclopedia of anthropology*, 911–39. London: Routledge.

Harding, J. 2000. Later Neolithic ceremonial centres, ritual and pilgrimage: the monument complex of Thornborough, North Yorkshire. In A. Ritchie (ed.), *Neolithic Orkney in its European context,* 30–46. Cambridge: The McDonald Institute for Archaeological Research.

Harding, J. 2003. *The henge monuments of the British Isles.* Stroud: Tempus.

Henshall, A. 1972. *The chambered tombs of Scotland, volume two.* Edinburgh: Edinburgh University Press.

Johnston, R. 1999. An empty path? Processions, memories

and the Dorset Cursus. In A. Barclay and J. Harding (eds), *Pathways and ceremonies: the cursus monuments of Britain and Ireland*, 39–48. Oxford: Oxbow.

Kelly, R. 1995. *The foraging spectrum.* Washington: Smithsonian.

Leach, J. and Leach, E. (eds) 1983. *The Kula: new perspectives on Massim exchange.* Cambridge: Cambridge University Press.

Lee, R. and DeVore, I. (eds) 1968. *Man the hunter.* New York: Aldine.

Lynch, F. 1975. Excavations at Carreg Samson megalithic tomb, Mathry, Pembrokeshire. *Archaeologia Cambrensis* 124, 15–35.

Malinowski, B. 1922. *Argonauts of the western Pacific: an account of native enterprise and adventure in the archipelagoes of Melanesian New Guinea.* London: Routledge and Kegan Paul.

McFadyen, L. 2002. Bodybuilding. In J. Macarthur and A. Moulis (eds), *Additions to architectural history. Society of Architectural Historians, Australia and New Zealand.* Brisbane: Brisbane University Press.

McFadyen, L. 2003. *A revision of the materiality of architecture: the significance of Neolithic long mound and chambered monument building practice, with particular reference to the Cotswold-Severn Group.* University of Wales, Newport: Unpublished PhD Thesis.

Piggott, S. and Powell, T.G.E. 1949. The excavation of three Neolithic chambered tombs in Galloway, 1949. *Proceedings of the Society of Antiquaries of Scotland* 83, 103–61.

Pollard, J. and Reynolds, A. 2002. *Avebury: the biography of a landscape.* Stroud: Tempus.

Price, T.D., Bentley, R.A., Lüning, J., Gronenborn, D. and Wahl, J. 2001. Prehistoric human migration in the *Linearbandkeramik* of central Europe. *Antiquity* 75, 593–603.

Ray, K. 2004. Axes, kula and things that were 'good to think'. In V. Cummings and C. Fowler (eds), *The Neolithic of the Irish Sea: materiality and traditions of practice*, 160–73. Oxford: Oxbow.

Richards, C. 1996. Henges and water: towards an elemental understanding of monumentality and landscape in late Neolithic Britain. *Journal of Material Culture* 1, 313–36.

Richards, C. 2003. *Dwelling among the monuments: the Neolithic village of Barnhouse, Maeshowe passage grave and surrounding monuments at Stenness, Orkney.* Cambridge: McDonald Institute of Archaeological Research.

Richards, C. 2004. Labouring with monuments: constructing the dolmen at Carreg Samson, south-west Wales. In V. Cummings and C. Fowler (eds), *The Neolithic of the Irish Sea: materiality and traditions of practice*, 72–80. Oxford: Oxbow.

Scarre, C. 2002. Coast and cosmos: the Neolithic monuments of northern Brittany. In C. Scarre (ed.), *Monuments and landscape in Atlantic Europe*, 84–102. London: Routledge.

Schulting, R. 2004. An Irish Sea change: some implications for the Mesolithic-Neolithic transition. In V. Cummings and C. Fowler (eds), *The Neolithic of the Irish Sea: materiality and traditions of practice*, 22–8. Oxford: Oxbow.

Schulting, R. and Richards, M. 2002. The wet, the wild and the domesticated: the Mesolithic-Neolithic transition on the west coast of Scotland. *European Journal of Archaeology* 5, 147–89.

Sherratt, A. 1991. Sacred and profane substances: the ritual use of narcotics in Later Neolithic Europe. In P. Garwood R. Jennings, J. Skeates, D. Toms (eds), *Sacred and profane*, 50–64. Oxford: Oxford Committee for Archaeology.

Spencer, R. and Jennings, J. 1977. *The Native Americans: ethnology and background of the north American Indians.* London: Harper and Row.

Thomas, J. 1998a. Economies of substance in earlier Neolithic Britain. In J. Robb (ed.), *Material symbols: culture and economy in prehistory*, 70–89. Carbondale: Southern Illinois University.

Thomas, J. 1998b. *Holm, Dumfries: excavations 1998.* Southampton: Interim report.

Thomas, J. 2003. Thoughts on the 'repacked' Neolithic revolution. *Antiquity* 77, 67–74.

Tilley, C. 1994. *A phenomenology of landscape: places, paths and monuments.* Oxford: Berg.

Watson, A. 2001a. Composing Avebury. *World Archaeology* 33, 296–314.

Watson, A. 2001b. The sounds of transformation: acoustics, monuments and ritual in the British Neolithic. In N. Price (ed.), *The archaeology of shamanism*, 178–92. London: Routledge.

Whittle, A. 1997. Moving on and moving around: Neolithic settlement mobility. In P. Topping (ed.), *Neolithic landscapes*, 14–22. Oxford: Oxbow.

Whittle, A. 2003. *The archaeology of people.* London: Routledge.

Whittle, A. 2004. Stones that float to the sky: portal dolmens and their landscapes of memory and myth. In V. Cummings and C. Fowler (eds), *The Neolithic of the Irish Sea: materiality and traditions of practice*, 81–90. Oxford: Oxbow.

Whittle, A., Pollard, J. and Grigson, C. 1999. *Harmony of symbols: the Windmill Hill causewayed enclosure, Wiltshire.* Oxford: Oxbow.

7 Monumental journeys: Neolithic monument complexes and routeways across Scotland

Gordon Noble

Introduction

Neolithic ceremonial complexes or monument complexes are loosely defined as the places where a wide range of monumental structures, often of more than one period, have been found in the same location (Barnatt 1989, chapter 3; Bradley 1993, 108–9). The largest monument complexes are often associated with concentrations of objects made from non-local materials (principally stone axes) and the monuments themselves may reference traditions more commonly found elsewhere in the British Isles (Bradley 1993, 110). The presence of non-local references and influences is undoubtedly due in part to the increasing contact between regions in the Later Neolithic (Barrett 1994; Bradley 1984, chapter 3; Bradley and Chapman 1986), and this can explain one of the most significant aspects of ceremonial complexes: their location on the major routeways that undoubtedly formed the main means of communication in prehistoric Britain. In this paper I want to examine this theme with a case study of some of the most significant monument complexes in Scotland. Three of the densest concentrations of Neolithic monuments in Scotland are found around Blackshouse Burn in the Upper Clyde Valley in Lanarkshire, at Dunragit in Wigtownshire, Dumfries and Galloway, and in the Kilmartin Glen, Argyll (Fig. 7.1). I want to outline the nature of these complexes to highlight the variety and numbers of monuments found at each location. However, while these places contain a diverse range of structures one of the unifying aspects of the complexes is their location on major routeways, and in particular their location at the heart of what are known as 'trans-peninsular' routes: where dangerous seas can be avoided through travel along inland river routes. These three complexes share this characteristic with the most famous concentration of Neolithic monuments in Britain and Ireland: the Wessex area of southern England. I will first outline the three complexes I want to look at in detail in this paper, before moving to a wider consideration of the relationship between monument complexes and routeways, showing how the location on routeways is part of a wider phenomenon and not merely restricted to the three examples outlined below.

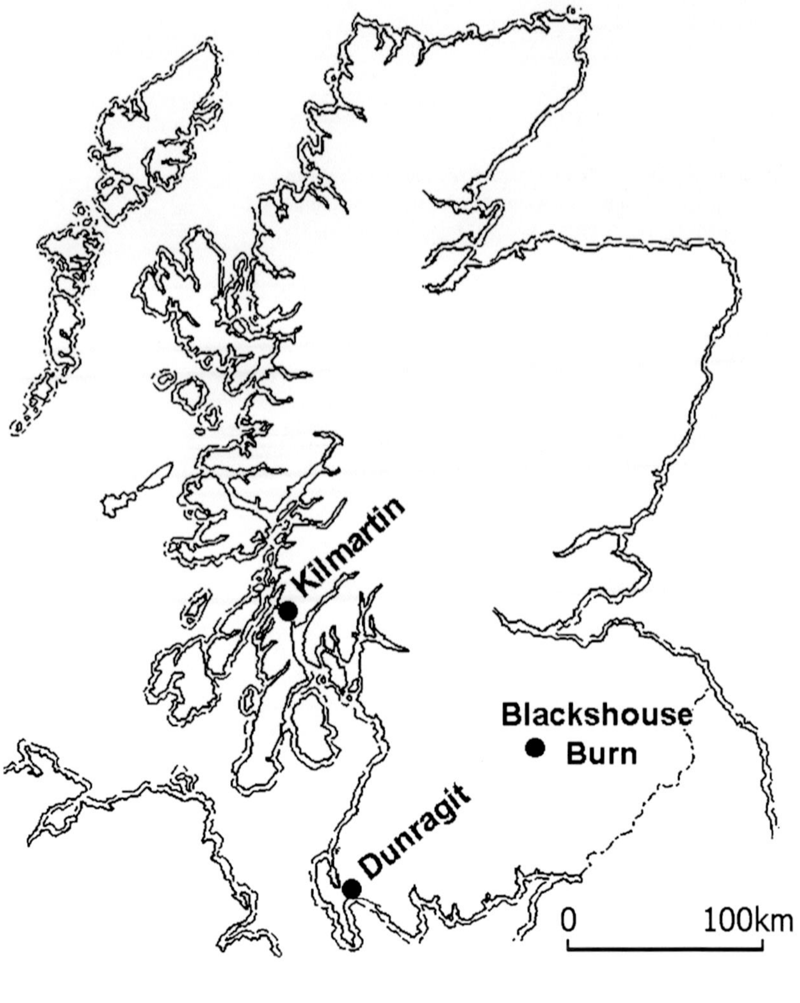

Fig. 7.1. The location of the three monument complexes outlined in the text

The location of monument complexes on routeways has important implications for the role of these places in Neolithic society and it may be that these monument concentrations had more complex roles in the maintenance of Neolithic society than has previously been argued. In short, I suggest these complexes were not merely the centralised power base of dominant social groups, but were instead crucial to the interaction *between* communities in the Neolithic and the monuments constructed there were symbols, and products, of those interactions. At the same time, monument construction was only part of the use of the landscapes in which complexes were set; in general, interactions would have been more mundane in nature, but nonetheless significant. Monuments were built at certain transitional times to reinforce, renew or change the nature of community interaction at these places. These places were neither in central or peripheral locations, but at points crucial to movement between regions.

Monument complexes in Scotland: three examples

Blackshouse Burn and the Upper Clyde Valley, Lanarkshire

The Upper Clyde area represents perhaps one of the densest concentrations of Neolithic monuments and settlement known in Scotland (Lelong and Pollard 1998; Fig. 7.2). The most spectacular and largest monument in the Upper Clyde, Blackshouse Burn, lies in an upland area, amongst the Pettinain Hill range, cradled in a broad bend of the River Clyde (RCAHMS 1978, No. 171). The monument originally consisted of two parallel rings of oak posts, joined by planking, with a stone bank in the centre of the rings of posts, enclosing an area almost 300m in diameter (Fig. 7.3; Lelong and Pollard 1998). The primary phase of Blackshouse would have been similar to palisaded enclosures at Dunragit, Forteviot and Leadketty in Scotland and examples in England and Wales (Gibson 2002). The stones used to construct the bank had been gathered from various sources on the surrounding Pettinain Hill range and the trees used in its construction were from a variety of different micro-climates (Lelong and Pollard 1998, 45). The single radiocarbon date for the large enclosure indicates construction around 2900–2300 BC. The size of the large enclosure at Blackshouse Burn compares with the great henges of Durrington Walls and Avebury in southern England (Wainwright 1989). There are six henge monuments in the adjacent valley and the routes leading to it (RCAHMS 1978, Nos. 169, 303, 324, 291, 170, 116). One of the few possible causewayed enclosures in Scotland is also located in the valley, along with a possible cursus monument (Nelson 2003; RCAHMS 1978, No. 323). The henges, causewayed enclosure and cursus sites are the only ones identified in the whole of South Lanarkshire. On the opposite side of the river to Blackshouse Burn another upland area, known as Biggar Common, has been found to contain extensive evidence for Early and Later Neolithic settlement as well as further monuments (Johnston 1997).

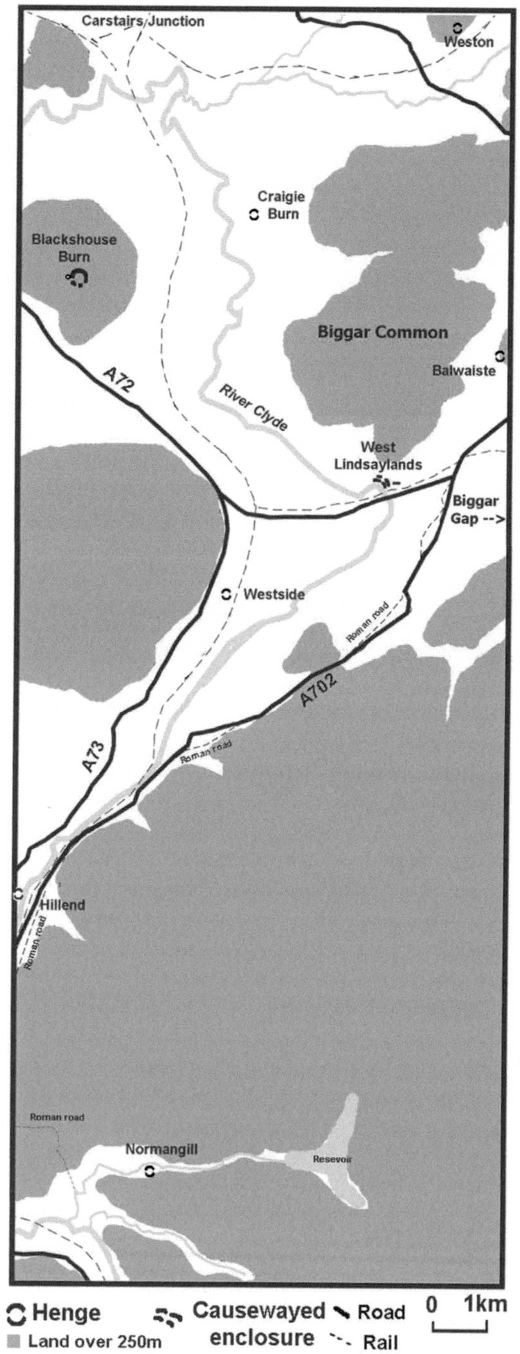

Fig. 7.2. The Upper Clyde Valley. The modern road and rail routes through the valley are marked

Dunragit, Wigtownshire, Dumfries and Galloway

At Dunragit, the remains of massive timber enclosures have been excavated in recent years (Thomas 1999; 2001a; 2001b; 2002). The site is on a flat expanse of gravel outwash, near to the

Fig. 7.3 (left). Blackshouse Burn. The monument encloses both heads of the Blackshouse Burn (after RCHAMS 1978, No. 171)

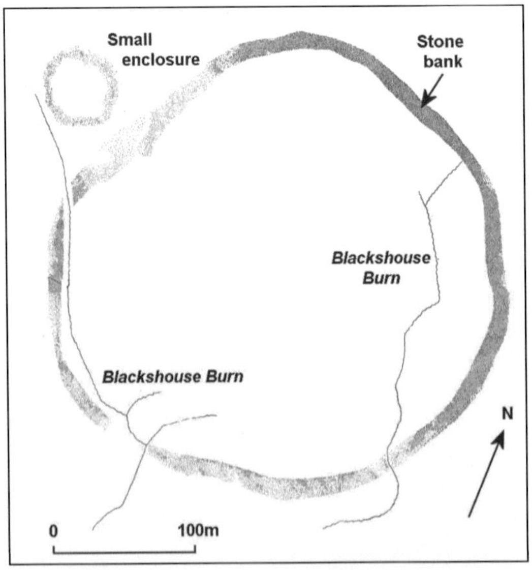

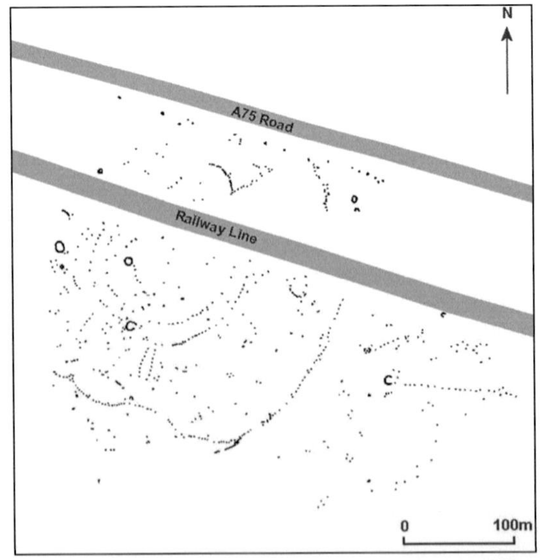

Fig. 7.4 (below). The Dunragit area. The outlined circles represent the Late Neolithic enclosures. The site is located next to the extensive dune system at Luce Sands, providing easy access to the sea

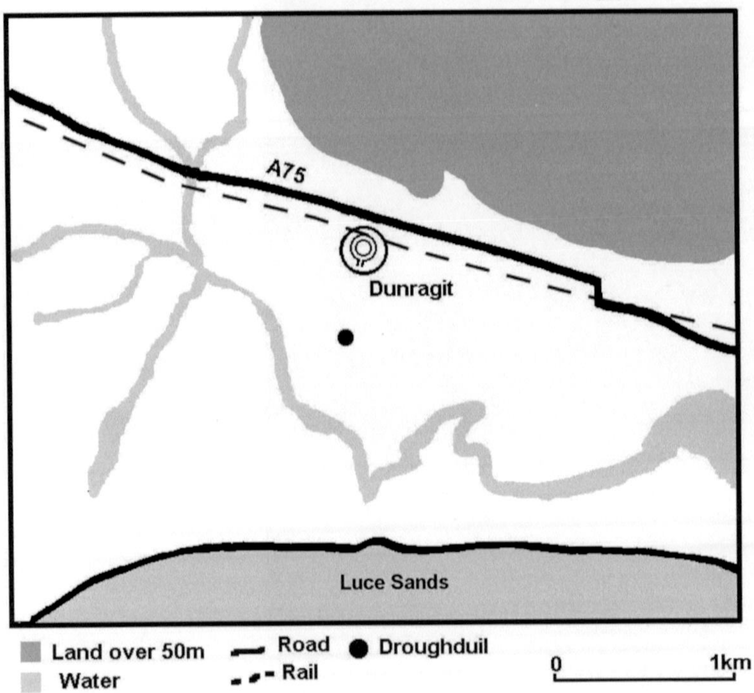

Fig. 7.5 (top right). Dunragit. The timber enclosures are bisected by the railway line and the A75. Droughduil mound in located a short distance to the southeast (after Thomas 2002, fig. 1)

Fig. 7.6 (bottom right). Droughduil mound

extensive dune system of Luce Sands (Fig. 7.4), where widespread evidence of Neolithic and Bronze Age activity has been uncovered over many years (Cowie 1996; Idle and Martin 1975; Wilson 1875–86; 1880–81; 1898–89). Earlier Neolithic activity is represented on the site by a post-defined cursus monument, over 200m long (Thomas 2001a). In the Later Neolithic, two large timber circles were constructed and surrounded by palisaded enclosures, the largest almost 300m in diameter (Fig. 7.5; Thomas 2001b). The inner freestanding timber circle was around 120m in diameter. The outer rings appear to have been of a single phase and were continuous fenced barriers. The middle ring was entered by a long avenue of posts, similar to avenues at other palisaded enclosures in Britain (Gibson 2002). The timber circle and enclosures were constructed around 2800–2500 BC (Julian Thomas *pers. comm.*). Between the timber enclosures and the Luce Sands lies a large prehistoric mound known as 'Droughduil' (Fig. 7.6; Thomas 2002). The entrance avenue of the middle timber palisade is aligned on the mound. Other smaller enclosures have been recorded in the immediate area and further enclosures and pit-defined monuments are located less than a kilometre to the west at Drumflower and in the wider area (Cowley and Brophy 2001; RCAHMS 1987, No. 161).

Kilmartin Glen, Argyll

The third monument complex I want to highlight in detail is that at Kilmartin Glen, Argyll. The dense

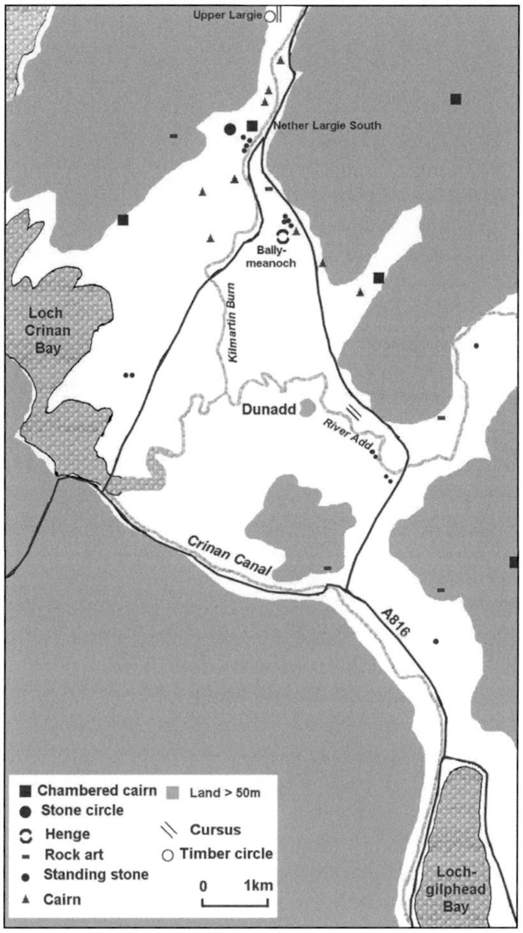

Fig. 7.7 (left). Kilmartin Glen

distribution of monuments and artefacts around Kilmartin is not easily paralleled elsewhere, and represents one of the best known and largest concentrations of prehistoric monuments in Scotland (Fig. 7.7; RCAHMS 1999, 12). Near the northern and southern entries to the valley, two cursus-type monuments were constructed in the Earlier Neolithic (Campbell 1996; Denison 1997; Ellis 2000; Terry 1997). These are the only identified cursus monuments in Argyll. A number of chambered cairns were also built around the edges of the valley (Henshall 1972; RCAHMS 1999). In the Later Neolithic a series of stone and timber settings were constructed at numerous locations in the valley, and the edges of the valley were marked with carvings on natural rock outcrops (RCAHMS 1999). Kilmartin contains the densest concentration and most elaborate rock art in Scotland. The only datable motifs are similar to those found in Later Neolithic passage tombs in Orkney and Ireland, and some of the carvings also include motifs found on Later Neolithic Grooved Ware pottery (Twohig 1981, chapter 4; Andy Jones *pers. comm.*).

The most extensively excavated monument at

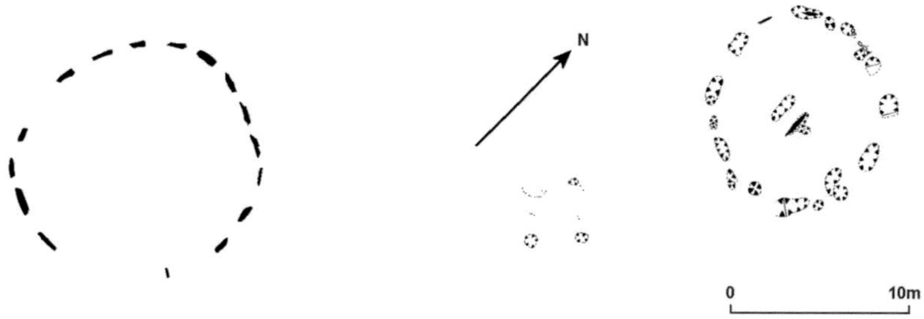

Fig. 7.8 (above). Temple Wood stone and timber circles (after Scott 1988–89, fig. 3)

Kilmartin is the stone circle at Temple Wood, towards the northern end of the valley (Fig. 7.8; Scott 1988–89). Two of the circle's stones were carved with passage grave-style motifs: one with concentric circles, the other with a double spiral carved across two faces of the stone. To the north of the stone circle there was a timber circle, subsequently replaced by a circle of freestanding monoliths. Further stone circles may have also stood in the valley in the Later Neolithic (Bradley 1993, 92–3; Craw 1930–31; Greenwell 1864–86) and a further timber circle, around 46m in diameter, was constructed at Upper Largie, near to one of the earlier cursus monuments (Denison 1997; Radley 1993; Terry 1997). There are also two major sets of stone alignments in the Kilmartin valley. One of these is a complex arrangement of over ten individual stones, 250m south of Temple Wood (RCAHMS 1999, No. 222). The other major alignment is at Ballymeanoch, where six stones are arranged in two parallel lines (RCAHMS 1999, No. 199). Nearby, there is a henge monument, the only known monument of this type in Argyll (RCAHMS 1999, No. 22). The Ballymeanoch henge comprises an outer bank with an inner ditch, and encloses an area of around 20m, with two entrances at the north and south.

Routeways and the location of monument complexes

While the three complexes outlined above contain a diverse range of monumental structures, there are many similarities between them. Each is a distinct regional concentration of monuments, and each has monuments that are unusual in the region, but common in distant regions. For example, Kilmartin contains the only known cursus monuments in Argyll and the henge monument at Ballymeanoch is one of the few known in western Scotland and again the only example in Argyll. The possible causewayed enclosure in the Upper Clyde Valley is of a type whose distribution is concentrated in the south of England and rare in Scotland (Oswald 2001). The six henge monuments in the valley are the only known examples in the region (Lelong and Pollard

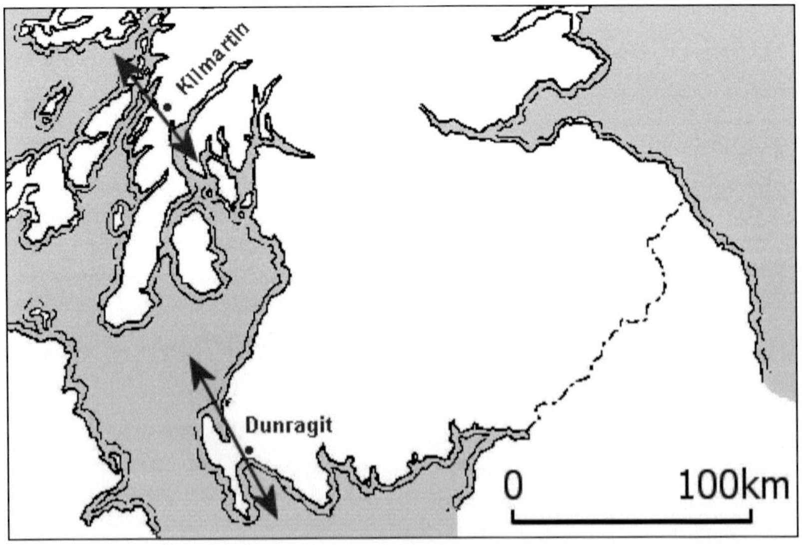

Fig. 7.9. The trans-peninsular routes adjacent to the monument complexes of Dunragit and Kilmartin

1998). The enclosures at Dunragit are of a type found in regions separated by great distances and there are few monuments of comparable size known in Dumfries and Galloway (Gibson 2002). There is also a striking relationship between these monument complexes and concentrations of non-local materials. In the vicinity of Dunragit there is a regionally distinct concentration of stone axes (Murray 1994, fig. 11.1; Williams 1970). The identified axes include a large number of Group VI axes from Cumbria and a smaller number of Irish axes (Williams 1970, 113). The Upper Clyde Valley also contains a remarkable concentration of imported axe heads (Clough and Cummins 1988; Lelong and Pollard 1998, 50). There has not been the same tradition of stone axe collecting around Kilmartin, due mainly to the dominance of pastureland in this area, but the rock art at Kilmartin contains an unusual concentration of passage grave-style motifs, motifs that have parallels with those found in Orkney and Ireland (Twohig 1981, chapter 4). The relationship between monument complexes and concentrations of non-local materials has been noted at other locations (e.g. Bradley 1984, 54; Stone and Wallis 1951).

However, while these observations are important, perhaps the most compelling similarity between these three complexes is their location on major natural routeways. For example, as Julian Thomas notes, Dunragit lies 'at the confluence of a series of natural routeways: northward up the valley of the Water of Luce, east and west along the Galloway coast, and north-west to Loch Ryan' (Thomas 2001a). The long established importance of this location in terms of routeways across the region is suggested by the relationship of the site to later routes. The site is bisected both by a railway line and by the A75, which are the main land routes through Dumfries and Galloway. These routes extend from Gretna in the east, near the English border, through Dumfries and along the coast to Dunragit and Stranraer in the west. The continuity of this route is demonstrated by aerial photographs, which show the route of the A75 is followed by a Roman road, the construction pits of which can be seen in aerial photographs near Dunragit (NMRS No. NX15NE 70.01). This route was also the major droveway in the region (Haldane 1997). Animals were brought by sea from Ireland to Portpatrick in the Rhinns before being driven through Glenluce towards Dumfries and ultimately to England. However, the importance of the Dunragit area does not rest merely on its proximity to land routes, the site is also closely related to one of the major sea routes around Scotland. The lowland area in which Dunragit sits, between the Rhinns of Galloway to the west and upland areas to the east, forms a natural routeway between the beach and dunes of Loch Ryan and Luce Sands, a major trans-peninsular route across Scotland (Fig. 7.9; Scott 1951). 'Trans-peninsular' routes or 'trans-isthmian' routes are routes that allow dangerous seas to be avoided through the use of inland river routes and/or by carrying boats across short stretches of land (Davies 1946; Scott 1951; Sherratt 1996a; 1996b). Over 50 years ago, before the discovery of the Dunragit enclosures, both Scott and Davies pointed to the importance of the Luce Sands to Loch Ryan route to prehistoric travel (Davies 1946; Scott 1951). Carrying a boat across the stretch of land between the two bays would have allowed the extremely treacherous seas around the Rhinns to be avoided (Scott 1951, 31).

Kilmartin, like the Dunragit area, also lies on a major trans-isthmian route (Fig. 7.9). The significance of the routeway has been used in the past to explain the unusual concentration of archaeological remains in the area: 'The geographical position of the area, controlling an important porterage from Loch Fyne and the western mainland of Scotland to Loch Crinan and the Atlantic coast, is one possible explanation of this localised wealth' (RCAHMS 1999, 12). The porterage (trans-isthmian route) between Loch Fyne and the western Mainland later became the Crinan Canal. The Crinan-Cairnbaan canal provides a 16km rather than a 150km journey between the west coast and the sheltered waters of Loch Fyne and the Clyde (RCAHMS 1999, 4). In prehistory the route could have been even shorter as smaller boats could exit at the bay of Lochgilphead rather than at Ardrishaig (as the canal does today), and travelled further inland from the Crinan end by navigating the River Add or simply crossing the flats at high tide. A prospectus published in 1792 attests to the importance of the Crinan route (Directors of the Chamber of Commerce and Manufacture in Glasgow 1792). This document outlines the difficulties in sailing around the bottom of Kintyre, through the Sound of Sanda. Vessels travelling from the Firth of Clyde had to wait for a

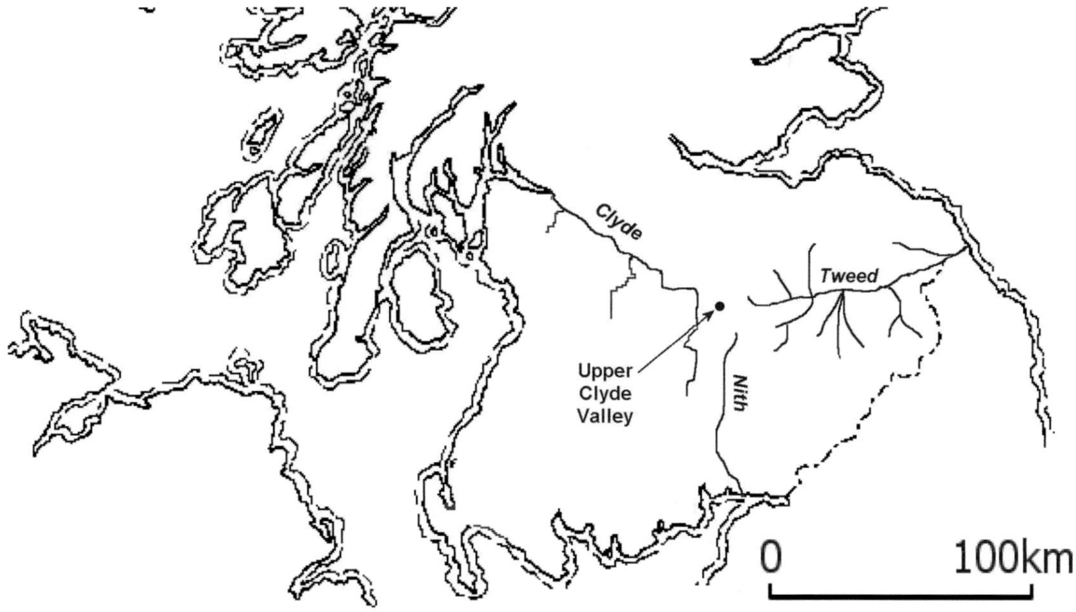

Fig. 7.10. The Upper Clyde Valley at the centre of lowland Scotland

favourable wind to carry them northwards up the west coast. Without the north winds, they had to head for Ireland and anchor there to wait for the right conditions. This apparently happened, on average, three out of four occasions and the use of this route often resulted in the loss of life. Neolithic boats were probably not sail driven, but navigating the notoriously dangerous currents and tidal pools around the Mull of Kintyre would not have been undertaken easily or lightly (Davies 1946, fig. 2). The landmass of Kintyre itself poses many problems to sailors. There are a distinct lack of natural bays and harbours on the west coast of Kintyre, and there are tremendous rocks and currents that frequently claimed ships and their crews along this coast (Directors of the Chamber of Commerce and Manufacture in Glasgow 1792, 3). There are further possible trans-isthmian routes in Kintyre (Scott 1951), but none provide as quick or as safe passage between west Scotland and the Firth of Clyde area.

Major land routes also pass through Kilmartin. The modern A816 travels northwards allowing access to the Great Glen and then on to Inverness and north-east Scotland. To the south the route is the main one through Kintyre towards Campbletown. One of the major drove routes in this part of Scotland also passed through the area at Kilmartin Glassary, close to the main concentration of monuments in the valley (Haldane 1997).

The Upper Clyde Valley is also located on a major trans-isthmian route, situated at the sources of three major rivers (Fig. 7.10; Scott 1951, 36). The River Clyde, to the west, links the area to the major water route of the Firth of Clyde and the western seaways. To the east, the River Tweed connects the valley to the North Sea. To the south, a few miles from the origin of the Clyde, lies the River Nith, which passes through Dumfries on its way to the Solway Firth, and then to the Isle of Man, northern England and Ireland (Davies 1946, fig. 2). The three rivers that radiate from the Upper Clyde Valley allow journeys by boat from western to eastern Scotland. Major land routes also converge at the Upper Clyde Valley and these modern routes were laid on the same course as a series of Roman roads, again highlighting the apparent continuity of these routeways. The Clyde has formed a broad, open corridor in the valley, forming a natural path across southern Scotland, extending from its origin in the Lowther Hills on the South Lanarkshire/Dumfries and Galloway border to its sea exit in the Firth of Forth (Lelong and Pollard 1998, 13). The floodplain known as the Biggar Gap joins the Clyde and the Tweed to the east and allows passage between these two major river valleys. The routes into the valley seem to have been marked in the Neolithic; as noted earlier, all of the six henge monuments are on the main routeways into and out of the valley.

Journeying beyond Scotland…

The relationship between monument complexes and routeways has previously been noted in a general manner and for individual sites without any real attempt at a synthesis (e.g. Atkinson 1956, 174–5; Bradley 1993, 108–112; Burl 1969, 18–19; Harding 2000). As early as 1951, Atkinson, Piggott and Sanders noted how large henge monuments were located in low-lying, easily accessible areas in riverine or waterside locations (Atkinson *et al.* 1951). Atkinson also later highlighted the possibility that Carn Meini, in the Presceli mountain range in south-west Wales, the source of the bluestones of Stonehenge and a significant monument complex in its own right, was on an important trade route linking Ireland and Wessex (Atkinson 1956, 174–5, 183–6). Atkinson proposed that the importance of Carn Meini was partly due to it being a source for stone axes and its use as an important landmark in sea journeys between Britain and Ireland: 'To the trader returning across the sea from Ireland, shielding his eyes from the spray as he peered across the bows of his laden boat, the same summit [Carn Meini] would be the first welcome sign of land ahead' (Atkinson 1956, 175).

Aubrey Burl (1976, 6), in a seminal publication on stone circles, wrote of the accessible locations of the largest monuments of this type. He noted that the largest and seemingly earliest circles were nearly always located next to rivers and in valleys, being situated 'along the seaways of the western coast of England or Scotland, or in north Wiltshire by the Ridgeway and the Oxfordshire prehistoric track connecting the eastern Cotswolds with Wessex' (Burl 1976, 36). Burl underlined the ease of movement by water in prehistory and associated the sites of large stone circles with land and riverine routes, with many circles (and henges) being located at the confluences of rivers (Burl 1976, 55). In a regional study and drawing on earlier observations, Burl also noted that stone circles in Cumbria were located on the trackways seemingly used to exchange stone axes. Manby and Plint in the 1960s had plotted the locations of flakes and rough-outs of stone axes in the Cumbrian area, and Burl correlated these locations with the major routeways through Cumbria and beyond, along which the main Neolithic monuments were distributed (Burl 1976, 65, fig. 12; Plint 1962; Manby 1965).

More recently, Sherratt (1996a, 214) has noted how the Wessex area is at the centre of a trans-isthmian route. Wessex is at the head of three rivers, all of which are called The Avon. Sherratt has suggested that these rivers have the same name as originally they conceptually formed part of the same route. The three Avons allowed the notorious seas around Land's End to be avoided, and he argues that the importance of Wessex was partly due to its position at the centre of the routes that linked a number of different regions, so extending its significance beyond the local area (Sherratt 1996a, 225). The similarities between the three Scottish complexes and the Wessex area are striking. The three Avons of Wessex are now followed by three major modern motorways, the M5, M6 and M4, again seemingly highlighting the continuity of these routeways (Sherratt 1996b, 6).

Other ceremonial complexes have also been noted for their positions at the centre of a number of land, river and sea routeways. Cooney notes that Brú na Bóinne, the location of the great passage graves of Newgrange and Knowth, is at the centre of important river routeways into and out of Ireland (Cooney 2000). Jan Harding has highlighted the location of the three henge monuments at Thornborough in North Yorkshire on the most accessible passage across the central Pennines, a major barrier to east-west movement in this part of northern England (Harding 2000, 42–43). The route was also used to move Cumbrian Group VI stone axes into eastern England. In total, six almost identical henge monuments are distributed along this route, which follows the flow of the River Ure (Harding 2000; Richards 1996a).

And back again…

Routes laid upon routes

The location of the three Scottish monument complexes outlined above is similar to many other monument complexes located across Britain and Ireland. Other monument complexes in Scotland are also located in relation to routeways (Noble 2006). In Orkney, for example, Colin Richards has commented on how the stone circles and burial monuments around the Stenness-Brodgar peninsulas on Mainland, the largest island of the archipelago, may have seemed conceptually and physically at the centre of the world in Later Neolithic Orkney (Richards 1996b, 190). In a similar manner, the Upper Clyde Valley may have been seen as the centre of prehistoric, lowland 'Scotland' (Fig. 7.10). Here, the heads of three rivers define the outer edges of the valley, creating connections with three different bodies of water. Consequently, the monuments in the Clyde valley are at a critical transitional point between regions, in a similar location to Wessex at the centre of the three Avons (Sherratt 1996a; 1996b).

Reconstructing prehistoric routeways is difficult; we have no preserved Neolithic routeways in Scotland. However, the proximity of monumental complexes to later routes is suggestive. Taylor (1979) underlined the continuity of routes and tracks: trackways are often laid on earlier paths, maintaining routes that were defined in more ephemeral ways millennia previously (Taylor 1979, 153). Taylor suggests that the very first routeways were tracks created by migratory animals following the 'best' routes and crossing rivers and waterways at the most easily forded locations; people would use these tracks to follow herds of animals (Taylor 1979, 1–4). In this way, routes would have formed over time through the interaction between animals, people and the natural topography.

The continuity of routeways is suggested by the preserved routes at many of the Scottish monument complexes. For example, at Dunragit it is remarkable how the modern A75, the railway line, the medieval drove route and a Roman Road all pass through the site of the monumental complex. These routes channelled movement from east to west across south-west Scotland for millennia. The location of Dunragit in relation to Roman sites is noteworthy and is a more widespread phenomenon. Most of the lowland complexes in Scotland are located in relation to Roman sites: Dunragit, Meldon Bridge, North Mains, the Upper Clyde Valley and Forteviot (Noble 2006). This is common outside Scotland too (e.g. the Hindwell and Walton enclosures; Gibson 2002, 12). In this respect it is significant that Hanson and Maxwell have noted that the Roman network of forts and camps were themselves built to dominate routeways in Scotland: 'The intention seems to have been not so much to coincide with concentrations of native population, but rather to control movement and thus localise any disaffection' (Hanson and Maxwell 1983, 37).

The occurrence of earlier monumental complexes and Roman routes and forts suggests that the locations of these phenomena shared similar objectives. One of the major centres of Roman activity in Scotland was in the Upper Clyde Valley where many Roman routes converged and where a concentration of camps and forts can be found (Hanson and Maxwell 1983, figs 2.3, 2.5 and 4.1). Many of these Roman roads are now followed or overlain by modern motorways, highlighting the continuity of these routes. Indeed, Taylor suggests that many prehistoric routeways are now modern roads (Taylor 1979, 12). This may explain why the distribution of the largest Later Neolithic henge monuments follows the same general routes of the major motorways of Scotland (Fig. 7.11). The major henges are located where river and land routes converge.

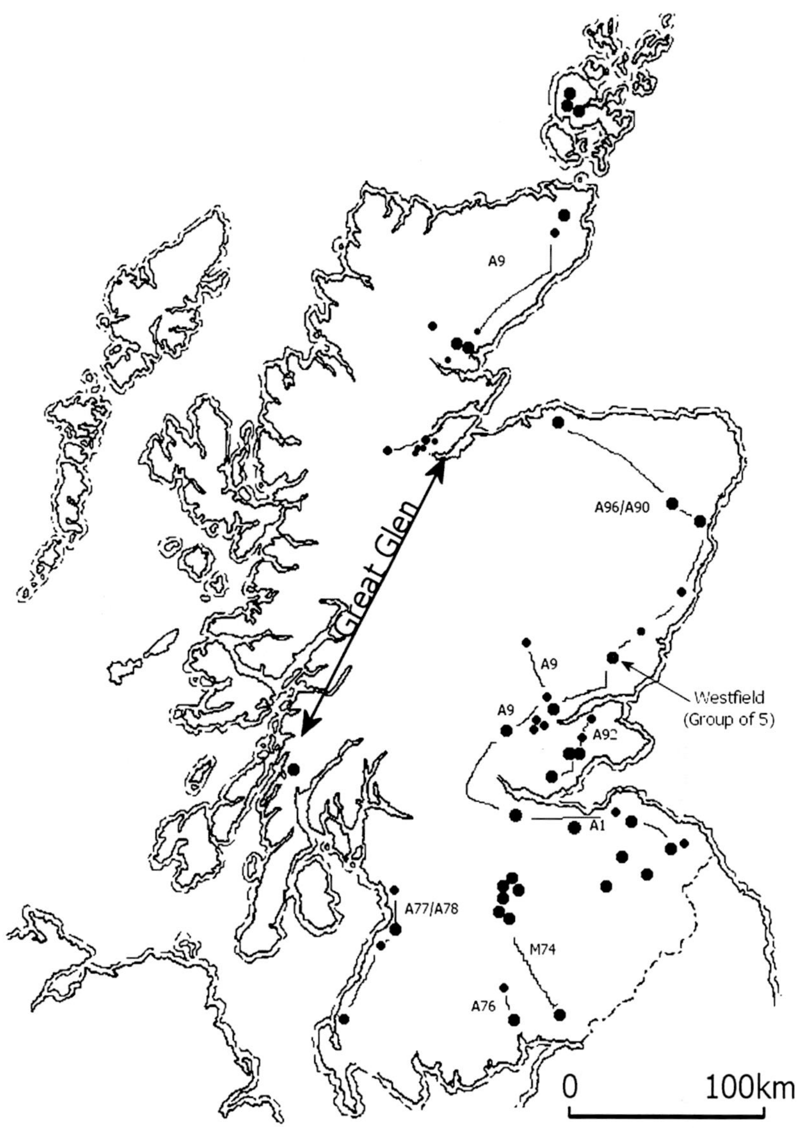

Fig. 7.11. Henges and motorways. The distribution of henges follows the main routes across modern Scotland.

Monument complexes and the social geography of Neolithic Scotland

The location of these monument complexes on routeways in places that were easily accessible from a number of different regions suggests that these complexes were not simply built by and for a local community (Burl 1976, 24). It has been suggested that monument complexes evolved due to a resident population intensifying agricultural production (Renfrew 1973; 1976; 1979; Sharples 1992; Telford 2002); this seems unlikely. Instead, complexes are more likely to have been created through the evolving and growing interaction between regional communities in the Neolithic. As Bradley and Burl have noted, monument complexes were not necessarily located at the heart of the settlement pattern, but in locations that were easily accessible, and in places that could draw on a wide catchment of people (Bradley 1993, 108–10; Burl 1976, 102).

Recent fieldwalking at Thornborough, North Yorkshire, seems to corroborate this observation. Fieldwalking around this complex has found that the raw materials used in this area included an extensive range of lithic types (Harding 2000, 43). Harding argues that this is not an indication of exchange, as the material includes materials inferior to the native gravel stone tool source, but represents the actual movement of people, an 'influx of distant peoples' to the Thornborough area; a position strengthened by the fact that the lithics seem to indicate short-term transient settlement (Harding 2000, 43). In this way the monuments at Thornborough were not the focus of an individual social group but the product of group interaction and social links, focused on a place that is on one of the most accessible routeways across the considerable barrier of the Central Pennines (Harding 2000, 42).

Monument complexes were not, however, simply gathering points, but places where contacts between communities were conducted. In this way, the great scale of the monuments found in these locations can be seen as a symbol, and product, of the interactions between people. Monuments in this respect were a means of negotiation: a way of symbolising, facilitating and materialising social relationships. The great monuments of the Later Neolithic are unlikely to have been symbols of personal power or the representations of powerful chiefdoms as has been suggested in the past (Renfrew 1973; 1976; 1979), but part of the interaction and communication between separate and dispersed small-scale groups of people. As Mark Edmonds has noted, such communties often 'recognise themselves as elements within extensive networks, webs of relations that they continually acknowledge and renew' (Edmonds 1999, 81). In this respect, monuments were part of this acknowledgment and renewal: symbols of the webs of relations that led to their creation.

The construction of monuments may have been only an intermittent and minor part of the use of these landscapes. At Blackshouse Burn, Lelong and Pollard (1998) have suggested that the monuments may have been built during seasonal gatherings, a tradition which began well before the main period of monument building: 'With groups from different settlements using different parts of these expansive uplands, gathering at the summer grazings may have been a central social event' (Lelong and Pollard 1998, 49). Monument building might then have been only a phase or limited event in a longer-term tradition of social gathering at places like Blackshouse Burn. In this respect, like the monuments, the surrounding landscapes may have developed through the gathering and labour of dispersed groups of Neolithic people. Monuments, were an important part of the landscape, but still only a component of a landscape that probably drew its main significance from seasonal gatherings of humans and animals engaged in agricultural and social activity. The products of communal grazing and agriculture may have been used at particular times to enable such great monuments to be built, but this was not always the case. The use of surplus produce created during the gatherings could be used to support the labour force required to build such great monuments at certain times, perhaps in periods of crisis or to celebrate significant events. In this way, Neolithic 'economy' and monumental landscapes may have been intimately linked, but not in the way that Sharples, Renfrew and others have suggested, where monuments were merely the by-products of economic intensification by a resident group (Renfrew 1973; 1976; 1979; Sharples 1992; Telford 2002). Instead, complexes may have been situated in areas that were traditionally used for (and were ideal for this purpose due to their position on natural routeways) the gatherings of dispersed populations during particular seasons. At times labour may have been invested and expended for the express purpose of monument building, but at other times less spectacular activities would have dominated the goings-on at these locations.

Conclusion

Archaeology has often sought to place monuments in a landscape context through an examination of their setting. While this is a valid and useful approach, we are perhaps failing to fully engage with the wider context of these monuments in a social, economic and regional sense. Three major examples of monument complexes from Scotland have been outlined above. All of these complexes had a range of large-scale monuments that were constructed throughout the Neolithic and were located in recurring landscape locations, positioned at, or near, the intersection of a number of land and sea routes. In the examples outlined here, the complexes were located at the centre of major trans-peninsular routes, in areas where communications between regions could be best facilitated. These locations emphasise that monument complexes cannot simply be examined in a purely local context. The location of monument complexes on routeways suggests that these places were not built by and for a resident community, but by extensive networks of dispersed communities who perhaps gathered periodically to affirm and renew social connections and relationships. We have to perhaps think more deeply about the scales of interaction that led to the creation of these monumental landscapes, and that requires a clearer conception of the social motivations that led people to journey to these landscapes in the Neolithic. While some journeys to and from monument complexes may well have been for purely ceremonial motives, many others would have been part of the cycles of movement that governed everyday life in the Neolithic: the movement of animals from summer to winter grazing or for the trade and exchange of animals. Other journeys would have perhaps been longer distance, undertaken by people procuring and exchanging stone axes and other materials, the evidence of which is demonstrated by the concentrations of non-local objects around these complexes. All of these activities were focused on monumental complexes and these landscapes would have developed through what might be termed economic motivations as much as ceremonial ones (if indeed we can separate these in any way). Many monumental complexes may have begun life as more mundane, yet nonetheless significant, places where people gathered to graze their animals, grow crops, to hunt, gather food, exchange ideas, to marry and to maintain kinship alliances. To associate monument complexes with the economic and agricultural cycles (and movements) of Neolithic communities is not to reduce the explanation of the location of these complexes to the relative agricultural potential of these areas as has been done in the past. This simply recognises that monument building was just a part of the use of these landscapes in the Neolithic. At significant transitional times in Neolithic society, monuments were built as a means of maintaining or reworking social bonds, but these relationships had probably grown over generations of activity prior to the construction of the monuments. The use of these landscapes was not just due to the quality of the land or the quantity of resources in these areas (although undoubtedly these were used), but reflected the openness of these locations to a wide catchment of people, who may have used these locations during regular, perhaps seasonal aggregations. Monument complexes were not empty ceremonial landscapes; the variety of activities that occurred here meant that Neolithic society was both maintained and renewed through gathering at these significant places. The recognition of the complexity of actions, journeys and motives that led to the construction of monumental complexes may well lead us to more fully engage with the wider context of these monuments in more ways than just the few social, economic and regional contexts that have been underlined briefly here.

Bibliography

Atkinson, R.J.C. 1956. *Stonehenge.* London: Hamish Hamilton.

Atkinson, R.J.C., Piggott, C.M. and Sanders, N.K. 1951. *Excavations at Dorchester, Oxon.* Oxford: Ashmolean.

Barnatt, J. 1989. *Stone circles of Britain: taxonomic and distributional analyses and a catalogue of sites in England, Scotland and Wales.* Oxford: British Archaeological Reports British Series 215.

Barrett, J. 1994. *Fragments from antiquity.* Oxford: Blackwell.

Bradley, R. 1984. *The social foundations of prehistoric Britain: themes and variations in the archaeology of power.* London: Longman.

Bradley, R. 1993. *Altering the earth: the origins of monuments in Britain and Continental Europe.* Edinburgh: Society of Antiquaries of Scotland Monograph Series No. 8.

Bradley, R. and Chapman, R. 1986. The nature and development of long-distance relations in the Late Neolithic of Britain and Ireland. In C. Renfrew and J.F. Cherry (eds), *Peer polity interaction and socio-political change,* 127–36. Cambridge: Cambridge University Press.

Burl, A. 1969. Henges: internal features and regional groups. *Archaeological Journal* 126, 1–28.

Burl, A. 1976. *The stone circles of the British Isles.* Yale: Yale University Press.

Campbell, E. 1996. Dunadd (Kilmichael Glassary parish), cursus. *Discovery and Excavation in Scotland,* 22.

Clough, T.H.M. and Cummins, W.A. 1988. *Stone axe studies, volume two.* London: Council for British Archaeology.

Cooney, G. 2000. Coping with death, changing the landscape: people, place and histories in the Irish Neolithic. In A. Ritchie. (ed.), *Neolithic Orkney in its European context,* 247–58. Cambridge: McDonald Institute for Archaeological Research.

Cowie, T.G. 1996. Torrs Warren, Luce Sands, Galloway: a report on archaeological and palaeoecological investigations undertaken in 1977 and 1979. *Transactions of the Dumfries and Galloway Natural History and Archaeology Society* 71, 11–106.

Cowley, D.C. and Brophy, K. 2001. The impact of aerial photography across the lowlands of Scotland. *Transactions of the Dumfries and Galloway Natural History and Archaeology Society* 75, 47–72.

Craw, C. 1930–31. Further excavations of cairns at Poltalloch, Argyll. *Proceedings of the Society of Antiquaries of Scotland* 65, 269–80.

Davies, M. 1946. The diffusion and distribution pattern of the megalithic monuments of the Irish Sea and north channel coastlands. *Antiquaries Journal 26,* 38–60.

Denison, S. 1997. News. *British Archaeology* 29, 5.

Directors of the Chamber of Commerce and Manufacture in Glasgow. 1792. *Prospectus of the advantages to be derived from the Crinan Canal.* Glasgow: William Reid and Co.

Edmonds, M. 1999. *Ancestral geographies of the Neolithic.* London: Routledge.

Ellis, C. 2000. Upper Largie, Argyll and Bute (Kilmartin parish), timber circle; sub-rectangular enclosure; cist. *Discovery and Excavation in Scotland,* 16.

Gibson, A. 2002. The Later Neolithic palisaded enclosures of Britain. In A. Gibson (ed.), *Behind wooden walls: Neolithic palisaded enclosures in Europe*: 5–23. Oxford: British Archaeological Reports International Series 1013.

Greenwell, W. 1864–66. An account of excavations in cairns near Crinan. *Proceedings of the Society of Antiquaries of Scotland* 6, 336–51.

Haldane, A.R.B. 1997. *The drove roads of Scotland.* Edinburgh: Birlinn.

Hanson, W. and Maxwell, G. 1983. *Rome's northwest frontier: the Antonine Wall.* Edinburgh: Edinburgh University Press.

Harding, J. 2000. Later Neolithic ceremonial centres, ritual and pilgrimage: the monument complex of Thornborough, North Yorkshire. In A. Ritchie (ed.), *Neolithic Orkney in its European context,* 31–46. Cambridge: McDonald Institute for Archaeological Research.

Henshall, A.S. 1972. *The chambered tombs of Scotland, volume one.* Edinburgh: Edinburgh University Press.

Idle, E.T. and Martin, J. 1975. The vegetation and land use history of Torrs Warren, Wigtownshire. *Transactions of the Dumfries and Galloway Natural History and Archaeology Society* 51, 1–11.

Johnston, D.A. 1997. Biggar Common, 1987–1993: an early prehistoric funerary and domestic landscape in Clydesdale, South Lanarkshire. *Proceedings of the Society of Antiquaries of Scotland* 127, 185–253.

Lelong, O. and Pollard, T. 1998. The excavation and survey of prehistoric enclosures at Blackshouse Burn,

Lanarkshire. *Proceedings of the Society of Antiquaries of Scotland* 128, 13–53.

Manby, T.G. 1965. The distribution of rough-out 'Cumbrian' stone axes. *Transactions of the Cumberland and Westmorland Antiquarian and Archaeology Society* 65, 1–37.

Murray, J. 1994. *The role of monuments in the Neolithic of the south of Scotland.* Department of Archaeology, University of Edinburgh: unpublished PhD thesis.

Nelson, C.J. 2003. *West Lindsaylands and Brownsbank: two geophysical surveys in the Upper Clyde valley, and their possible Neolithic context.* Department of Archaeology, University of Glasgow: unpublished undergraduate dissertation.

Noble, G. 2006. *Neolithic Scotland: timber, stone, earth and fire.* Edinburgh: Edinburgh University Press.

Oswald, A. 2001. *The creation of monuments: Neolithic causewayed enclosures in the British Isles.* Swindon: English Heritage.

Plint, R.G. 1962. Stone axe factory sites in the Cumbrian Fells. *Transactions of the Cumberland and Westmorland Antiquarian and Archaeology Society* 62, 1–26.

Radley, A. 1993. Upper Largie (Kilmartin parish). *Discovery and Excavation in Scotland*, 75.

RCAHMS 1978. *The Royal Commission on the Ancient and Historical Monuments of Scotland. Lanarkshire: an inventory of the prehistoric and Roman monuments.* Edinburgh: The Royal Commission on the Ancient and Historical Monuments of Scotland.

RCAHMS 1987 *The Royal Commission on the Ancient and Historical Monuments of Scotland: the archaeological sites and monuments of East Rhins, Wigtown District, Dumfries and Galloway Region.* Edinburgh: The Royal Commission on the Ancient and Historical Monuments of Scotland.

RCAHMS 1999 *The Royal Commission on the Ancient and Historical Monuments of Scotland. Kilmartin: prehistoric and early historic monuments.* Edinburgh: The Royal Commission on the Ancient and Historical Monuments of Scotland.

Renfrew, A.C. 1973. Monuments, mobilisation and social organisation in Neolithic Wessex. In C. Renfrew (ed.), *The explanation of culture change: models in prehistory,* 539–58. London: Duckworth.

Renfrew, C. 1976. Megaliths, territories and populations. In S. De Laet (ed.), *Acculturation and continuity in Atlantic Europe*, 198–229. Bruges: De Tempel.

Renfrew, C. 1979. *Investigations in Orkney.* London: Thames and Hudson.

Richards, C. 1996a. Henges and water: towards an elemental understanding of monumentality and landscape in Late Neolithic Britain. *Journal of Material Culture* 1, 313–36.

Richards, C. 1996b. Monuments as landscape: creating the centre of the world in Late Neolithic Orkney. *World Archaeology* 28, 190–208.

Scott, J.G. 1988–89. The stone circles at Temple Wood, Kilmartin, Argyll. *Glasgow Archaeological Journal* 15, 53–125.

Scott, L. 1951. The colonisation of Scotland in the second millennium BC. *Proceedings of the Prehistoric Society* 17, 16–82.

Sharples, N. 1992. Aspects of regionalisation in the Scottish Neolithic. In N. Sharples and A. Sheridan (eds), *Vessels for the ancestors: essays in honour of Audrey Henshall,* 332–31. Edinburgh: Edinburgh University Press.

Sherratt, A. 1996a. Why Wessex? The Avon route and river transport in later British prehistory. *Oxford Journal of Archaeology* 15, 211–34.

Sherratt, A. 1996b. Linking Wessex with the three rivers Avon. *British Archaeology 20*, 6.

Stone, J.F.S. and Wallis, F.S. 1951. Third report of the sub-committee of the south-western group of museums and art galleries on the petrological determination of stone axes. *Proceedings of the Prehistoric Society* 17, 99–158.

Taylor, C. 1979. *Roads and tracks of Britain.* London: Orion.

Telford, D. 2002. The Mesolithic inheritance: contrasting Neolithic monumentality in eastern and western Scotland. *Proceedings of the Prehistoric Society* 68, 289–315.

Terry, J. 1997. Upper Largie (Kilmartin parish), prehistoric ritual and funerary complex. *Discovery and Excavation in Scotland*, 19–20.

Thomas, J. 1999. Excavations at Dunragit, Wigtownshire, 1999. http://orgs.man.ac.uk/research/dunragit/dunragit_1999.htm

Thomas, J. 2001a. Excavations at Dunragit: 2001. http://orgs.man.ac.uk/research/dunragit/dunragit_2001.htm

Thomas, J. 2001b. Neolithic enclosures: reflection on excavations in Wales and Scotland. In T. Darvill and J. Thomas (eds), *Neolithic enclosures in Atlantic Northwest Europe*, 132–43. Oxford: Oxbow.

Thomas, J. 2002. Excavations at Dunragit: 2002. http://orgs.man.ac.uk/research/dunragit/dunragit_2002.htm

Twohig, E.S. 1981. *The megalithic art of western Europe.* Oxford: Clarendon.

Wainwright, G.J. 1989. *The henge monuments: ceremony and society in prehistoric Britain.* London: Thames and Hudson.

Williams, J. 1970. Neolithic axes in Dumfries and Galloway. *Transactions of the Dumfries and Galloway Natural History and Archaeology Society* 47, 111–22.

Wilson, G. 1875–76. Notice on a collection of stone implements and other antiquities from Glenluce, Wigtownshire, now presented to the museum. *Proceedings of the Society of Antiquaries* 11, 580–87.

Wilson, G. 1880–81. Notice on a collection of implements and ornaments of stone, bronze, from Glenluce, Wigtownshire. *Proceedings of the Society of Antiquaries* 15, 262–77.

Wilson, G. 1898–99. List of antiquities of Glenluce, Wigtownshire, with descriptive notes. *Proceedings of the Society of Antiquaries* 33, 170–85.

8 Ritual journeys and landscapes of the afterlife: a cognitive mapping approach to the Middle Kingdom Coffin Texts of the Ancient Egyptian afterlife

Peter Robinson

Introduction

For many, ancient Egypt is characterised by richly decorated tombs, pyramids and the mummified remains of its former inhabitants. Whilst the burials of the earliest Egyptians, some seven thousand years ago, were simple graves cut into the sands of the desert edge, over the millennia tombs and their associated funerary paraphernalia developed and became richly imbued with sacred significance. By the end of the Old Kingdom Pyramid Age (*c.* 2100 BC), many Egyptians regarded their tombs as 'houses of life', an indication perhaps that they perceived their afterlife as an extension of their mortal lives, which was reached by a journey through the liminal gateway of death. At this time, the coffins containing the preserved remains of the deceased were often richly decorated with images and texts, known by Egyptologists as the 'Coffin Texts'. These were religious and ritual texts written on numerous examples of coffins, many of which date from about 2100 BC to 1795 BC, the periods known as the First Intermediate Period and the Middle Kingdom – although there are examples of Coffin Texts that have been suggested to date from the end of the Old Kingdom (Hornung 1999, 7).

Unlike the texts that appeared within the burial chambers of some of the pyramids, most of the Coffin Texts were placed upon coffins associated with the funerary cult of non-royal persons, although they can also be found on other funerary objects and tomb walls. The texts consisted of 'spells' inscribed or written on the inner (and in some cases, the outer) surfaces of the coffin. Not all coffins contained the same spells, and some only occur as unique examples on single coffins. Generally, however, a number of themes appear amongst the various spells of the Coffin Texts. These include a combination of funerary rites, magical 'transformations' and actions required to enable the deceased to travel from this life to the next. Many of the texts contain descriptions of the afterlife that the deceased was hoping to enter, as well as details of its landscape and inhabitants, whether they were benign or demonic. In addition, the coffins, like the images upon the walls of the tombs at this time, often included depictions of activities denoting the yearly cycle of events such as harvest, or descriptions of the cosmos, in an attempt to ritually describe the universe for the deceased.

Source documents

A number of Middle Kingdom coffins take this conceptual representation of landscape and cosmography one stage further. These coffins include some that come from Bersheh in Middle Egypt and Gebelein in Upper Egypt (Fig. 8.1), and portray what can perhaps be called 'maps' or certainly some form of pictorial representation of afterlife landscapes and their features within sections of their texts. They can be best described as *aides memoires* for the deceased, enabling him or her to achieve a blessed existence in the metaphysical world of an eternal afterlife.

The coffins from the necropolis of Bersheh include various representations of afterlife landscapes. They are now to be found on display in a number of museums around the world. Coffins from Bersheh primarily used in this paper are those of the general Sepi, Cairo coffin CG 28083, (de Buck (1954; 1956; 1961) designated this coffin B1C) and Gwa, London coffin BM 30840 (numbered by de Buck as B1L). The second necropolis location is that of Gebelein, south of Luxor. Here, associated with the tomb of a priest called Ini, were found the remains of the inner coffin of a certain Iker (Porter and Moss 1937, 163). Porter and Moss suggest dating the coffin to the reign of Pepy I, who reigned at the end of the Old Kingdom. Willems, however, has suggested that this coffin belongs instead to a

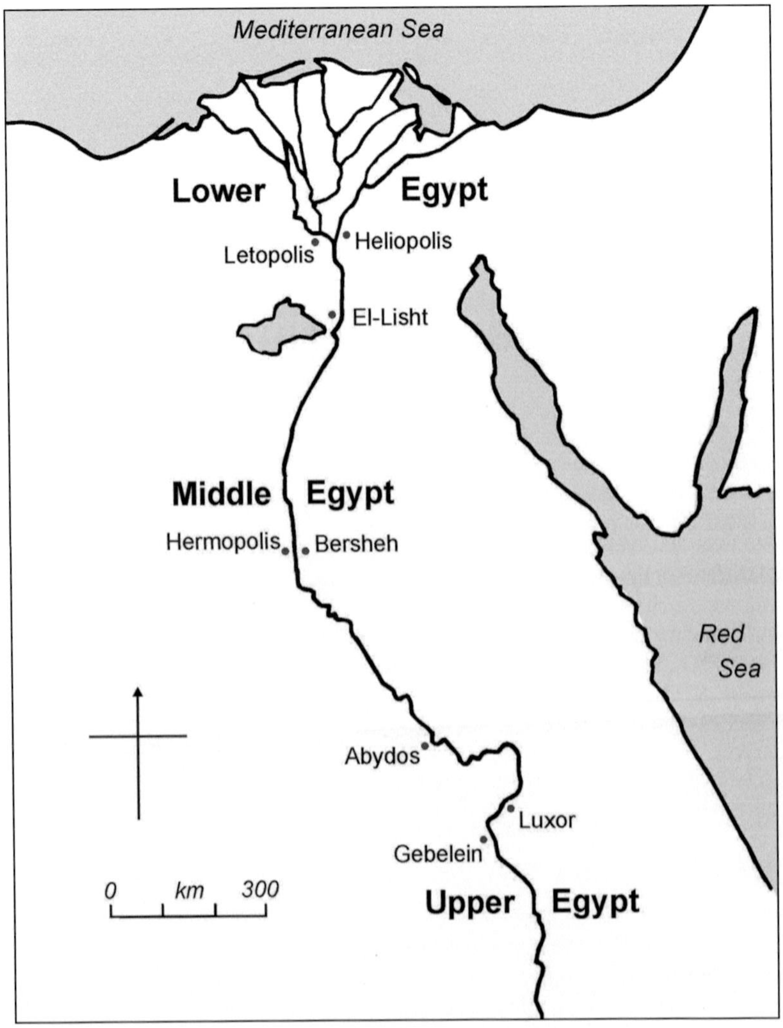

Fig. 8.1. Map of Egypt showing places mentioned in the text

late First Intermediate school of artists, based in the south of Egypt (Willems 1988, 109). The coffin of Iker is now on display in the Egyptian Museum in Turin catalogued as object 15.774, and numbered by de Buck as G1T.

Methodologies and terminologies

The term 'cognitive mapping' is one that describes how, both in humans and non-human species, the brain builds up and stores images of spatial information with which the organism is familiar. It especially defines the deliberate encoding of data within memory in order to determine one's location or ways of getting from one place to another (Golledge 1999, 15). A useful introduction to and review of the methods of using cognitive mapping techniques can be found in Kitchin and Blades (2002, 11–83). 'Cognitive mapping' is, however, more than just the 'cognitive' paradigm of ideas and processes that characterises modern holistic and theoretical philosophies. Thus 'cognitive archaeology' is seen as 'the study of the ways of thought of past societies...based on the surviving material remains' (Renfrew 1993, 248). Where little cultural remains survive, the interpretation of such ways of thought must necessarily be speculative (Flannery and Marcus 1993, 261). The 'cognitive' aspects of the present study, and in cognitive mapping in general, relate not to an interpretation of past culture or our present understanding of its features, but to the processing of information about landscape and travel within neurological systems of the brain. In essence, cognitive mapping relates, amongst other concepts and ideas, to how we find our way in the physical world and how we communicate directions to others in order for them to find their way around an environment (Gluck 1991, 117).

Whilst most cognitive maps depict real space and geographical locations directly experienced and familiar to the living individual, instances can be envisaged where mythological and legendary space could be mapped and recorded by way of texts or other symbolic codes. These landscapes, though, are clearly artificial environments rooted in the realms of fantasy and fable, with little or no truly 'real-world' substance. Furthermore, such landscapes might have some religious connotations (Laslo *et al.* 1993, 12–13), and may be more than just a personal perception of the world, forming instead part of a shared culturally perceived landscape of a group (or groups) of people from a particular society. Societies and cultures other than that of dynastic Egypt have conceptualised such metaphysical and fabulous (or 'ideational') landscapes for the purposes of religion or stories associated with their belief systems (Barnes 1999, 113; Knapp and Ashmore 1999, 12). It is with this concept – that of a shared 'experience' of a fantasy world, albeit one that no living human had successfully visited and returned from and especially one where the landscape and environment has not been properly described or documented – that I wish to concentrate upon within this paper.

Such 'mental maps' can be shown to exhibit a measurable distance decay. Thus, the further away from one's own home space one is, the less is known about the location and consequently the more general, or even fantastic, the descriptions of the landscape. For the people of Ancient Egypt, who, we may assume, had little means of rapid transport or mass media familiar to the modern age, this distance decay would have limited the knowledge of many places beyond their immediate personal space. The land of Egypt itself provided for most of the Egyptians' needs, with an abundance of food grown in the Nile Valley, and the deserts either side of the Nile providing stone and semi-precious materials for their architecture and craftwork. At times of empire building and expansion, the Egyptians invaded neighbouring areas, such as

Nubia and the Levant, but they generally recognised these places as 'foreign' and non-Egyptian and therefore to be avoided. With their particular beliefs in an afterlife as a metaphysical environment in which they were to continue their existence, however, the Egyptians needed to conceptualise their post-mortem landscape. We can surmise that they used their experiences of the 'real' world and its geographies to express the mythical regions of the afterlife, where none had gone to and successfully returned, in order to describe this metaphysical environment to the living.

Returning to the cognitive constructs of this physical world in which we inhabit, one should note that what we learn of beyond our immediate environment is generated by both actively visiting locations or through passive activities, for example, by hearing about or meeting people from far-off places (Goodey 1971, 5–7). In an Ancient Egyptian context, people could have visited neighbouring locations, maybe to trade or to undertake state-required *corvée* work. On the other hand, talking with traders, visitors from other locations or soldiers home from fighting in distant lands would have enabled the population to gain something of a knowledge of far-away places, either second-hand or more indirectly (Fig. 8.2). Of course, knowledge of the Afterlife could not have come from direct experience; it would have been somewhat esoteric or mythic in nature, perhaps disseminated by priests or other learned men and developed in a scholarly institution such as the temple library or royal palace (Quirke 2003, 178).

Route-based learning is perhaps one of the most common ways an environment or landscape is learnt. It takes place when one follows a path or route between points and is fundamental to the way we all make our way around the surface of the landscape. By starting off in a known environment, we explore new places by looking forwards and creating 'vistas' onto new landmarks before progressing on towards one of these new points. The process is then repeated until we reach our goal at the end (Fig. 8.3; Stern and Portugali 1999, 107–9). Over time, people undertake increasingly overlapping journeys until they can progress confidently around a fully integrated environment and encode the detail into a map-like cognitive structure. This journeying methodology is the basis of many maps, both ancient and modern. Indeed, much of our knowledge of the Ancient Egyptian afterlife is as a journey, whether it be the sun-god's journey through the hours of darkness and night painted on tomb walls, or the ordinary deceased person's journey down the Winding Waterway of the Coffin Texts or other 'Books of the Dead'. Of course, in interpreting the Ancient Egyptians' afterlife books, one must always bear in mind that what they are

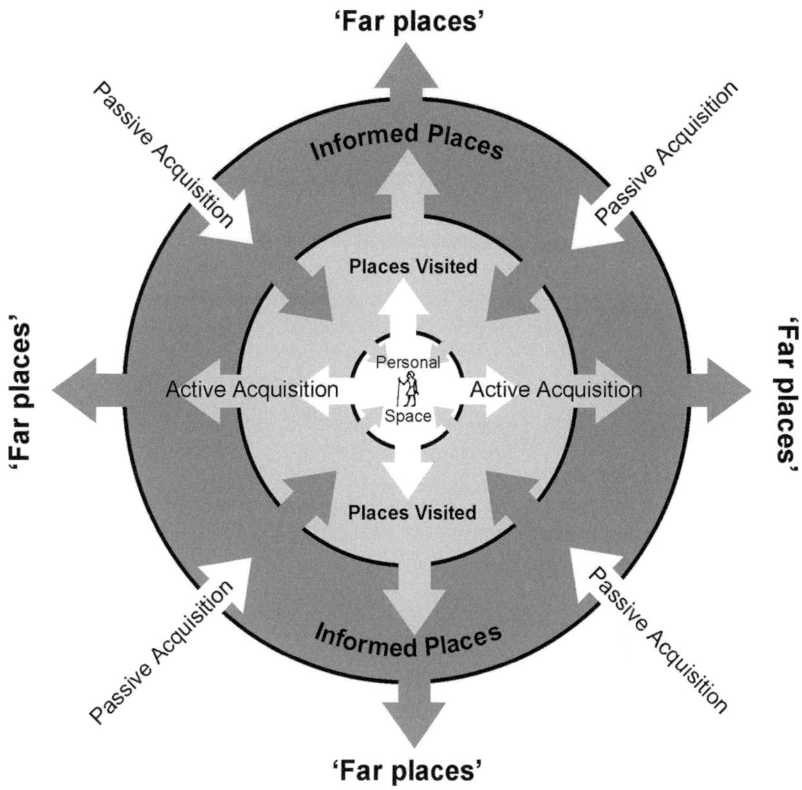

Fig. 8.2. A model of cognitive knowledge acquisition (after Goodey 1971, fig. 1)

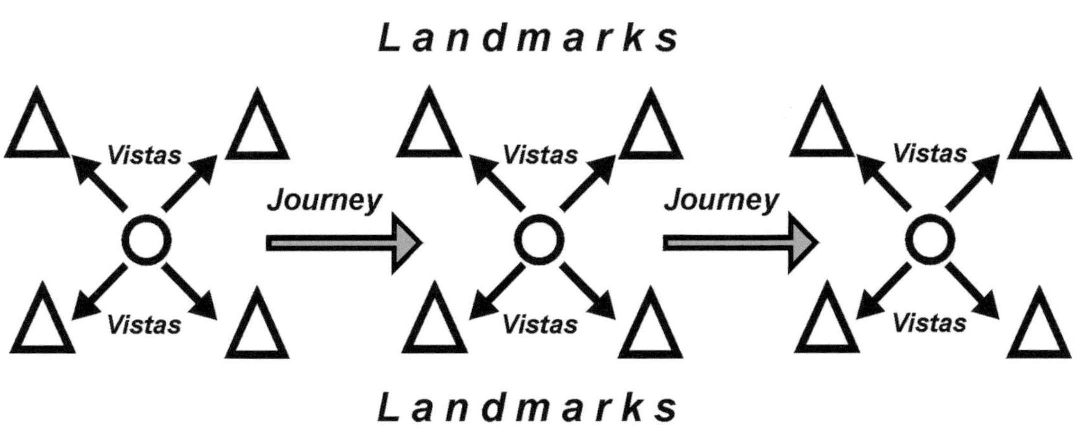

Fig. 8.3. A perceptual model of the environment (after Stern and Portugali 1999, fig. 4.5)

describing is not necessarily a real place on the Earth's surface, but instead a rather nebulous and metaphysical group of locations which had never been directly experienced by the living.

Journeys are not the only way that people describe the world around them. Working in a number of post-war American cities, the geographer-architect Lynch identified five landscape elements that people regularly use to describe their environment (Lynch 1960, 46–49). These elements can be summarised as follows:

1. *Paths* – the routeways along which people move. They can be either roadways or waterways.
2. *Edges* – linear elements that act as boundaries between regions. They can join regions or function as barriers.
3. *Districts* – medium to large sections of the city that have a two dimensional extent. Each usually has some unifying common feature that identifies it to the individual.
4. *Nodes* – focal points into which people enter. In urban contexts they might be road junctions or gateways. They might also be where people change from one transport mode to another, for example from foot to boat at a quayside.
5. *Landmarks* – points not entered by the individual and therefore somewhat external to the immediate landscape. They are often used as waymarkers along routes.

Others have simplified these five features into landmarks, districts and paths. Nonetheless, these conceptual geographical entities have relevance not only in the Coffin Texts and other afterlife topographies, but also in other texts from Egypt and elsewhere where people may describe the landscape they inhabit or visit, for example in records of military campaigns or autobiographical images of texts.

Coffin G1T

The coffin of Iker, from Gebelein, contains a number of vignettes and illustrations of what are described as 'ferryman texts' (Willems 1988, 234). These images, showing boats the deceased was supposed to use in his journey to the afterlife, appear on the inner coffin surface close to a depiction of a landscape of routeways, divine shrines and gardens, and various monstrous and divine beings (Fig. 8.4). This landscape image, and the accompanying spells form the group numbered CT649 to 653 (references to individual Coffin Text spells throughout this paper refer to the transcription editions in de Buck volumes V to VII (1954; 1956; 1961) and translations in Faulkner 1977 and 1978). The opening spell of this sub-text consists of repeated invocations to divinities, seemingly at the threshold of a sacred space, such as: 'O you Ram-man, open a path for me, for I am the young child; let me pass unharmed'. Clearly, this is liminal space and a barrier at the commencement of a journey. Spells 652 and 653, however, declare and depict a series of locations within this landscape. So the text records an area of shrines and gardens: 'This is the allotting of the field of the gods'; and a number of divine beings: 'This is this man of his, whose name is "Loud-

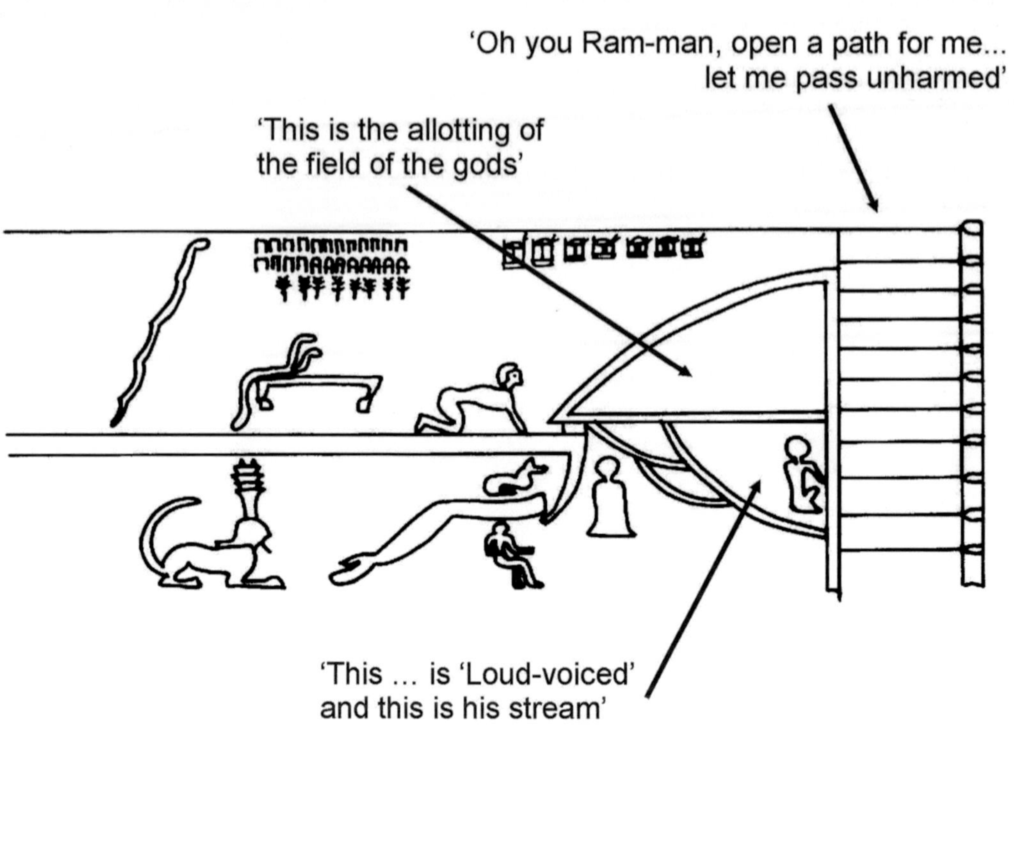

Fig. 8.4. Example locations in Spells CT 649–653 – coffin G1T

Voiced", and this is his stream'. These features of the landscape are obviously simple landmarks that the deceased, Iker, is expected to familiarise himself with, and the spells in this section of the coffin clearly assume that the deceased is already in some form of afterlife existence. The proximity of this landscape to the spells of the ferryman text suggests that entry to this location was as a result of travelling on the ferryman's boats. The description of this landscape therefore apparently illustrates places without much attempt to synthesize a more complex environment. Hornung, however, also suggests that this image might represent 'chambers of the sanctuary of Thoth', containing images of divinities which are described in other magical texts of the period (Hornung 1973, 34–35).

Bersheh Coffins

About 300km north-west of Gebelein, in Middle Egypt, lies the necropolis of Bersheh. Whilst the coffin and the Coffin Texts of Iker seems to be part of a southern tradition of artistic design (Willems 1996, 22–25), the Coffin Texts from Bersheh appear to stem from a separate tradition, with the inclusion of a different set of themes and texts. As a result, the coffins from Bersheh seem to be much more geographically aware and cartographically experimental than that of Iker's.

One text appearing exclusively in the Bersheh coffins is a graphical representation of the Field of Hetep (Fig. 8.5), also described as the Field of Reeds in the coffin of another Bersheh mummy, Sen (Lesko 1971–72, 100). Mention is made of this location on many Middle Kingdom coffins and even as far back as texts written in some of the Pyramids (the 'Pyramid Texts'): for example, Pyramid Text Utterance 519 includes the words 'the Field of Rushes is inundated, the Field of Offerings is filled with water' (Faulkner 1969, 192). But Bersheh, it seems, is the only place to have given a cartographic representation of the text where it appears in the Coffin Text spells CT464 to 467. Hetep is a land of waterways and towns, of fields where the deceased ploughs and reaps and of divine inhabitants.

The texts that describe the Field of Hetep include a number of invocations and spells similar to those from Iker's coffin. For example, the opening lines of CT465 include the phrases: 'Lord of the Field of Offerings. This is Horus of the Tree...This is Hetep'. These texts also give us detailed information about localities in Hetep, enumerated in spell CT466 in the form of an annotated map (Lesko 1971–72, 99). These localities take the form of place names (for example, the mythological Kenkenet), objects found ('Offerings'), regions or routeways ('The Waterway of the White Hippopotamus'), inhabitants ('Mistress of the Two Lands') and actions taking place at localities ('Ploughing and reaping barley and emmer of the gods' estate).

Clearly this text, a forerunner and direct antecedent of the later 'Book of the Dead' Spell 110, was perceived to be a living, functioning environment (Allen 1974, 87–90). It uses a complex imagery of pathways, regions and landmarks to describe the detail of the landscape of Hetep and its waterways and cities. Such explanations in the accompanying spells CT464 and CT467 further indicate the activities and locations within this area. The deceased rows along the waterways of the region, lives by eating and drinking and performs agricultural activities, proving he is alive and well in this environment beyond mortal death. The texts go on to describe the individual regions within Hetep and even justify the assertion of the purpose of this text: 'I know the names of the towns, districts and waterways within the Field of Offerings in which I am' (CT467).

The Field of Hetep, therefore, was undoubtedly to be used by the deceased as another map of a district of the afterlife. Unlike the example from Gebelein, however, the texts do not simply represent a static series of landmarks, but an environment with pathways and districts that the deceased explored and wandered through. The Gebelein example might justifiably be a pictorial *aide memoire* of an environment which the deceased was only expected to recognise, and with which they had no interaction. The Bersheh texts, on the other hand, explicitly indicate that the Field of Hetep was to be

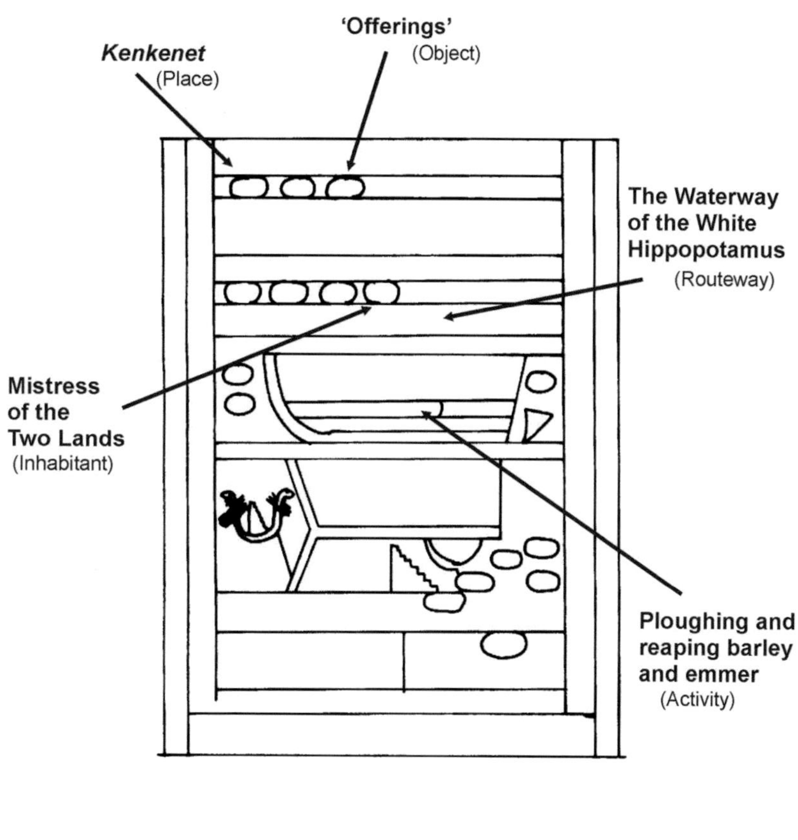

Fig. 8.5. Example locations in Spells CT 466 – coffin B1L

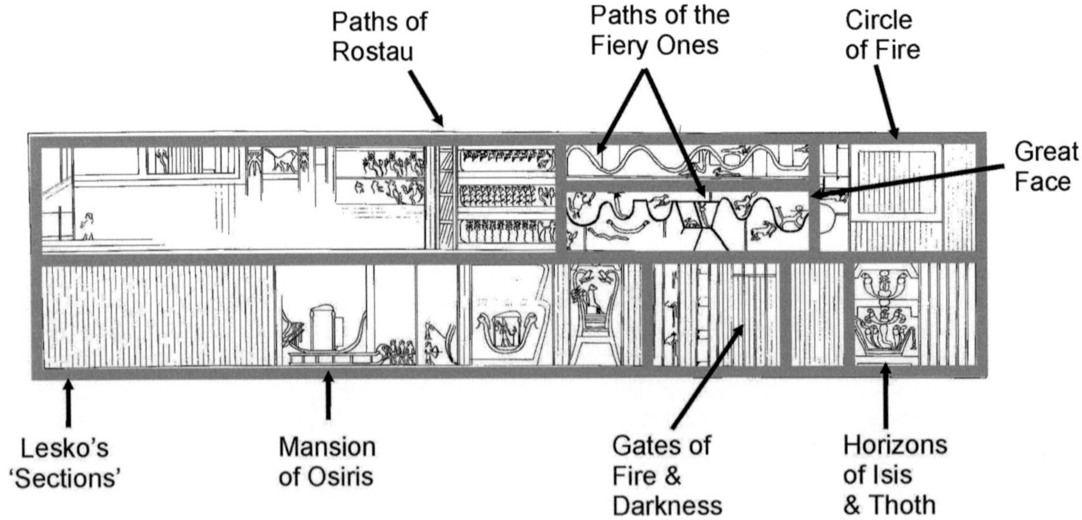

Fig. 8.6. Example locations in the Book of Two Ways – coffin B1C

seen as a world inhabited by the deceased, who existed there as a living and invigorated being capable of travel around his afterlife.

The floor section of a number of the Bersheh coffins is occupied by a complex series of spells, which provide a detailed description of a journey from this mortal life to the next (Fig. 8.6). These texts, called the Book of Two Ways, are a description of liminal regions with many gates of fire and darkness, and paths of sky, earth and water. Along the route of the journey, the deceased encounters various gatekeepers, watchers and strange and dangerous divinities, some armed with knives. De Buck (1961, plate 1) includes a plan of the image on the floor of B1C depicting a number of reptilian, mammalian and avian composite demons in various parts of the text. The Book of Two Ways has been described as the first Egyptian cosmography (Hornung 1999, 11). In most copies, it contains over 100 separate spells that can be split into eight separate sections. Each section appears to correspond to a different part of the journey from this life to an eternal afterlife. Lesko (1972, 4–5), states that the Book of Two Ways contains nine sections. Lesko separated the texts into three versions: two versions, which he designated A and B, containing the eight sections of one hundred spells, and the third (C) version contains four sections, one of which (Section II) is unique to the C version. In addition, the three C version coffins contain fifty-four spells similar to, but not exactly the same as, those spells in the other A and B version coffins. The text itself takes its name from the two prominent pathways separated from each other by a 'Lake of Fire' and depicted in sections III and IV of the texts.

The landscape depicted by the Book of Two Ways clearly indicates the pathways of particular journeys. There are detailed descriptions of features along the route the deceased must pass by, for example the 'Path of the Fiery Ones' and a 'Lake of Fire'. Demons and monstrous beasts are encountered in some parts of the text whilst demonic guardians are explicitly named in others. The texts also contain regions such as Rostau, and the Mansion of Osiris, the god of the Dead, mentioned as lying beyond gateways that occur at some point along the journey.

The deceased must also travel through a number of nodal points – for example, the many gates of fire and darkness, often explicitly drawn as doorways of red or black to indicate their natures. Actual depictions of doors are also included in the images drawn upon the coffin floors. Edges are represented as liminal entities such as the 'Horizons of Isis and Thoth' and boundaries of regions into which the text can be divided (Lesko 1972, 4).

Although some Egyptologists consider that the Book of Two Ways represents a celestial journey, with its allusions to sunrise and the Milky Way, nonetheless it is clearly also a landscape of journeys, barriers and regions. There are places that demons inhabit, structures such as Rostau, with its images of snake-charming demons, confused pathways and walls of flint. There are also many gateways and barriers appearing within the text and associated images. The three 'C version' examples begin with the double doors of a 'mansion of many faced' being thrown open, thus releasing the spirit of the deceased onto his or her journey. Further along the journey, more liminal regions occur until the deceased reaches his or her aim of an eternal blessed existence.

Conclusions: symbolic visibilities and accessibility of knowledge

It has been noted many times that in pharaonic Egypt there is often a geographical connotation in the placement of the coffin within its burial chamber

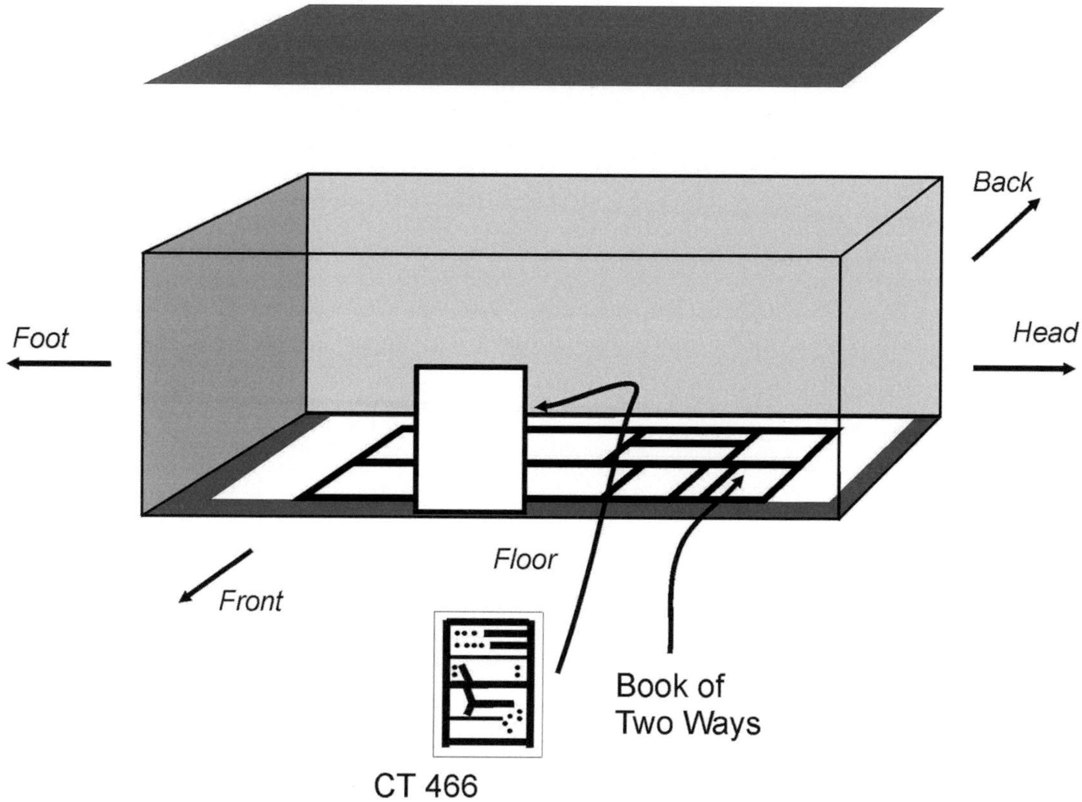

Fig. 8.7. Decorated coffin surfaces – Bersheh coffin types

and also with the texts on the inner and outer sides of the coffin itself. Such text probably also had a ritual use, performing more than just a decorative function (Willems 1996, 363–5). In some instances, these ritual functions enabled the deceased to perform activities connected with his or her rebirth or transmission to an afterlife. They also sustained the deceased once he or she attained the afterlife existence desired. Clearly, such texts were meant to be hidden from living mortals. It is also possible that the route to the afterlife itself and the topography of the afterlife may have been closely guarded secrets, kept from most mortals and only really available to those most needy of them – the deceased. Hence, the 'maps' that have been the subject of this paper were depicted upon the insides of the coffins for the exclusive and private benefit of the coffin's occupant and no-one else. Furthermore, they are arranged at places within the coffin perhaps readily accessible to the deceased and would probably have been thought of as way-pointers and guidebooks.

In most cases, Bersheh coffins (Fig. 8.7) place the 'Netherworld map' of the Book of Two Ways on the coffin floor (Lesko 1979, 24 for B1C, 38–39 for B1L; Willems 1988, 235). Images of the Field of Hetep are painted on the inner front surface of the coffin, approximately at arm level (Lesko 1979, 23 for B1C, 38 for B1L). This is all the more significant as these images are said to be in the vicinity of depictions of offering tables, enabling the deceased to partake of whatever provisions he or she desired (Lesko 1971–72, 89–90; Willems 1988, 233, 235).

Whereas Bersheh's maps underlie and face the deceased, Iker's coffin is floored by a wooden framework, raising the mummy up and taking the form of a garden (or perhaps the hieroglyphic symbol for 'garden' or 'floor'). On the inner surface of the lid, the coffin depicts a star clock, recalling the positions of stars at various times of the year. No doubt both these had one clear purpose, which was to orientate the deceased within physical space. The 'gardens' and 'shrines' appear behind the deceased at the back of his head (Fig. 8.8), perhaps visible if the re-animated deceased were to have turned his head in his coffin (Lesko 1979, 56; Willems 1988, 234). In general, people feel great anxiety when faced with traversing unknown places or when located in unfamiliar places, and this is also clearly evident in the way the Ancient Egyptians perceived a potentially topsy-turvy chaotic world in the afterlife where the deceased could potentially be orientated upside down and forced to eat faeces and drink urine, as numerous spells within the Coffin Texts testify and guard against. The use, therefore, of these images to orientate the deceased could have ritually alleviated the dangers and stresses faced by the deceased in the initially unfamiliar environment of the afterlife.

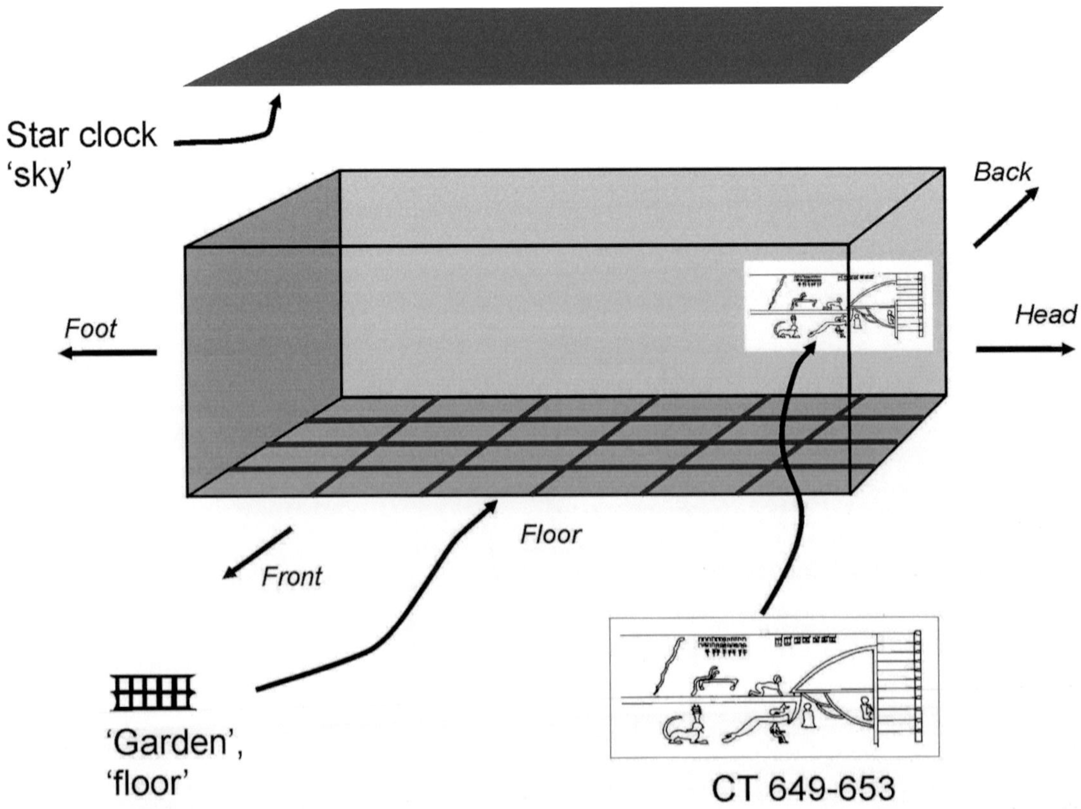

Fig. 8.8. Decorated coffin surfaces – coffin G1T

Cartography at Bersheh

Most of the texts discussed in this paper have come from amongst the coffins found at Bersheh, which seems to have had a tradition of depicting the afterlife in the form of graphical 'maps'. The complex ways of depicting the afterlife here show a good use of graphical and representational forms of art in a cartographical sense. The priests presiding over the necropolis of Bersheh, and the makers of the funerary equipment, it would appear were experimenting with novel ways of cartographical design, since not only were simple locations depicted upon coffins, but also illustrations of journeys.

As within many cultures and their conceptions of fantastic landscapes, the descriptions of the afterlife represented within the Coffin Texts, both in Bersheh and elsewhere, might have had some physical basis in the known landscape. Pathways, gates, regions and significant landmarks all exist in the 'real world', and if some spells from the general corpus of Coffin Texts were to be analysed, it would be possible to envisage a real-world journey not just from hypothetical or mythological locations but also from significant ritual and pilgrimage locations in Egypt, such as Abydos, Heliopolis and Letopolis or even geographical entities, such as the western and eastern horizons in the case of the Field of Hetep (Willems 1996, 368–9). Equally, however, the somewhat esoteric generalities of the texts studied within this paper can also be considered as indicating purely mythical locations, or at least locations whose significance for the Egyptians was more abstract, in much the same way as the cosmologies represented in Tantric Buddhism contrasted to more concrete locations depicted within other branches of Buddhism (Barnes 1999, 113–17).

These afterlife texts are apparently confined to a narrow group of individuals. Whilst it is not possible to show that this group were especially allowed greater access to the hidden knowledge of the landscape of the afterlife, if that might have existed in some form or other, it is nonetheless tempting to suggest that the rulers of Bersheh at this time, as well as selected members of their households, did have a somewhat unique concept of the afterlife otherwise inaccessible to others either in the region or in the Nile valley as a whole. In a modern-day parallel to the Bersheh coffin maps, however, the anthropologist-surveyor Brody discusses the way specific individuals are able to create dream-maps, as part of his study of a Native American hunter-gather people, the Beaver tribe of north-east British Columbia. Whilst many of these dream-maps are related to hunting and to potential sources of food, his discussions with members of the tribe whilst out on a hunting expedition are perhaps illuminating with regard to the Ancient Egyptian perceptions of journeying towards the afterlife: 'good men… could dream of more than animals. Sometimes they saw heaven and its trails' (Brody 1988, 46). This knowledge, however, was put to use for the benefit of the whole community: 'a strong dreamer can tell others how to get to heaven' (Brody 1988, 47). But the clear aim of some of these dreams is to direct the person to an afterlife, and furthermore, the 'maps' so created were given a tangible and physical form as an aid to the deceased: 'Heaven is reached only by careful avoidance of the wrong trails. These must be shown so that the traveller can recognize and avoid them…a person can take a map with him…[some] choose to have a map buried with them. They can thus remind themselves which ways to travel' (Brody 1988, 47). Although the hunter-gatherer society of the Beaver is far removed culturally, spatially and chronologically from that of the Egyptians of four millennia ago, nonetheless the 'maps' within the coffins of both groups clearly define some common conceptions of routeways and mechanisms for the transition between this world and the afterlife.

Bersheh was the necropolis of Hermopolis, the sacred city of Thoth, god of writing and knowledge, and capital of the local region, or *nome*. It is possible that as a central place, Hermopolis itself could have been a centre of learning, with perhaps a sacred library of texts, and that such 'maps' were designed and developed there by those knowledgeable in the content of those texts (Quirke 2003, 178). These texts could well have been intended for secular use outside of the sacred sphere.

Further evidence for Hermopolitan learning and wisdom might be provided by the 'map' on the Gebelein coffin, which is associated with Thoth and his 'field' as well as other divinities and afterlife locations in an image similar perhaps in purpose to that of the Field of Hetep (Hornung 1973, 34). However, there are sufficient differences between coffins from Bersheh and other contexts to suggest that sub-genres might have arisen independently in various localities. Indeed, the Hermopolitan origin of the Book of Two Ways itself has been disputed (Hoffmeier 1996, 49–50). But without specific contemporary source libraries and scriptoria, as well as original exemplars of the texts themselves, it would be difficult to ascribe particular localities as the origins of these various texts.

On the other hand, since the development of such esoteric thought might equally have developed elsewhere, for example in a scribal centre attached to the royal residence in the capital city of that time, Lisht, it might be that some other reason could have led to the development of the geographical treatises within the Coffin Texts of Bersheh, such as greater trading links between nearby Hermopolis and the rest of the Nile Valley. Such linkages with a greater hinterland would undoubtedly have led to greater cosmopolitan awareness amongst the population. As a consequence, the geographical knowledge and personal space of those responsible for the manufacture of funerary equipment would have undoubtedly increased. Of course, it is equally possible that as a centre of knowledge and a regional capital, Hermopolis itself, with its aristocratic family of local rulers, attracted scholars and artists from along the Nile Valley, and thus the Bersheh world-view and perceptions of the landscape of the afterlife itself would have developed as a result, with the consequent depictions of such afterlife environs as the Book of Two Ways, and the Field of Hetep. Without further documentary evidence of this, however, such ideas must unfortunately remain speculative at present.

It has been said that 'the cognition of geographic space is fundamental to our daily living' (Kitchen and Blades 2002, 203). This is as true for historic and prehistoric societies as it is for our modern culture. Although prehistoric societies have left little or no documentary evidence, it is apparent that ancient landscapes would have created frames of reference for their inhabitants, and that in traversing these landscapes, those inhabitants would have used what can be described as 'cognitive markers'. These markers, whether they were habitation sites, food production or acquisition sites, locations where 'industrial' activities were carried out, or places of sacred or ritual significance, would have needed to have been internalised by some sort of cognitive processes. The descriptions of the afterlife in the Egyptian Coffin Texts discussed in this paper stem from a literate and well-documented, if long-dead, culture. They nonetheless can be analysed in much the same way as the 'world knowledge' of modern, technologically more-advanced groups. Furthermore, since such concepts can be paralleled in a number of societies and their belief systems, it is possible that the same methodologies might be equally applicable to societies and landscapes elsewhere. Although the ritual and environmental concepts of the cultures involved may differ, the general idea of cognitive mapping applied to journeys and landscapes, whether these be ritual or 'real-world', will undoubtedly be similar. Having regard for cognitive mapping and the processes behind the way we all map landscapes and journeys in our minds, the archaeologist can therefore begin to come to a better understanding of the world-view, if not cosmology, of former cultures.

Acknowledgements

I am grateful to Vicki Cummings and Robert Johnston for their invitation to contribute to these proceedings, and for their comments, along with those of the anonymous referee, upon an earlier draft of this paper.

Bibliography

Allen, T.G. (ed.) 1974. *The book of the dead or going forth by day: ideas of the Ancient Egyptians concerning the hereafter as expressed in their own terms*. Chicago: SAOC.

Barnes, G.L. 1999. Buddhist landscapes of East Asia. In W. Ashmore and A.B. Knapp (eds), *Archaeologies of landscape*, 101–23. Oxford: Blackwell.

Brody, H. 1988. *Maps and dreams*. Vancouver: Douglas and McIntyre.

de Buck, A. 1954. *The Egyptian Coffin Texts V. Texts of Spells 355–471*. Chicago: University of Chicago Press

de Buck, A. 1956. *The Egyptian Coffin Texts VI. Texts of Spells 472–786*. Chicago: University of Chicago Press

de Buck, A. 1961. *The Egyptian Coffin Texts VII. Texts of Spells 787–1185*. Chicago: University of Chicago Press

Faulkner, R.O. 1969. *The Ancient Egyptian pyramid texts*. Oxford: Clarendon.

Faulkner, R.O. 1977. *The Ancient Egyptian Coffin Texts, volume II*. Warminster: Aris and Phillips.

Faulkner, R.O. 1978. *The Ancient Egyptian Coffin Texts, volume III*. Warminster: Aris and Phillips.

Flannery, K.V. and Marcus, J. 1993. Cognitive archaeology. *Cambridge Archaeological Journal* 3, 260–67.

Gluck, M. 1991. Making sense of human wayfinding: review of cognitive and linguistic knowledge for personal navigation with a new research direction. In D. M. Mark and A.U. Frank (eds), *Cognitive and linguistic aspects of geographic space*, 117–35. Dordrecht: Kluwer Academic Publishers.

Golledge, R.G. 1999. Human wayfinding and cognitive Maps. In R.G. Golledge (ed.), *Wayfinding behavior*, 5–45. Baltimore and London: John Hopkins University Press.

Goodey, B. 1971. *Perception of the environment: an introduction to the literature*. Birmingham: Birmingham University (Centre for Urban and Regional Studies).

Hoffmeier, J.K. 1996. Are there regionally-based theological differences in the Coffin Texts? In H. Willems (ed.), *The world of the Coffin Texts*, 45–54. Leiden: Nederlands Instituut voor het Nabije Oosten.

Hornung, E. 1973. Die 'Kammern' des Thot-Heiligtumes, *Zeitschrift für Ägyptische Sprache und Altertumskunde* 100, 33–35.

Hornung, E. 1999. *The Ancient Egyptian books of the afterlife*. (trans. D. Lorton). Ithica: Cornell University Press.

Kitchin, R. and Blades, M. 2002. *The cognition of geographic space*. London: I.B. Tauris.

Knapp, A.B. and Ashmore, W. 1999. Archaeological landscapes: constructed, conceptualised, ideational. In W. Ashmore and A.B. Knapp (eds), *Archaeologies of landscape*, 1–30. Oxford: Blackwell.

Laslo, E., Masulli, I., Artigiani, R. and Csány, V. (eds) 1993. *The evolution of cognitive maps*. Luxemburg: Gordon and Breach.

Lesko, L.H. 1971–72. The Field of Hetep in Egyptian Coffin Texts. *Journal of the American Research Center in Egypt* 9, 89–101.

Lesko, L.H. 1972. *The Ancient Egyptian Book of Two Ways*. Berkeley: University of California Press.

Lesko, L.H. 1979. *Index of the spells on Egyptian Middle Kingdom coffins and related documents*. Berkeley: BC Scribe Publications.

Lynch, K. 1960. *The image of the city*. Cambridge (Mass.): MIT Press.

Porter, B. and Moss, R.M. 1937. *Topographical bibliography of Ancient Egyptian hieroglyphic texts, reliefs and paintings*. Oxford: Clarendon Press.

Quirke, S. 2003. Measuring the underworld. In D. O'Connor and S. Quirke, (eds), *Mysterious lands*, 161–81. London: UCL Press.

Renfrew, C. 1993. Cognitive archaeology: some thoughts on the archaeology of thought, *Cambridge Archaeological Journal* 3, 248–50.

Stern, E. and Portugali, J. 1999. Environmental cognition and decision making in urban navigation. In R. G. Golledge (ed.), *Wayfinding behaviour,* 99–119. Baltimore and London: John Hopkins University Press.

Willems, H. 1988. *Chests of life: a study of the typology and development of Middle Kingdom standard class coffins*. Leiden: Ex Oriente Lux.

Willems, H. 1996. *The coffin of Heqata (Cairo* JdE *36418): a case study of Egyptian funerary culture of the Early Middle Kingdom*. Leuven: Uitgeverij Peeters Departement Oriëntalistiek; Orientalia Lovaniensia Analecta 70.

9 Journeying into different realms: travel, pilgrimage and rites of passage at Graig Lwyd

Bronwen Price

Introduction

Graig Lwyd, the Group VII 'axe factory' in Gwynedd, North Wales, has been neatly slipped into the succession of modern archaeological narratives depicting the nature of British Neolithic life (e.g. Darvill 1987, 54). It was a source of flakable rock, and as such was utilised for the production of polished axes which in this paradigm, both symbolised and facilitated the role of early farmers in their battle against the native woodland (Lynch *et al.* 2000, 54). Seen as prized material forms by archaeologists on the basis of their frequent deposition at monuments and supposedly inherent aesthetic appeal, growing demand for polished Group VII stone axes in the Late Neolithic was both generated and met by increasingly well-established exchange networks (Renfrew 1986, 6). The axes' desirability may have been enhanced by Graig Lwyd itself (Bradley 1993, 26). Indeed, the extraction face is situated in a landscape setting that includes the remnants of seven stone circles aligned with one another, numerous cairns and standing stones, votive axe deposits, a prehistoric track-way and several large glacial erratics which are biographically named in local folklore. The axes' aesthetic characteristics were often distinctive to their source (Whittle 1995, 253), and the Group VII examples may have metonymically drawn from Graig Lwyd's cosmological and mythological significance at the juncture between sea, sky and land (Cooney 1998, 192).

What if, however, Group VII axes were not the cause but the consequence of the popularity of the site? I argue that we continue to apply a formalist economic rationale in assuming that axes were the most important aspect of prehistoric experiences at Graig Lwyd based on the significance attributed to their form and find-spots in the modern day. What if the *journey* was more important than its product? What if *each experience* lent significance to *each axe*? What if, crucially, the cliff face at Graig Lwyd was itself an active material agent? Perhaps a re-assessment of the 'significance ranking' of particular forms of material culture and agency evident in recent approaches can aid our comprehension both of the individuality of axe biographies, and the subsequent possibilities for these extraction sites.

As a peripheral element of taskscape (Ingold 1993), I intend to develop the idea that Graig Lwyd worked in opposition to the security of the confines of *habitus* (Bourdieu 1977, 79) and social structure (Giddens 1984, 25). At a time when everything beyond the boundaries of 'home' may have been associated with concepts of danger, profanity, disorder and transience (Helms 1988, 22–23; Hodder 1990, 54), Graig Lwyd may have represented distant realms, bound to foreign and amorphous configurations of the world. This association with other times, places and mentalities may have caused passage to Graig Lwyd to become capable of transforming identities, thereby enhancing its perceived threat. As a sacred place on the edges of the earth, Graig Lwyd may have also been liminal, and thus conveyance through the site may have been regarded as equally dangerous. I explore how the site operated in its wider context; as an active material agent within Giddens' recursive dialectic between structure and agency (Giddens 1984, 17).

This chapter is a shortened version of my Masters dissertation which explores these themes and the site in far greater depth. Here I will briefly introduce the site and why it and the wider topic of axe distribution/deposition demands a re-examination before sharing with you my physical and interpretive journey. I would like to stress that my engagement with this incredible landscape does not offera definitive conceptual ordering of it. Equally, I could never hope to tap into all the perceptions of the many people who visited this place at different times in the past. I accept many of the theoretical and methodical flaws with phenomenological approaches (e.g. Fleming 1999, 120). I simply try to present and interpret how and why I related with and comprehended the prehistoric route way that leads to and from Graig Lwyd.

Introduction to the site

Graig Lwyd ('grey rock' in English), is situated on the northern coast of Gwynedd in North Wales, and lies at an altitude of 429m AOD at its highest peak above the modern town of Penmaenmawr, meaning 'head of the big stone' (Fig. 9.1). All known prehistoric quarrying faces and working floors were discovered along the eastern scarp of the igneous intrusion and at the nearby Dinas and Garreg Fawr outcrops which, along with the southern edge of Graig Lwyd, contain the seam of very fine-grained, pale-grey augite granophyre used to create the axes (Williams *et al.* 1998, 3–5). Most of the faces have been lost to repeated quarrying since the nineteenth century (Hazzledine Warren 1922; Fig. 9.2).

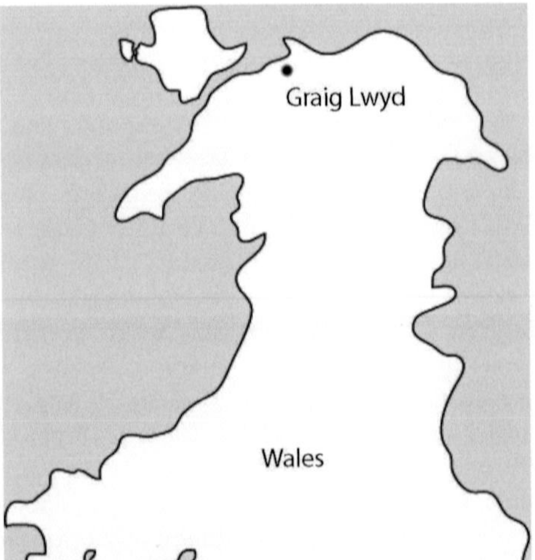

Fig. 9.1. Location of the Penmaenmawr circles and Graig Lwyd face

Fig. 9.2. (right) Graig Lwyd taken from the bank north of Meini Hirion. Note the modern quarrying plateau, tip of south-east Anglesey to the west and Great Orme's Head to the east

Recent excavation by Williams *et al.* (1998) built on Hazzledine Warren's field-walking, and confirmed that axe flaking debitage and rough-outs are scattered throughout the local area. This indicates that the preliminary phases of production occurred on-site. Extraction events have been dated from the very end of the terminal Mesolithic through to early in the Late Neolithic (in North Wales, this is equivalent to roughly 4350–2900 BC; Peterson 1999).

Group VII axes have been found across the UK in various archaeological contexts although, unlike other source sites such as Great Langdale in Cumbria, the highest concentration of find spots occur locally in the Conwy Valley. However, the depth of time and events these 'distribution', or deposition, maps encompass renders interpretation problematic. For example, the possible Late Neolithic peak in deposition may correlate with changes in the treatment and determination of axe deaths rather than a 'major expansion in axe production and exchange' (Bradley and Edmonds 1993, 179).

To the immediate south and south-east of Graig Lwyd lies the gentler moorland of Cerrig Gwynion (meaning 'white stone'; Fig. 9.3). Upon this Ordovician shale and slate bedrock sits numerous large glacial erratic blocks, some of which have been utilised in the construction of various forms of prehistoric monuments. A line of six stone circles is sited across the rolling moorland of Cerrig Gwynion, running approximately east-west from a standing stone on the Tal-y-fan ridge to the Graig Lwyd face. Dating is difficult due to later funerary insertions and a lack of modern excavation. However, on the somewhat tenuous basis of rough typological affinities with other dated monuments, three of these circles were probably built in the Late Neolithic (*c.* 2900–2300 BC) whilst the others are more likely to derive from the Beaker period (*c.* 2300–1800 cal BC). Later Early and Middle Bronze Age cairns are also scattered throughout the moorland respecting and overlooking the linear alignment of the earlier stone circles. Five of the stone circles and approximately eight of the cairns are situated along a one kilometre stretch on the Cefn Coch ridge, immediately to the south-east of

Fig. 9.3. (below) View across the Cerrig Gwynion moorland facing north

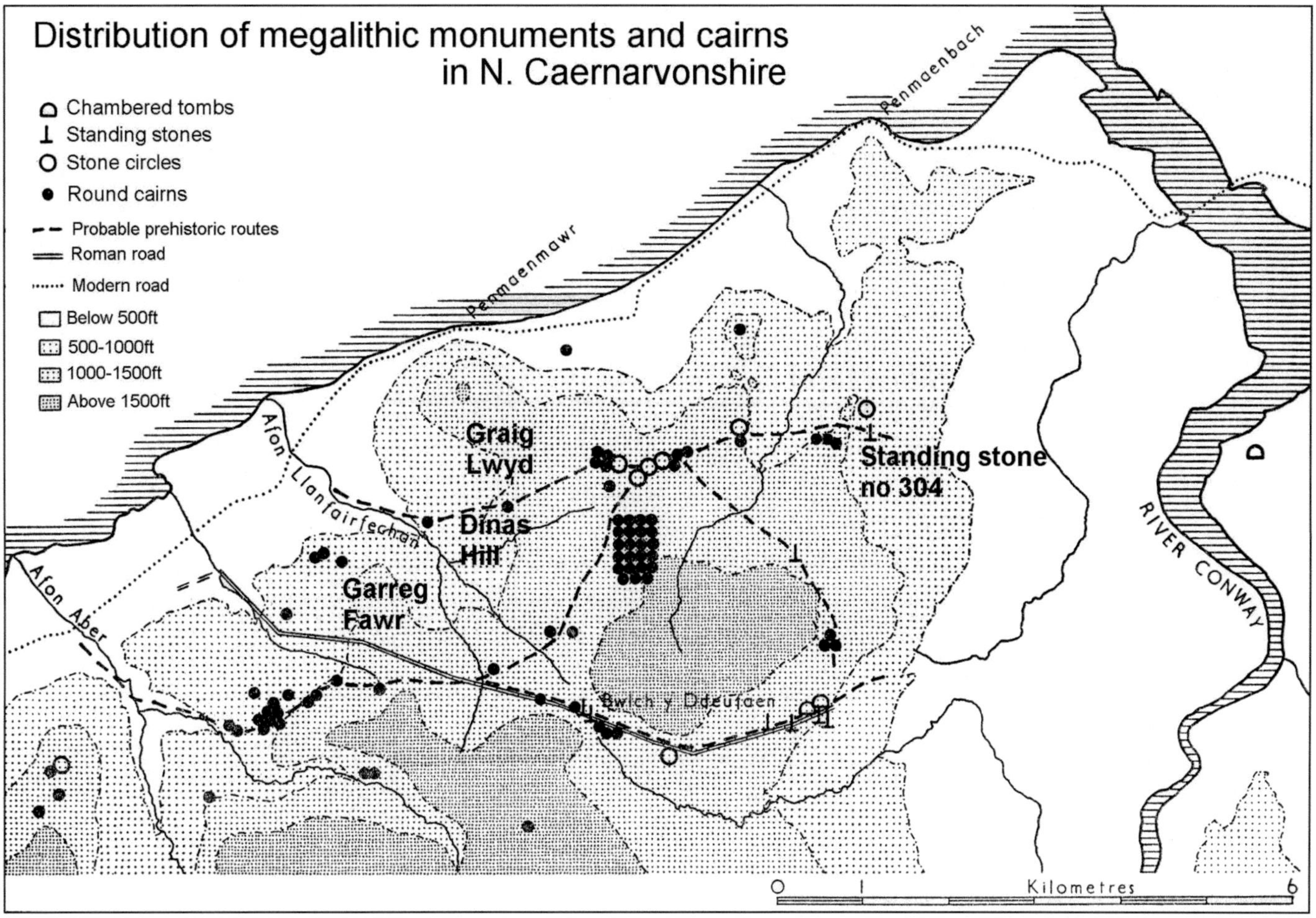

Fig. 9.4. Plan of prehistoric track-ways and monuments in the Graig Lwyd area (after Griffiths 1960, 334)

Graig Lwyd. Many of the largest glacial erratics on the sweeping Cerrig Gwynion moorland are demonstrably orientated with the arrangement of stone circles.

This alignment has been recognised as a probable route way that links up with a much longer prehistoric track, eventually formalised in the Roman period (Gresham and Irvine 1963, 55–6). This longer track runs from mid Wales, across the Conwy valley, along the southern scarp of the Tal-y-fan dolerite ridge way and on towards the Aber estuary (one of the easier places to navigate the Menai Straits). The Graig Lwyd route way can most easily be viewed at Meini Hirion stone circle, where the arc of stone settings is visibly flattened in its north-western corner to accommodate the path (Griffiths 1960, 313). It was plotted by Griffiths (1960, 334) from the standing stone (no. 304) at the Cefn Llechen region of the Tal-y-fan ridge way, due west across the Cerrig Gwynion moorland, past the stone circles and Graig Lwyd itself at the gentler Cefn Coch ridge, and onwards west to Dinas Hill (Figs 9.4 and 9.5).

The unrelenting preoccupation with axes, axe factories and formalist economics: an outline of the problem and review of the literature

The axes and particularly axe 'factories' of Neolithic Britain are subjects that have been largely under-investigated since the formalist and systemic modelling of trade and exchange by Renfrew (1973) and Clarke (1968) during the 1960s and 1970s. These approaches, respecting Clark (1952, 248) and Childe (1958, 169), saw extraction sites and their 'products' as resources that were subjected to 'rational' acts of manipulation and distribution by early sedentary farmers who utilised agricultural surplus to create and control prestige goods, and ultimately jostle for position as elites.

Following Hodder and Orton's (1976) classic rejection, based on equifinality, of the modelling of trade processes from the spatial distribution of products, discussing trade and exchange has become a somewhat unpopular topic. This has been supported by the abandonment of social evolutionary theory and economic rationalism in archaeology, and more recently, the questioning of the relevance of

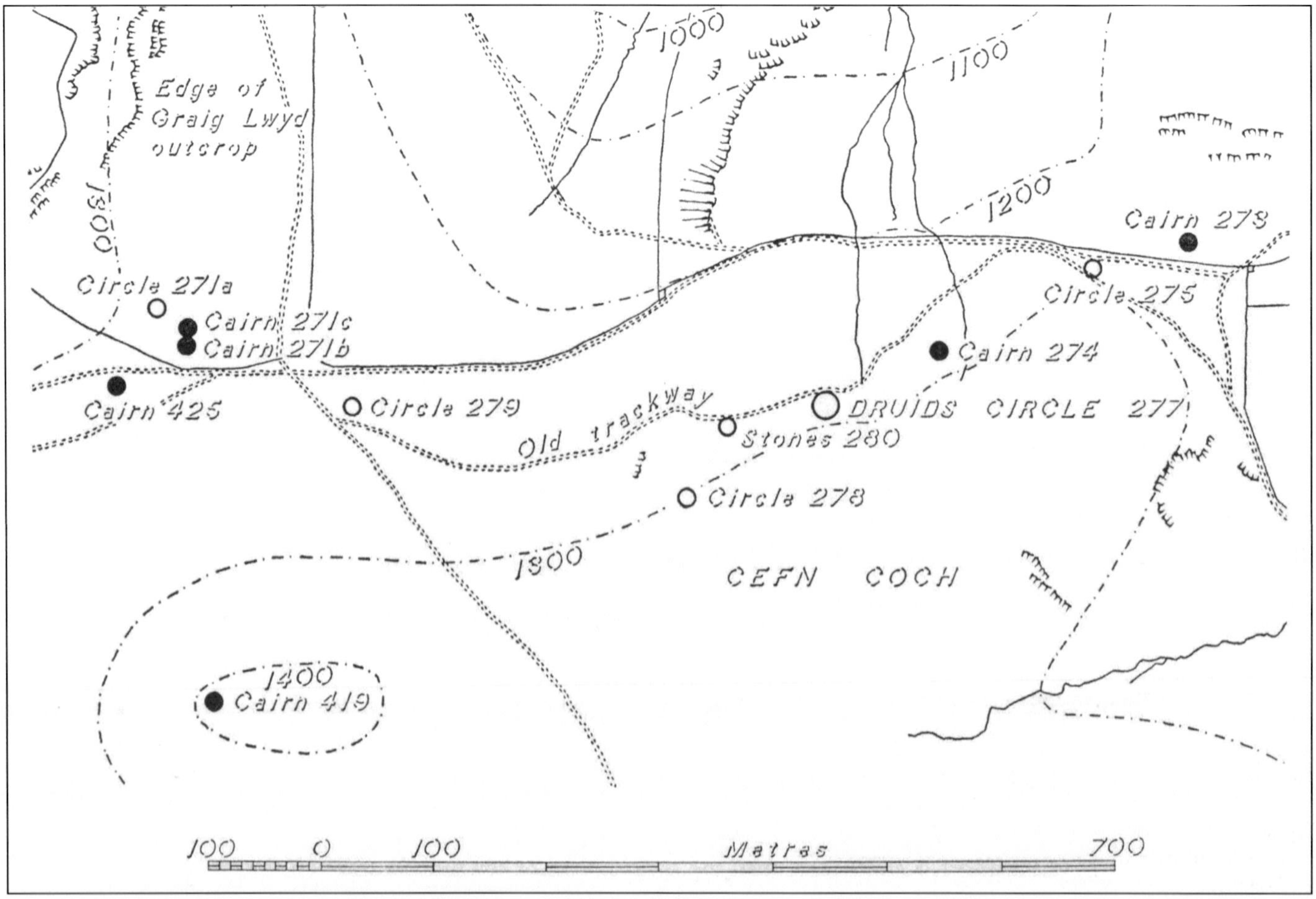

Fig. 9.5. Plan of the Cefn Coch section of the Penmaenmawr monuments after the 1958 and 1959 excavations (after Griffiths 1960, 304)

sedentism in Neolithic Britain (Bradley 1993; Thomas 1991, 25) and the rejection of a clear dichotomy between economy and society (Sherratt 1997).

Bradley and Edmonds (1993) have provided the most systematic appraisal of the issue in the last fifteen years in their discussion of the Great Langdale axes from Cumbria, although they still maintained that these objects were classic 'prestige items'. Consequently extraction sites were interpreted as 'valued' commodities: foci for ongoing power struggles (Bradley and Edmonds 1993, 143). The evidence, however, simply does not fit this deterministic understanding: there is nothing in the archaeological record to support the existence of an 'elite'; extraction pockets within 'quarries' are focused on the most obscure and dangerous faces of the sites (Bradley and Edmonds 1993, 131); most distribution maps plotting axes and sources do not follow the straightforward fall-off pattern often associated with down-the-line trade; and many sites are associated with contemporary ritual or mortuary complexes (e.g. the Group XIII Preseli 'axe factory' in Dyfed; David and Williams 1995, 433). There was clearly much more to these quarries than simple extraction, production and distribution activity centres, and much more to axes than inanimate prestige goods, polished to enhance their exchange potential and status (Pétrequin *et al.* 1998, 295).

More recently, most archaeological perspectives have worked within the frameworks set out in Giddens' (1984, 16–25) structuration theory and Bourdieu's (1977, 78–87) concept of *habitus*. In both, very broadly speaking, structural conditions of society (e.g. norms and values) are locked in a perpetual discursive relationship with forces of agency (i.e. the capability to exercise some sort of influence). Thus, people continually constitute their worlds by constructing, deconstructing and reconstructing normative rules. This ongoing discourse between 'structure' and 'agency' underpins the nature of human existence, where *habitus* forms both the dynamic generative principles *and* site of the dialectic (Bourdieu 1977, 78). In this way, *habitus* is the multi-faceted nature of existence at any given point, for any given agent, and is continually reproduced and reconfigured through daily life. It follows that material culture, as a constituent of *habitus*, is both the actualisation of this dialectic, and an agent in its own right (Hodder 1982).

Subsequently, most work on axes from the last fifteen years has either embraced variations of Mauss' (1954) concept of gift exchange where the axe becomes active (e.g. Patton's (1993) work on axe exchange in the Armorican Neolithic), or instead focused on elements of their biographical symbolism (e.g. Skeates' (1995) work on axe amulets in the Mediterranean). Edmonds (1995, 55) describes how axes provide metaphors for 'some of the qualities and roles that defined people in the Neolithic world'. In these mindsets, axes are material agents. Whilst they may have been created for specific reasons or purposes, their roles and symbolism changed and developed recursively with innumerable strata of social contexts immediately after their conception. For example, Cooney (2002, 101) describes how porphyry axes created at Lambay Island, off the central-east coast of Ireland, originally drew meaning from the deliberate emphasis of their whiteness, achieved through grinding using red sandstone. He argues that this act represented the activation of life through forces of blood/vitality, since white and red/brown are common cross-cultural metaphors for these concepts respectively. For Cooney, this symbolism was paralleled in the coastal attrition of the porphyry seams, and combined an understanding of how the world worked with a desire to use this powerful rock. In this perspective, axe production (as a constituent of *habitus*) provided a critical forum for dialectical discourse between structural conditions and agency: in this case to reinforce, maintain or challenge metaphysical knowledge. Equally, upon conception, axes momentarily actualised the dialectic and instantly became embedded agents in their own right. It is inferred that axes subsequently continually reworked these, and new meanings throughout their life histories.

Axe factories have been similarly re-incorporated as nodal points in the wider Neolithic taskscape (Edmonds 1999, 36–50). Bradley (1993, 26) first suggested that the settings of axe extraction sites established the significance of their 'products'. Whittle (1995, 253) went on to emphasise the metaphoric and metonymic symbolism axes may have recalled, compromised or confirmed through their aesthetic distinctiveness specifically derived from a known source. Cooney (1998, 110) has more recently gone further by suggesting that in some cases 'part of the attraction of the place chosen for production was the nature of the location itself' (Cooney 1998, 110). Mythology associated with remote locations like Le Pinacle on Jersey, Tievebulliagh in County Antrim and Great Langdale in Cumbria may pre-date the production of axes (Bradley 2000, 41). Extracting stone from such sites could have provided contact with the spiritual world (Cooney 1998, 110).

Reactive axes, animated axe factories

Whilst these approaches have generated a great deal of thought on specific aspects of axes' significance, all have preserved their 'superior' status compared to other elements of Neolithic material culture and agency. The polished stone axe is maintained as a classic and almost iconic item of prestige through its treatment as a generic and independent material form in the literature, despite an acknowledgement of the specific life experiences entangled and enmeshed in each and every example (e.g. Bradley 2000, 82; Edmonds 1998, 262; Patton 1993, 19; Rudebeck 1998, 326). For example, Edmonds (1998, 262) implies a hierarchy amongst both material culture and social contexts by suggesting 'axes and certain forms of specialised arrowhead may have served…as weapons of exclusion'. Similarly, Ray (2004, 170) describes how stone axes' aesthetic, metaphorical and functional attributes made them ideal candidates for kula-type exchange. Such stances imply that axes were somehow inherently more important to the ongoing negotiation of life than other material agents and situations, and are based on a rather out-dated 'form equals function' typology. This is highly problematic because the ranking of the role of particular material forms, and the corollary ranking of social places and times in which these different material forms act, undermines the complexity of discursive social relations at every resolution. In fact, one could argue that the two sentiments are entirely contradictory, since if material culture is locked in perpetual discursive relationships with structural conditions, the biography and persona of each example is therefore individually unique and cannot be pre-determined by form (Barrett 2001, 152; Thomas 2001, 177). Indeed, the sustained emphasis of these paradoxical trajectories, combined with the widespread application of the postprocessual shibboleth of the 'meaningful constitution of material culture' (Appadurai 1986; Barrett 2001; Hodder 1982; 1992; Thomas 2001), has had the perverse effects of abstracting axes from their social contexts and 'over-animating' them. After all, axes cannot be perceived as truly active unless they are bound to humanly endowed meaning, and thus a discursive dependency exists between humanity and materiality (Gosden and Marshall 1999, 172).

I argue that for the animation of material culture to operate theoretically, one has to fully abandon the ever-implicit idea that particular predetermined times, places, agents and materialities were necessarily more 'significant' in the dialectical renegotiation of *habitus* than others. Ultimately, I argue that the biographies of material culture were not determined primarily by form. Although this may have affected some of the social contexts material culture inhabited, the significance of all dialectical renegotiations of *habitus* remained irrespective of it. This might aid our comprehension of the fact that Neolithic stone axes have been found deposited or abandoned in many different archaeological contexts, with a huge variability in the degree of 'wear' evident on their surfaces (e.g. the 'pristine' surface of the jadeite axe blade found beside the Sweet Track in Somerset can be contrasted with axe-cut marks preserved on timbers nearby: Coles and Coles 1986).

So why bother scaling these highly inaccessible 'axe quarry' faces if an 'influential' life history was neither guaranteed, nor particularly probable? Cooney's suggestion that the perceived 'quality' of the stone may have been enhanced by the 'special setting from which they came' (1998, 112) hints at an answer. What if the creation of axes was subsidiary to the primary intentional aim of visits to these sites? Perhaps the only meaning specific axes immediately drew from was their knappers' experiences approaching and engaging with these forums of activity as very real taskscapes. Thus if axes do derive initial, and perhaps for some, sustained, meaning from their respective sources (Cooney 1998, 112; Whittle 1995, 253), a localised appreciation of these sites is imperative because ultimately, the journey and the moment may have been more significant than the end result.

An experience, one journey

I am now going to briefly outline my two-hour journey towards Graig Lwyd from the Conwy Valley following the aforementioned prehistoric route plotted by Griffiths (1960, 334). There are various issues with choosing to describe this particular route such as whether access was originally obtained from an alternative cliff path to the north. Also, even if Griffiths' route way was the only original approach, the return journey may have been as, or even more, significant. Ultimately, there are no definitives, I simply relay my journey for the purpose of analysis.

My journey therefore commenced at standing stone 306 (numbered in the Royal Commission on Ancient and Historical Monuments in Wales (1956) inventory), which was probably erected in the Early Bronze Age although dating isolated monoliths is notoriously difficult (Burl 1993, 183; Fig. 9.6). This narrow stone is over two metres tall and commands views exclusively to the east across the Conwy Valley (between the bearings of 0° and 180°). Proceeding almost exactly due north in the direction of Hafodty Circle (no. 304), it remained visible until I had just gained a view of the circle, at which point it disappeared beneath the gradient of the incline.

This circle (304), with seven surviving orthostats and a diameter of 12.2m, is probably Late Neolithic/ Beaker period in date (Burl 1976, 47–48; Fig. 9.7). Again, views to the east (between the bearings of roughly 30° and 190°) were extensive, but to the west, visibility was extremely limited. Ascending westwards, I passed a small group of ring cairns and encountered my first view of the Cerrig Gwynion moorland. Descending the opposite side of the dolerite ridge and onto the moor itself, I crossed the streams at the most fordable spot, directly overlooked by a large erratic containing seams of glittering quartz. Continuing roughly due west across the northern section of the moorland, Red Farm Circle appeared (no. 276; Fig. 9.8).

This Late Neolithic circle survives as an arc of four knee high orthostats with an original diameter of 30.1m (Burl 1976, 268). To the east of this circle, the recently traversed moorland and ridge were fully visible, but from a bearing of 219° to 50°, Cefn Coch ridge and Craig Hadfodwen Hill blocked visibility. This was demonstrably intentional in the siting of the circle as a short climb north-westerly revealed no such inhibition to the west. A 200m walk at a bearing of 219° brought me to the upright erratic named Maen Crwn (Round Stone) on the OS map (Fig. 9.9).

Fig. 9.6. (left) Standing stone 306, taken facing north-east

Fig. 9.7. (right) Hafodty Circle (no. 304), taken facing north

Continuing westwards, I passed a huge plateaued stone and a cairn (273) and arrived at Circle 275, which consists of five large, low boulders set lengthways with an internal diameter of only 3.2m (Fig. 9.10). Early Bronze Age in date, it is probably the remains of a cist-less cairn circle, although both the excavator (Griffiths 1960, 318) and Burl (1976, 268; 1995, 177) are adamant that it is a stone circle similar to the south-west Irish 'five-stone rings'. Quartz fragments were found scattered internally (Griffiths 1960, 318). As the latest of all monuments thus far mentioned, it was interesting that the previous trend for inhibited visibility to the west and open views to the east was not adhered to. The next stone circle and Graig Lwyd itself were, for the first time, visible. Proceeding westwards, I passed a ruinous ring cairn (no. 274) before encountering Meini Hirion ('Druid's Circle', no. 277).

This circle is the most famous and complete of those at Penmaenmawr. It has an average diameter of 25m, and in the WSW section of the circumference, a break in the bank was originally flanked by two large orthostats forming a portalled entranceway (Griffiths 1960, 313–14; Fig. 9.11). Local dolerites were used for its construction and quartz lumps were originally spread throughout its interior (Fig. 9.12). Various cremation burials of juveniles, including one placed in an urn within a central cist, were added to the circle in the early second millennium BC (Griffiths 1960, 322–5). The excavator attributed the circle's construction to the later Early Bronze Age, based on these cremation deposits (Griffiths 1960, 322–5). However, they were probably inserted post-construction and the circle is more likely to have been built at the end of the Late Neolithic since its portalled entrance and large diameter share typological affinities with other dated sites such as Long Meg and her Daughters in Cumbria (Burl 1995, 178). Again, at this earlier circle, visibility is blocked to the west. Conwy Bay and Graig Lwyd are both invisible from the centre of the circle, but visible from immediately north of it. In 1846 it was observed that the orthostats in the north-westerly quadrant of the circle were notably taller than their counterparts, perhaps enhancing the blocking of visibility in this direction (Burl 1993, 39).

Continuing westwards along the route of the track way I encountered Stones 280, which is the only visible monument from Meini Hirion (Fig. 9.13). Although nineteenth century destruction has rendered it an unrecognisable array of low stones, its original 'H' formation set perpendicular to Meini Hirion's portalled entranceway is detailed in an engraving dated 1846 (Griffiths 1960, 313). It is possible that this site may have been an avenue terminus or screen across the track way, soliciting or restricting travellers between Meini Hirion, the subsequent two circles and Graig Lwyd itself. Such

Fig. 9.8. Red Farm Circle (no. 276), taken facing south

Fig. 9.9. The Maen Crwn erratic, taken facing north

Fig. 9.10. Circle 275 with Meini Hirion in full view, taken facing south-west

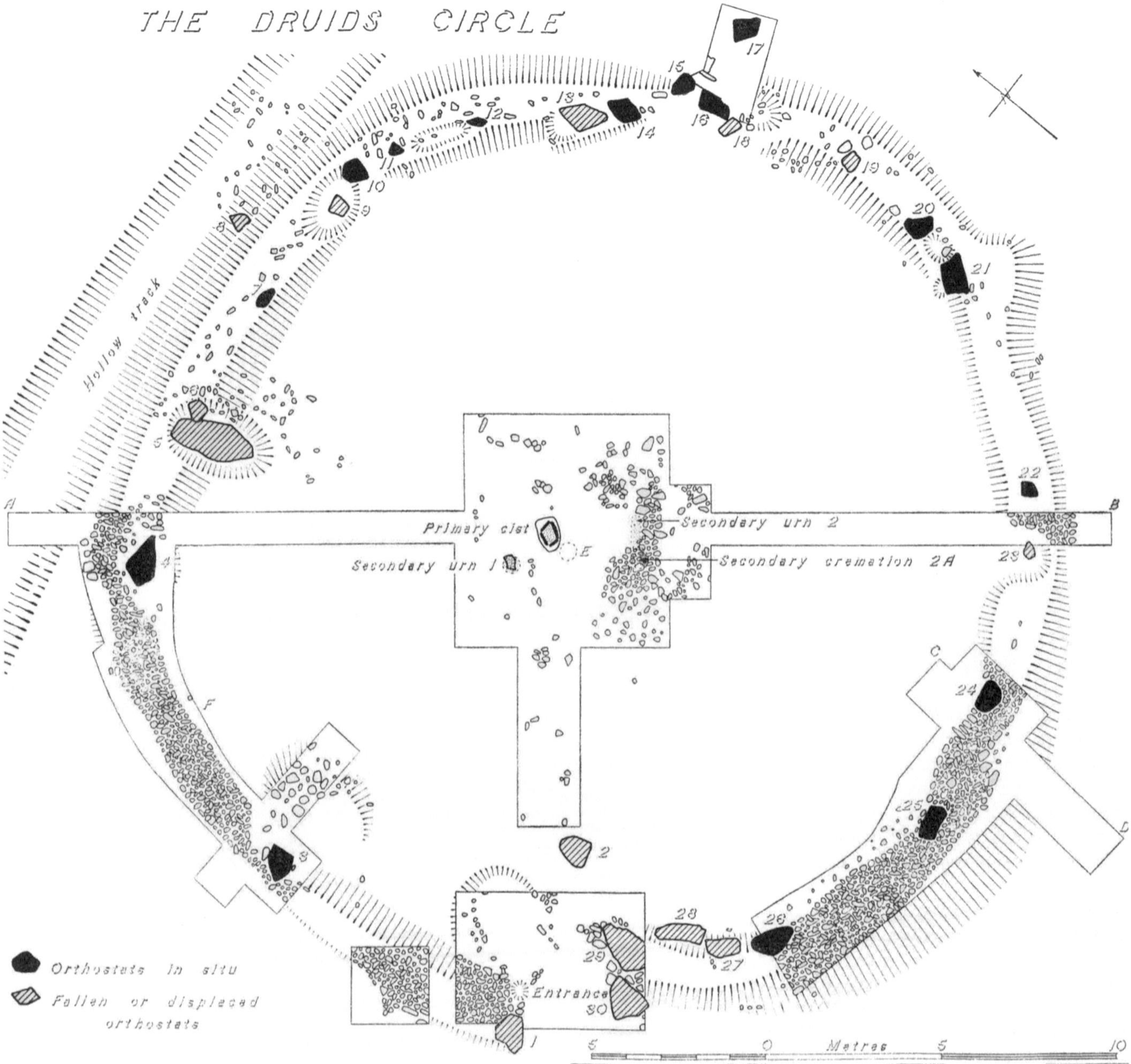

Fig. 9.11. Plan of Meini Hirion (no. 277/Druid's Circle) (after Griffiths 1960, 307)

Fig. 9.12. Meini Hirion (no. 277/Druid's Circle), taken facing south-west

Fig. 9.13. Stones 280, taken facing north-east

'detached avenues' date from the middle of the Early Bronze Age (*c.* 2200 BC to 1800 BC) and a more complete example can be found 60km from Penmaenmawr at Rhos y Beddau, Gwynedd (Burl 1993, 75–7). Visibility at this site is again blocked to the west and open to the east, but Graig Lwyd is visible to the north-west.

Passing the type-site for small kerbed Welsh ring cairns (no. 278), which is invisible from Stones 280 despite its proximity, I proceeded downhill due west along the trackway, in full view of Graig Lwyd. Here, Circle 279 originally stood, now unrecognisable in a sea of dismantled debris. Visibility once again conformed to the west/east trend. I proceeded uphill at a bearing of 300° to Circle 271a and two adjacent cairns (271b and c). This monument, similar in shape, size and structure to Circle 275, is also probably a small Early Bronze Age cist-less cairn circle without its stony mound (Fig. 9.14). This later 'circle' also does not adhere to the west/east visibility trend. Leaving Circle 271a behind me, a 125m walk uphill due north leads me to the working face of Graig Lwyd's most southerly edge (Fig. 9.15).

My journey, executed in around two hours, seems to have been carefully orchestrated. The Graig Lwyd face was hinted at visually and emotively (and perhaps during the Neolithic, sonorously) but was not revealed until I was almost upon it. Banks, tall stones and localised hillocks seemed to be selected for the earlier stone circle locations due to their restrictive capabilities to the west, rendering movement through each monument full of intrigue and curiosity about the final destination. Equally, the completed parts of the journey were almost always recognisable behind me, as if their potential was exhausted and no longer subject to mystery. Punctuated throughout this journey was a kaleidoscopic sense of place that repeatedly re-focused as I moved from the path into the proximity of the stones and circles. These 'nodes' seemed to demand rest, reflection and anticipation prior to a continuation back into the less architecturally ordered sense of place beyond and between (Thomas 2001, 173). The journey from east to west followed the movement of the sun, which I witnessed setting over Graig Lwyd near midsummer's day in June.

Fig. 9.14. Circle/cairn 271a, taken facing west

Fig. 9.15. The surviving south-easterly section of the Graig Lwyd face as it appears, walking north-west from Circle/cairn 271a

Fig. 9.16. The two portal outliers to Lissyvigeen stone circle and henge, Co. Cork, Ireland

Themes

I will now consider aspects of sociality which struck me as partly constitutive of my comprehension of this journey. A fictional narrative of a Neolithic journey to this site will then be presented, based both on the themes I have addressed and certain so-called 'empirical' evidence I consider relevant (which is an acknowledged contradiction in terms). Whilst this will probably inform the reader a little about me, it should predominantly highlight one way in which the Penmaenmawr monuments and Graig Lwyd can be re-integrated as a dynamic and inter-linked prehistoric landscape.

The anthropology and archaeology of pilgrimage: towards an understanding of identity in transition

Travelling, mobility and movement have become maxims for the nature of existence in Neolithic Britain (Edmonds 1995). Despite the plurality of literature dedicated to typologies of modes of movement (e.g. Whittle 1997), one rarely encounters discussion considering why people chose to move that probes deeper than simple environmental determinism. This is especially surprising when one considers that much of our movement-related terminology centres on motivational aspects of it. 'Exile' denotes 'forced' political travel, 'migration' perhaps refers to more pressing economic factors, whilst 'walkabout' implies emotive, spiritual and societal motivations. Ulysses' struggle between the security of home and the challenge of adventure is perhaps a common human predisposition (Helms 1988, 3). All 'reasons to move' refer to a sense of ethnically specific rationale, and thus are entirely justifiable in specific social contexts. A subtle and under-explored motivation may, however, lie behind some of these reasons to travel. The re-negotiation of identity could be founded on trajectories of here and there, 'I' and 'not-I', present and future and hence on metaphors of movement and place (Robertson 1994). By introducing the concept of alternative 'heres', movement makes explicit current senses and dimensions of being which may otherwise have been more inherent. Indeed, normality and its counterpart abnormality are socially-specific constructs which are certainly not universal in either nature or appearance. In some cases, these concepts may be first conceived through the dialectical negotiation of multiple perceptions of on-route experiences; the resulting interpretation of events then becoming integrated into long-term communal memory once 'home'.

Movement also introduces metaphysical and metaphorical thresholds, borderlines, limits, margins and fringes, beyond which co-emerging 'I' and 'not-Is' are perhaps more at liberty to develop (Lichtenberg-Ettinger 1994, 40). By travelling outside 'normality', one encounters and experiences space and difference, potentially provoking new concepts, mentalities and ways of being or subtly unravelling previously institutionalised knowledge (Bourdieu 1977). By expanding or reconfiguring *habitus* through travel, personhood can become unwound and re-pliable. Past travels are frequently cited by people today as 'life-changing experiences', and demarcate social agents through their negotiated esoteric knowledge (Helms 1988, 3).

Perceptions of space and distance have long been discussed as political, social and ideological constructs, rather than neutral or homogenous entities (Durkheim 1915; Giddens 1979, 198–225; Ingold 1993, 157; Thomas 2001, 173). Humans order the landscape into micro and macro dimensions by organising individual/kin/affine units within daily, monthly and yearly rhythms, themselves situated within terrestrial and celestial place (Helms 1988, 22). That which lies beyond the spatial borders of 'here' and 'I' is often equated with distant times and cognitions (Helms 1988, 30). For example, residents of Quito in Ecuador perceive the Amazonian Montaña forest and its people as a surviving repository for ancestral knowledge that has been repeatedly expelled from the highlands by Christianity (Helms 1988, 41). Eliade (1959) points out that many societies conceive of the local as the central heartland of social and ideological life and the focal point for communication with the sacred. Distance from the heartland invokes an interval of separation, beyond which distance and the distant can convey a range of spatial, temporal and relational concepts. Indeed, Helms (1988, 4) suggests people and places beyond this heartland are often perceived as increasingly different and are therefore conceptually more invisible, dangerous, impure, transient; entwined with mythical and supernatural realities.

Either in the forms of strict dichotomies (e.g. the Hebrew wilderness/settlement) or vaguer zones (e.g. the Bashu of Zaire's categories of near and distant neighbours), organising the landscape in this way institutionalises the identity of 'otherness'. By delineating 'us' and 'them' through temporal, spatial and emotive categories, and rules governing any transcendence, emphasis becomes increasingly focused on the potential dangers of boundaries.

The danger of liminality

These junctures, the points at which one crosses the borderline between here and there, 'I' and 'not-I', incurs a period of what van Gennep would term 'liminality' (1960). Temporal, spatial and cognitive, such contexts fundamentally involve the abstraction from present being prior to any integration with future being. Thus, van Gennep (1960, 11) sandwiches liminal (or transitional) rites between rites of separation (e.g. funerals) and rites of reincorporation (e.g. marriage). Liminality is essentially a conditionof being in neither one state nor another; it is an anomalous, indefinite and ambiguous mentality, place or time. However, it is always temporary and therefore permeable. Most popularly symbolised by the desert in the Old Testament, when passing through liminality one finds oneself 'physically and magico-religiously in a special situation for a period of time…waver[ing] between two worlds' (van Gennep 1960, 18). Van Gennep (1960) argues that this symbolic and spatial area of transition can be found in all the ceremonies that accompany passage from one social situation to another. Such periods, places and states of mentality can become feared and therefore carefully managed, perhaps because they emancipate the limits of being. This can result in societal ordering and restriction of the times, places and mentalities in which liminality is encountered, such as rites concerning the use of hallucinogens (e.g. Amazonian Yanomamo abenae) and architecture formalising boundary zones (e.g. Etruscan boundary sanctuaries). In nineteenth century Hawaii, icons of deities and rulers were periodically marched around peripheral nodal points in the landscape such as mountains, shrines and borders (Sahlins 1981, 18–9). This purification of transcendental points between 'us' and 'not-us', and the identification of areas beyond which ritual protection was necessary, emphasises a common structuralist dichotomy between here – safe and pure, and there – dangerous and profane (Douglas 1966, 120–1; Helms 1988, 28). Navajo traders returning from Pueblo and Ute festivals in Midwest America during the fifteenth century AD would perform ceremonies at their border to 'remove such malignant influences in them as would result from dangerous contact with the outside' (Hill 1948, 385). Thus, at the very point in a metaphorical or metaphysical journey when ways of being during here and now are destabilised, conscious social dictat orchestrates change.

The journey is always a symbol of the narrative where the fulfilment of conscious and subconscious purpose is always the result (Curtis and Pajaczkowska 1994, 198). The movement beyond liminality is literally a movement outside 'normal' spatial, temporal and cognitive realms. At the destination especially, time and space are less ordered, and displeasing aspects of mundane existence such as status related behaviour are quelled or quashed completely (hence 'getting away from it all'). For example, Bhardwaj (1973, 151–52) describes how caste distinctions melt away at Hindu shrines and Pilgrims of the lower orders can escape the limits of position and enjoy the freedom of the semblance of equality. This perhaps leads us nearer to answering specifically how journeys facilitate the reconfiguration of identity, since they suppress the 'norm' (structure) and familiarise the foreign (there, not-I and then). Ultimately, journeys reveal less restrained choice because experiences and thus knowledge formation are situated there rather than here. However, by its very nature *habitus* dialectically constrains and is constrained by experience, and thus agents' interpretations of postliminal events are never truly free. Encountering 'newness' demands comprehension and incorporation both into, and by, dialectics between agency and structure (Giddens 1984, 17). Thus, the moment abstraction from normality occurs is critical in how dimensions of agency and structure are specifically reconfigured, and may be central to how, when and why identity is reconstituted during journeys.

Pilgrimage as intensified journey

If travelling incurs a forum for the subconscious reconfiguration of identity, one can begin to appreciate how significant a journey might become if the explicit motivation for travel is pilgrimage. An 'outer' journey of physical and spatial mobility can function as a metaphor for the 'interior' journey of the soul, the mind or consciousness (Curtis and Pajaczkowska 1994, 200). Thus a religious quest for spiritual redemption takes the form of pilgrimages to 'special' places, and the transition to adulthood takes the form of a rite of passage such as leaving home. Davies (1988) has discussed many of the reasons pilgrims give for making their journeys. These include a desire to participate in gatherings, to educate oneself, to ensure safe passage to the afterlife, to ask specific favours including forgiveness and aid, to validate religious beliefs, to give thanks and to gain prestige and power upon return (Davies 1988, 6). Self-realisation away from the confines of village society may have also motivated pilgrims. In medieval Europe, 'a surprisingly large number of pilgrims seemed to have left their homes solely in order to deny their parish priest his monopoly over their spiritual welfare' (Sumption 1975, 76). Objects are also often sought out (e.g. relics) or acquired to materially symbolise the completed task (e.g. cockle shells at Compostela and conch shells at Rameshwaran). In nineteenth century Australia, for example, Aboriginal men occasionally ventured on quests for sacred shields from distant lands, lured by their 'magical power' (Helms 1988, 119). However, I argue that it is the emotive experience of the journey, culminating in rites at the destination, that constitutes the exercise, rather than the fulfilment of any intentions or the acquirement of material representations of it. It is the less explicit which is crucial to negotiating changes in identity and perception, and it is this emotive rather than literal aspect of the journey that is negotiated into long-term memory.

Raghubir Singh (1992) highlights the fundamentality of the emotive impact of the journey over material metonyms of it, or conscious achievements from it, in his discussion of pilgrimages to the Ganges River in northern India and Bangladesh. The geography of the Ganga interplays so acutely with Hindu origin beliefs that the mountains, the lakes and the celestial world beyond become synonymous with divinities, paradise and heaven. Just as the Kailas Mountain in the Himilayas mythically channels life forces into earth via the Ganga, so temples along its route symbolise and facilitate these nodes of connectedness with cosmology: 'As life developed along the Ganga and her sister streams, temples arose. They were modelled after Kailas. The river and the temple dissolve the boundary between heaven and earth' (Singh 1992, 10). Singh participates in numerous pilgrimages along the stretch of the Ganga, including to the mythical and actual sources of its four tributaries and to the various shrines along its banks. All are recalled as emotions, rather than as epic narratives, and specific experiences are highlighted above general movement. He talks of 'being tested' (Singh 1992, 11), and the mental strain of the journey seems ever apparent in his references to high altitudes, gorges, waterfalls, blizzards and recent deaths on route (Singh 1992, 13). Many of the experiences focus on nodes where here and there, now and then, 'I' and 'not-I' becomes ambiguous and indistinct. Whether these are communally discernible (i.e. temples, his dead father being 'fed' Ganga water) or otherwise (e.g. dreams, hallucinations, being under spells; Singh 1992, 13), they correspond to van Gennep's (1960) concept of liminality. These are periods or places in which normality becomes disentangled, and together they comprise, constitute and symbolise metaphorical and 'actual' transition. Where and when predictable and/or common, such liminal experiences can be formally structured (e.g. visits to temples, origin stories linked to place). However, when and where these liminal places and periods are less customary, they can be more open to personal, albeit still structurally-bound, interpretation. The test, the purification, the fasting, the movement, the consecration and the veneration all represent journeys, and are remembered through highly specific sights, smells, tactilities, sounds and tastes.

However, Singh's recollection is also based in the context of his society's beliefs and collective memory. By placing himself temporally and spatially within bodies of collective knowledge such as Hindu origin beliefs and the biography of the river, Singh (1992) contextualises and defines both his identity and the world in which he lives. Although one of his conscious aims seems to be becoming 'purified' (Singh 1992, 11), the journey yields more general implicit consequences. It facilitates his understanding and appreciation of one of the most fundamental questions of existence, 'why?', by enabling him to experience life at crucial junctures, designated by his society's doctrine. In these ways, the journey can both challenge and/or reinforce *habitus*. Newness is encountered, and this can be incorporated to augment institutional facts, or it can be destabilising and even capable of contradicting core elements of *habitus*. During this process of re-categorising and understanding life in the light of experiencing the unknown, how Singh (1992) conceives of himself is re-negotiated, bullied, imposed, requested and re-asserted. By structuring his personal experiences around the general ideology of the Ganga, he subconsciously negotiates between his instilled knowledge of who he is and should be, and the enlightenment his personal experience has given him. In this way, the emotive rather than literal experience is negotiated into long-term memory, and perceptions of self and life become inextricably linked to periods of liminality.

Rites of passage; spatial, temporal and mental dimensions of liminality: a consideration of the implication of metaphysical knowledges

Journeys associated with rites of passage have particular relevance to the renegotiation of identity. Indeed, journeys may incur rites of passage without ever being their explicit aim. However, by equating the physical journey with the mental one the process of transcendence can become explicit, and therefore regulated, through its symbolic rhetoric. Incorporating separation, transition and re-integration rites (van Gennep 1960, 11) with territorial passage ultimately familiarises, and therefore sanctifies, 'new' places since it is performance that constitutes taskscape as landscape embodied (Ingold 1993, 161–2). In this way, the threat of 'there' and 'not-I' would diminish, and the experience of travel would become increasingly choreographed through repeated return to places, times and mentalities perceived as liminal.

Thus the symbolism of initiation could become materialised in taskscape, and this has the potential to be archaeologically visible. For example, both Bradley (1993, 32) and Tilley (1994, 200–1) have suggested that the cursus monuments of Middle Neolithic Britain were used for processional rites connected to separation, transition and re-incorporation. In reference to the Dorset Cursus, Tilley argues that the monument formally structures the experience of the landscape by acting 'not only as a conduit of movement, but as a barrier blocking a less structured encounter with [nearby] barrows' (Tilley 1994, 199). By channelling movement, it may have operated as a route-way for the passage and purification of bones and bodies from the land of the living in the east, to the long barrows of the dead in the west (Tilley 1994, 200). In this way, linearity may have come to represent funerary rites and transition to death, and through the material actualisation of both metaphysical and metaphorical journeys, entrance into the 'unknown' may have become institutionalised, and therefore controlled.

Religion is fundamental to initiation because it thematically structures and contextualises specific rites (Cox 1992, 24). It is integral to the fabric of the process because, through its status as a body of difficult to dispute 'institutional facts' (Searle 1995) it validates the actions of its participants and the knowledge they imbue. Rites which negotiate transition between here/'I' and there/'not-I' are often situated in places associated in collective memory with hierophanies (symbols of the manifestation of the sacred into the profane e.g. the Christian Cross; Eliade 1959, 62–65). These places are therefore 'liminal' in the sense that they are perceived as intermediate, perhaps between terrestrial and celestial space, present and ancestral realms or childhood and adulthood. Pilgrimages, explicitly or implicitly initiatory in nature, are often made to such places.

The puberty rites (Bora) of the Kamilaroi people of Queensland, eastern Australia, involved the creation of a sacred area and isolation camp in the bush (Matthews 1895, 412). Neophytes (young men) were marched from their homes and forced to lie face down under a cover of leaves for many hours (the separation rite). In the midst of bull-roarers and sky-pointing, elders revealed the name and creation myths of the 'Great Master' Daramulun; information which was to remain concealed from women and the uninitiated (Matthews 1896, 320). A great journey to distant mountains ensued, punctuated by dances where 'medicine men cause[d] their magical influence to enter the novices, thus making them pleasing to Daramulun' (Matthews 1896, 320).

Upon arrival, novices set up camp, observing certain dietary and behavioural taboos, whilst the elders prepared and sanctified a scrub clearing. They then constructed two circles comprising of earth-cut banks and ditches. The larger of the two was roughly seventy feet in diameter, with a central pole topped with emu feathers. The second circle had two uprooted trees fixed centrally. A path was constructed connecting the two, along which were positioned various clay icons and painted figures representing Daramulun, mythical ancestors, animals and the twelve young men from Daramulun's first camp (Matthews 1895, 413). The initiates were brought along the path to the larger circle, forcibly looking only at the floor. Circumcision or tooth extraction then occurred, throughout which initiates were forbidden from flinching (van Gennep's transitional rites), and they were then told many secrets about Daramulun which they must never reveal to women or children (the reintegration rites). The group then stayed on site for several weeks, observing various behavioural taboos and performing dances and magical rites including burning the figurines (Matthews 1895, 414).

Throughout these rites, it is possible to observe a clear parallel between the metaphysical and the metaphorical journey. Travelling to the mountains represents the journey from the first circle (ignorance and childhood) to the second (enlightenment and adulthood). Along these paths is chaos (liminality), which is purified by rites (dancing), behavioural taboos (looking only at the ground), and the subsequent burning of iconography. Entrance to the second circle, and thus exiting liminality, was marked by pain, after which gradual re-incorporation took place. Thus, on multiple spatial and cognitive scales, the movement into and out of liminality (the bush on route, the path between the circles and the mountains connecting the terrestrial and celestial worlds) is controlled. Whilst both the explicit and implicit aim of this Kamilaroi Bora journey is the renegotiation of identity, there is also a manifestation of the 'familiarisation' of the unknown, the 'not-I' and ultimately the dangerous (cf. Hodder 1990). Without wishing to apply a simplistic model of social dynamics, there is an undeniable suppression of alternative agencies through the imposition of behavioural norms and the categorisation of spatial, temporal and cognitive states. Sustained connectedness to religion objectified the experience, but it is the materialisation of the symbolism that I believe is key to the process and the performance, and it is this symbolism that is potentially archaeologically accessible, particularly in the hierophany of the threshold.

Spatial boundaries between 'I', 'here' and 'now', and 'not I', 'there' and 'then', can be defined by visible (e.g. architectural) and invisible constructs (e.g. religious). They are usually distinguishable by the requirement of ritual protection beyond it, and the necessity for purification upon re-entry (Helms 1988, 30). Boundaries can be marked by stakes, upright stones or other recognised signs that are sometimes installed by rites of consecration and enforced by frontier deities, for example, the Greek god Hermes (van Gennep 1960, 15–6). Portals are however, the most common symbol of transition from 'here' and 'I' to 'there' and 'not-I', and they can be found on a variety of scales from the lintel beam of a door to the pass in a mountain ridge (van Gennep 1960, 19–20). One could tentatively suggest that portal iconography can be found across prehistoric Europe; for example the two stone outliers at Lissyvigeen stone circle and henge, Co. Cork, Ireland (Fig. 9.16). Such thresholds mark the boundaries between the familiar, profane and normal worlds and foreign, sacred and abnormal worlds in contemporary realities. In ethnographic examples, this 'neutral' or 'liminal' place is frequently subjected to, or utilised for, rites of transition (e.g. carrying a newly wed bride through the door of her new home). It is this symbol that brings us back to Graig Lwyd.

The journey to Graig Lwyd: an interpretation

Fundamentally, I believe not just that the place itself enhanced the perception of the axes extracted from it (Cooney 1998, 112), but that from the Mesolithic, Graig Lwyd was a focus of religious pilgrimage: a hierophany for the deity-driven emergence of order from chaos, and ultimately a liminal place which communed between here and there, 'I' and 'not-I', and the terrestrial and celestial. This was initially localised knowledge, but as seafarers journeying across the Irish Sea (Cummings 2004, 6) or across the North Wales track (Gresham and Irvine 1963, 55–56) picked up on these myths, Graig Lwyd became increasingly infamous. Its prominent cliff, vertical extraction face and alignment with the setting of the sun at midsummer when viewed from the south, caused Graig Lwyd to represent the end or start of a dangerous journey at the threshold to the land, sea and sky. It was a place where ancestral, spiritual, identity, spatial and temporal transgression, transmission and transition occurred.

Graig Lwyd became so perceptually focal in trips around the North Wales coast that by the Early Neolithic, a diversion was made from the track to the Aber estuary. Large erratics were initially used as sight lines, and during the Later Neolithic, dolerites were dragged from the nearby ridge to construct three stone circles roughly equidistant along the route way. Each stone in this dynamic landscape had its own unique biography and character in these creationist mythologies (cf. Gillings and Pollard 1999, 180).

From very early in Graig Lwyd's Neolithic history, axes were extracted and flaked on site (Williams *et al.* 1998, 19). It would be naïve to suggest that this liminal and sacred place also happened to have a seam of rock running through it 'possess(ing) a remarkable combination of physical properties not very unlike flint' (Hazzledine Warren 1922, 4). The flakable properties of this seam were recognised by experienced knappers early on in the history of localised journeys to the site. This amplified and consolidated the liminality of Graig Lwyd, since extracting stone from the earth was seen as 'providing contact with the spirit or ancestral world' (Cooney 1998, 110). This additional dimension to the site may have facilitated its durability in local collective memory, and was one cause of the expansion of the popularity of myths about the site which occurred during the Later Neolithic. Pilgrimages to this dangerous, transient place steeped in mythology would have been uplifting, life changing experiences that empowered visitors with esoteric knowledge to take home.

However, with heightening numbers of pilgrimages and associated extraction events, visits became increasingly choreographed and formalised with an emphasis on thresholds to and through the site. The earlier circles were built as nodes in a dangerous landscape, carefully located in positions where the future route to the west could not be viewed. Meini Hirion's portalled entrance and the later 'H' shaped detached avenue screen of Stones 280 both face westwards towards the extraction face itself, testifing to this emphasis on controlling visual and physical access to Graig Lwyd. Movement through each node, accompanied by rites and behavioural taboos, purified the recently crossed terrain between the circles and therefore allowed the opening up of visibility behind to the east. I have already demonstrated that the emotive dimension of pilgrimage can be the most empowering force for emancipating agency. Through newness, *habitus* can be challenged and personhood re-negotiated. By emplacing engagements with liminality firmly within recognisable religious imagery (i.e. the portal as a symbol of the hierophany), the process of re-negotiating identity and the cosmos can become imposed and bullied rather than self-driven. Thus, by the Early Bronze Age, the liminality of Graig Lwyd was deemed less potentially dangerous, which is why it is visible from most of the later monuments. It is at this time that axe extraction diminishes.

Following examples from ethnography (e.g. the Kamilaroi), the mechanism for asserting social norms during these visits may have been through the action of elders, although this is a fairly crude understanding of social dynamics and agency and is somewhat functionalistic. Bourdieu's 'structured dispositions' (i.e. material and societal constructs) are dialectically engaged with agency and institutional facts, and to unravel the three in assessing motivation is arguably impossible. Ultimately, those local or distant peoples who built the stone circles had a desire to familiarise and sanctify the foreign by regulating transcendence to it. The physical journey to, through and from the site was linked to a metaphorical transition of identity, and I argue that by the Late Neolithic pilgrimages to the site were explicitly initiatory in nature. The maturation to adulthood was facilitated through both the admission to this sacred place and the revealing of the secrets of axe manufacture. Associated facilitating rites of spatial, temporal and cognitive passage were performed under the architects' control, through the monumental thresholds in place. Towards the very end of the period in which axes were extracted from Graig Lwyd, human burials began to be emplaced in its vicinity. It is from this period that the two juvenile cremations found at Meini Hirion date, representing the bodies of those who did not survive to become initiated into this dying realm of creation myths, liminality and danger.

Implications; a conclusion

I hope I have illustrated why and how we should re-assess the generic role assumed of axe-factories and axes in British and Irish prehistory. Graig Lwyd may have been a focus for pilgrimage: a site offering a diverse spectrum of meanings to the many visitors it attracted, and continues to draw. Its monuments undoubtedly orchestrate engagement with the innumerable experiences on offer, whenever they occurred. Its axes may have drawn equally as unique initial meanings from these journeys and the hands involved in their creation, and some may have retained a souvenir-like quality linked to their conception for the rest of their lives. Graig Lwyd may have been viewed as a sacred and dangerous place: a threshold to distant worlds, knowledges and ways of being that could yield spiritual and personal enlightenment, in an albeit increasingly pre-determined manner.

Other 'axe factories' and 'axes', 'places' and 'material cultures' of the Later Neolithic and Early Bronze Age may have been similarly discursively linked to ideas of liminality, unfamiliarity and metaphysical knowledges. For example, both the curvilinear rock art (commonly linked to altered states of consciousness) and architectural emphasis of thresholds evident in many Irish Sea and Scottish Late Neolithic and Early Bronze Age passage tombs could have been material conveyors of transgressions into and out of unknown worlds. Rites of passage were probably also performed at these tombs, and it is likely that at least some of these were associated with death prior to the interment of bodies. The threshold and spiral symbols may have formalised experiences with unfamiliar and/or taboo aspects of mortuary journeys, reinforcing the categorisation of the unknown and known in worldviews and effectively making-safe on-site activities.

However, I argue that passage grave architecture and its constituent symbolism were rather than the medium focus of rites performed there. The taskscape setting of some of these constructs may have prompted the transcendental status of on-site performances, or more likely this was derived from narratives and ways of being associated with monuments in a manner which is inaccessible to us now. Similarities in monument and hierophany form (e.g. passage grave, stone circle, threshold, pecked spiral) were therefore not necessarily as significant to their meaning as one might assume. Each engagement, material construct and agent had a unique and socially embedded flavour which cannot be presumed from the significance placed on form in the present. We must accept that just as different passage graves probably shared very few universal connotations to its prehistoric visitors, Graig Lwyd has and continues to represent innumerable definitions depending on the context of its interactions. Thus, whilst some of the experiences manifested through these monuments and symbols would have shared similarities and significances, others most certainly would not.

Ultimately, whether the conceptual dichotomies, themes and social dynamics I have outlined hold true at Graig Lwyd, or at any other place, time or way of being is neither particularly relevant nor conceptually resolvable. What matters is the re-incorporation of places, materialities and people as active agents living through real and dynamic taskscapes and world-views.

Acknowledgements

I am grateful to Alasdair Whittle for his assistance and perseverance, Vicki Cummings for giving me this opportunity, and my father for carrying all the equipment on one of my visits.

Bibliography

Appadurai, A. (ed.) 1986. *The social life of things: commodities in cultural perspective.* Cambridge: Cambridge University Press.

Barrett, J.C. 2001. Agency, the duality of structure and the problem of the archaeological record. In I. Hodder (ed.), *Archaeological theory today*, 141–64. Cambridge: Polity Press.

Bhardwaj, S.M. 1973. *Hindu places of pilgrimage in India.* Berkeley: University of California Press.

Bourdieu, P. 1977. *An outline of a theory of practice.* Cambridge: Cambridge University Press.

Bradley, R. 1993. *Altering the earth: the origins of monuments in Britain and continental Europe.* Edinburgh: Society of Antiquaries of Scotland Monograph 8.

Bradley, R. 2000. *An archaeology of natural places.* London: Routledge.

Bradley, R. and Edmonds, M. 1993. *Interpreting the axe trade: production and exchange in Neolithic Britain.* Cambridge: Cambridge University Press.

Burl, A. 1976. *The stone circles of the British Isles.* Yale: Yale University Press.

Burl, A. 1993. *From Carnac to Callanish: the prehistoric stone rows and avenues of Brittany, Ireland and Britain.* Yale: Yale University Press.

Burl, A. 1995. *A guide to the stone circles of Britain, Ireland and Brittany.* Yale: Yale University Press.

Childe, V.G. 1958. *The prehistory of European society.* Harmondsworth: Penguin.

Clark, J.G.D 1952. *Prehistoric Europe: the economic basis.* Methuen: London.

Clarke, D.L. 1968. *Analytical archaeology.* Methuen: London.

Coles, B. and Coles, J. 1986. *From Sweet Track to Glastonbury.* London: Thames and Hudson.

Cooney, G. 1998. Breaking stones, making place: the social landscape of axe production sites. In A. Gibson and D. Simpson (eds), *Prehistoric ritual and religion,* 108–18. Stroud: Sutton.

Cooney, G. 2002. So many shades of rock: colour symbolism and Irish stone axeheads. In A. Jones and G. MacGregor (eds), *Colouring the past: the significance of colour in archaeological research*, 93–107. Oxford: Berg.

Cox, J.L. 1992. *Expressing the sacred: an introduction to the phenomenology of religion.* Harere: University of Zimbabwe Publications.

Cummings, V. 2004. Connecting the mountains and sea: the monuments of the eastern Irish Sea zone. In V. Cummings and C. Fowler (eds), *The Neolithic of the Irish Sea: materiality and traditions of practice*, 29–36. Oxford: Oxbow.

Curtis, B. and Pajaczkowska, C. 1994. 'Getting there': travel, time and narrative. In G. Robertson, M. Mash, L. Tickner, J. Bird, B. Curtis and T. Putnam (eds), *Travellers' tales: narratives of home and displacement*, 198–215. London: Routledge.

Darvill, T. 1987. *Prehistoric Britain*. London: Routledge.

David, A. and Williams, G. 1995. Stone axe-head manufacture: new evidence from the Preseli Hills, West Wales. *Proceedings of the Prehistoric Society* 61, 433–60.

Davies, J.G. 1988. *Pilgrimage yesterday and today*. London: SCM Press.

Douglas, M. 1966. *Purity and danger*. London: Routledge.

Durkheim, E. 1915. *The elementary forms of religious life*. London: Allen and Unwin.

Edmonds, M. 1995. *Stone tools and society*. London: Batsford.

Edmonds, M. 1998. Sermons in stone: identity, value and stone tools in Later Neolithic Britain. In M. Edmonds and C. Richards (eds), *Understanding the Neolithic of north-western Europe*, 248–75. Glasgow: Cruithne Press.

Edmonds, M. 1999. *Ancestral geographies of the Neolithic: landscapes, monuments and memory*. London: Routledge.

Eliade, M. 1959. *The sacred and the profane: the nature of religion*. London: Harcourt Brace Jovanovich.

Fleming, A. 1999. Phenomenology and the megaliths of Wales: a dreaming too far? *Oxford Journal of Archaeology* 18, 119–25.

Giddens, A. 1979. *Capitalism and modern social theory*. Cambridge: Cambridge University Press.

Giddens, A. 1984. *The constitution of society*. Cambridge: Polity Press.

Gillings, M. and Pollard, J. 1999. Non-portable stone artefacts and contexts of meaning: the tale of Grey Wether (www.museums.ncl.ac.uk/Avebury/ stone4.htm). *World Archaeology* 31, 179–93.

Gosden, C. and Marshall, Y. 1999. The cultural biography of things. *World Archaeology* 31, 169–78.

Gresham, C.A and Irvine, H.C. 1963. Prehistoric routeways across north Wales. *Antiquity* 37, 54–58.

Griffiths, W.E. 1960. The excavation of the stone circles near Penmaenmawr, North Wales. *Proceedings of the Prehistoric Society* 16, 303–39.

Hazzledine Warren, S. 1922. The Neolithic stone axes of Graig Lwyd, Penmaenmawr. *Archaeologia Cambrensis* 77, 1–34.

Helms, M.W. 1988. *Ulysses' sail: an ethnographic odyssey of power, knowledge and geographical distance*. Princeton: Princeton University Press.

Hill, W.W. 1948. Navajo trading and trading rituals: a study of cultural dynamics. *SW Journal of Anthropology* 4, 371–96.

Hodder, I. 1982. *Symbols in action: ethnoarchaeological studies of material culture*. Cambridge: Cambridge University Press.

Hodder, I. 1990. *The domestication of Europe*. Oxford: Blackwell.

Hodder, I. 1992. *Theory and practice in archaeology*. London: Routledge.

Hodder, I. and Orton, C. 1976. *Spatial analysis in archaeology*. Cambridge: Cambridge University Press.

Ingold, T. 1993. The temporality of the landscape. *World Archaeology* 25, 152–75.

Lichtenberg-Ettinger, B. 1994. The becoming thresholds of matrixial borderlines. In G. Robertson, M. Mash, L. Tickner, J. Bird, B. Curtis and T. Putnam (eds), *Travellers' tales: narratives of home and displacement*, 38–62. London: Routledge.

Lynch, F., Aldhouse-Green, S. and Davies, J.L. 2000. *Prehistoric Wales*. Stroud: Sutton.

Matthews, R.H. 1895. The Bora, or initiation ceremony of the Kamilaroi tribe. *Journal of the Royal Anthropological Institute* 14, 411–27.

Matthews, R.H. 1896. The Bora of the Kamilaroi tribes. *Proceedings of the Royal Society of Victoria* 9, 137–73.

Mauss, M. 1954. *The gift: forms and functions of exchange in archaic societies*. London: Cohen and West.

Patton, M. 1993. *Statements in stone: monuments and society in Neolithic Brittany*. London: Routledge.

Peterson, R. G. 1999. *The construction and use of categories of Neolithic pottery from Wales: volumes 1 and 2*. University of Southampton: Unpublished PhD thesis.

Pétrequin, P., Pétrequin, A-M., Jeudy, F., Jeunesse, C., Monnier, J-L., Pelegrin, J. amd Praud, I. 1998. From the raw material to the Neolithic stone axe: production processes and social context. In M. Edmonds and C. Richards (eds), *Understanding the Neolithic of north-western Europe*, 277–312. Glasgow: Cruithne Press.

Ray, K. 2004. Axes, kula and things that were 'good to think' in the Neolithic of the Irish Sea. In V. Cummings and C. Fowler (eds), *The Neolithic of the Irish Sea: materiality and traditions of practice*, 160–73. London: Routledge.

Renfrew, C. 1973. Monuments, mobilisation and social organisation in Neolithic Wessex. In C. Renfrew (ed.), *The explanation of culture change*, 539–58. London: Longman.

Renfrew, C. 1986. Introduction: peer polity interaction and socio-political change. In C. Renfrew and J.F. Cherry (eds), *Peer polity interaction and socio-political change*, 1–18. Cambridge: Cambridge University Press.

Robertson, G. 1994. As the world turns: introduction. In G. Robertson, M. Mash, L. Tickner, J. Bird, B. Curtis and T. Putnam (eds), *Travellers' tales: narratives of home and displacement*, 1–6. London: Routledge.

Royal Commission on Ancient and Historical Monuments in Wales 1956. *An inventory of the ancient monuments in Caernarvonshire, volume 1: east*. HMSO: London.

Rudebeck, E. 1998. Flint extraction, axe offering and the value of the cortex. In M. Edmonds and C. Richards (eds), *Understanding the Neolithic of north-western Europe*, 312–28. Glasgow: Cruithne Press.

Sahlins, M.D. 1981. *Historical metaphors and mythical realities: structures in the early history of the Sandwich Islands kingdom*. New York: Aldine.

Searle, J. 1995. *The construction of social reality*. Harmondsworth: Allen Lane.

Sherratt, A. 1997. *Economy and society in prehistoric Europe: changing perspectives*. Edinburgh: Edinburgh University Press.

Singh, R. 1992. *The Ganges*. London: Thames and Hudson.

Skeates, R. 1995. Animate objects: a biography of prehistoric 'axe-amulets' in the central Mediterranean region. *Proceedings of the Prehistoric Society* 61, 279–301.

Sumption, J. 1975. *Pilgrimage: an image of medieval religion*. Totowa: Rowman and Littlefield.

Thomas, J. 1991. *Rethinking the Neolithic*. Cambridge: Cambridge University Press.

Thomas, J. 2001. Archaeologies of place and landscape. In I. Hodder (ed.), *Archaeological theory today*, 165–84. Cambridge: Polity Press.

Tilley, C. 1994. *A phenomenology of landscape: places, paths and monuments*. Oxford: Berg.

van Gennep, A. 1960 (1909). *The rites of passage*, trans. M.B. Vizedom and G.L. Caffe. Chicago: University of Chicago Press.

Whittle, A. 1995. Gifts from the earth: symbolic dimensions of the use and production of Neolithic flint and stone axes. *Archaeologia Polona* 33, 247–59.

Whittle, A. 1997. Moving on and around: Neolithic settlement mobility. In T. Darvill (ed.), *Neolithic landscapes: Neolithic Studies Group Seminar Papers 2,* 15–22. Oxford: Oxbow.

Williams, J.L., Davidson, A., Flook, R., Jenkins, D.A., Muckle, P., and Roberts, T. 1998. Survey and excavation at the Graig Lwyd axe-factory, Penmaenmawr. *Archaeology in Wales* 38, 3–21.

10 Short journeys, long distance thinking

John Roberts

Forecast

During the first fortnight of May 1958 the weather at Waun Llanfair, an area of upland moorland above Penmaenmawr on the north coast of Wales, was 'extremely bad'. So W.E. Griffiths (1960, 305) informs us in his account of the excavation of a number of stone circles at Cefn Coch, at the north edge of Waun Llanfair. In thinking about the relationship between the sites he was working on and the numerous cairns and standing stones in the wider area, Griffiths invokes journeys along trackways between and past them. I wonder if his experience of walking to site on a cold, damp morning and spending the day in sodden clothing may have influenced him to think about the impact of the weather on his prehistoric subjects and their journeying when he ended his discussion with the comment that the position of two standing stones 'must surely have been intended to mark the head of the pass in misty weather and to assure the weary traveller that he had chosen the correct exit from the high ground' (Griffiths 1960, 334).

I have spent quite a bit of time at Waun Llanfair as part of broader research into monuments, landscape and society in the third and second millennia BC of north-west Wales, and can sympathise with Griffiths' experience of the weather. However, I am unconvinced by his image of a weary prehistoric traveller crossing an inhospitable area and relying on way-markers. Is this an appropriate way of thinking about the way people moved through this upland district, and does it provide a useful context for understanding the construction of monuments and their locations? The prehistoric traveller seems to have rather a lot in common with a modern rambler or outdoor pursuits enthusiast, furnished with an Ordnance Survey map and perhaps a copy of Poucher's (1962) popular guide to the Welsh hills.

The prehistoric trackways at Waun Llanfair and Moel Goedog

Waun Llanfair is a moorland plateau covering *c.* 8km^2 between the Llanfairfechan and Conwy valleys and stretching 3km from the outcrops of Graig Lwyd and Penmaenmawr stone above the north coast to the peaks and ridges of Tal y Fan and Foel Lwyd, behind which the higher peaks of the Carneddau massif rise to the south.

There are a number of monuments of iconic status within the archaeology of the Neolithic and Bronze Age in the area: an axe 'quarry' (Graig Lwyd and its associated outcrops, Williams and Davidson 1998), and the Cefn Coch complex of 'ceremonial' and 'funerary' monuments, which includes an embanked stone circle, a ring cairn – both investigated by Griffiths – and a number of large barrow cairns (Griffiths 19600. There is also a plethora of smaller monuments, so-called 'cairn variants', with forms ranging from simple stone piles to those with slab-lined cists, rings of edge/end set stones, platformed interiors and kerbing.

Griffiths' work is an exercise in landscape archaeology in that he dedicates a good chunk of the paper to a discussion of the broader context of the excavated sites. He noted that the embanked stone circle, known as the 'Druid's Circle', is flattened at its northern part where it respects a trackway, implying that the trackway predates the circle. The direction of approach to the circle may also have been carefully orchestrated, as it is positioned so as to only be visible on approach from the east, where it forms a striking presence outlined against the sky. Finally, the monuments at Cefn Coch form only one element in a series of linear monument distributions 'clearly related to the existence of east-west routes across the hills' and to possible cross-tracks connecting these two main routes (Griffiths 1960, 333; Fig. 10.1).

Griffiths is explicit about who is moving along these routes and why: 'Bronze Age travellers, and traders bringing gold and copper from Ireland, crossed the north Caernarvonshire [sic] hills and gained the Conway [sic] valley while avoiding the precipitous headlands of Penmaenmawr and Penmaenbach' (Griffiths 1960, 333). He went on to interpret the artefacts as evidence of cultural contact between indigenous 'food-vessel societies' and the

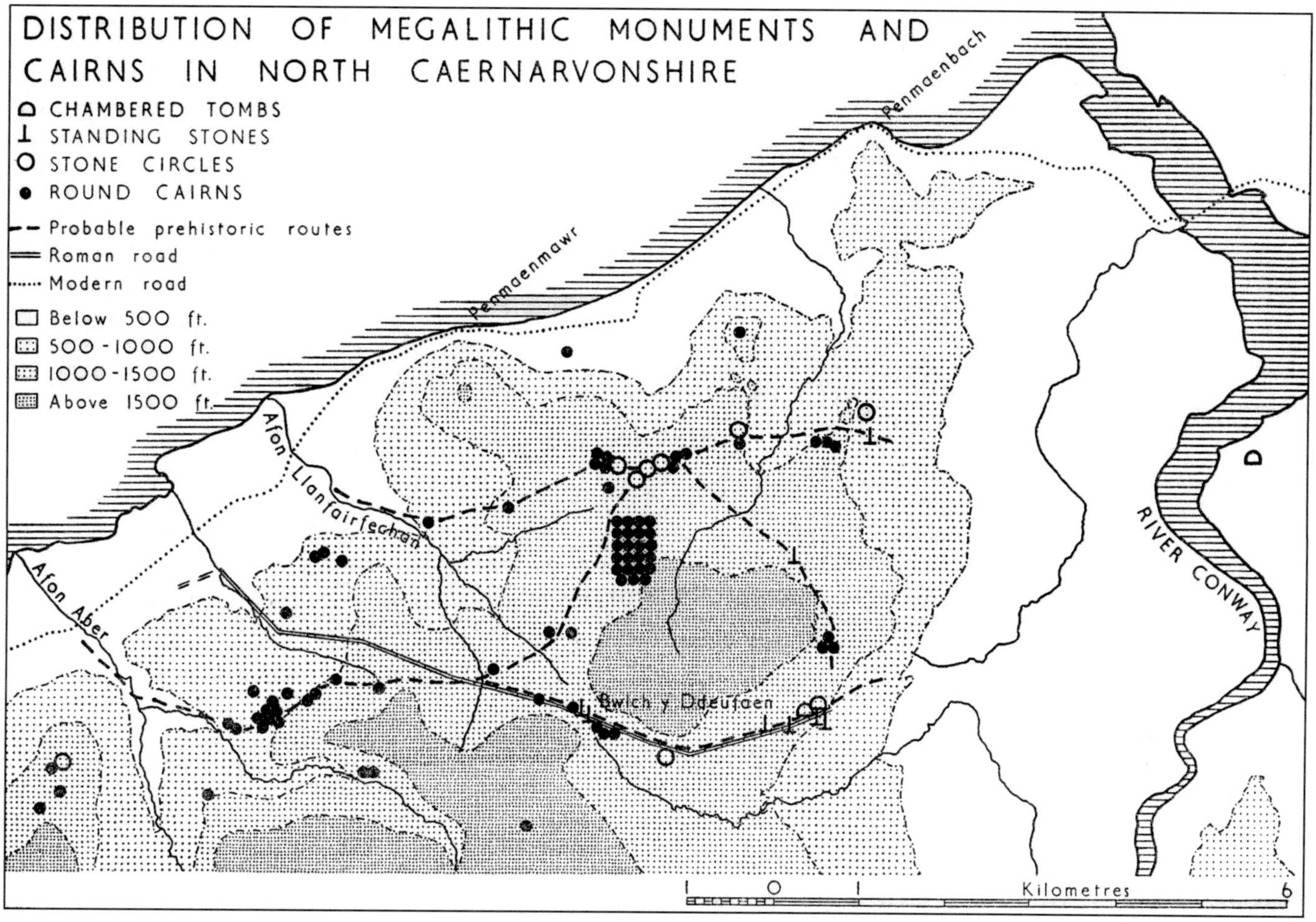

Fig. 10.1. Monuments and trackways (Reproduced from Griffiths 1960)

distant 'Wessex Culture', and the trackways themselves as migration and trade routes controlled by Wessex chieftains. These ideas are couched in the prevalent culture-historical discourse of the time and it seems glib to criticise them from today's perspectives. Nonetheless, it is interesting to see how Griffiths ties the trackways and the monuments into a sense of the district as remote and hostile, an area crossed through necessity rather than by desire. If people linger at all they only seem to do so at the monuments themselves for the esoteric purposes of the ceremonial activities carried out there.

A number of other prehistoric trackways have been identified or imputed in north Wales and the Marches, including those discussed by Bowen and Gresham (1967), Chitty (1963), Gresham and Irvine (1963) and Lynch (1984). The most recent of these, by Frances Lynch, concerns the excavation of a ring cairn, Moel Goedog Circle 1, in the mountains above and to the east of Harlech. Lynch introduces the 'Ardudwy trackway' in her discussion of the landscape setting of the site and its relationship to other monuments (cairns of various kinds and standing stones). The track is marked by cairns and standing stones, and as with Waun Llanfair, there is good evidence with which to argue that the monuments were meant to be approached from a particular direction. Moel Goedog 1, for instance, is one of a pair of ring cairns located a short distance apart either side of the trackway. Despite their proximity, the ring cairns are not intervisible, and they are each only visible on approach along the track from opposite directions (when moving south and north for Circles 1 and 2 respectively; Lynch 1984, 10). Bryn Cader Faner, a cairn further north along the trackway, has a ring of tall slabs set radiating outwards around its edge and is positioned on the side of a hill such that it forms a dramatic silhouette when approached from the south, but is invisible on approach from the north (Lynch 1984, 36).

An important and interesting feature of Moel Goedog 1 is the presence of soil of foreign origin adhering to bone in two of the pits at the site. Heavy mineral analysis indicated that the soil may derive from an area close to the coast several miles to the south, and one interpretation of this is that the bone was dug up from a lowland context and reburied in the ring cairn (Lynch 1984, 28). For Lynch, the suggestion of reburial, together with the clustering of architecturally elaborate monuments at two key points along the trackway indicates that the 'high ground above Harlech may have been an area of special importance to the Bronze Age population of Ardudwy' (Lynch 1984, 34), and that the monuments may be related 'to a population who were living at some distance away from them, although they may have been using the surrounding ground for grazing' (Lynch 1984, 36). There is more ambiguity over the possible identities and motivations of the people moving along the trackway in her account: they are abstract and undifferentiated travellers, and it is unclear whether they are, for example, locals or outsiders, or are engaged in short or long journeys.

Lynch's account draws on the by then familiar concept of prehistoric trackways (specifically, Bowen and Gresham 1967), but it arises out of a different interpretive milieu to the culture-historical perspectives of earlier work. Her account of the trackway and the monuments is unusual in that she shows an awareness of the different scales over which people move, and that there might be a tension between those travelling from afar attracted by the 'ritual landscape', and those who built the monuments and whose animals grazed the upland pastures. However, while Lynch may have revealed these tensions, they effectively exist as contradictions in her argument. On the one hand, there is a sense (as there is in Griffiths' discussion of Waun Llanfair) of this upland area as hostile and remote, somehow beyond the margins of usual experience – it is described as 'beautiful but inhospitable' and it is concluded that a key quality of the place might be as a distant burial ground or ceremonial centre (Lynch 1984, 36). On the other hand, it was also the context for upland grazing, a subsistence practice that would imply occupation and familiarity. There is an apparent opposition between connotations of distant-as-valued and local-as-mundane. This leads to a second contradiction, between linearity of movement along the trackway by 'travellers', and the diffused patterns of movement which would presumably accompany organised grazing. Linear movement along trackways implies journeys *through* the area whilst grazing implies journeys *around/within* it.

Distance and linearity: a short critique

I do not intend to deny that linear routes such as trackways existed in prehistory; both Griffiths and Lynch detail strong evidence for deliberately structured linear movement through upland areas. Yet, the tensions concerning the relationships between trackways, monuments and society that are observed in the above examples perpetuate a sense of the uplands as distant and remote (for example, as inhospitable or as ritual 'sanctuaries') removed from the world of everyday experience.

It has already been noted that Griffiths' travellers' obsession with their destination appears to have a lot in common with a twentieth century rambler/walker. But Griffiths was not alone in adopting this uncritical perspective. In the concluding section of *Life and death in the Bronze Age*, Sir Cyril Fox evokes journeys between monuments that are just as unconvincing to the modern reader as are Griffiths' travellers (Fox 1959). Here, Bronze Age elites on horseback travel long distances between ceremonial events much like the aristocrats of the eighteenth century touring between each others' country properties to admire and be seen in the right place with the right company (Fox 1959, 185). Placing undue emphasis on notions of linear movement *towards* a particular destination or *between* significant places draws in part on an anachronistic (modernist) perception of travel. Ingold (2004) describes this as 'destination oriented travel'; a set of novel spatial practices, such as aristocratic movement between places by carriage, emerging out of the Enlightenment. In contrast to movement in and around the terrain (particularly movement on foot as part of everyday practices), linear travel closes the gap between embarkation and destination and so collapses interest in the specificity and local context of the places being traversed.

These places were in some respects distanced still further from the everyday lives of those using the trackways by their characterisation as marginal and inhospitable. The attribution of the label marginal to prehistoric upland Britain has been challenged by a number of authors, based on a lack of evidence for economic fragility and abandonment of the landscape in times of environmental stress, together with a theoretical critique of a universal concept of 'marginality' (e.g. Tipping 2002; Young and Symonds 1995). It is especially important to question these assumptions in the context of Welsh prehistory as not only is much of Wales, particularly the north-west, upland in character, but the shadow of Fox's 'personality' of the 'highland zone' persists (Fox 1932). Older syntheses of Welsh prehistory draw directly on Fox's value-laden 'rule' (e.g. Grimes 1951, 112; Savory 1965, 71) concerning cultural conservatism in which stimuli for social change are invariably a result of external influence. The most recent synthesis (Lynch *et al.* 2000) retains some of these connotations of conservatism, and of the dominance of distant influences, which one could describe in terms of the shifting 'Irish-ness' and 'English-ness' of Welsh prehistory. This is not to say that things and ideas from distant places were not a feature of Wales during the third and second millennia BC, but rather that Wales' prehistoric inhabitants should not be seen as backward or passive recipients of distant influence.

At a smaller scale than the distinction between upland and lowland, we can see in Griffiths' and Lynch's accounts a spatial and temporal separation of ritual and routine, whereby the monuments form part of ceremonial centres in the landscape. The possible context for people's presence in the area, namely organised grazing, is contradicted by notions of the district as a place remote from society and the world of the everyday. However, it is unlikely that 'ritual' and 'rational' were held apart in the kinds of small scale societies characteristic of the third and second millennia BC in the way that they are seperated in the west today (Bradley 2005; Brück 1999a). This does not mean that places were special in spite of their likely use for practical activities such as grazing, but that they were important precisely because of them.

This perception of the uplands as set apart from everyday life is also to be found in some of the most recent interpretations of Neolithic and Bronze Age monuments. In *The significance of monuments*, Bradley links the creation and elaboration of stone circles and other monuments in upland areas to the occupation of newly open landscapes (Bradley 1998, 129–30). This allowed greater integration of monuments and the wider world because of the opportunities to construct visual linkages between monuments across considerable distances, and with astronomical alignments in areas with strong topographical variation. However, whilst Bradley claims that this is an increasingly 'settled' landscape, we get very little sense of the practical context of people's presence. In fact, despite the differences in their theoretical positions, Lynch (1984) and Bradley (1998) reproduce some similar assumptions about the relationship between monuments, landscape and routine practice. These are 'ritual' landscapes set apart from the everyday. The practical context for people's presence in the uplands, whether grazing or 'settlement', is taken for granted. Again, there is a sense of distant-as-important and local-as-mundane. This is problematic in terms of perceptions of upland areas as 'other' places removed/detached from everyday experience. The importance of the place appears to be derived from things that happen elsewhere.

Local and distant at Waun Llanfair

It is possible, therefore, to identify a variety of reasons why the interpretation of Waun Llanfair – and also, by implication, Moel Goedog and the 'Ardudwy trackway' – is problematic. I wish to suggest an alternative model for the prehistory of Waun Llanfair during the third and second millennia BC. It takes some of the elements of extant interpretations but recasts them within a discussion of the shifting balance of 'local' and 'distant' resources (practical and symbolic) in mediating social relationships. Above all, it focuses on the reworking of the relationship between people and land.

The Neolithic stone source of Graig Lwyd forms the starting point for the model; an outcrop in a dramatic upland setting, whose products – mainly polished stone axes – were arguably imbued with qualities of the distant and exotic. The potential relationship between Graig Lwyd and the Cefn Coch monuments is downplayed by Griffiths. Despite finds of Graig Lwyd material made during the excavation at the Druid's Circle (a rough out, axe fragments and a number of flakes albeit in stratigraphically ambiguous contexts and interpreted as residual), he comments that '[t]he necropolis that thus arose on the plateau behind Graig Lwyd...had no connection with the defunct stone-axe industry' (Griffiths 1960, 332). However, more recent work on stone circles suggests earlier dates than previously suspected with many of the monuments originating in the Late Neolithic (Bradley 1998, 129). While at Graig Lwyd itself, an axe was found beneath a small, simple cairn on land close to the stone source (Williams and Davidson 1998, 18–9). This argument is strengthened still further by the recent discovery of an unusual narrow flaked axe/pick and several flakes of Graig Lwyd stone, along with a large flint flake, serrated blade and oblique arrow head (minus tip), beneath one of the small cairns at the north-east edge of a large peaty basin at the west side of Waun Llanfair, which is known locally as Padall Llanfair (G. Smith *pers. comm.*). This might suggest that the activities associated with visits to the stone source were not limited to the immediate vicinity of the source but spread across the moorland plateau of Waun Llanfair.

This evidence makes it possible to argue that acts of quarrying were probably implicated in reworking the relationship between people and land on a local basis. Persistent associations between family/extended kin groups and certain places may have been established in the Neolithic in the context of stone procurement. By the Late Neolithic and into the Early Bronze Age, these associations were reworked as open spaces were occupied within the routines of organised grazing – there is pollen evidence for an increasingly open environment in north Wales at this time (Caseldine *et al.* 2001). Residential mobility need not imply that these populations were entirely mobile, but that dwelling was constituted by a range of practices rather than by the enduring occupation of, for example, permanent 'homes'(Brück 1999b; Edmonds 1999; Whittle 2003). People's presence in these upland areas may have been seasonal but it was not necessarily defined in relation to a permanent lowland base. Rather than being ancillary to lowland locations, for part of the year at least, upland pastures may have become the key sites of occupation.

A network of paths and places is likely to have been created through both human and non-human reworking of the landscape, for example, through the movement of stock along habitual routes. The appearance of monuments could be interpreted as the formalisation of patterns of movement to and from the stone source in the Late Neolithic/Early Bronze Age, with the construction of circular ceremonial monuments drawing on the significance of the stone source and acting as gathering places and arenas for formalised ritual action. Griffiths' stylised depiction of the cairn 'cemetery' at Waun Llanfair, south of the monument complex at Cefn Coch is at the expense of recognising other possible patterns of movement (Fig. 10.1). The complex and localised settings of these monuments that one becomes aware of on walking around the area refutes any sense of linearity. They seem instead to be set in clusters around Padall Llanfair. Smith (2002, 27–9) identifies these clusters as possible occupation areas consisting of fairly regular associations between cairn(s)/cairn variant, platforms (for buildings or other structures), burnt stone mounds and in some cases, lengths of patchy wall footings (Fig. 10.2). Their distribution suggests non-linear journeys and a sense of 'going around' the area (cf. Gray 1999) in contrast to the 'destination oriented' movements suggested by Griffiths' (admittedly large scale) plan. The clusters of sites may be related to the establishment of 'stints', grazing areas with persistent associations with a herd. These smaller monuments, in particular, may have been the focus for small-scale, ongoing funerary and ceremonial activities and have been bound up with the constant reworking of relationships between kin which might be expected to have underpinned tenurial relations.

This model may swing too far towards considering the non-linear distributions of monuments at Waun Llanfair and away from the larger sites at Cefn Coch. What might these larger monuments and the trackway with which they appear to be associated represent in terms of the preceding discussion? The larger size of the Cefn Coch monuments would suggest that they were intended for larger audiences/groups. However, rather than gatherings of people in remote places with distant associations, might they relate to small kin groups and their herds coming together at significant points in the herding calendar, such as at the start of grazing during the opening up of seasonal pastures, or at the end of the seasonal cycle to mark closure of the pastures?

In their discussion of Nuristani calendrical time and its relationship with herding practices, Edelberg and Jones (1979, 91–8) note that while cultivation imposes a fairly rigid set of thresholds onto the annual cycle, the timings of practices associated with grazing have to be carefully constructed, measured and maintained. Whilst key dates such as the beginning and ending of the grazing season are similar across a wide area, the length (and even the number) of calendar months within the summer grazing period varies locally as the months inform the length of time herds will stay in any one pasture/part of a pasture system, and this in itself is dependent on the size and qualities of that place. Ceremonial monuments of British prehistory during the third and second millennia BC frequently have astronomically significant alignments, and one wonders whether the complex arrangements of calendrical time within seasonal grazing regimes as outlined above establish a possible context for activities at some of these monuments.

By the Early Bronze Age, a few of the monuments at Cefn Coch were the focus for the deposition of cremated human bone, pottery vessels and charcoal. This has been interpreted elsewhere in Britain as a process whereby open monuments which had once served wide communities were closed off or appropriated for the burials of a restricted section of the population, as part of strategies to legitimise social authority and claims to power (Bradley 1998). I am not convinced that these ideas apply here. For Lynch (1984, 29 quoting Griffiths 1960, 335–6), the small quantities of bone (incomplete individuals) present in the Druid's Circle cremations and the fact that those identifiable were of children are indicative of 'token' deposits. Similar examples of partiality and of the reworking of burials can be observed at other excavated monuments in north Wales (see for example Lynch 1991, 145–208; 1993). The sense here is of plasticity, play and ongoing activity rather than stability and closure. Others have suggested that prehistoric monuments should be interpreted as projects where social identities are in a constant state of emergence out of the activities conducted at them (see McFadyen 2003 for discussion of this point in the context of Neolithic monuments).

Rather than envisaging an inevitable accumulation of power through the appropriation of monuments during the earlier Bronze Age, ongoing activities at, and changes to the form of, monuments may have served to sustain a set of tenurial relations and occupational practices bound up with pasturing that remained very stable over a long period of time. Distant material and symbolic resources (including monumental architecture, pot forms, burial practices and grave goods) clearly did feature during this period at Waun Llanfair and across upland north Wales more widely, but these were bound into fundamentally localised discourses.

The end of the monumental sequence was not dependent upon environmental catastrophe or the appropriation of monuments by social elites, but came when local monuments and the activities carried out at them no longer played an active role in sustaining local tenurial relations. This is not to say that the subsistence context of Waun Llanfair changed. Indeed it is likely that it was still exploited for seasonal pasture. But tenurial arrangements concerning people's presence there and its use were now established somewhere else. In the balance of

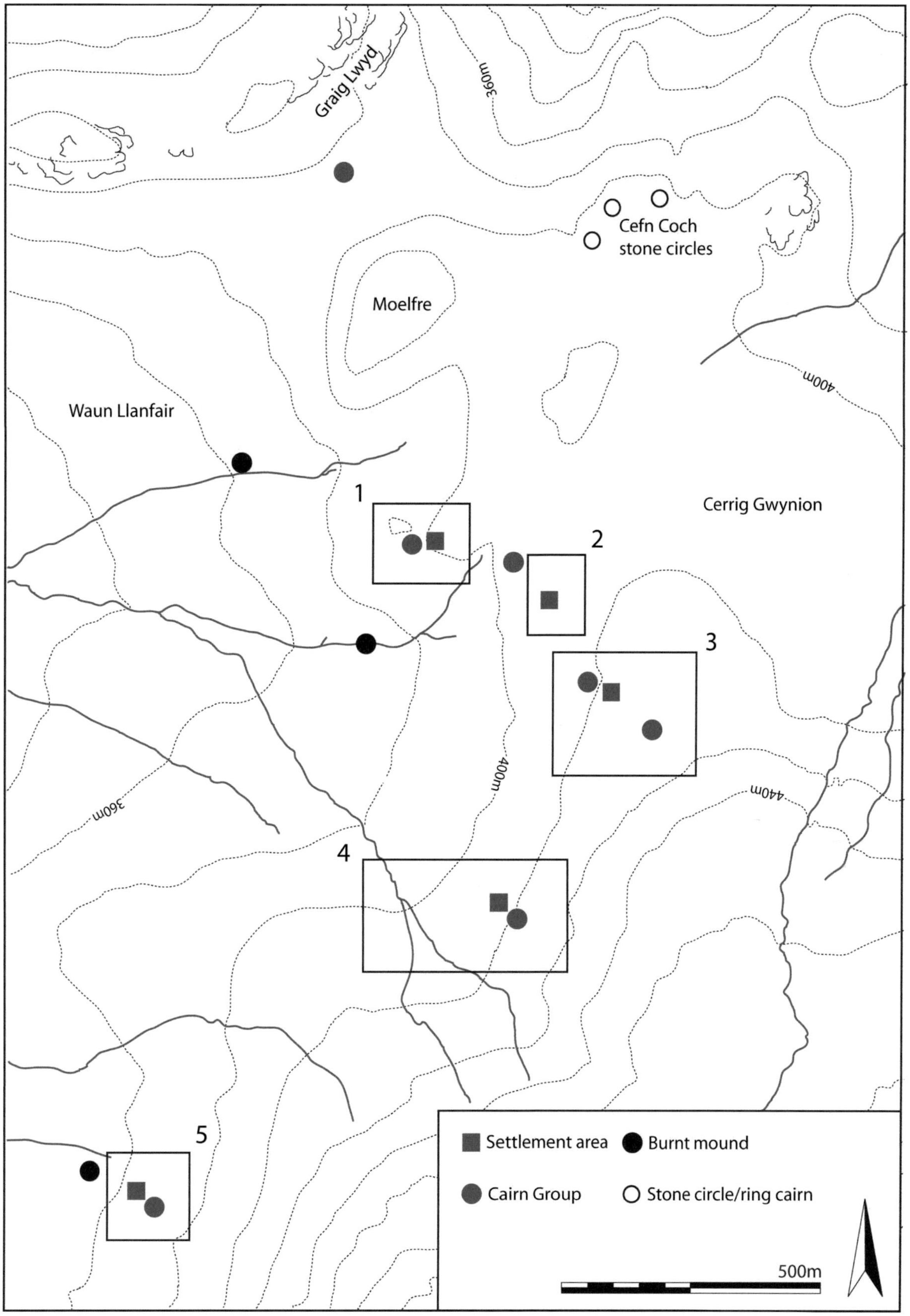

Fig. 10.2. Monument clusters (after Smith 2002)

notions of local and distant, Waun Llanfair had become 'elsewhere'.

Conclusion

This paper has investigated a series of tensions between 'local' and 'distant' inherent within the idea of a journey. It has done so in relation to ceremonial and funerary monuments of the third and second millennia in an area of upland north Wales. The identification of prehistoric trackways is a particular feature of the archaeology of the region. The idea of the 'trackway' as an interpretive construct has a number of implications. In particular by focussing on the linear movement of people *passing through* it reinforces the perception of upland areas as distant places remote from everyday experience. It sidelines other patterns which may relate to different, more diffused ways of *moving around* these areas. Similar problems are manifest within certain contemporary approaches to the 'landscape' setting of monuments.

Journeys continue to form key interpretive elements of accounts of prehistory. However, journeys operate at different geographical, temporal and social scales and it is important to look not just to the role of long distance specialists (cf. Kristiansen and Larsson 2005) but to local journeys and to places from within.

Acknowledgments

Thank you to the editors for their patience. Mark Edmonds, Bob Johnston, Emily La Trobe-Bateman and Graham Robbins are all gratefully acknowledged for reading and commenting on drafts. Bob Johnston's encouragement in particular ensured that the paper made it as far as publication.

Whilst this paper has not been prepared in consultation with them, and the views expressed within it should in no way be taken as representative of their perspectives, it is a continuing pleasure to collaborate on work at Waun Llanfair with George Smith (Gwynedd Archaeological Trust) and Astrid Caseldine (University of Wales, Lampeter).

I am grateful to Cliff Hughes, Tanja Harding Jones, Neil McGuinness, Anthony Pritchard, Anne Marie Oattes, Maxine Bailey and Shirley Williams for their help (and good company) during fieldwork – sorry about the weather.

This paper was written whilst I was in receipt of an AHRC doctoral award. I gratefully acknowledge the permission of The Prehistoric Society and George Smith/Gwynedd Archaeological Trust to reproduce figures 10.1 and 10.2 respectively.

Bibliography

Bowen, E.G. and Gresham, C.A. 1967. *History of Merioneth. Volume 1: from earliest times to the age of the native princes.* Dolgellau: The Merioneth Historical Record Society.

Bradley, R. 1998. *The significance of monuments.* London: Routledge.

Bradley, R. 2005. *Ritual and domestic life in prehistoric Europe.* London: Routledge.

Brück, J. 1999a. Ritual and rationality: some problems of interpretation in European archaeology. *European Journal of Archaeology* 2, 313–44.

Brück, J. 1999b. What's in a settlement? Domestic practice and residential mobility in Early Bronze Age southern England. In J. Brück and M. Goodman (eds), *Making places in the prehistoric world*, 52–75. London: UCL Press.

Chitty, L.F. 1963. The Clun-Clee ridgeway: a prehistoric trackway across south Shropshire. In I. Ll. Foster and L. Alcock (eds), *Culture and environment: essays in honour of Sir Cyril Fox*, 171–92. London: Routledge and Kegan Paul.

Caseldine, A.E., Smith, G. and Griffiths, C. J. 2001. Vegetation history and upland settlement at Llyn Morwynion, Ffestiniog, Meirionnydd. *Archaeology in Wales* 41, 21–33.

Edelberg, L. and Jones, S. 1979. *Nuristan.* Graz: Akademische Druele-u. Verlagsanstalt.

Edmonds, M. 1999. *Ancestral geographies of the Neolithic: landscapes, monuments, and memory.* London: Routledge.

Fox, C. 1932. *The personality of Britain.* Cardiff: National Museum of Wales.

Fox, C. 1959. *Life and death in the Bronze Age.* London: Routledge and Kegan Paul.

Gray, J. 1999. Open spaces and dwelling places: being at home on hill farms in the Scottish borders. *American Ethnologist* 26 (2), 440–60.

Gresham, C.A. and Irvine, C.H. 1963. Prehistoric routes across North Wales. *Antiquity* 37, 54–58.

Griffiths, W.E. 1960. The excavation of stone circles near Penmaenmawr, North Wales. *Proceedings of the Prehistoric Society* 26, 303–39.

Grimes, W.F. 1951. *The prehistory of Wales.* Cardiff: National Museum of Wales.

Ingold, T. 2004. Culture on the ground: the world perceived through the feet. *Journal of Material Culture* 9 (3), 315–40.

Kristiansen, K. and Larsson, T.B. 2005. *The rise of Bronze Age society: travels, transmissions and transformations.* Cambridge: Cambridge University Press.

Lynch, F.M. 1984. Moel Goedog circle I: a complex ring cairn near Harlech. *Archaeologia Cambrensis* 133, 8–50.

Lynch, F.M. 1991. *Prehistoric Anglesey.* Llangefni: The Anglesey Antiquarian Society.

Lynch, F.M. 1993 *Excavations in the Brenig Valley: a Mesolithic and Bronze Age landscape in North Wales.* Cardiff: Cambrian Archaeological Monographs 5.

Lynch, F.M., Aldhouse-Green, S. and Davies, S. (eds) 2000. *Prehistoric Wales.* Stroud: Sutton.

McFadyen, L. 2003. *A revision of the materiality of architecture: the significance of Neolithic long mound and chambered monument building practice, with particular reference to the Cotswold-Severn*

Group. Unpublished PhD Thesis, University of Wales College, Newport.

Poucher, W.A. 1962. *The Welsh peaks*. London: Constable.

Savory, H.N. 1965. The Bronze Age. In I. Ll. Foster and L. Alcock (eds), *Prehistoric and early Wales*, 71–107. London: Routledge and Kegan Paul.

Smith, G. 2002. *Prehistoric funerary and ritual sites project: West Conwy and North Gwynedd*. Unpublished report. Gwynedd Archaeological Trust report 449.

Tipping, R. 2002. Climatic variability and 'marginal' settlement in upland British landscapes: a re-evaluation. *Landscapes* 3 (2), 10–29.

Whittle, A. 2003. *The archaeology of people: dimensions of life in the Neolithic*. London: Routledge.

Williams, J.Ll. and Davidson, A. 1998. Survey and excavation at the Graiglwyd Neolithic axe-factory, Penmaenmawr. *Archaeology in Wales* 38, 3–21.

Young, R. and Symonds, T. 1995. Marginality and the nature of later prehistoric upland settlement. *Landscape History* 17: 5–16.

11 Journeys through the seascapes of Scilly

Gary Robinson

Introduction

The idea for this paper came about through the observation that numerous prehistoric monuments on Scilly are used on modern and historical navigational charts and pilot guides (Admiralty 1998; Brandon 1999; Corporation of Trinity House 1749; 1808; Rowett 1869) demonstrating that the settings of these monuments are significant, both today and within recent history, to maritime movement within the archipelago. This observation poses the question of whether meaningful correlations might once have existed between the landscape settings of prehistoric monuments and their visibility from the ancient seascape. Whilst archaeologists have theorised the concept of landscapes, the concept of seascapes has received little attention. Through a consideration of patterns of movement within the inshore and offshore waters of Scilly, this paper will explore the concept of prehistoric journeys within the seascapes of Scilly and how these might shed new light upon the landscape settings of prehistoric monuments. The fieldwork on which this research is based was carried out both on land and on the sea (where a sea kayak was used).

Fig. 11.1. The Isles of Scilly are located 48 km south-west of Lands End, Cornwall

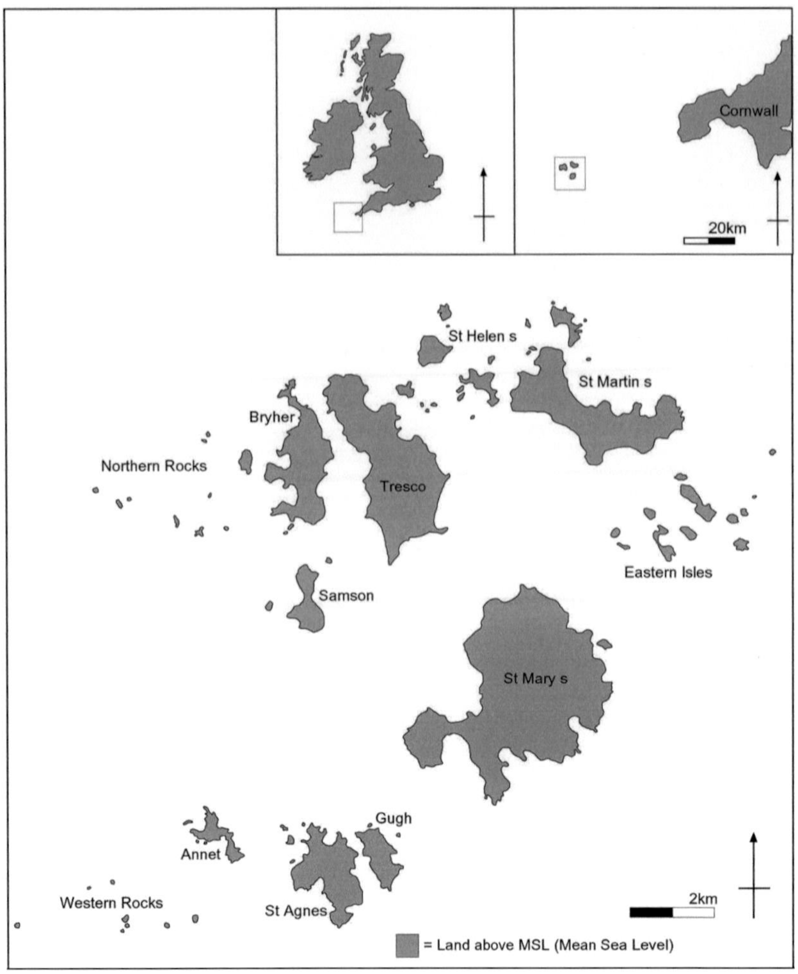

Scilly and the Scillonian entrance grave

The Isles of Scilly are a small archipelago of granite islands located 48km south-west of Land's End, Cornwall (Fig. 11.1). Today Scilly comprises *c.* 200 'named' islands, although the vast majority of these are devoid of terrestrial vegetation and soil and project only a few metres above Mean Sea Level (MSL). The seven largest islands of the archipelago are Annet, Bryher, Samson, St Agnes, St Martin's, St Mary's and Tresco. To the east and north of the archipelago the Eastern Isles and St Helen's group form small clusters of islands and islets, whilst to the north-west and south-west are the infamous Northern and Western Rocks – substantial rocky islets, pinnacles and ledges and the scene of numerous shipwrecks.

In this article I will consider the landscape settings of one type of monument, the Scillonian entrance grave. These entrance graves are Late Neolithic/Early Bronze Age (3000–1600 cal BC) chambered cairns comprising roughly circular mounds of stone and earth, revetted by a kerb and containing a burial chamber (Fig. 11.2). Chamber walls are constructed of orthostats or coursed walling covered by large capstones. The chambers occupy the centre of the mound and are accessed via an entrance within their kerb. 83 entrance graves have been found on Scilly in contrast to nine on the

Cornish mainland (Barnatt 1982; Ratcliffe 1989). Of the 83, nine are only alleged and have been excluded from further study. Of the remaining, three have been destroyed, although these are included within this discussion as accurate accounts exist (Borlase 1756; Grimes 1960).

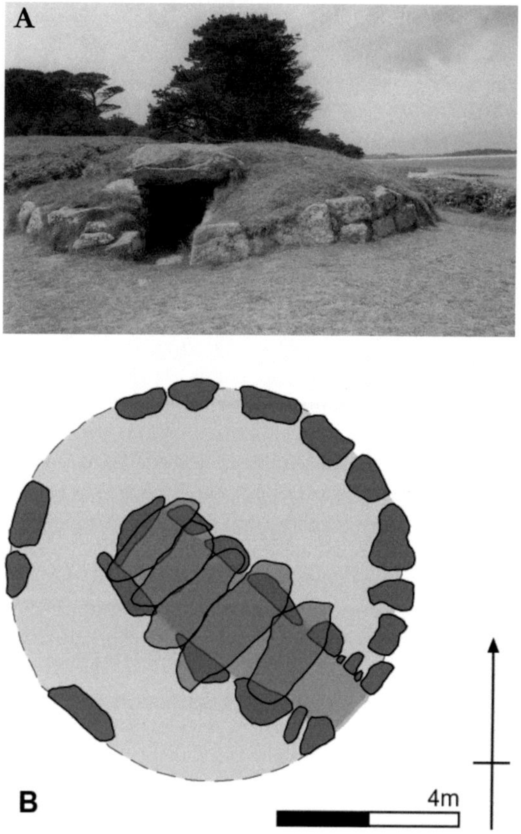

Fig. 11.2. The Scillonian entrance grave: A: Photograph of Innisidgen Carn, St Mary's (camera facing WNW). B: Plan of Innisidgen Carn, St Mary's (redrawn and modified from Ashbee 1974, 81, fig.10)

From landscape to seascape

The study of prehistoric landscape enjoys a central place within contemporary British archaeology, a point demonstrated in the proliferation of publications, conference sessions, field projects and post-graduate courses (Bender 1993; Brück 2001; Ucko and Layton 1999). In part, this interest has come about through a growing awareness of indigenous peoples' perceptions of landscape and the realisation that such landscapes are deeply ingrained with meaning for the people who inhabit them (Basso 1984; Morphy 1995). A central theme within studies of prehistoric landscapes has been the focus on the settings of monuments and how they emphasise and signify certain aspects of the lived landscape (Cooney 2000; Cummings 2002; Richards 1996; Tilley 1994). Much of this work has considered how people may have experienced monuments and the ways in which formal patterns of movement link together sites across the landscape (Barrett 1994; Thomas 1993; Tilley 1994).

The majority of archaeologists today accept that landscapes are invested with a range of meanings, and sites may be positioned in relation to a mythological and symbolic landscape (Cummings 2002; Tilley and Bennet 2001). In contrast, the sea continues to be thought of as empty, featureless and liminal, or as an obstacle or conduit to movement (Branigan and Foster 2002; Mithen and Lake 1996). A few archaeologists have noted the significance of the sea to the settings of monuments, where the sea is interpreted as a symbolic or metaphorical backdrop to life (and death) on the land (Scarre 2002a, 2002b; Woodman 2000). For example, Woodman (2000) demonstrates that the distribution of Neolithic chambered tombs on Orkney is predominately coastal, with views from such settings dominated by the sea. She concludes that Orcadian chambered tombs are located in regard to visibility, and that visibility *from*, rather than visibility *of*, a tomb appears as an overriding concern in their landscape setting. Although Woodman emphasises the importance of views over the sea in the placement of tombs, she ignores the fact that her findings also imply that such tombs are equally visible *from* the sea, and that the key to their settings may be linked to maritime rather than terrestrial perceptions of the environment.

Such studies, enlightening as they are, remain 'landlocked', ignoring the potential of the sea as a social '*seascape*'. We must remember that islanders did not just gaze across the sea, but physically engaged with it on a daily basis. In this way, the sea was not inherently symbolic but achieved significance through people's active engagement with it, acquiring an intimate knowledge of its currents, wave patterns and locales through the daily practices of seafaring and fishing. Through such activities, the sea, like the land, becomes socially constructed.

In contrast to how archaeologists have studied the sea, anthropological studies demonstrate the potential of the sea as an embodied social, symbolic and mythological environment. This social construction of the sea is well illustrated by Cordell (1989) in his study of sea tenure amongst modern 'small scale' fishing communities. He notes 'It is one thing to contemplate the inshore sea from lands end as a stranger to observe an apparently empty, featureless, open accessed expanse of water. The image in a fisherman's mind is something very different. Seascapes are blanketed with history and imbued with names, myths and legends and elaborate territories that sometimes become exclusive provinces partitioned with traditional rights and owners much like property on land' (Cordell 1989,1).

The seascape may become socialised through systems of wayfaring, such as the observation and correct interpretation of stars, animals and their behaviours, the appearance of landmarks when viewed from the sea, wave patterns, and wind directions (Akimichi 1984; 1996; Feinburg 1988; Gaffin 1996; Gell 1985; Goodenough 1953; Sopher 1965). Similarly, anthropological studies demonstrate that the seascape and journeys made within it may be embroidered with stories and mythological events, and comprise named places frequently inhabited by powerful spirits and ancestral beings (Cosentino 1995; Davis 1989; Rasmussen 1979; Thompson 1995).

The capacity of the sea to contain meanings and mythologies is clarified by Davis' work with coastal aboriginal communities in Arnhem Land, Northern Australia (Davis 1989). During fishing trips locals would assiduously, but inexplicably, avoid certain water spaces, consistently turning back when their boats drifted across seemingly imaginary lines (Davis 1989, 44). Davis was able to correlate these invisible boundaries with undersea ridges and configurations of the sea floor – some under 30m of water – and was able to establish that these locales and lines within the sea were considered to be created during the *Dreamtime* by ancestral beings. Many of these sacred sites were so powerful that they had to be approached with caution and respect, for transgression could bring about dire physical and psychological consequences (Davis 1989, 46).

Whilst archaeologists have made extensive use of accounts of ancestral geographies of the Australian aborigines (e.g. Morphy 1995) to inform a different way of thinking and conceptualising prehistoric landscapes (Bradley 1993; Tilley 1994), little or no attention has been given to the sea. Yet Davis' work demonstrates that the seascape, like the landscape, might comprise a web of named and significant locales whose meaning is constructed through both the actions of ancestral beings and the daily activities of present day fishing communities. These sacred sites create an ancestral geography within the sea that link together the movements and activities of *Dreamtime* beings with those of modern aboriginal fishing communities. These sacred sites are located through the correct interpretation of a boat's position in relation to specific landmarks, reefs and water currents; knowledge of how to locate these sites being restricted to specific individuals who had earned this right through age, status and initiation.

A similar scenario is highlighted in Cordell's (1989) study of the Bahia fishing communities of north-east Brazil. Here, Cordell shows how the sea is filled with fishing locales (*pesqueiros)* and how, through the correct identification of these important sea places, meaning and history is mapped within coastal waters. These *pesqueiros* are only accessible to those with knowledge of how to locate them through the correct interpretation of relationships between landscape and seascape features (such as coastal headlands, reefs, tidal currents and so on) and precise knowledge of the effects of lunar tide on the behaviour of fish. Access to this knowledge is controlled through family and personal networks, apprenticeships and initiation. Cordell (1989) demonstrates that through daily activities on the sea the seascape is inscribed with biographies, places, patterns of movements, and histories. The separate concepts of seascape and landscape become intimately entwined and inseparable through this process of socialisation.

Whilst archaeologists have been keen to embrace the concept of landscape, particularly in their interpretations of the settings of monuments, few have considered the concept of seascape as a viable or worthwhile field of research. I wish to argue that the sea, like the land, would have held great significance to people in the past, and whilst providing challenges to its study, should be considered in accounts of prehistory. The following discussion will consider the significance of the sea, and how journeys made within the seascape might be linked to the landscape settings of Scillonian entrance graves.

The drowned landscapes of Scilly

It is essential, if we are to explore the relationship between the landscape settings of Scillonian entrance graves and the sea, that we can confidently demonstrate the relationship between these monuments and the ancient coastline. I have provided a consideration of this theme in my doctoral thesis and a further account of Scilly's submergence will be published separately elsewhere (Robinson 2005; in prep.); for the purpose of this paper I aim to provide a summary of the salutary points.

Ashbee has noted that the question of the submergence of Scilly is unavoidable in any study of the islands' prehistory (Ashbee 1974). The effect of sea-level change, and the presence of archaeological remains within the present day intertidal zone, has been noted since the mid eighteenth century (Borlase 1753). Various efforts have been made to define and model the 'drowned landscape' of Scilly (Ashbee 1974; Crawford 1927; Fowler and Thomas 1979) but only Thomas (1985,17–64) has provided a comprehensive model for the archipelago's submergence.

Recently, the discovery of intertidal peat deposits on Scilly has allowed Thomas' model of submergence to be refined (Ratcliffe and Straker 1996). The dating and analysis of these intertidal deposits suggests a much slower rate of sea-level change than previously thought predicting that Mean Sea Level (MSL) was: -5.29m O.D. at 5000 cal BC; -3.79m OD at 3000 cal BC; -2.29m OD at 1000 cal BC and -

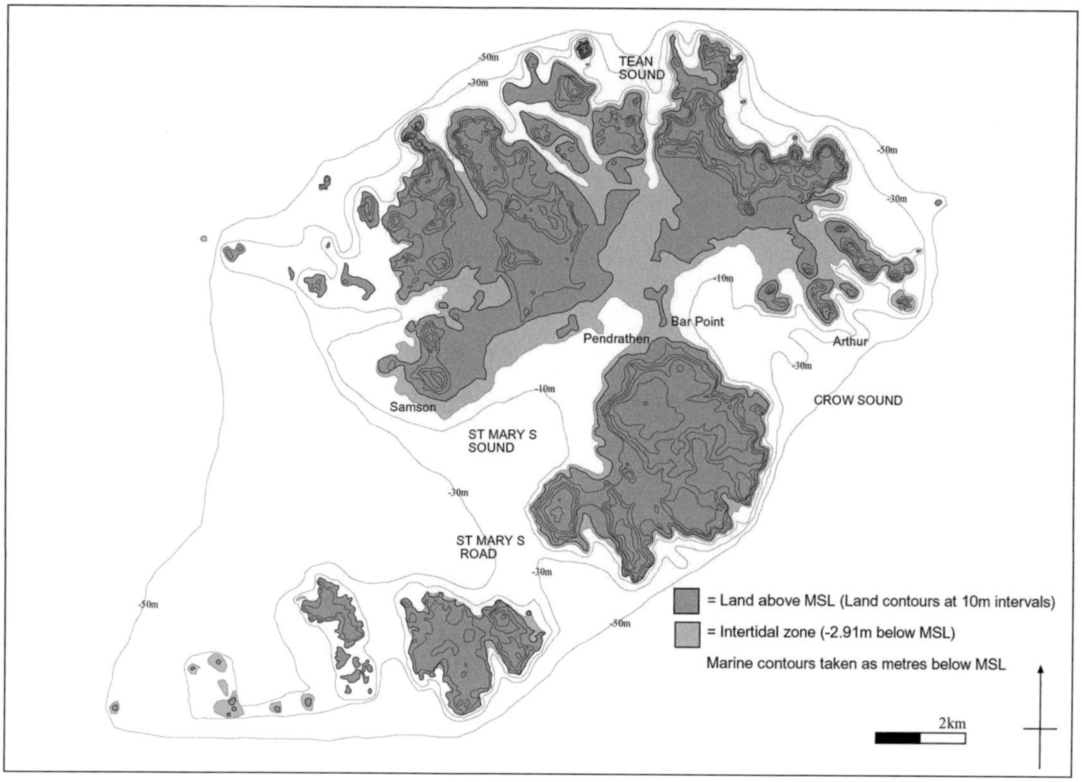

Fig. 11.3. The prehistoric island landscape of Scilly

1.79m OD at 0 cal BC/AD (Ratcliffe and Straker 1996, 50, fig. 36). This rate of sea-level change is comparable with sea-level curves produced elsewhere in south-west Britain and north-west Europe (Healy 1995; Heyworth and Kidson 1982; Morzadec-Kerfourn 1998; Selwood *et al.* 1999). These findings suggest that during the third millennium BC the highest normal tide (Mean High Spring Tide) was only -1m below modern Ordnance Datum. The significance of these findings for the reconstruction of the Scillonian coastline of Scilly is that, based upon changes in sea-level alone, the archipelago need not have looked substantially different from that experienced today. However, coastal morphology is not only affected by changes in sea-level, as the complex and transformative processes of erosion and deposition also need to be considered.

We can state with confidence that little erosion has taken place along the outer Atlantic coastline of the archipelago, as this is comprised of granite cliffs set in deep water. Where erosion has occurred along this outer coastline it has been restricted to coastal inlets and bays, characterised by cliffs of degraded granite. The recognition of Quaternary maritime features (e.g. wave cut notches located above present day MSL) suggests that the majority of coastal erosion that has occurred happened during the Quaternary, and that subsequent erosion has not significantly altered the shape of the coastline since the third millennium BC.

Erosion within the central lagoon of the islands is primarily from the south-west, instigated by the prevailing south-westerly wind and resulting wave regimes. This pattern of erosion can be detected in the island landscape by the presence of extensive sand flats and dunes along the northern and eastern inner shoreline of the archipelago. When attempting to reconstruct the configuration of the ancient coastline it is important to consider the effect of Atlantic storms on the formation and destruction of storm beaches and coastal barriers. Healy (1995; 1999) has argued that the crenulated coastlines of west Cornwall are particularly prone to the cyclical formation and breaching of such coastal geomorphological features. Once formed, storm beaches and coastal bars allow terrestrial habitats to form at, or potentially below, MSL. However, Atlantic storms will eventual breach these sea defences causing a return to marine conditions. The implication of this for a study of the ancient island configuration of Scilly is that the amount of land above MSL at any point need not be solely linked to relative sea-level. The island landscape that emerges is dynamic and shape shifting.

Figure 11.3 represents an attempt to reconstruct the ancient coastline of Scilly based upon available archaeological and geomorphological data. The main geographical features that comprise this island landscape are two large bays: the first to the east, spanning between Bar Point and Arthur; and the second to the west between Pendrathen and Samson.

To the north, a small bay/inlet may once have existed within the deep channel of Tean Sound. The significance of this data for our interpretation of the prehistoric landscape of Scilly is that, whilst sea-level change and coastal erosion has altered the archipelago's coastline, the overall shape and configuration of the islands during prehistory need not be substantially different to that illustrated in Figure 11.3. Thus we can confidently relate the landscape settings of entrance graves in relation to the archipelago's ancient coastline.

Scillonian entrance graves and the island landscape

Entrance graves are a feature of higher ground around the Atlantic coastline of the archipelago (Fig. 11.4). It could be argued that the present distribution of these monuments is deceptive, as low-lying sites may have been lost through inundation. The destruction of entrance graves through inundation is unlikely as the amount of land lost through sea-level change amounts to only 15–20% of the present day landmass (the majority of which is from around the islands' coastline). Entrance graves are not found within the present day intertidal zone. The absence of these substantial stone monuments from the intertidal zone is in marked contrast to other intertidal remains, such as prehistoric houses, field boundaries and cists (Ratcliffe 1989; Thomas 1985). On balance, it would seem that very few entrance graves have been destroyed by sea-level change and their present distribution accurately mirrors that of prehistory.

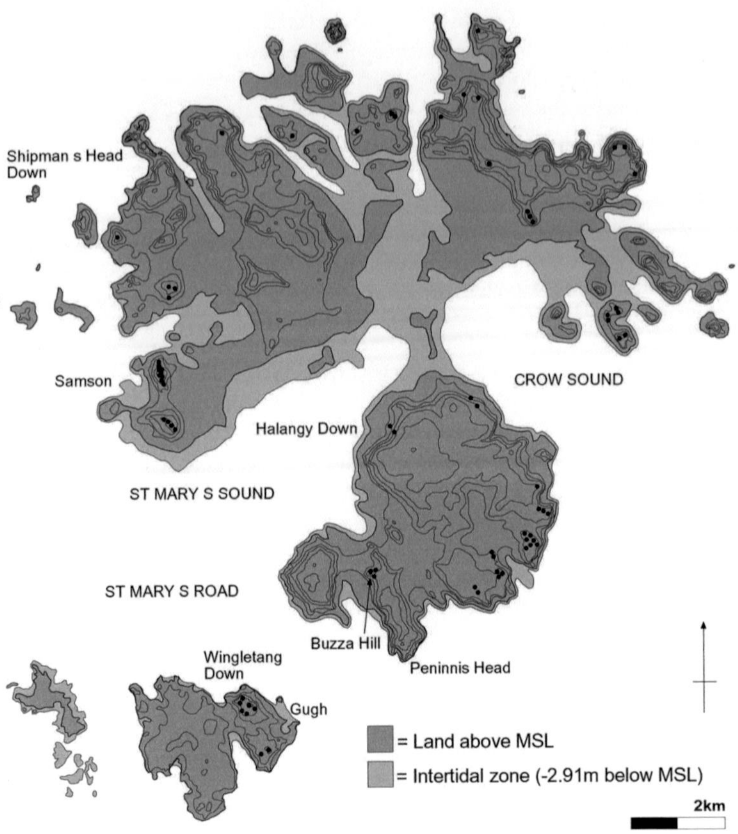

Fig. 11.4. The distribution of entrance graves on Scilly

Whilst a prehistoric coastal distribution pattern can be identified for entrance graves, they are not evenly distributed throughout the archipelago, being absent from islands such as St Agnes, Ganilly and Annett, and with restricted distributions on Bryher and Tresco. Over 40% of the monuments occur in only three locations: Porth Hellick, Kittern Hill, and Samson. The location of entrance graves in close proximity to the ancient coastline means that the sea is an ever-present element of their settings. One consequence of this is that intervisibility between monuments is low when viewed across the interior of the islands (such as between Porth Hellick Down and Bant's Carn) but high when viewed over the sea between them (such as between Bant's Cairn and Samson).

Whilst proximity to the sea was important in the choice of setting for entrance graves, they did not command the most extensive views over the sea. This is demonstrated by the absence of monuments from locales on the periphery of the archipelago, such as Shipman's Head Down, Wingletang Down and Peninnis Head (Fig. 11.4). Instead, entrance graves are sited to command specific and localised views. This pattern of intervisibility between groups of entrance graves might suggest that particular views over water are being emphasised. For example, a monument on the south-west slopes of Buzza Hill has been located so that it has views across St Mary's Road towards Gugh, but only limited views in other directions. Similarly, intervisibility between entrance graves on Samson and Halangy Down emphasise St Mary's Sound.

One interpretation of this data is that entrance graves are being located within specific landscape settings to emphasise significant areas of the seascape. This interpretation argues that the sea (as a metaphoric or symbolic resource) is not important in itself, but rather that particular areas of the sea are highlighted. I will argue that the key to interpreting these monuments is, firstly, to explore their landscape settings from the sea, and secondly to relate their distribution and settings to potential prehistoric sea-borne movement within the archipelago.

Journeys in the seascape

It can be shown that prehistoric Scillonians were making sea journeys during the third and second millennia BC. Journeys between the archipelago and the mainland are demonstrated through the presence of imports, such as axes, pottery and animals (Ratcliffe and Straker 1996; Robinson 2005). Similarly, localised movement within coastal waters is shown through the presence of offshore and coastal fish species identified from prehistoric midden deposits (Neal 1983; Ratcliffe and Straker 1996; Robinson 2005; Turk 1967; 1978; 1984a; 1984b). The identification of these species of fish show that prehistoric seafarers, in the pursuit of fish and sea mammals, visited both coastal and offshore waters.

Archaeologists identify movement and journeys within a landscape through the identification of significant cultural features such as settlements, burial monuments and so on, and how they may have structured the experience of movement and the creation of pathways. Whilst physical obstacles such as mountains, cliffs and rivers restrict movement within the landscape, archaeologists tend to place emphasis upon cultural constraints such as the correct way to move along a stone row or enter a stone circle (Thomas 1993; Tilley 1994; 1996). In contrast, movement on the sea around Scilly is primarily structured by the cyclical patterns of the tides (Admiralty 1998). These cycles form a predictable temporal pattern of movement around the archipelago that both restricts and facilitates local journeys on the sea. Those making safe passage, entry and pilotage within the archipelago needed to heed these natural cycles and accurately predict and identify tidal currents and wayfaring points.

Success at sea would have been determined by the seafaring capabilities of a crew and their ability to locate themselves and their relationship to known locales within the seascape. Such knowledge would have been fundamental to both safe passage on the sea and success in locating fishing areas. Whilst the landscape is experienced through the body as its contours enter our muscular consciousness (Ingold 1993), experience of the seascape (and therefore our experience of the landscape *from* the sea) is mediated through the boat. Whilst journeys made within a landscape are difficult to isolate, movement within the sea is structured both spatially and temporally by the shifting patterns of tide and current. Through this structuring of movement we can begin to discuss the times, places and problems of movement in and around the coastal and offshore waters of the archipelago.

Initial approach to the islands from the mainland would have been from the north-east. We can rule out a western or southern approach to the islands as this would have to contend with the innumerable rock pinnacles, ledges and dangerous currents that comprise the Western and Northern Rocks – where tides run strong with confusing eddies and overfalls. These waters rank amongst the most dangerous in the world (Doodson and Warburg 1973; Royal Yachting Association 1981). This is not to deny that people might, on occasions, have ventured into the seas to the west and north-west of the islands. However, such journeys would be limited to the few times within the year when conditions allowed: such journeys would be the exception rather than the rule. Thus, the dangerous nature of the seas around Scilly structured how people approached and moved around the seascapes.

Once within the relatively sheltered water of the eastern seaboard of the islands, access to the interior would be channelled through either Crow Sound or St Mary's Road to the west, or through the deep water channel of Tean Sound to the north (Admiralty 1998; 2001; Brandon 1999). As well as entry points into the archipelago, potential landing places can also be recognised through the exclusion of areas of coastline where the landing of small boats would have been impossible or seriously prohibited. Such places include steep and rocky shorelines and areas of coastline exposed to the prevailing wind, wave surges and strong current races. The resultant map, here compiled, shows that only a limited number of places around the coastline of the islands would provide a sheltered landing and harbour (Fig. 11.5).

The major entry points into the archipelago, Crow Sound, St Mary's Road, St Mary's Sound and Tean Sound, correspond well with the distribution

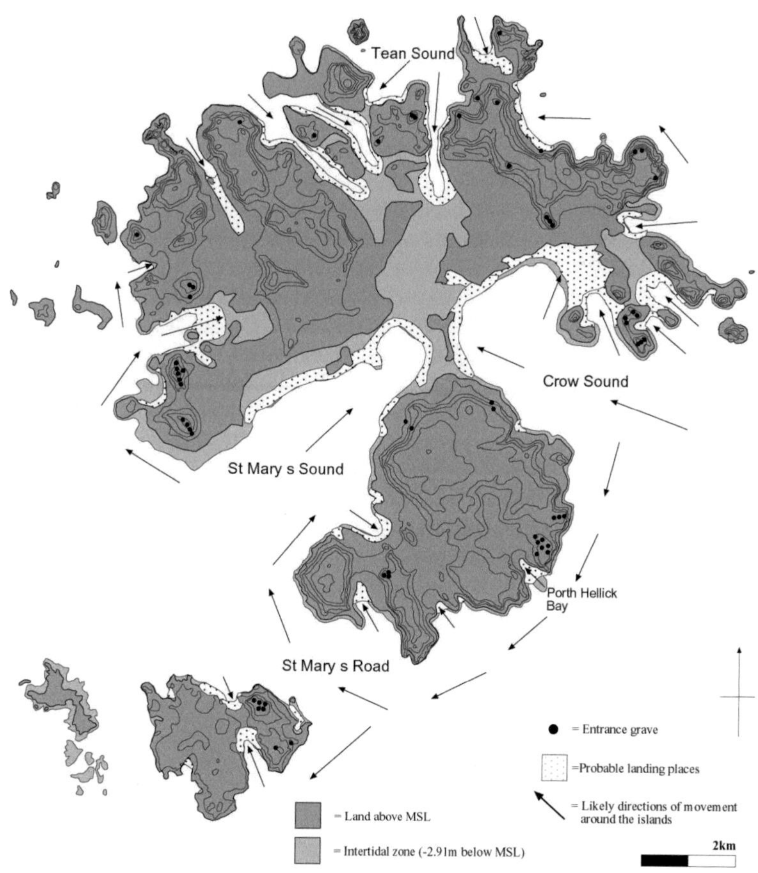

Fig. 11.5. Potential movement patterns and landing places within the prehistoric seascape of Scilly

of entrance graves. The implication developed in this chapter is that the locations of entrance graves marked out movement on the sea and, in particular, approach and entry into the archipelago. The presence of entrance graves on Arthur and Innisidgen mark an eastern entry into Crow Sound; monuments on Gugh, the western limit of an eastern approach into St Mary's Road; monuments on Samson, the western limit of a southern approach into St Mary's Sound; and monuments on White Island, Tean and St Martin's, a northern approach into Tean Sound. Similarly, the high concentration of entrance graves along the eastern coast of St Mary's might relate to the importance of this coastline as the first landfall encountered during a crossing from the mainland.

The marking of these locales through the construction of entrance graves highlights the significance of these places for safe movement on the sea. The significance of these journeys is further emphasised through the powerful presence of both cremation and inhumation burials within the chambers of the entrance graves (Ashbee 1974; Hencken 1932, 1933; O'Neil 1954). By placing ancestral remains at the entry points to the archipelago they guided the living (both practically and symbolically) to the safety of harbour, and through this relationship safe passage on the sea was communicated through the physical presence of past islanders. Furthermore, by emphasising these significant island locales through the construction of monuments, connections were being drawn between the seafaring activities of the living and those of the ancestors, thereby creating a genealogy of the seascape.

If the distribution of entrance graves relates to movement and activities within the seascape, we need to account for the absence of these monuments from within specific areas of the archipelago. Wingletang Down, Annet and Shipman's Head, where monuments are absent, are associated with exposed coastlines which offer little shelter or harbourage and where sea-borne movement would be restricted (Brandon 1999). Similarly, the absence of entrance graves from locales such as along the eastern coastline of Tresco might be accounted for by the potential for extensive areas of towan (sand dunes) here and thus the inability to launch or land boats.

Whilst the landscape settings of entrance graves provided a powerful visual discourse for activity on the sea it would be misleading to suggest that all of these monuments are visible from the sea around the islands. Whilst an attempt was made to establish which of these were visible, the sea-based logistics of this proved beyond the scope of this article. What was made clear during fieldwork was that from the sea the most visually significant elements of the island landscape were the granite tors that punctuate the archipelago's Atlantic coastline. In order to explore further the significance of the coastal distribution of entrance graves attention must be focused on these tors and their relationship with entrance graves and movement on the sea.

The land as viewed from the sea

The tors on Scilly form the most visible elements of the island landscape: many can be picked out and identified kilometres offshore (Brandon 1999). The importance of such wayfaring points for modern seafaring is clearly demonstrated in their inclusion on both modern and historical charts and pilot guides (Admiralty 2001; Brandon 1999; Corporation of Trinity House 1749; 1808; Rowett 1869). Of particular importance are pilotage guides produced for the training of navigators for the islands' tourist and fishing vessels (Brandon 1999; Norm 1980). These guides demonstrate the importance placed upon local knowledge, which is required to correctly identify landmarks in order to avoid dangerous rocks and currents and to locate important locales within the seascape, such as holes within the seabed into which lobster or crab pots are placed. Through wayfaring, a detailed and intimate knowledge of both surface and seabed topography is directly informed through the correct identification of significant landmarks.

In order to develop this argument further we must briefly leave *terra firma* and explore the islands from the sea. Granite tors are found along the Atlantic coastline of Scilly where they dominate cliff tops and headlands; these tors have been mapped and characterised by Mitchell and Orme (1967) and Scourse (1986). Whilst tors have a wider distribution within the archipelago than entrance graves, a strong correlation exists as entrance graves are located in close proximity to coastal tors (Fig. 11.6). For example, entrance graves at Innisidgen, Tinker's Hill, Gweal Hill, and Middle Arthur are located in close proximity to tors (Fig. 11.7); whilst on Samson and Cruther's Hill, St Martin's, the linear arrangement of entrance graves mimic the sinuous spines of granite that dominate the summit of these hills. At Works Carn, Bryher, an entrance grave has been sited directly on top of a hillside tor (Fig. 11.7). The relationship between tors and entrance graves suggests that whilst correlations exist, tors are not inherently significant. The correlation demonstrated suggests that only specific tors have significance within the island landscape and that only these are emphasised through the construction of monuments.

The significance placed upon coastal tors can be further recognised at a number of sites through the intentional deposition of artefacts. At Yellow Rock Carn an urn was found within a crevice of a tor (Lewis 1948, 7), whilst at English Island Carn a Late

Fig. 11.6. (left) The close proximity between entrance graves and granite tors: A: Innisiden Carn, St Mary's. B: Lower Innisidgen, St Mary's. C: Middle Arthur, Eastern Isles. D: Works Carn, Bryher.

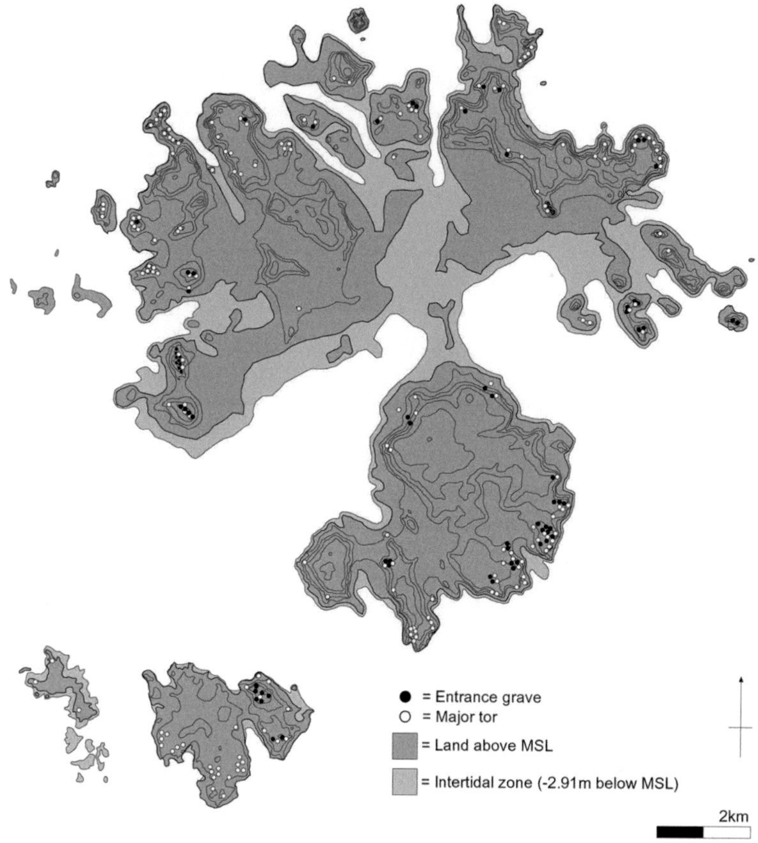

Fig. 11.7. (above) A comparison between the distribution of entrance graves and granite tors

Neolithic/Early Bronze Age dolerite shaft-holed adze and an urn were found (Ransom 1984, 194). At Carron Rock's, St Martin's, an Early Bronze dagger and a comb-impressed urn were found within the crevice of a tor and at Block House, Tresco, a stone mace head was recovered from immediately below a rocky prominence (Ashbee 1974; Hencken 1932; Lewis 1948; Ratcliffe 1989). By constructing entrance graves in close proximity with tors, and through the deposition of associated artefacts, the importance of these 'natural' features to prehistoric Scillonians was emphasised.

Wayfaring and the Scillonian seascape

Today lighthouses and marker buoys aid wayfaring, however, natural landmarks, such as tors, remain the principal means by which seafarers locate themselves within the islands' dangerous waters. Evidence for the present day and historical importance of coastal features (many of which are only apparent from the sea), such as cliffs, inlets, tors and islets, is illustrated through the naming of these features on maps and charts (Admiralty 1998; Thomas 1979a; 1979b). In prehistory, everyday activities on the sea around Scilly, such as fishing, would primarily have been carried out within coastal waters. In these waters, the tors and outcrops that encircle the Atlantic coastline of the islands would have provided the most prominent wayfaring points. Through an intimate knowledge of the island landscape and its shifting perspectives prehistoric Scillonians would have acquired knowledge of the sea, and through this process the sea would have become invested with significant locales and seaways. Tors would have played an important role in this socialisation of the sea. Tors may have become associated with sea tenure, ancestral fishing grounds, pilotage routes and mythological events upon the sea (Cordell 1989; Davies 1989). Whilst the precise location of significant locales within the ancient seascape cannot be reconstructed, through the identification of prominent coastal landmarks, embellished through the construction of monuments, we can appreciate the potential practical, social and symbolic importance that these locales might have held.

The significance of coastal tors on Scilly associated with movement on the sea is likely to predate the construction of entrance graves (perhaps dating back to the Mesolithic). But through the construction of monuments the knowledge and significance of these tors became socialised and embedded within the lives of prehistoric islanders. If the location of entrance graves relate to movement on the sea, and particularly to entry into the archipelago, we can postulate that only tors that were significant to sea routes were emphasised through the construction of monuments. Therefore, each entrance grave was associated with a particular point within the landscape (usually a tor) that was readily visible from the sea and may therefore have functioned as a wayfaring marker.

Conclusion

Wayfaring would have been crucial for negotiating the dangerous waters of the archipelago and this knowledge of the sea was intimately linked to knowledge of the land. Whilst knowledge of wayfaring carries socio-economic significance in sustaining life in an offshore island environment, the necessity of a system of wayfaring cannot be separated from a meaningful and symbolic ancestral geography. The location of entrance graves at significant locales along the coastline, emphasising landing places and pilotage routes, draws the monuments out beyond the confines of the land and into the sea. Through the construction of monuments containing ancestral remains within these locales, connections were made between generations of prehistoric islanders (both living and dead) and safe passage on the sea. The entrance graves therefore represented a material confirmation of the social relationships between people and places. The construction of monuments, and the correct interpretation of their settings, thus constructed a spatial and temporal geography of the sea (where and when journeys were possible on the seascape). Likewise, the landscape settings of entrance graves can only be understood from journeys made on the sea. Therefore, the island landscape of Scilly was and is created through a dialectic relationship between landscape and seascape. Thus, the seascape shares many attributes with landscape in that both are socially constructed and comprise named places, mythologies, biographies and social networks.

In this paper I have aimed to demonstrate that only by studying the archipelago from the sea, through journeys made within the seascape, can we appreciate how the landscape settings of entrance graves relate to the sea. Through the identification of entry points into the archipelago, landing places, journeys made and wayfaring skills, I have explored the prehistoric social production of both landscapes and seascapes of Scilly. The sea was not merely backdrop for human action but was an active medium through which people lived, experienced and ordered their worlds.

Bibliography

Admiralty 1998. *Isles of Scilly, Saint Mary's and the principal off-islands: chart 883*. Taunton: National Hydrographic Office Publications.

Admiralty 2001. *Isles of Scilly chart SC 34*. Taunton: National Hydrographic Office Publications.

Akimichi, T. 1984. Island orientation and the perception of sea areas in Satawal (Central Caroline Islands). *Bulletin of the National Museum of Ethnography* 9, 651–709.

Akimichi, T. 1996. Image and reality at sea: fish and cognitive mapping in Carolinean navigational knowledge. In R. Ellen and K. Fukui (eds), *Redefining nature: ecology, culture and domestication,* 493–514. Oxford: Berg.

Ashbee, P. 1974. *Ancient Scilly: from the first farmers to the early Christians.* Newton Abbot: David and Charles.

Barnatt, J. 1982. *Prehistoric Cornwall: the ceremonial monuments.* Wellingborough: Turnstone.

Barrett, J. 1994. *Fragments from antiquity*. Oxford: Blackwell.

Basso, P. 1984. Stalking with stories: names, places and moral narratives among the western Apache. In E. Bruner (ed.), *Text, play and story,* 19–55. Prospect Heights: Waveland Press.

Bender, B. (ed.) 1993. *Landscape: politics and perspectives.* Oxford: Berg.

Borlase, W. 1753. Of the great alterations which the Isles of Scilly have undergone since the time of the ancients. *Philosophical Transactions of the Royal Society* 46, 55–67.

Borlase, W.C. 1756. *Observations on the ancient and present state of the Isles of Scilly,* Oxford: W. Jackson.

Bradley, R. 1993. *Altering the earth: the origins of monuments in Britain and continental Europe.* Edinburgh: Society of Antiquities of Scotland.

Brandon, R. 1999. *The Isles of Scilly Pilot.* St Ives: Imray, Laurie, Norie and Wilson.

Branigan, K. and Foster, P. 2002. *Barra and the Bishop Isles: living on the margin.* Stroud: Tempus.

Brück, J. (ed.) 2001. *Bronze Age landscapes: tradition and transformation.* Oxford: Oxbow.

Cooney, G. 2000. *Landscapes of Neolithic Ireland.* London: Routledge.

Cordell, J. (ed.) 1989. *A sea of small boats.* Cambridge, Massachusetts: Cultural Survival.

Corporation of Trinity House 1749. *Lighthouses and navigation.* London: Corporation of Trinity House (The Corporation of London, Guildhall Library MS. v9685548).

Corporation of Trinity House 1808. *Pilotage.* London: Corporation of Trinity House (The Corporation of London, Guildhall Library MS. v9686128).

Cosentino, D. 1995. Water spirits: Agwe and La Siren. In D. Cosentino (ed.), *The sacred arts of Hatian vodou,* 148–152. Los Angeles: UCLA Fowler Museum of Cultural History.

Crawford, O.G.S. 1927. Lyonesse. *Antiquity* 1, 5–14.

Cummings, V. 2002. Between mountains and the sea: a reconsideration of the Neolithic monuments of south-west Scotland. *Proceedings of the Prehistoric Society* 68, 125–46.

Davis, S. 1989. Aboriginal tenure of the sea in Arnhem Land, Northern Australia. In J. Cordell (ed.), *A sea of small boats,* 37–59. Cambridge, Massachusetts: Cultural Survival.

Doodson, A.T. and Warburg, H.D. 1973. *Admiralty manual of tides.* London: Her Majesty's Stationary Office.

Feinburg, R. 1988. *Polynesian seafaring and navigation.* Honolulu: Honolulu University Press.

Fowler, P. J. and Thomas, C. 1979. Lyonesse revisited: the early walls of Scilly. *Antiquity* 53, 175–89.

Gaffin, D. 1996. *In place: spatial and social order in the Faeroe island community.* Waveland: Prospect Heights

Gell, A. 1985. How to read a map: remarks on the practical logic of navigation. *Man* 20, 271–86.

Goodenough, H.W. 1953. *Native astronomy in the Carolines.* Philadelphia: University of Pennsylania.

Grimes, W.F. 1960. *Excavations on defence sites, 1939–1945.* London: Ministry of Works Archaeological Reports No.3.

Healy, M.G. 1995. The lithostratigraphy and biostratigraphy of a Holocene coastal sediment sequence in Marizion Marsh, West Cornwall, with reference to relative sea-level movements. *Marine Geology* 24, 183–89.

Healy, M.G. 1999. Relative sea-level change in west Cornwall. In J.D. Scourse and M.F.A. Furze (eds), *The Quarternary of Cornwall: field guide.* London: Quarternary Research Association.

Hencken, H. 1932. *The archaeology of Cornwall and the Isles of Scilly.* London: Methuen.

Hencken, H. 1933. Notes on megalithic monuments in the Isles of Scilly. *Antiquaries Journal* 13, 13–29.

Heyworth, A. and Kidson, C. 1982. Sea-level changes in south-west England and Wales. *Proceedings of the Geologists' Association* 93, 91–111.

Ingold, T. 1993. The temporality of landscape. *World Archaeology* 25, 152–72.

Lewis, H.A. 1948. *St Martins, St Helens and Tean in legend and history.* St Martin's (Published privately by the author).

Mitchell, G.F. and Orme, A.R. 1967. The Pleistocene deposits of the Isles of Scilly. Quarterly *Journal of the Geological Society of London,* 489 (123), 59–92

Mithen, S. and Lake, M. 1996. The South Hebrides Mesolithic project: reconstructing Mesolithic settlement in western Scotland. In T. Pollard and A. Morrison. (eds), *The early prehistory of Scotland,* 123–51. Glasgow: Glasgow University Press.

Morphy, H. 1995. Landscape and the reproduction of the ancestral past. In E. Hirsch and M. O'Hanlon (eds), *Anthropology of landscape,* 184–209. Oxford: Clarendon Press.

Morzadec-Kerfourn, M. 1998. L´évolotion de la Ligne de Rivage. In P. Giot, J. Monnier and J. L´Helgouach (eds), *Préhistoire de la Bretagne,* 437–40. Rennes: Ouest-France.

Neal, D.S. 1983. Excavations on a settlement at Little Bay, St Martins, Isles of Scilly. *Cornish Archaeology* 22, 27–34.

Norm. 1980. *A yachtsman's guide to Scilly.* Cambourne: Protempts Agency Service.

O'Neil, B.H.St.J. 1954. Excavations at Knackyboy Carn. *Antiquaries Journal* 32, 21–34.

Ransom, V.I. 1984. *A catalogue of perforated implements from Cornwall and the Isles of Scilly.* University of Exeter: Unpublished M.Phil thesis.

Rasmussen, K. 1979. A shaman's journey to the sea spirit. In A.W. Lessa and E.Z. Vogt (eds), *Reader in comparative religion: an anthropological approach,* 308–11. New York: Harper and Row.

Ratcliffe, J. 1989. *The archaeology of the Isles of Scilly: an assessment of the resource and recommendations for its future.* Truro: Cornwall Archaeological Unit.

Ratcliffe, J. and Straker, V. 1996. *The early environment of Scilly.* Truro: Cornwall Archaeological Unit and English Heritage.

Richards, C. 1996. Monuments as landscape: creating the centre of the world in late Neolithic Orkney. *World Archaeology* 28, 190–208.

Robinson, G. 2005. *The prehistoric island landscape of Scilly.* University College London: Unpublished PhD thesis.

Robinson, G. in prep. Dynamic environments: exploring the prehistoric coastal morphology and intertidal archaeology of the Isles of Scilly.

Rowett, W. 1869. *Sailing directions for approaching the islands of Scilly.* London: Unknown publisher (British Library ref. 10496-6-37).

Royal Yachting Association 1981. *RYA manual of navigation* London: Royal Yachting Association.

Scarre, C. 2002a. A pattern of islands: the Neolithic monuments of north-west Brittany. *European Journal of Archaeology* 5, 24–41.

Scarre, C. 2002b. Coast and cosmos: the Neolithic monuments of northern Brittany. In C. Scarre (ed.), *Monuments and landscape in Atlantic Europe,* 84–102. London: Routledge.

Scourse, J.D. 1986. *The Isles of Scilly field guide.* London: Quaternary Research Association.

Selwood, E.B., Durrance, E.M. and Bristow, C.M. (eds) 1999. *The geology of Cornwall and the Isles of Scilly.* Exeter: University of Exeter Press.

Sopher, D.E. 1965. *The sea nomads: a study based on the literature of the maritime boat people of south-east Asia.* Singapore: Government Press

Thomas, A.C. 1979a. An archaic place name element from

the Isles of Scilly. *Bulletin of the Board of Celtic Studies* 28, 229–33.

Thomas, A.C. 1979b. Coast and cliff names of Gwithian and the northern cliffs. *Journal of the Royal Institution of Cornwall* 3, 291–6.

Thomas, A.C. 1985. *Exploration of a drowned landscape: archaeology and history of the Isles of Scilly.* London: Batsford.

Thomas, J. 1993. The politics of vision and the archaeologies of landscape. In B.Bender (ed.), *Landscape, politics and perspectives*, 19–48. Oxford: Berg.

Thompson, R.F. 1995. From the isle beneath the sea. In D. Cosentino (ed.), *The sacred arts of Hatian vodou*, 91–119. Los Angeles: UCLA Fowler Museum of Cultural History.

Tilley, C. 1994. *A phenomenology of landscape: places, paths and monuments.* Oxford: Berg.

Tilley, C. 1996. The power of rocks: topography and monument construction on Bodmin Moor. *World Archaeology* 28, 161–76.

Tilley, C. and Bennett, W. 2001. An archaeology of supernatural places: the case of West Penwith. *The Journal of the Royal Anthropological Institute* 7, 335–63.

Turk, F.A. 1967. Report on the animal bone remains from Nornour. *Journal of the Royal Institute of Cornwall* 5, 250–66.

Turk, F.A. 1978. The animal remains from Nornour: a synoptic view of the finds. *Cornish Archaeology* 17, 99–103.

Turk, F.A. 1984a. A study of the vertebrate remains from May's Hill, St Martins. *Cornish Studies* 1, 69–80.

Turk, F.A. 1984b. *The sub fauna of Cornwall and the Isles of Scilly.* Redruth: Cornish Biological Records, Institute of Cornish Studies.

Ucko, P. and Layton, R. (eds) 1999. *The archaeology and anthropology of landscape.* London: Routledge.

Woodman, P.E. 2000. Beyond significant patterns towards past intentions: the location of Orcadian chambered tombs. In, C. Buck, V. Cummings, C. Henley, S. Mills and S. Trick. *UK Chapter of Computer applications and quantative methods in archaeology: proceedings of the fourth meeting at Cardiff University, 27th and 28th February 199,* 91–105. Oxford: British Archaeological Reports, International series 844.

12 Prehistoric sea journeys and port approaches: the south coast and Poole Harbour

Eileen Wilkes

Introduction

Travel over water is a different experience from travel over land, involving other fundamental elements such as tides, currents, wind and waves. Journeys by sea do not have the benefit of paths or trackways, but rather rely on different signs such as water colour and depth, the nature of the sea-bed, the sound of waves breaking, the smell of the land, the sight of birds, and other almost intuitive perceptions to guide the passage. Landmarks and sea-marks are important navigation aids both *en route* and for safe pilotage to the destination. There, artificial structures such as quays, jetties or hards dictate the direction of movement through the bay or harbour area. Many of these factors have not changed since later prehistory. This paper sets out how they can still be used to identify the possible locations of late prehistoric sites on the south coast of Britain, and examines in detail features at the Iron Age port of Poole Harbour in Dorset.

The northern coast of the English Channel, between Land's End and Dover, extends for *c.* 1600km along the high water mark. This stretch has a very varied geology and landform. Coastal topography ranges from low-lying sand or shingle beaches to dramatic rock or chalk cliffs rising sheer from the sea.[1] This variety in the coast to a great extent dictated the form of settlement or construction along it. However, when viewed from a maritime perspective it is clear that, despite the variety in topography, common natural physical features can be recognised at coastal sites.

A maritime perspective on port approaches

Sea journeys in the Iron Age were undertaken for a variety of purposes including trade, conflict, fishing and gathering resources, and travel for social reasons. Earlier writers, drawing on written sources from the classical period onwards, have concluded that ancient mariners tended to 'hug the coast' or 'move crabwise from rock to rock' (Eric de Bisschop 1939, quoted by Braudel 1972, 103), staying within sight of land for as much of the journey as possible, and only crossing open water such as the English Channel by the shortest routes (e.g. Braudel 1972; Davis 1997; Piggott 1979; but see also Winslade 2001). Such strategies would permit landmarks, water depths and colour changes to be more easily observed and keep the vessel in close proximity to shelter.

It is clear that this process would have required a series of landfall sites along the south coast, and it is also clear that these were not limited to the sites discussed most frequently in the literature: Hengistbury Head in Dorset and Mount Batten in Devon. In later prehistory, as now, different scales of harbour facilities each served particular needs. A variety of coastal site types, which included breakwaters, waterfronts, and other artificial facilities, are known from the Mediterranean from the early first millennium BC and probably before (for example, Carthage, Delos, Massalia, Ostia, Puteoli, and the Piraeus: Casson 1971, 362–70). It is suggested here that the English Channel was similarly served with maritime facilities, albeit generally, though not always, of less monumental form. As well as large complexes with established harbours, such as Dover (Rigold 1969; Wilkes 2004, 114–17; 392–4), smaller sites will have provided temporary safe havens on long coasting voyages or places for local trading activities. The coast varied and the sites along it were also different in size, physical characteristics, infrastructure and features: diverse needs were addressed and there were different scales of operation. However, all required particular natural conditions, often enhanced by artificial developments.

When undertaking journeys over water, Iron Age mariners had available types of vessel which were each suited to different conditions and environments. Evidence for various forms of craft (log boats, hide boats and plank boats) can be found in

Table 12.1. Physical traits of later prehistoric coastal nodes (after Wilkes 2004, 104)

1	Position on the coast with favourable tides and currents, and safe and easy entrance that was free from hazards at a location accessible from known along and across Channel routes .
2	Access to river/s, often via a tidal estuary/harbour.
3	Promontory or headland location to serve as a sea-mark, demarcated area, and to offer shelter (to vessels on the water and facilities on land).
4	Presence of a prominent land mark identifiable from sea (if not a promontory or headland location).
5	Shelter from winds, especially the predominant westerlies.
6	Safe haven with good anchoring/mooring locations, often in a harbour, with space for manoeuvring vessels.
7	Beaching points and/or formal waterside facilities such as jetties, quays or maintained hards.
8	Capacity for securely storing imports and exports.
9	Capacity for facilities to serve people and pack animals.

the archaeological record and classical texts (see Wilkes 2004, 79–86). Log boats (e.g. the Poole Harbour log boat: Peers 1965) were generally for use on inland waters and rivers (but see McGrail 1995, 261). They were propelled by paddle or by pole in shallow waters and could be beached on a suitable foreshore or brought alongside a quay, jetty or larger vessel. Similarly, small hide boats, with skins stretched over a wicker or wooden frame, were for inland and coastal use, but larger hide vessels were equipped with masts and sails and some also with oars, making them sturdy vessels suitable for off-shore use. Although no vessels of this type have yet been found in British waters, their use in later prehistory is suggested by classical references[2] and illustrated by the gold Broighter model (Farrell and Penny 1975) and the Caergwrle model, the latter made of shale inlaid with precious metal (Green 1985; Meyrick 1827). Plank boats of different sizes were also designed for use in rivers and estuaries or on the open sea, some with paddles or poles, others with sails and/or oars.[3] Several examples of plank boats have been found in Britain, including at Brigg (McGrail 1981), Caldicot (Parry and McGrail 1991), Dover (Clark 2004), Ferriby (Wright 1990), Goldcliff (Bell *et al.* 2000) and Kilnsea (Van de Noort *et al.* 1999).

The investigation of prehistoric boats and seafaring has developed substantially in the late twentieth century. The term 'maritime perspective' was first used by Keith Muckelroy (1981) and subsequently incorporated into the idea of a 'maritime cultural landscape' by Westerdahl (1992) and Hunter (1994), a concept which in turn has recently been reviewed by Parker (2001). Muckelroy did not specifically define the term but it is generally taken, and used here, to mean the view of the land from the sea, as much as from traditional terrestrial approaches (see Cooney 2003).

The present writer adopted this perspective in recent doctoral research which examined the Iron Age coast of southern Britain in order to identify suitable locations for use by contemporary shipping (Wilkes 2004). These locations, the arenas of along- and across-Channel interactions where sea journeys start and finish, were defined as 'coastal nodes'. They are contact points within the maritime network and between the coast and inland networks, based on the concept of 'transit points' (see Westerdahl 1992, 6). 40 nodal locations were identified which conform, to a greater or lesser degree, with a suite of common physical characteristics (summarised in Table 12.1) that were recognised as necessary both for contemporary shipping and occupation on land (Fig. 12.1). The suite of consistent characteristics was distilled from earlier works (including Davis 1997; McGrail 1993; Westerdahl 1992) and from factors arising from vessel requirements and nautical considerations.

Although identified by their correspondence with the suite of physical characteristics, the 40 locations are diverse in scale and use. They range from large sites with artificial facilities, such as at Dover and Poole Harbour, which were probably primary journey destinations, to small 'safe havens' which might have been little more than shelter points on the coastal network, such as Mullion, Cornwall. Some of the locations had earlier origins with evidence of use as a 'coastal node' during the Bronze Age (as at Hayling Island in Hampshire and the Kingsbridge Estuary in Devon), and many exhibit continuity of use into the Roman period (including Dover and Topsham). Nearly all were associated with one or more high ground enclosures (including monuments classified as hillforts) which served a variety of purposes such as control/monitoring points on routes to/from the coast, places for communal gatherings, and for manufacturing activities and storage.

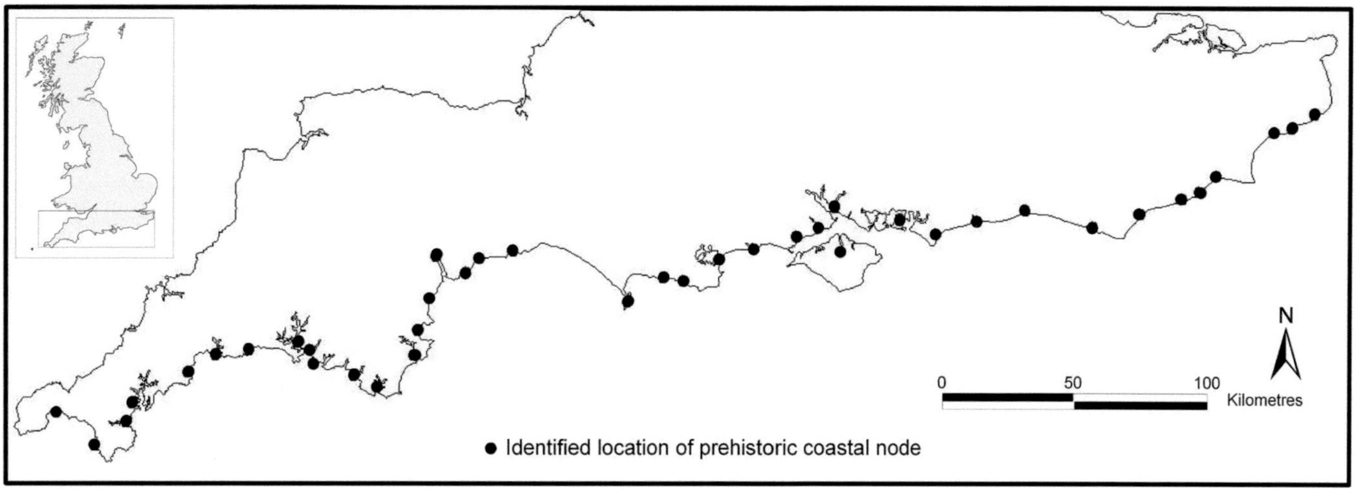

Fig. 12.1. Locations of the 40 Iron Age coastal nodes on the south coast (after Wilkes 2004, fig. 76)

Navigating to the right place and making a safe arrival at land are the principal requirements for any voyage. A location on or near the coast which is suitable for occupation and inland communications is not necessarily appropriate for safe access from the sea. The use by vessels of a coastal site on the south coast would have been heavily dependent on the criteria listed in Table 12.1, essentially concerned with issues of accessibility, visibility, shelter, and infrastructure (although not all of the listed criteria are present or expected at all coastal node locations).

Analysis of the common physical traits at certain coastal sites sheds light on how prehistoric mariners viewed the land from the sea. Land is the most dangerous thing for a mariner: it has to be approached carefully with attention to detail to make the right passage, avoiding hazards *en route* and navigating the closing zone (area of immediate approach) to the beaching spot or berthing facility. Landmarks are used in different ways: lined up to direct passage through hazards, used to indicate where to change course, make landfall, etc. Familiarity with landmarks is usually essential to follow a route between places. The names of significant landmarks are often based on physical descriptions of features as perceived from the sea. Such knowledge could be passed between mariners and handed on, given form by the naming of places both on the coast and in the sea (cf. Waters 1967). These names can be very long-lived and often the names applied to navigation marks and indicators in the past persist in the names of land sites today (Griffith and Wilkes 2007).

There are thus a wide range of factors that affected both the execution and the experience of a sea or coastal journey in the later prehistoric period. These will now be examined in the case study of Poole Harbour, an important element of the late Iron Age coastal network of southern Britain.

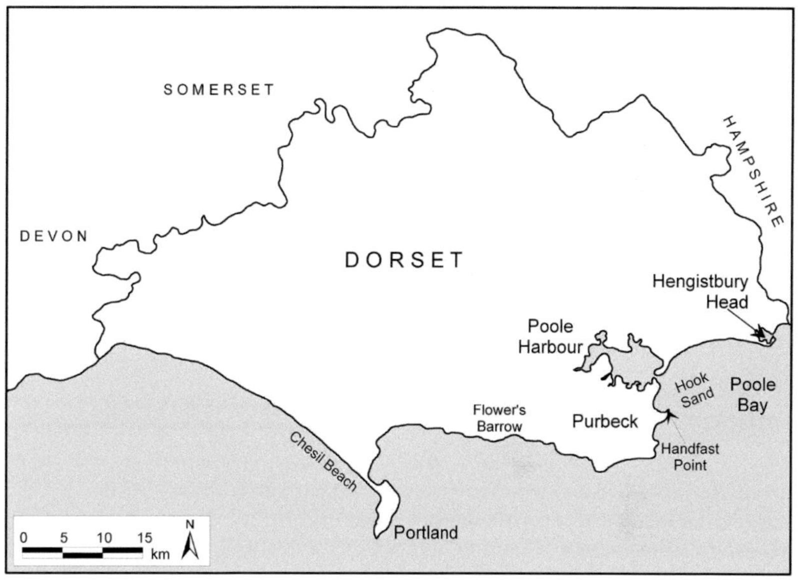

Fig. 12.2. Natural and artificial landmarks observed on the outer approaches to Poole Bay and Poole Harbour

Poole Harbour, Dorset

Poole Harbour is located half-way along the English Channel on the west side of Poole Bay. It covers almost 4000ha and is one of the largest, yet shallowest, harbours in the world (Fig. 12.2). It is fed by four rivers, the Corfe, Frome, Piddle (or Trent) and Sherford, which together drain over 77,500ha of Dorset and adjacent areas. The harbour experiences a double tide in each 24 hours with a current range of just 1.3m between low and high springs (*c.* 0.5m AOD and 1.8m AOD respectively) – one of the lowest ranges on the English Channel coast. Within the harbour today there are three main islands, Brownsea, Furzey and Green Island (Fig. 12.3). Two deep water channels (Middle Ship Channel and South Deep) provide corridors for water flow and access for vessels of all sizes. Modern

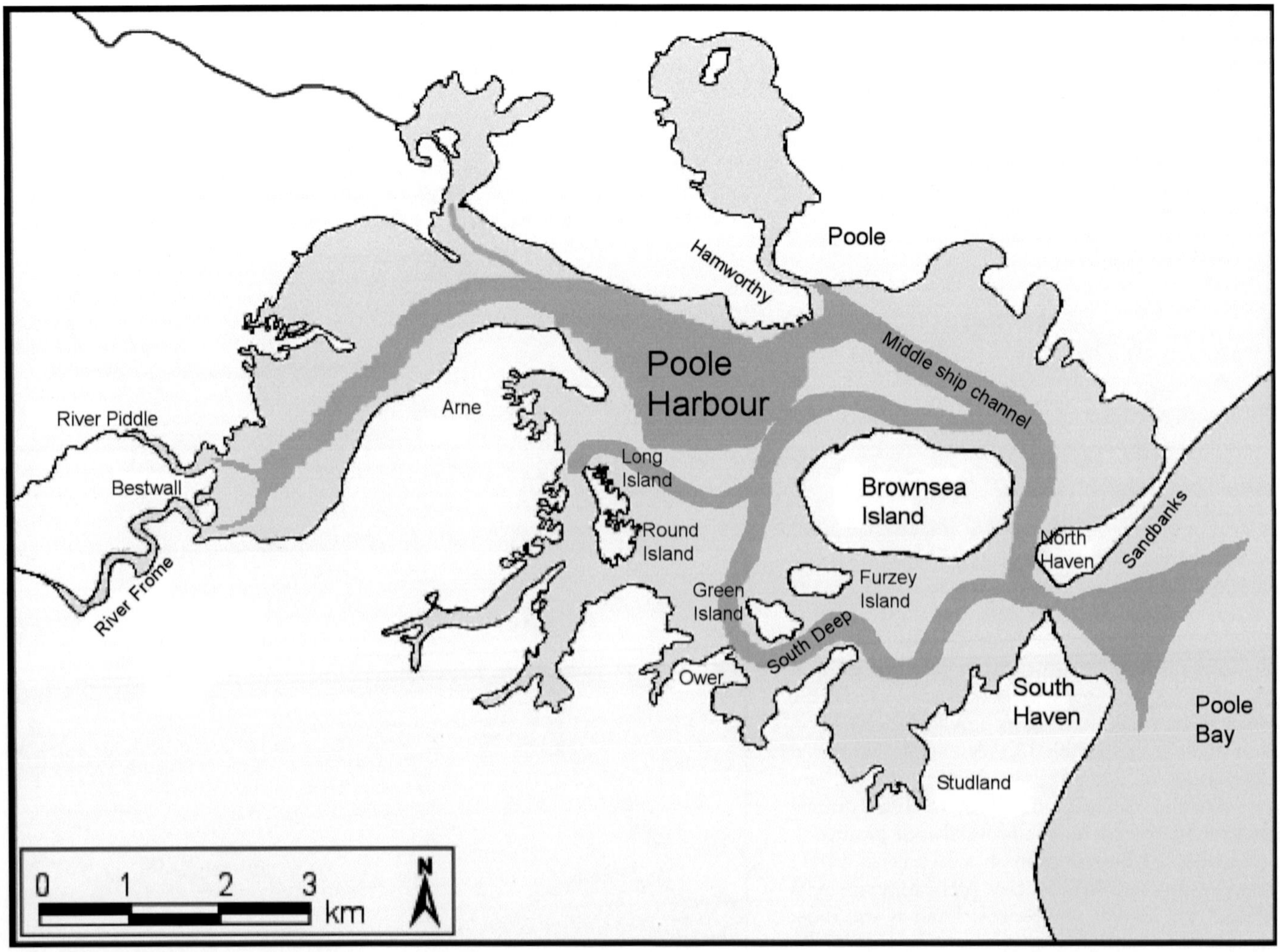

Fig. 12.3. Plan of Poole Harbour and places mentioned in the text

dredging regimes mean that the northern channel, the Middle Ship Channel, is now the preferred route from the harbour entrance to the main port facilities of Poole. Emerging evidence in Poole Harbour hydrographic studies indicates that in antiquity, prior to dredging and the use of mechanically powered craft, the more sheltered South Deep channel leading directly to the Corfe River, Upper Wych, Wareham Channel and rivers Frome and Piddle, was probably the favoured route (G. Wareham, former Poole Harbour Master *pers. comm.*).

Poole Harbour contains a number of the elements which have been identified as characterising an Iron Age coastal node complex (Table 12.2), and it appears to have been an important destination for prehistoric journeys. Earlier studies (including Hawkes 1953 and Piggott 1979) identified Poole as a terminus of prehistoric cross-Channel routes. It offered a safe haven for seafarers and was the transit point between maritime and riverine networks. It was also a focal point for maritime trade, where imports were received from other parts of Britain and the continent, and material for export was gathered and prepared.

Traders were attracted to Poole Harbour by the natural resources extracted from the harbour's hinterland, including good quality clays, Purbeck stone, shale and salt, and objects which were produced locally from those resources. From the Bronze Age onwards items manufactured from Kimmeridge shale were distributed throughout southern Britain and further afield: for example, the Farway cup in Devon (Fox 1948); the Caergwrle model boat in Wales (Green 1985; Meyrick 1827); and hand-made and lathe-turned armlets recovered from locations in Britain and north-west France. The manufacture of shale items is known at various sites around Poole Harbour including Green Island, where both hand-working and lathe-turning practices were employed to produce the distinctive shale armlets in the late Iron Age (Calkin 1955; Wilkes 2004). Pottery produced around the harbour during the middle Iron Age was the precursor to Black Burnished Ware, widely distributed in the late

1	It is located at a convenient point along the English Channel coast, on known routes and with favourable (double) tides for frequent access and beaching.
2	The tidal harbour provided access to inland waterway routes.
3	The harbour entrance was identifiable to vessels at sea as a break in the low cliff line.
4	Land marks such as Hengistbury Head and Old Harry served to guide mariners in to Poole Bay and towards the harbour.
5	The harbour offered shelter from winds, including westerlies.
6	It was a safe haven with good anchoring/mooring locations.
7	Formal waterside constructions are suggested by the 'Green Island causeway' (see text).
8	There was capacity on the mainland and islands for securely storing imports and exports and to accommodate people and animals.
9	Iron Age material (locally produced and imported from other regions of Britain and from the continent) has been found on the mainland and the islands.

Table 12.2. Coastal node characteristics of Poole Harbour

Iron Age and Roman periods (see Allen and Fulford 1997; Holbrook 2001). Production sites are known at Worgret (Hearne and Smith 1991) and other locations in the immediate hinterland of the harbour (Farrar 1977; 1982), including Bestwall Quarry where excavation has recently been completed (Ladle 2003).

Later prehistoric activity is well attested, particularly in the southern littoral of the harbour area. On the mainland at Ower a planned settlement was established, it has been suggested, in 20 BC (Cox and Hearne 1991; Woodward 1987) although an earlier date for the occupation of this strategic harbour-side location cannot be dismissed (Wilkes 2004, 179). The late Iron Age settlement is associated with local, regional and international maritime trade, receiving continental imports and exporting locally produced wares. The resources of the harbour and its hinterland provided the materials to manufacture items for trade or exchange along the coast and across the Channel which sustained harbour settlements in an agriculturally poor area.

The approach to Poole Harbour and the 'port' within

The coastal approach to Poole Bay is recognised by outlier landmarks which are distinctive when viewed from the sea. Travelling from the east, the approach passes The Solent, the entrance to which is marked by the Isle of Wight with its distinctive white chalk cliffs facing towards Poole. From the west, the coastal journey passes the prominent point of Portland Bill and follows the line of Purbeck cliffs, past the recognisable earthworks of Flower's Barrow hillfort and numerous tumuli which can be seen against the skyline from vessels at sea.

At the end of the voyage, the closing zone to Poole Harbour is through Poole Bay, which is reached from the east by rounding the headland of

Fig. 12.4. Handfast Point and Old Harry as seen on the approach to Poole Harbour (Photo: Eileen Wilkes, 2002)

Hengistbury Head and following the low sand cliffs of the Bournemouth and Poole heaths. From the west, the bay is approached from the dramatic line of sheer Purbeck cliffs, past landmarks such as the chalk promontory of Handfast Point, now a series of stacks at Harry Rocks (Fig. 12.4), which signal the proximity of the harbour entrance. Immediately outside the harbour it is necessary to navigate around Hook Sand, a submerged sand bar, but otherwise the approach is generally clear of obstacles and sheltered by land from winds in all directions other than the east.

The current entrance to Poole Harbour is narrow, less than 300m wide between the two low sand banks of North Haven and South Haven (Sandbanks and Studland). This creates a funnelled run of water at spring tides that can be utilised advantageously by small craft, depending on wind direction, if the approach is timed to coincide with the flood. Surface currents run through the harbour mouth at *c.* 4 knots at spring tides and *c.* 2.5 knots at other times (HMSO 1943, 100). When the harbour first formed in the immediate post-glacial period, the entrance was over two miles wide (Robinson 1955, 35). The sand banks which define the present harbour mouth appear as spits with opposed directions of growth (Robinson 1955, 35). Current research (Cook forthcoming) has suggested that the harbour entrance may have been *c.* 1.5km to the north in later prehistory and less than 500m wide (R. Cook *pers. comm.*; see also Green 1940; Robinson 1955; Ward 1922, 97). However, the approach through Poole Bay would have followed the same route past Hook Sand, and within the harbour the entrance channel fed directly into the southern channel leading to South Deep.

Iron Age vessels passed through the entrance and would have faced directly towards the low mass of Brownsea Island. The main channel in antiquity, South Deep, curved away to the south, meandering through mud flats with open heath beyond (Fig. 12.5). Mariners travelled past 'South Island' (the combined landmass of what has now separated into Green Island and Furzey Island) following the line of South Deep as it ran between Ower and the Island. It is here that voyagers were confronted with what is currently thought to be a unique sight in British coastal waters. Leading out from both the mainland at Ower and the western shore of what is now Green Island was a pair of stone and timber moles.

The structures have recently been interpreted as jetties (Markey *et al.* 2002). These are erroneously labelled on Admiralty charts as a single structure, the 'Green Island causeway'. The moles were described in antiquarian texts as the remains of a bridge connecting Ower and Green Island (Hutchins 1774), and their first investigation was undertaken by a group of Boy Scouts in 1959 which revealed the timber and stone construction of the 'causeway' (Taylor 1959). However, recent excavation and survey (Markey *et al.* 2002) has confirmed that the two structures are on slightly different alignments so are unlikely ever to have formed one continuous 'causeway', and the 70m gap between them is too large to have been spanned by a bridge in antiquity. In addition, each 'jetty' has clearly constructed seaward terminals and an investigation by divers of the channel between the two terminals revealed no structural evidence or any loose material beyond their ends (Markey 2001). Oak timbers retrieved from both structures have so far provided ten radiocarbon determinations (Fig. 12.6) which suggest a middle Iron Age date for the construction of the 'jetties'.[4] The structures survive today intact, as far as is known, beneath more than a metre of accumulated mud, silt and the higher water level in Poole Harbour (Fig. 12.7).

Fig. 12.5. Aerial view across South Deep to the entrance of Poole Harbour (Photo: Eileen Wilkes, 2003)

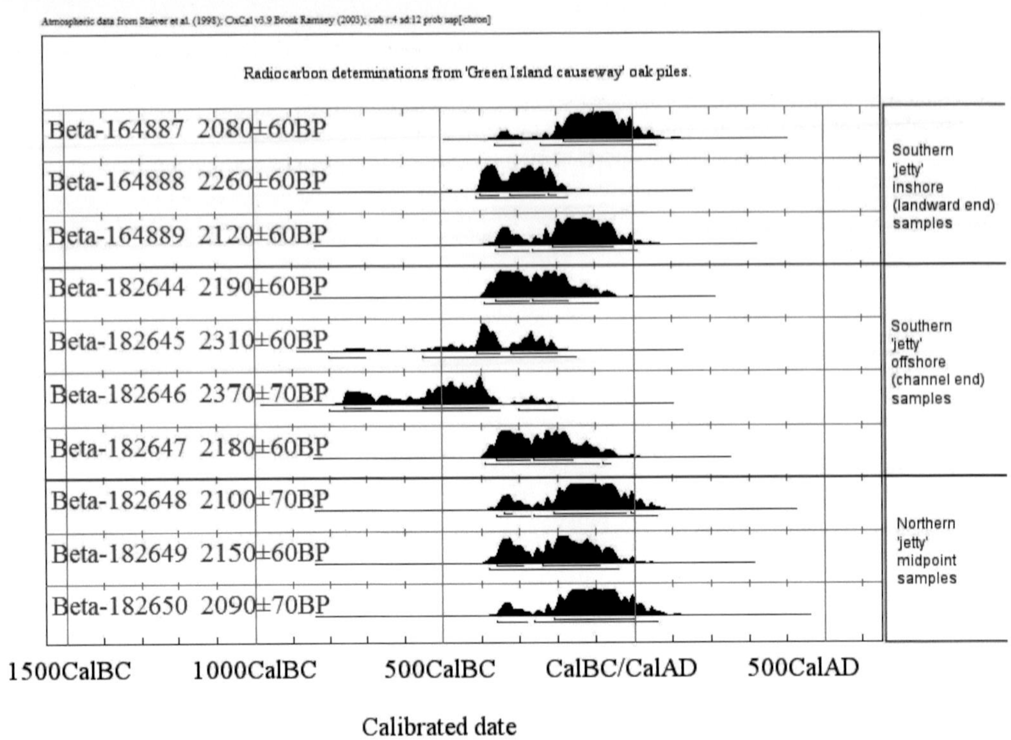

Fig. 12.6. Radiocarbon determinations from timbers retrieved from the 'jetties' in South Deep (after Wilkes 2004, fig. 40)

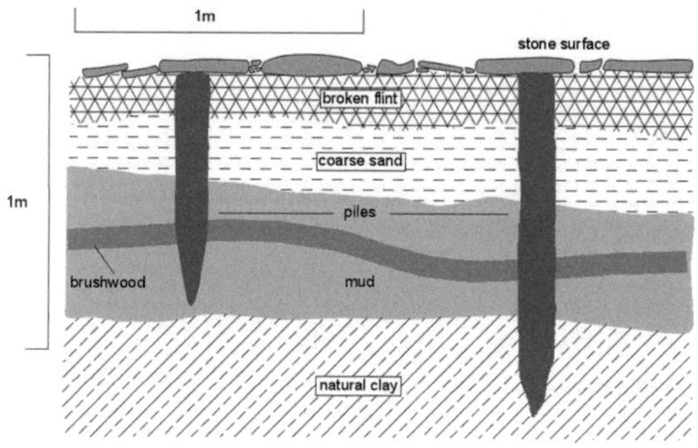

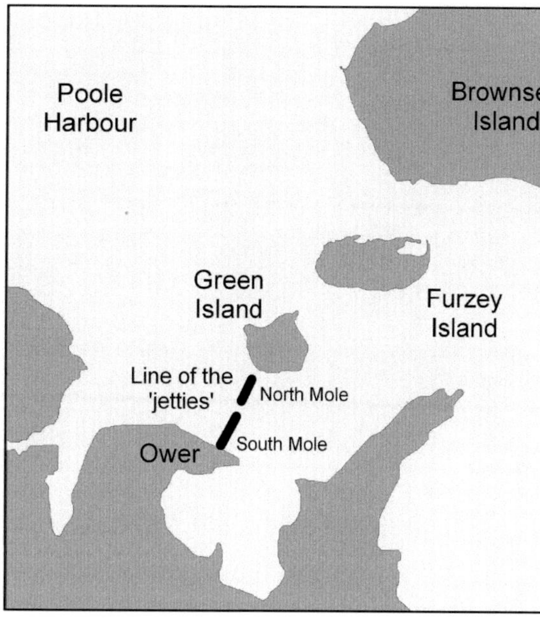

Fig. 12.7. (top left) View along the southern 'jetty' towards South Deep and Green Island, 27 March 2002. The conditions required for the 'jetties' to break the water surface in this way at low water rarely occur (Photo: Eileen Wilkes)

Fig. 12.8. (bottom left) Schematic illustration of section through the southern 'jetty' as recorded during excavation in August 2001 (after Markey 2001, fig. 7)

Fig. 12.9. (above) Location of the two structures in South Deep. The southern mole is c. 165m long; the northern mole is c. 65m long and terminates c. 70m from the current shore of Green Island. Both moles are c. 8m wide across their top surfaces.

The design of the moles is complex and they would have required considerable labour to construct. They are built around a framework of vertical oak piles (from which the radiocarbon determinations were obtained) and horizontal cross-members which contains a sequence of consolidating layers of gravel, sand, clay (silt/mud) and flint (Markey *et al.* 2002; Fig. 12.8). They were prominent features and appear to have been constructed to create a striking impression on approaching mariners. They are massive structures, at least eight metres wide across their top surface, and capped along that surface and a short way down the sides with the local Purbeck 'marble' which has been fashioned into slabs. These dimensions are greater than would have been necessary for purely functional reasons either as jetties or as moles to protect an inner harbour from the weather. A functional jetty, then as now, could have been constructed from timber piles and planking, which would permit water to flow under the pier and vessels to tie-up alongside. The rubble, sand and flint infill, and Purbeck marble capping are not essential to provide a sturdy operating jetty, and this suggests they were constructed for purposes other than use solely as jetties.

An alternative interpretation can now be proposed which reflects the symbolic and formal elements of the structures, as well as their practical function. It is difficult to see why, in functional terms, a jetty from Green Island would be needed in addition to one from Ower, as port activity appears to have been confined to the mainland site. While it is clear that the shore of Green Island has retreated significantly since the Iron Age (Fig. 12.9), no evidence for port activity has ever been identified. In 1967, Bugler, in one of the first papers to discuss the submerged remains, listed seven proposals for the function of the 'Green Island causeway', one of which was that it was a boom defence for protection against possible Viking raids during the Saxon period (Bugler 1967, 160). The complexity of the structure meant that a prehistoric date was not considered at that time. It is not suggested here that the structures were purely defensive, but rather that the moles may be considered as control points to monitor waterborne traffic into and out of the main harbour area (Wilkes 2004, 210–3). These complex timber and stone structures are located at the narrowest point of South Deep channel and, as they project into the water, serve to narrow that gap further to just 70m (Fig. 12.9). This would be an obvious location for access control, with the striking appearance of the Purbeck marble topped structures further enhancing the 'gateway' entrance to an inner harbour basin and the riverine routes. As such, the structures marked the entrance to the heart of the harbour complex and paralleled the entrance from the sea between two extended sand spits, so providing visual continuity between natural and artificial grandeur (Fig. 12.10). The monumentality of their appearance could also have reflected the importance attributed to the maritime/trade function and/or the status of the community operating the node. They mark the achievement of the voyage's destination and provide a visual statement of the 'gateway' function of the port and the transition to the inner harbour network.

Fig. 12.10. Artist's impression of the approach to the two Iron Age moles in South Deep (Mike A'Court)

The use of such structures was a feature of Mediterranean harbours, as at fifth century BC Piraeus (the port of Athens) and Motya (a Phoenician harbour on Sicily) where the entrances were deliberately narrowed by the construction of moles (Shaw 1972). In both cases, immediately within the narrowed entrance was a 'cothon', a holding basin for vessels arriving to unload or preparing to leave through the gap (Shaw 1972), and work is in hand to investigate whether such a feature existed at Poole (Wilkes in prep a). At Piraeus, the access was further protected by a chain that could be drawn up between the two moles. The 70m span between the South Deep moles could easily be closed by a chain in this way. Although in northern Europe no channel-blocking chains are recorded, we know that chains were in use for other purposes by the late Iron Age. They are described by Caesar (*de Bello Gallico* III.13) and a probable Iron Age example was found with an anchor at Bulbury Hill (Cunliffe 1972; Cunnington 1884), approximately five kilometres north of the harbour.

The location of the control point was important to safeguard people and goods at the settlements, production sites and trade areas around the harbour. Adequate security and control is a recognised feature of 'port of trade' sites (see Polanyi 1963). The output from the hinterland was fundamental to the economy of individual sites and the area as a whole. Access to the hinterland and manufacturing sites was primarily by the harbour and riverine waterways, the outflows of which all lie within the area of the harbour beyond South Deep and 'inside' the line of the two structures.

The reinterpretation of the structures as impressive monumental statements and access control points rather than operational jetties does not diminish the role of Poole Harbour as a major coastal node and port. Rather, it reinforces the importance of the port of Poole Harbour, and the need to control access to the sites, ships and cargo within. While the location of the moles is topographically dictated at the narrowest crossing point across what was in antiquity the main channel into the inner harbour, it also provides, in terms of perception of the arriving mariner, a striking effect. After the entrance to the harbour between two sandbanks, the symbolic effect of the artificial barrier in South Deep would have been that of the second pair of doors of a vestibule. Here was the human control to match the natural. Fig. 12.10 shows the view from the water looking up the channel. The 'double door' effect emphasised the control of overall access to the harbour. While this is at present unparalleled in a north European context, if this interpretation is correct it tells us both about the importance of the interior of Poole Harbour in the later prehistoric period and also the levels of social control that can be postulated.

Conclusion

Nowadays, the sea is perceived not as a barrier to prehistoric interactions but as a facilitator of communications. Later prehistoric journeys over water were undertaken as the most efficient means by which to transport people and goods locally, regionally and internationally. Some journeys would have lasted for many days, others were direct sailings of a few hours' duration. Both the destinations and stop-off points *en route* needed to be identifiable from the sea and accessible to vessels in all weather conditions. By combining nautical and terrestrial considerations, it is possible to identify what locations on the coast would have been most suitable for use as ports and safe havens. The maritime perspective – viewing the land from the sea – is important to understand how movement across water was guided by features on land.

The coastal locations utilised by prehistoric mariners shared common physical traits of visibility, access, shelter and infrastructure, and were suitable for use by boats as well as serving the needs of people and animals on land. This paper has outlined how, after sea routes which were determined by elements, natural forces and conditions, the start and end of sea journeys were guided and controlled by natural and artificial features. A phenomenological view of sea approaches, as adopted for Poole Harbour, can usefully be applied to the other node locations which have been identified along the south coast (Wilkes in prep b). The example of Poole Harbour illustrates both how the landmarks can still be followed to guide the mariner and has highlighted the complexity, design and attention to detail with which port features were constructed to guide, and in this case possibly control, movement through the harbour.

Acknowledgements

This paper derives directly from the writer's PhD research which was carried out at Bournemouth University, supported by a studentship from the Arts and Humanities Research Board. The preparation of this paper was undertaken during the writer's tenure as the A.H.A. Hogg Fellow at the University of Wales, Lampeter. The work in Poole Harbour is supported by the Poole Harbour Heritage Project, and the underwater investigation of the 'jetties' has been undertaken by the Poole Bay Archaeological Research Group. The group's founder, Mike Markey, is particularly thanked for ongoing discussions and cooperation. Fig. 12.10 was prepared by Mike A'Court of the PHHP. The writer would like to thank all the groups, organisations and individuals mentioned, and Frances Griffith who commented on drafts of this paper.

Notes

1 One important consideration in reconstructing prehistoric coastal features is that the hard rocks of the south-west coasts (such as granite) have remained much more stable than the easily eroded sand and chalk shores of the south east where, according to May (1966), the shoreline has in some places changed by as much as 0.75 m per annum.

2 Although this subject has engendered much debate, it is useful to consider the comments of writers in antiquity regarding sea transport. Timaeus (quoted by Pliny 4.104) stated that hide vessels were used to carry exported tin from south-west Britain on sea voyages. Similarly, Aviensus, in Ora Maritima, related that the sixth century BC inhabitants of Ushant undertook trade in lead and tin by sea using hide boats (see Murphy 1977).

3 Flat-bottomed plank boats with leather sails were described by Caesar (de Bello Gallico III.13) and Strabo (Geography IV.41) as the type of vessel used by the Veneti of north-west France in the first century BC for journeys along and across the English Channel. The flat-hull design made them particularly suited for travel in the tidal waters of the Channel and beaching along the coast.

4 This matches the date determined for the Poole Harbour log boat found off Brownsea Island in 1964 (Peers 1965). Organic caulking provided a radiocarbon determination of 2245±50 BP (Q-821), subsequently re-calibrated to 397–176 BC (see McGrail and Switsur 1975).

Bibliography

Allen, J. and Fulford, M. 1996. The distribution of south-east Dorset black burnished category I pottery in south-west Britain. *Britannia* 27, 223–81.

Bell, M., Brunning, R., Johnson, S., McGrail, S., and Morgan, R. 2000. Boat planks of c. 1170 BC. In M. Bell, A. Caseldine and H. Neumann, *Prehistoric intertidal archaeology in the Welsh Severn Estuary*, 74–82. York: Council for British Archaeology.

Braudel, F. 1972. *The Mediterranean and the Mediterranean world in the age of Philip II.* London: Collins.

Bugler, J. 1967. Poole Harbour "causeway". *Proceedings of the Dorset Natural History and Archaeological Society* 88, 158–60.

Calkin, J. 1955. 'Kimmeridge coal-money': the Romano-British shale armlet industry. *Proceedings of the Dorset Natural History and Archaeological Society* 75, 45–71.

Casson, L. 1971. *Ships and seamanship in the ancient world.* Princeton: Princeton University Press.

Clark, P. 2004 (ed.). *The Dover Bronze Age boat.* Swindon: English Heritage.

Cook, R. forthcoming. *Spatial and temporal scales of the morphodynamic evolution within the Studland complex.* Bournemouth University, unpublished PhD thesis.

Cooney, G. 2003. Introduction: seeing land from the sea. *World Archaeology* 35, 323–8.

Cox, P. and Hearne, C. 1991. *Redeemed from the heath: archaeology of the Wytch Farm Oilfield (1987–90).* Dorset: Dorset Natural History and Archaeological Society.

Cunliffe, B. 1972. The late Iron Age metalwork from Bulbury, Dorset. *Antiquaries Journal* 52, 293–308.

Cunnington, E. 1884. On a hoard of bronze, iron, and other objects found in Belbury Camp, Dorset. *Archaeologia* 68, 115–20.

Davis, P. 1997. Some navigational considerations of pre-medieval trade between Cornwall and north-west Europe. *Cornish Archaeology* 36, 129–37.

Farrar, R. 1977. A Romano-British black-burnished ware industry at Ower in the Isle of Purbeck, Dorset. In J. Dore and K. Green (eds), *Roman pottery industries in Britain and beyond*, 199–228. Oxford: British Archaeological Reports.

Farrar, R. 1982. The Black Burnished ware factory at Redcliff, Arne. *Proceedings of the Dorset Natural History and Archaeological Society* 104, 186–7.

Farrell, A. and Penny, A. 1975. Broighter boat: a re-assessment. *Irish Archaeology Research Forum* 2.2, 15–26.

Fox, A. 1948. The Broad Down (Farway) necropolis and the Wessex Culture in Devon. *Proceedings of the Devon Archaeology and Exploration Society* 4, 1–19.

Green, F. 1940. *Poole Harbour: a hydrographic survey*. London: Geographical Publications.

Green, S. 1985. The Caergwrle bowl – not oak but shale. *Antiquity* 59, 116–7.

Griffith, F.M. and Wilkes, E.M. 2007. The land named from the sea? Coastal archaeology and place-names of Bigbury Bay, Devon. *Archaeological Journal* 163.

Hawkes, C. 1953. English Channel harbours for pre-historic trade. *Proceedings of the Isle of Wight Natural History and Archaeological Society* 4, 257–9.

Hearne, C. and Smith, R. 1991. A late Iron Age settlement and black-burnished ware (BB1) production site at Worgret, near Wareham, Dorset (1986–7). *Proceedings of the Dorset Natural History and Archaeological Society* 113, 55–105.

HMSO 1943. *Channel pilot for south coast of England and French coasts*. London: Her Majesty's Stationary Office.

Holbrook, N. 2001. Coastal trade around the south-west peninsula of Britain in the later Roman period: a summary of the evidence. *Proceedings of the Devon Archaeological Society* 59, 149–58.

Hunter, J. 1994. 'Maritime Culture': notes from the land. *International Journal of Nautical Archaeology* 23, 261–4.

Hutchins, J. 1774. *The history and antiquities of the county of Dorset*. London: Nichols and Sons.

Ladle, L. 2003. Bestwall Quarry. *Current Archaeology* 186, 268–73.

McGrail, S. 1981. *Brigg 'raft' and her prehistoric environment*. Oxford: British Archaeological Reports.

McGrail, S. 1993. Prehistoric seafaring in the Channel. In C. Scarre and F. Healy (eds), *Trade and exchange in prehistoric Europe*, 199–210. Oxford: Oxbow.

McGrail, S. 1995. Celtic seafaring and transport. In M. Green (ed.), *The Celtic world*, 254–81. London: Routledge.

McGrail, S. and Switsur, R. 1975. Early boats and their chronology. *International Journal of Nautical Archaeology and Underwater Exploration* 4, 191–200.

Markey, M. 2001. *Green Island causeway: 2001 fieldwork*. Unpublished report of the Poole Bay Archaeological Group.

Markey, M., Wilkes, E. and Darvill, T. 2002. Poole Harbour: Iron Age port. *Current Archaeology* 181, 7–11.

May, V. 1966. A preliminary study of recent coastal changes and sea defences in south-east England. *Southampton Research Series in Geography* 3, 3–24.

Meyrick, S. 1827. An ancient British cup. *Archaeologia* 21, 542–3.

Muckelroy, K. 1981. Middle Bronze Age trade between Britain and Europe: a maritime perspective. *Proceedings of the Prehistoric Society* 47, 275–97.

Murphy, J. 1977. *Rufus Festus Avienus, Ora maritima*. Chicago: Ares.

Parker, A. 2001. Maritime landscapes. *Landscapes* 1, 22–41.

Parry, S. and McGrail. S. 1991. A prehistoric plank boat fragment and a hard from Caldicot Castle Lake, Gwent, Wales. *International Journal of Nautical Archaeology* 20, 321–4.

Peers, R. 1965. Dugout canoe from Poole Harbour, Dorset. *Proceedings of the Dorset Natural History and Archaeological Society* 85, 131–4.

Piggott, S. 1979. South-west England – north-west Europe: contrasts and contacts in prehistory. *Proceedings of the Devon Archaeological Society* 37, 10–20.

Polanyi, K. 1963. Ports of trade in early societies. *Journal of Economic History* 23, 30–45.

Rigold, S. 1969. The Roman haven of Dover. *Archaeological Journal* 76, 78–100.

Robinson, A. 1955. The harbour entrances of Poole, Christchurch and Pagham. *Geographical Journal* 121, 33–50.

Shaw, J. 1972. Greek and Roman harbourworks. In G. Bass (ed.), *A history of seafaring based on underwater archaeology*, 87–112. London: Omega/Thames and Hudson.

Taylor, W.H. 1959. *Green Island causeway*. Privately published for the Boy Scouts' Association.

Van de Noort, R., Middleton, R., Foxon, A. and Bayliss, A. 1999. The 'Kilnsea Boat', and some implications from the discovery of England's oldest plank boat remains. *Antiquity* 73, 131–5.

Ward, E. 1922. *English coastal evolution*. London: Methuen.

Waters, D.W. 1967. *The rutters of the sea: the sailing directions of Pierre Garcie*. New Haven and London: Yale University Press.

Westerdahl, C. 1992. The maritime cultural landscape. *International Journal of Nautical Archaeology* 21, 5–14.

Wilkes, E. 2004. *Iron Age maritime nodes on the English Channel coast: an investigation into the location, nature and context of early ports and harbours*. Bournemouth University, unpublished PhD thesis.

Wilkes, E. in prep a. Coastal and intertidal survey of inner Poole Harbour.

Wilkes, E. in prep b. Later prehistoric coastal nodes in south-west Britain.

Winslade, R. 2001. Navigational considerations of pre-medieval trade between Cornwall and Brittany: a reply to Mr P.R. Davis. *Cornish Archaeology* 39–40, 228–30.

Woodward, P. 1987. Excavations of a late Iron Age trading settlement and Romano-British BB1 pottery production site at Ower, Dorset. In N. Sunter and P. Woodward, *Romano-British industries in Purbeck*, 44–124. Dorchester: Dorset Natural History and Archaeological Society.

Wright, E. 1990. *The Ferriby boats*. London: Routledge.

13 Trackways, hooves and memory-days – human and animal movements and memories around the Iron Age and Romano-British rural landscapes of the English north midlands

Adrian M. Chadwick

Introduction – the journey begins

I want to take you with me on a journey around some of the settlements and field systems of the Iron Age and Romano-British periods, examining the routine movements of people and animals around these landscapes. I will explore how the biographies, identities and memories of animals and people were interwoven through mutually interdependent seasonal rhythms of life and movement, and animal and human agency. These mundane movements were, in the alternative sense of the word 'mundane', worldly and grounded pathways of place. It is also a means of considering the social, historical, political and symbolic significance of these landscapes to the people who inhabited them. This will be a temporal journey too, through the seasons and across over 1400 years of human and animal history, and alighting upon particular places and features within these landscapes.

The landscapes of the north midlands – open spaces and wet places

The focus of this paper is Nottinghamshire, South Yorkshire and West Yorkshire, which for convenience I term the north midlands (Fig. 13.1). Aerial photographs of this region have revealed extensive field systems, trackways and enclosures dating to the later Iron Age and Romano-British periods (Chadwick 1998; Cox 1984; Deegan 1996; 2001a; Riley 1980; Whimster 1989). From the Trent Valley in Nottinghamshire and up to the Rivers Don, Thorne and Idle in South Yorkshire, there are broad, shallow alluvial valleys interspersed with gentle gravel ridges. Sherwood sandstones are the principal hard geology, and the soils are light and well drained on higher ground. To the north and west of the Rivers Trent and Don, the ground rises onto Magnesian limestone and Coal Measures forming more undulating landscapes, cut by occasional river valleys, with greater topographic contrasts and sharper ridgelines. The Lower Coal Measures form an elevated plain with localised folds of ground and lines of small hills. Further west again, the land rises higher to the Millstone Grit shelves and Carboniferous limestone plateau of the Pennines and Peak District. The soils are wetter and more acidic to the west, but drier and more calcareous to the east. One problem hampering archaeological interpretation is that bone and palaeo-environmental preservation is poor, except from sites on the Magnesian limestone.

I first became interested in the Iron Age and Romano-British archaeology of this region during the early 1990s when I was working for the South Yorkshire Archaeology Unit. Along with colleagues, I became very frustrated at the marginalisation of this archaeology in the literature. For example, Cunliffe's supposedly magisterial *Iron Age Communities in Britain* volume only devoted a few lines of text to the Magnesian Limestone areas of West Yorkshire (Cunliffe 1991, 279), and he made no mention of Coal Measures or Sherwood Sandstone areas and river valley systems. This archaeology effectively did not exist, simply because there was no mention of it in general or national publications (Cumberpatch and Robbins 1995; Robbins 1998). I hope that my own writing, some of it produced as the result of PhD research, goes some way to redressing this imbalance.

By the late Iron Age, these landscapes were essentially open in character, with farmsteads interspersed with fields and possibly hedges, and

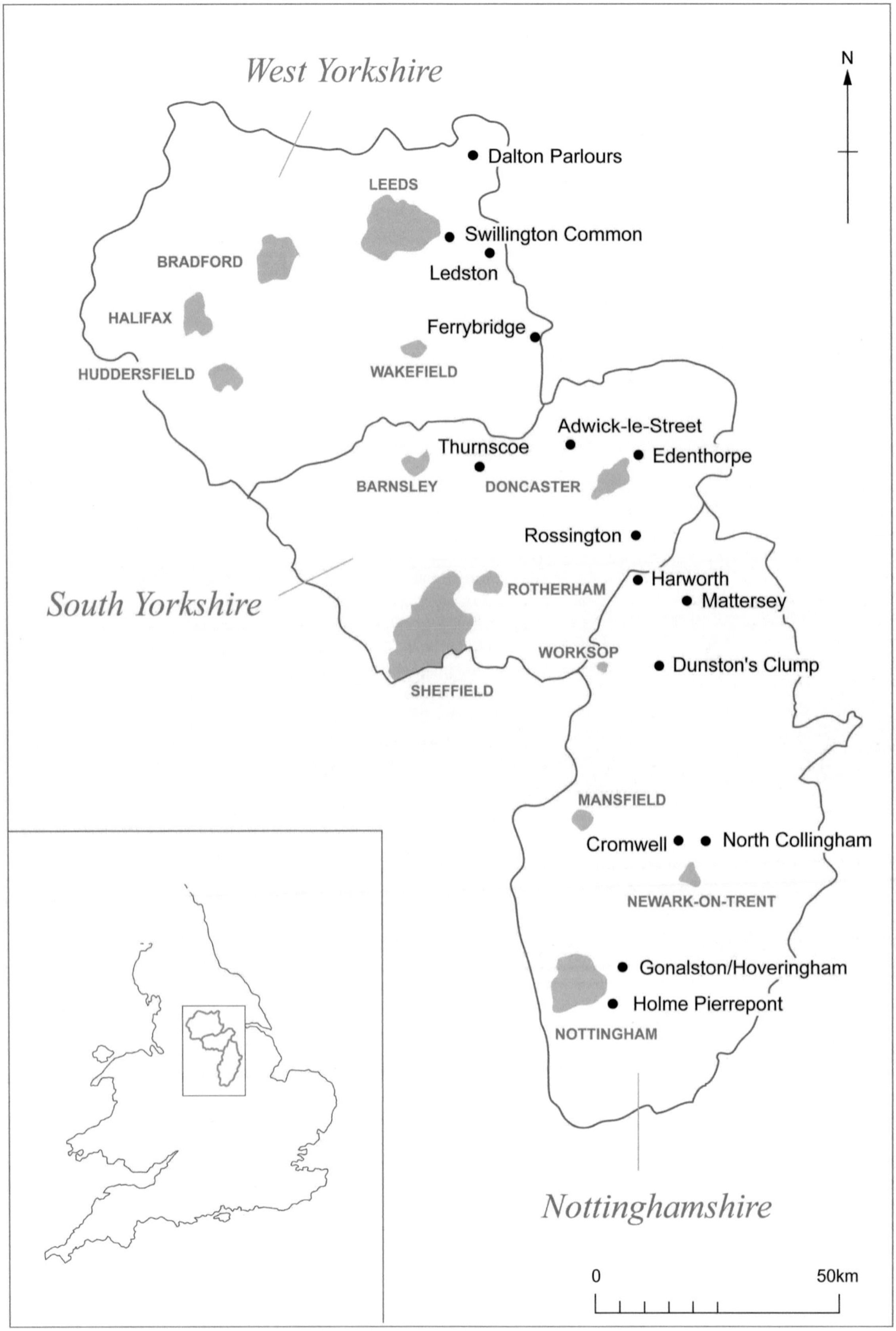

Fig. 13.1. Location map of study region, with some of the sites mentioned in the text (drawing: A. Leaver)

small copses of managed woodland (Berg 2001, 8–9; Buckland 1986, 4; Garton *et al.* 1988, 29; Garton and Salisbury 1995, 40–1; Yarwood 1981). Palaeo-environmental work suggests that although some wildwood might have remained on hills and upland areas, on the lowlands most had disappeared by the late Iron Age, and flooding and increased alluvial deposition in the Romano-British period may reflect this loss of woodland cover (Eccles *et al.* 1988; Knight and Howard 2004; Knight and Priest 1997; Samuels and Buckland 1978). There would have been large areas of drier grassland in many places, but also damper grass meadows in the valleys, and heather and heath vegetation on ridges, hilltops and more elevated ground (Bastow and Murray 1990; Berg 2001; Bogaard 1997; Garton 1987; Giorgi 2004).

Many of the river valleys were peaty and prone to winter flooding until nineteenth century drainage, but during the study period their floodplains would have provided lush summer grazing. The Rivers Don, Thorne, Idle and Trent all drain north-eastwards into the larger region known as the Humberhead Levels, an area of once extensive wetlands (Van de Noort 2004; Van de Noort and Ellis 1997). Peat formation in areas like the Thorne and Hadfield Moors probably began in earnest during the mid to late Bronze Age (Buckland 1979). Although tree clearance contributed to this, it was exacerbated by rising sea levels and a concomitant rise in water tables from around 500 BC, which also affected many low-lying areas of East Anglia (Evans 1998; Scaife 1992). Place names such as 'carr' reflect areas that were likely to have been standing water or marsh, where alder carr, willow and birch scrub would have formed the dominant vegetation by the early Iron Age (Buckland 1979; Parker Pearson and Sydes 1997). Around open water and reed swamp, willow, sedges, rushes, reeds, water lily, arrowhead and water plantain would have served for food, thatch, matting or basketry. Fish, wildfowl and even beavers might have been important resources, although biting insects and disease may have been a problem.

There have been finds of Bronze Age and Iron Age boats as at Ferriby, Hasholme, Scotter, Appleby and Brigg in Lincolnshire and Humberside, and at Holme Pierrepont in Nottinghamshire (MacCormick 1968; McGrail 1981; 1987; 1990; Millett and McGrail 1987; Wright 1990; Wright *et al.* 2001). Sewn plank boats such as the Ferriby examples were capable of sea voyages, but the logboats such as Hasholme, Brigg and the three examples from Holme Pierrepont were also very large, well-made vessels. The stern of the Hasholme logboat, and perhaps the bows of the Brigg and one of the Holme Pierrepont examples, had carved decoration. These were craft of considerable status that had taken great skill and time to produce (McGrail 1987; Millett 1999). The loss of these boats is normally attributed to accidental sinking. However, there is contextual evidence that the Hasholme vessel and perhaps one of the Holme Pierrepont examples were deliberately sunk, either as part of 'decommissioning' rites, or as votive offerings (Ransley 2002, 39–40).[1] In a wider regional context, such watery practices also involved the Roos Carr early or middle Iron Age wooden figurines from the Humber wetlands (Coles 1990), which featured a stylised boat; and Fiskerton in Lincolnshire, where Iron Age and Romano-British bronze and iron weapons and tools, jewellery, pottery, human and animal bones and two logboats were deposited from a timber causeway into a palaeo-channel of the River Witham (Field and Parker Pearson 2003; Rylatt *pers. comm.*).[2] This may have represented beliefs in water as a mysterious, ever-changing and liminal substance, an entrance to other worlds or other realms of being (Chadwick 2004c).

These rivers and waterways would also have been vital communication routes, and indeed for many of these 'hydraulic communities' (q.v. Evans 1997a), water and movement along it would have been crucial to concepts of place and identity. Water-courses were not barriers, but vital arteries connecting places and peoples. Several excavated settlements were close to the edge of the Humber wetlands (Roberts 2003; Rose 2003). At some, more specialised practices may have included the summer grazing of livestock. These people were not eking out a miserable existence in marginal areas, but instead had very sophisticated understandings of their landscapes involving networks of social contacts, trade and seasonal journeys (Evans 1987; Willis 1997). Such aquatic archaeologies and fluid movements deserve a paper in their own right.

The character of the archaeology

On the Sherwood sandstone areas of north Nottinghamshire and southern South Yorkshire, Derrick Riley identified three types of fields: irregular, nuclear, and brickwork. The latter formed extensive, north-south orientated co-axial field systems. Some fields on the Coal Measures and Magnesian limestone also show similar co-axiality and regularity, such as those to the east of Barwick in Elmet in West Yorkshire (Deegan 2001b, 21). There are many differences apparent across the region, however. Most other field systems on the Coal Measures and limestone areas were more irregular and/or nucleated. Linear, sinuous trackways and boundaries appear to have been more important in these areas than blocks of rectangular fields. This may reveal variations in agricultural regimes and social practices between these areas, or even social differences based on kinship, clan or tribal identities.

A few concentrations of enclosures are known, as at Ledston, Dalton Parlours and Aberford in West Yorkshire, and South Muskham, North Collingham and Cromwell in Nottinghamshire (Deegan 2001b, 21; Faull and Moorhouse 1981; Whimster 1989, 75–9; Wrathmell and Nicolson 1990). These may simply result from stratigraphic and historical depth, rather than reflecting larger, nucleated settlements, although it is significant that at Cromwell and Dalton Parlours, villas were later constructed at these locales. For much of the study area though, the settlements were predominantly dispersed farmsteads within subrectangular or rectangular enclosures.

Post-PPG16 developer-funded excavations have demonstrated that some of the major trackways, boundaries and farmsteads had their origins in the later Iron Age, with pottery of Iron Age type or of Iron Age tradition now recovered from many sites (Chadwick 2004a).[3] Some Iron Age pottery found in Nottinghamshire and South Yorkshire was East Midlands Scored Ware, which was probably moved up from the Trent Valley (Elsdon 1992; Knight and Howard 2004). Other fabrics and vessels came from Lincolnshire, or were produced locally in South and West Yorkshire (Cumberpatch 2001; *pers. comm.*; Evans 1995; Runnacles and Buckland 1998). Gritstone querns from Wharncliffe near Sheffield were widely distributed (Challis and Harding 1975, 21–5). The region is particularly interesting because of these diverse procurement and production traditions. This suggests longer distance trade rather than simple 'down-the-line' exchange, and for some people at least, these journeys would have required great flexibility in routines and extensive social contacts. Boat journeys and travels along trackways would have been vital to this.

The regularity of even the brickwork field systems is often illusory. More detailed analyses of the cropmarks have shown more localised, subtle variations in slope, aspect and alignment (Deegan 1996; 1998; Robbins 1998), with rivers and the lines of valleys and ridges affecting trackway and field orientations. Excavations also suggest that in some cases, the apparent regularity was actually a product of many different phases of ditch cutting and recutting. The supposed 'planning' may have been the result of traditional, communal practices based on shared seasonal and daily routines (Chadwick 1995; 1999; Davies *et al.* 1997; Robbins 1998). Some Roman forts and roads were superimposed across earlier fields and enclosures (Buckland 1986, 8; Riley 1980, 94–5; O'Neill 2001a, 110–3), but later fields were clearly orientated to Roman roads. Although some trackways and boundaries were laid out in the Iron Age, in places there was an expansion of land enclosure in the third and fourth centuries AD (Knight and Howard 2004; O'Neill 2001b, 276–7). The Roman presence would have been most marked at roads, forts, and urban settlements, but in the early decades following the invasion of the north in AD 70–71, it may have been mostly Roman military units, officials and traders using the Roman roads (Petts 1998, 88). Away from them, there was relatively little impact on the landscape, and people continued to use traditional trackways.

In previous articles I have suggested that the creation, maintenance and reworking of trackway, field system and enclosure ditches was part of the reproduction of personal and community identity (Chadwick 1997; 1999). The acts of digging ditches, and of constructing and maintaining field systems, were socially meaningful activities. I have also begun to explore patterns of both everyday discard and placed deposits, in order to consider how people, material culture and the landscape were bound together through such practices, and how these relations were maintained, changed and re-worked over time, in different landscape settings (Chadwick 2004b, 20–3; Petts 1998, 79–80; Taylor 1997, 192–4; 2001, 47). These depositional practices cannot be separated from the habitual movements of people and animals, as both placed deposits and dumps of household refuse occurred in very specific areas around enclosures, fields and trackways, particularly entrances and gateways (Chadwick 2004a). In order to pursue this theme of movement in more detail and to write such archaeologies, we must first consider the relationships between animals and humans more critically.

Actor-networks and hybrid geographies

Until relatively recently, in the many critical reconsiderations of social agency in social theory, human beings seemed to be the only actors who were able to act knowledgeably and purposefully *upon* their environment. However, Harvey (1996) suggested that physical and biological processes work together with social, economic and political factors, and non-human organisms can be regarded as active subjects, eroding the culture : nature divide. 'Nature' is itself understood and mediated *through* culture, and so cannot be considered separate to it (Macnaghten and Urry 1998, 30).

Actor Network Theory has proposed that humans are enmeshed within webs or networks of relational agency. People give form to non-humans, but are themselves acted upon and given shape by non-humans, partly through expanding the means available to people for conceptualising their own humanity (Latour 1993, 137). Rather than seeing agents or actors as centres of self-aware intentionality, agency is actually the outcome of the relationships between humans and the living and material worlds (e.g. Harvey 1996; Law and Hassard 1999; Murdoch 1997; Thrift 1996). The actions of plants and animals can be considered to be active and transforming, in that the growth of plants and the behaviour of animals can impact upon landscapes and human activities. Although usually less purposive than human agency, this constitutes agency nevertheless. Agency is not a pre-given attribute applicable only to humans, but is the outcome of a series of constraints and affordances mutually constituted through these relations between people, plants and animals, and the material world.

'Animal geographies' have examined how historically and culturally specific constructions of 'nature' and animality have affected how animals have been defined, regarded as food, pets or pests, or how they have been constricted within or excluded from areas of the landscape by humans (e.g. Elder *et al.* 1998; Ingold 1988; Noske 1989; Philo and Wilbert 2000; Wolch and Emel 1995; 1998). It has also been suggested that trees are actants within landscapes (Jones and Cloke 2002). Non-human agency has also been considered in studies of material culture, which is both a medium for agency, and may at times also become imbued with it (Gell 1998). All this recent critical work has employed metaphors of networks and hybridity, whereby humans are just part of a series of complex, meaningful and interlinked relationships, where meaning and agency are created and flow along these interactions.

For Tim Ingold, however, Actor-Network Theory is merely a 'way of stating a problem, and of making a rhetorical point' (Ingold and Jones 2002, 10), and it does not explain *how* the relational links between beings and the material world are constituted. Instead, Ingold suggests that there should be a wider project investigating the dwelled-in world, obviating the epistemological and theoretical differences between social and biological anthropology, psychology, archaeology and anthropology (Ingold 2001). This intertwining of human, animal and plant bodies, touch, smell, vision and materiality, experiences of emotion and memory, are all part of 'the messy heterogeneity of being-in-the-world' (Whatmore 2002, 147). By reconfiguring the ways in which we consider our human engagements with the living and non-living components of the physical world, we can move towards a unifying theory of practice which allows us to understand the diverse ways in which human self-identity and embodiment is constructed, maintained and experienced.

In anthropology too, the oppositions between culture : nature, human : animal, mind : body and subject : object have been criticised (e.g. Descola and Pálsson 1996; Ingold 1986; 2000; MacCormack and Strathern 1980; Noske 1989; Sökefeld 1999; Strathern 1988). People who have close relationships with plants and animals often regard these relations in terms of mutualism, interdependence and trust, and to speak of non-humans in terms of kinship or exchange acknowledges an underlying ontological equivalence between human and non-human beings (Ingold 1996b; 2000). The notion of relational personhood therefore conceives each human not as a unique, indivisible and individual unity, but as an entity in continuous connectivity with multiple selves in multiple contexts, in reciprocal relations with other *persons* (Battaglia 1990; Bird-David 1999; Ingold 2000; Strathern 1980; 1988).

These relationships may be conceived of through either totemism or animism. Such relational epistemologies occur in many gatherer-hunter and small-scale pastoral and cultivating communities, where people do not distinguish between human 'cultural' identities, and animals or plants as part of some separate 'natural' world (Battaglia 1990; Bird-David 1990; Bourdieu 1977; Brody 2001; Fowler and Turner 1999; Gudeman and Rivera 1990; Guenther 1988; Ingold 1996b; 2000; Kayano 1994; Sillitoe 1983; Strathern 1980; Watanabe 1972; 1999). Their landscapes are conceived of as unities of perception and dwelling, shared by humans, animals and plants alike, where animals and plants have to agree to be killed or harvested by human beings. Animals intentionally offer themselves up to hunters, in a spirit of goodwill or even love (Hallowell 1960; Ingold 1988; Tanner 1979).

Herders and their relationships with animals

Ingold argued in his earlier work that pastoralism or herding involves domination, where the control of animals' destinies has passed to humans, and where the animals' compliance is achieved by people imposing their will upon them. Unlike their relationships with gatherer-hunters, animals do not sacrifice themselves *to* people, but rather are sacrificed *by* them (Ingold 1986, 273; 1996a, 18–20; 2000, 72–73; Tapper 1988, 53). Domestication is thus equated with slavery. However, this seems too simplistic, and indeed Ingold now sees herders regarding animals as 'endowed with powers of sentience and autonomous action' (Ingold 2000, 74), albeit akin to infants or children. The changes in Western agriculture since the end of the nineteenth century have removed livestock from the experiences of most people. Animals are either pets, or the relatively shapeless lumps of processed flesh bought in supermarkets, yet raising, caring for and slaughtering animals was once a common experience of the lifeworlds of many people. In many extant societies throughout the world, these more intimate engagements persist. Animals of herders are guarded and cared for benevolently and attentively, albeit in a paternalistic and ultimately hegemonic fashion.

Most importantly, pastoral peoples rarely see animals in these terms. This is manifested in very close relationships that go far beyond the utilitarian demands of husbandry. Cattle in particular are often held in high regard, partly because of their value as 'wealth on the hoof', and also because the individual animals and herds are often physical embodiments of complicated networks of reciprocity and obligation between different people, clans and lineages within a community, or between different communities (e.g. Crandall 1998; Parker Pearson 2000). These relationships between people and animals are the basis for many human words, metaphors, songs, stories and myths (e.g. Ingold 1988; Serpell 1985; 1986; Tambiah 1969; Vitebsky 2005; Willis 1990). Human groups within societies often distinguish themselves through differences based on attributes of their livestock, and the names of owners' families and descent groups, and the names or descriptive terms of animals, may be interlinked. The Maasai of Kenya have matrilineal descent groups, and the structure of human lineages and clans is actually based upon that of cattle (Galaty 1989).

Close attention is often paid to the colour and patterning of cattle, horse and reindeer skins, or to the shape of cattle and reindeer horns and pig tusks. Many cattle-keeping peoples have dozens or hundreds of terms for the colours, patterns and sheen of cattle hides, and the shape of their horns and bodies (Coote 1992, 250–1; Galaty 1989; Parker Pearson 2000, 224). For the Siberian Eveny, each herder has his or her own *kujjai*, a reindeer consecrated to protect its owner from harm, even to die in their place (Vitebsky 2005). People recognise the behavioural idiosyncrasies of many individual animals, in the same way that cattle, reindeer and horses, and even pigs, sheep and goats, come to know, recognise and trust individual humans. Animals may be named, and respond to the call. Calving, tending, milking, leading, slaughtering and skinning are practical human interventions in animal's lives, but are nonetheless emotional and meaningful, though this should not be confused with sentimentality. In parts of New Guinea, piglets are raised within the house, and are named, petted and accorded great affection and respect (Gillison 2002; Rappaport 1984). Orphaned piglets may be suckled by human women, and follow their mistresses attentively around settlements and gardens. Yet most of these pigs are later killed and eaten when fully grown. Similarly, the Saami, Nenet and Eveny care for orphaned or sick reindeer (Alexander and Alexander 1996; Ingold 1980; Vitebsky 2005), but these animals are still slaughtered later on.

For the Turkana of north-east Kenya, cattle, camels, and to a lesser extent sheep and goats, are the basis of their social values, beliefs and practices, and of their wealth. Men mimic in dance the curves of the horns of their favourite cattle, which are often artificially shaped (Dyson-Hudson 1973, 94), and notch their cattle's ears 'to make them glad', after they have killed a human enemy. The Samburu men sing to their cattle, and decorate their favourite animals with geometrical designs of mud or ochre (Pavitt 1991). Amongst the Dinka, favoured animals have horns decorated with tassels or with ash during rituals, and forked-branch shrines imitate the shapes of cattle horns. Designs etched onto pottery and gourds, and even patterns scarified on human skin, may be based on horn representations (Coote 1992, 259). Many dance movements amongst the Nuer, Dinka and Atuaot are, like the Turkana, based upon patterns of cattle horns, or the movements and behaviour of cows and bulls (Burton 1980; 1982; Evans-Pritchard 1940). Human bodies and animal bodies, human lives and animal lives, are thus linked materially and symbolically through performed practices and decorative schemes.

Humans and animals are linked and inter-dependant in their agency. In an evocative article on reindeer herding in the Cairngorms of Scotland, Hayden Lorimer examined the relations between herders and herd. In their regular movements around a known landscape, both herders and animals come to share intimate memories of particular places and imbue them with significance. Memories of the most favourable areas for shelter, shade, water and food form part of a phenomenal and elemental geography of the herd (Lorimer 2004, 9). Animals come to know and trust certain people, and humans come to know and trust certain animals within the herd. When animals and people move together, authority does not lie solely with the herders, but also with herd leaders – particularly favoured animals who, in return for affection and respect, act as intermediaries during drives or round-ups. Herders trust these beasts to lead the way at times, to make the decisions as to where to ford rivers or scramble up steep hillsides. Sometimes it is the animals that show people the best paths to take. When herding sheep or cattle, dogs may often be employed by people, and here too, people place a measure of trust in their trained companions. In these movements between fields, through droveways or up into areas of highland transhumance, agency resides in the reciprocal relations between human and herd, in their collective will.

Despite metaphors to the contrary, even sheep possess agency, and particularly in upland areas, older sheep look after and lead younger animals, to show them the safest paths, and the best places for grazing, shelter and lambing. This process is known as heeafing or hefting (Hart and Ingelby 1990). Even in intensive modern dairy farming, older cattle can bring younger animals in for milking or take them out to pasture, with comparatively little human intervention. Lorimer tells the story of Sarek, a lead reindeer with the Cairngorm herd who, close to the point of death, descended from the mountains so that he could die close to the trusted hands of his human herder (Lorimer 2004, 9). Keith Basso narrates how Dudley Patterson, an old Western Apache cowhand, had a long-standing antagonism with a particular maverick bull, which always broke out of corrals and quite literally led other animals astray. Although most animals were eventually rounded up, the bull was extremely difficult to find and catch, and would only rejoin the herd when 'it suited him' (Basso 1996, 82). The relationship between man and bull was nevertheless seen as one of mutual respect by Dudley Patterson and other people in his community. After Dudley's death, the maverick bull stayed for two days and nights on a bluff overlooking the cemetery, before mysteriously disappearing for good. Along with animals' experiences of places and paths in the landscape, such knowledge and memory is all part of an 'earthbound geography' that animates what is effectively a lived culture of the herd. It is 'a sentient geography of impermanent points, forces, flows and energies that confounds any representational cartography' (Lorimer 2004, 8). Movement through landscapes thus enculturates people *and* animals.

Non-human, relational agency and agencies

So non-human and relational agency is not simply a trend of recent academic enquiry, or a means of merely (re)presenting the world that reflects postmodern ideas of blurred boundaries and multiple perspectives. Rather, for many people around the globe, this is how they actually engage with their landscapes and the beings within it. For them, the world is not constituted in terms of their subsistence techniques, but through their social relationships. The differences between hunting and herding may merely be 'the relative scope of human involvement in establishing the conditions for growth' (Ingold 1996a, 21).

The post-Enlightenment western concept of the individual as a bounded, autonomous agent is thus very culturally and historically specific (Chadwick 2004b; Geertz 1983, 59). For many cultures, people are part of wider networks of obligations and connections. Fields of relationships between beings and the landscape continually emerge as a series of cross-cutting, progenerative encounters (Ingold 2000, 142). Routine embodied movements and practices, significant life events such as births and deaths, relations with plants, animals and spirits, memories of these and the places in the landscape where they occurred, take place *within* this movement, as part of dynamic and meaningful engagements with the materiality of the lived-in world. Animals, plants and other beings are drawn into human social life, and through their agency affect human societies. People are likewise drawn into webs of relationships with non-human persons, and their identities may be composed partly or largely through their continuous relationships with other human, plant and animal beings.

Animals in the Iron Age and Romano-British periods

In the Iron Age and Romano-British periods, and probably in earlier prehistoric periods too, it is likely that for many rural communities the numbers and health of cattle, sheep and pigs would have been indicators of identity, wealth and status. Favoured animals might have been named and highly valued. They would have been a rich source of symbolism, cosmological meanings and myths, and in other regions of Britain, cattle, sheep and pigs seem to have been used to mark gender, age, status or other aspects of identity in human burials (Fitzpatrick 1997; Giles 2000; Parker Pearson 1999; Stead 1992). Along with horses and dogs, these animals, or parts of them, often formed part of deliberately structured, placed deposits in pits, ditches, entranceways and watery contexts (e.g. Grant 1984; 1991; Hill 1992; 1995). Horses might have had connotations of high status, long-distance movement, speed and hunting, and the socially ambiguous nature of dogs in many cultures and complex beliefs surrounding them probably also meant the special treatment of their remains on occasion (q.v. Serpell 1985). There is increasing recognition that such practices continued or were re-worked and re-interpreted during the Romano-British period (Dobney 2001; Fulford 2001; Woodward and Woodward 2004). Despite the problems with organic preservation in the study region, there are several striking examples of placed deposits involving animal remains, or animal burials, on both Iron Age and Romano-British sites (Chadwick 2004a, 98–102). Although this treatment of animal remains originated in pre-Roman customs, it had many resonances with Roman cosmological beliefs and practices.

Swillington Common, West Yorkshire

At Swillington Common near Leeds (Fig. 13.2), in advance of the M1-A1 link road project, aerial photographic analysis, geophysics and extensive open-area excavation undertaken by the West Yorkshire Archaeology Service revealed a prominent double-ditched trackway (Deegan 2001b, 31; Howell 2001, 54, fig. 29). This trackway was on the same alignment as the line of a bank and ditch

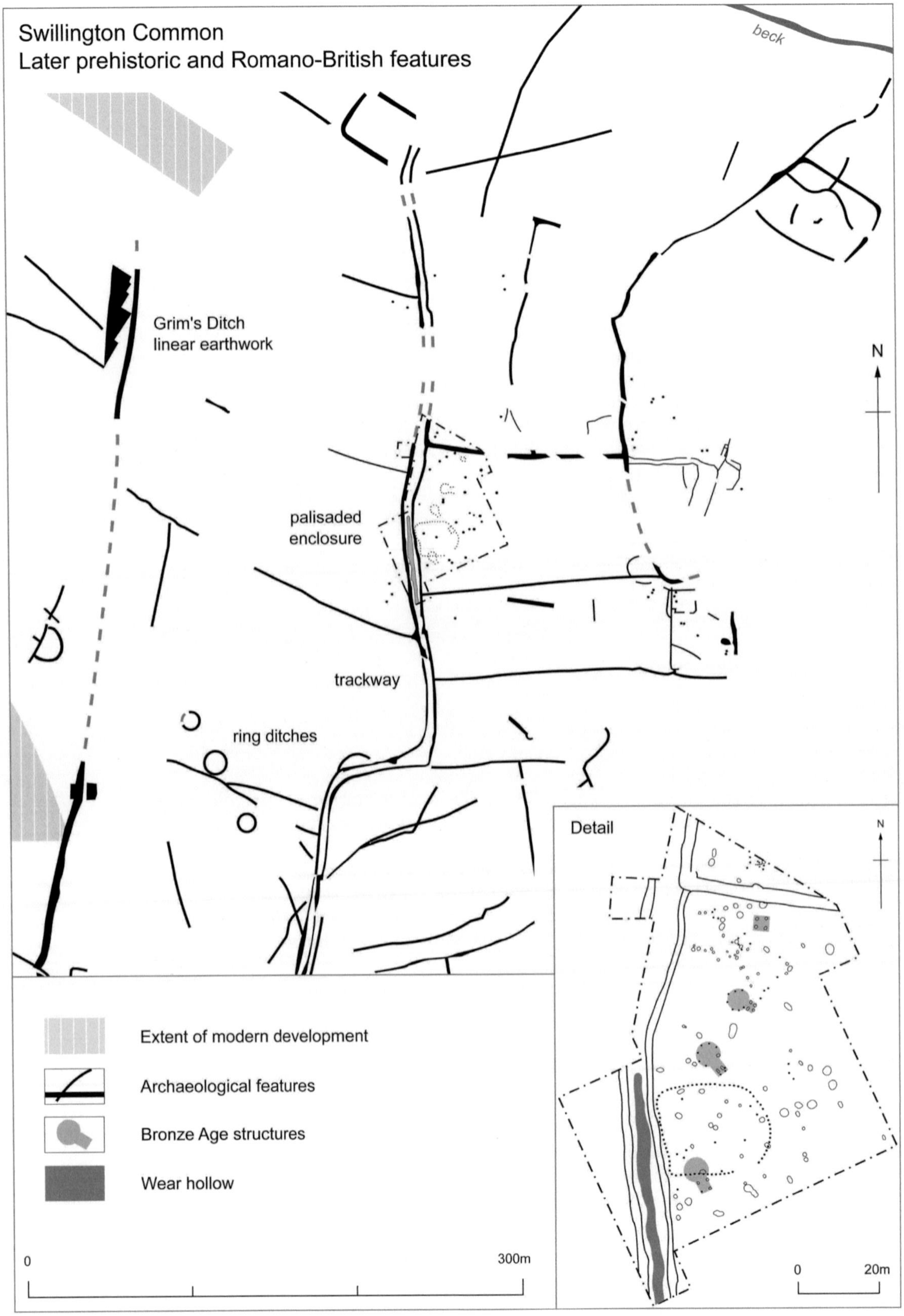

Fig. 13.2. A simplified plan of later prehistoric and Romano-British features at Swillington Common (drawing: A. Leaver, after Roberts et al. *2001, 31, 50, figs 13 and 30)*

earthwork – Grim's Ditch, of later Bronze Age or earlier Iron Age date. Between them were three unexcavated possible Bronze Age ring ditches or round barrows, plus two more irregular features. An open settlement of early to mid-Bronze Age roundhouses and rectangular structures was excavated just to the east of the trackway itself, whose ditches may have been dug in the early Iron Age. It had a pronounced kink or 'dogleg', which might have been aligned on the ring ditches, deliberately cutting one of the more irregular features; or the dogleg might have been caused by a realignment of fields on either side of the trackway at this point. Alternatively, the kink may have been caused by the avoidance of a landscape feature such as a once-prominent tree, and/or by tenurial factors, in the same way that medieval lanes sometimes turned at right-angles to respect different land-holdings.

Following the construction of the trackway, a D-shaped palisade enclosure was built immediately to the east (Howell 2001, 56–57, figs 30 and 45), tucked in close to the side of the trackway. This had a gap or entrance in the south-eastern side, and a possible entrance structure to the east, and was dated to the middle Iron Age. The trackway was then incorporated into a later Iron Age and Romano-British landscape of fields, enclosures and more minor tracks, the major trackway nevertheless acting as an axial spine for this later land division. The wear hollow in between the trackway ditches, and the samian pottery recovered from the upper ditch fills, showed it was maintained and used for many centuries after it was first laid out (Howell 2001, 54–56).

We begin our journey on a heath-covered ridge, one of many in an open, undulating landscape, with just a few copses of surviving woodland, and small becks running in the shallow valleys between the ridgelines. Behind us lies the past, and the distance we and our animal charges have walked in half a day, a north-south path that has also been trod by many previous generations of people and animals. If we stop on the ridge and look around us, we can see and smell the smoke from the cooking fires of several farmsteads, which are situated at the heart of their infields, defined by ditches, hedges and fences. The more open grazing country lies beyond. These lineages are all known to us, we inter-marry, and we share the same clan name. Further afield, in journeys that are measured in several days and nights, are lineages from other clans. Sometimes our relationships with them are friendly, sometimes tense and strained, but at times of crop failure, famine or war we still count them as brothers and sisters. But the lead beasts are now raising their heads with impatience, and our dogs too are puzzled by the delay. So we must press on, moving southwards through the landscape, and also passing through the weave of time itself, for we have some distance and considerably many years to cover in but a short telling.

Ledston, West Yorkshire

Five kilometres to the south-east of Swillington Common, at Ledston, two major trackways led southwards from enclosures on higher ground, running past some earlier Bronze Age ring ditches to converge at a double-ditched, low-lying enclosure near a beck (Deegan 2001b, 21, 26, figs 4 and 9). This enclosure was of an unusual, subtriangular form. Partially excavated, to the north of this middle to later Iron Age enclosure was at least one roundhouse and several four-post structures, in addition to a minimum of 70 large pits cut into the limestone, out of a possible original total of around 280 such features (Burgess 2001b, 266; Faull and Moorhouse 1981, 119–20; Roberts 2005b). The pits and four-post structures may have provided communal grain storage on a massive scale, although there is no evidence that the pits were ever used for this (Roberts 2005b, 31–2)

The excavation of at least two Iron Age human pit burials from the site, which are rare in the region, together with evidence of placed deposition (Roberts 2005b), also suggest that this central locale was a very important focus for local families. Here, before the spring sowing and autumn harvest, people and animals travelled from more local settlements and fields, meeting up along the way, and exchanging greetings and gossip. In and around the enclosure, gatherings were marked by feasts and small-scale votive deposits, some people were honoured with burial there, and such events were as much about social practices and sociality as about 'social storage' or the redistribution of wealth.

They say a bloodline's wealth can be measured by their animals. The curved grace of cattle horns, the patterning of their shaggy hides, their strength. The twisted spirals of sheep and goat horns, their milk and wool, their resilience in numbers. The tusks and stiff hairs of pigs, their especially prized meat, their power and half-wildness. The speed and agility of horses, their stamina, their use in the hunt and in war. Dogs for herding, guarding and to send messages to the gods. Milk and blood, meat and bone, life and limb, hearth and home.

Ferrybridge, West Yorkshire

At Ferrybridge in West Yorkshire (Fig. 13.3), a late Neolithic henge was the focus for six or more Neolithic and Bronze Age hengiform monuments, timber circles and barrows, several of them roughly 20–30m in diameter (Burgess 2001a, 258; Wheelhouse 2005, 21–49). Several pit alignments later surrounded the henge and barrows and defined their extent, yet apparently also kept a respectful distance from them. These may have been late Iron Age in origin, although they contained structured deposits of Iron Age and Romano-British pottery and metalwork, but also a series of human burials

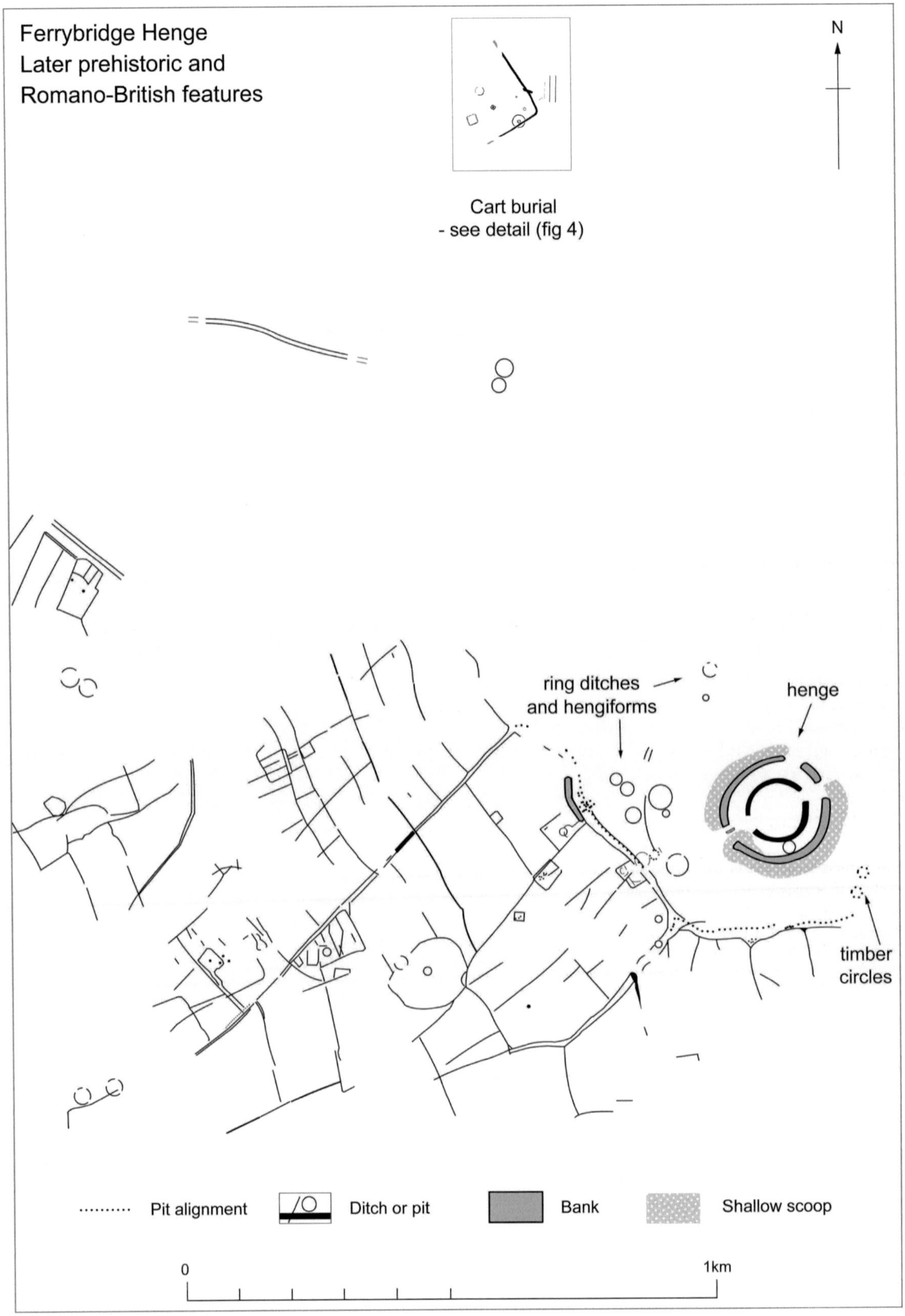

Fig. 13.3. A simplified plan of later prehistoric and Romano-British features at Ferrybridge Henge (drawing: A. Leaver, after Roberts 2005a, 71 fig. 60, and unpublished digital information provided by Oxford Archaeology North, to be published in Brown et al. *forthcoming)*

ranging from the late Iron Age to the earlier medieval period (Richardson 2005, 53–70), an incredible length of time for the pits to have remained such significant landscape and social features. Some of these pit alignments were incorporated within a landscape of ditched trackways, enclosures and co-axial field boundaries, in the later Iron Age and Romano-British periods. But the area around the henge and barrows was still largely respected by these later features, whilst at the same time forming the focus for the funnel-shaped entrances of at least one, possibly two trackways, perhaps linked to another trackway curving round the earlier monuments. These trackways ran past several enclosures and pit groups, some of the former possibly shrines or mortuary enclosures. Excavations by the West Yorkshire Archaeology Service revealed a late Iron Age domestic enclosure with evidence for copper working, whilst another earlier enclosure had evidence for placed deposits (Roberts 2005a, 215).

Another trackway ran off to the north, towards a further, more scattered group of round barrows. Here, approximately 600m to the north-west of the henge, recent excavations by Oxford Archaeology North found an unusual palisaded enclosure, and in between two round barrows, a square-ditched barrow (Fig. 13.4). This contained a cart or chariot burial, with an adult male body laid on the vehicle platform accompanied by half a pig's head and a leg joint, horse fittings, and possibly a spear (Boyle 2004a; 2004b). This is a unique rite for the study area. The cart itself was interred whole in a large pit, similar to the Newbridge cart burial in Scotland (Carter and Hunter 2003), and different to the burial practice in East Yorkshire, where the vehicles were dismantled (Giles 2000; Stead 1992). It seems to have been assembled from parts of different carts, and it is not clear if it was ever a 'working' vehicle. Just above the primary silts on the base of the square ditch were four partial cattle skulls, which may have been displayed elsewhere before they were deposited. At a later date however, up to 250 cattle were butchered and eaten, then their bones deposited in the square ditch surrounding the central pit, but this might have been in more than one episode.

It was originally proposed that like Newbridge, the Ferrybridge burial may have been quite early, possibly dating to the fifth century BC (Boyle 2004a, 26). Radiocarbon determinations seem to indicate a date of around 400–200 BC for the burial of the man and the pig bones, but the deposition of the butchered cattle bone in the second or fourth centuries AD (F. Brown *pers. comm.*). Isotope analysis has suggested the man was not raised locally, and might have been born and lived some of his early life further north, maybe as far as Scotland. An involuted, later Iron Age style brooch found with the man might suggest a slightly shorter gap between the burial and the later feasting event(s). Further post-excavation work in advance of publication will have to elucidate this (Brown and Boyle in prep.). Nevertheless, stories or even myths might have all been implicated in the subsequent events, which would still have taken place many generations after the primary inhumation. As at Swillington Common, memory and tradition was continually being caught up and reworked in relationships between landscape features, and between people and the land. The square barrow would not have been an obvious landscape feature, especially compared to the henge and round barrows, so for it to be chosen in this way implies some persistent memory, no matter how distorted, of the original unique burial. The large feast(s) may have been linked to activities in the palisaded enclosure (F. Brown *pers. comm.*), which is similar to some Romano-British shrines. The man

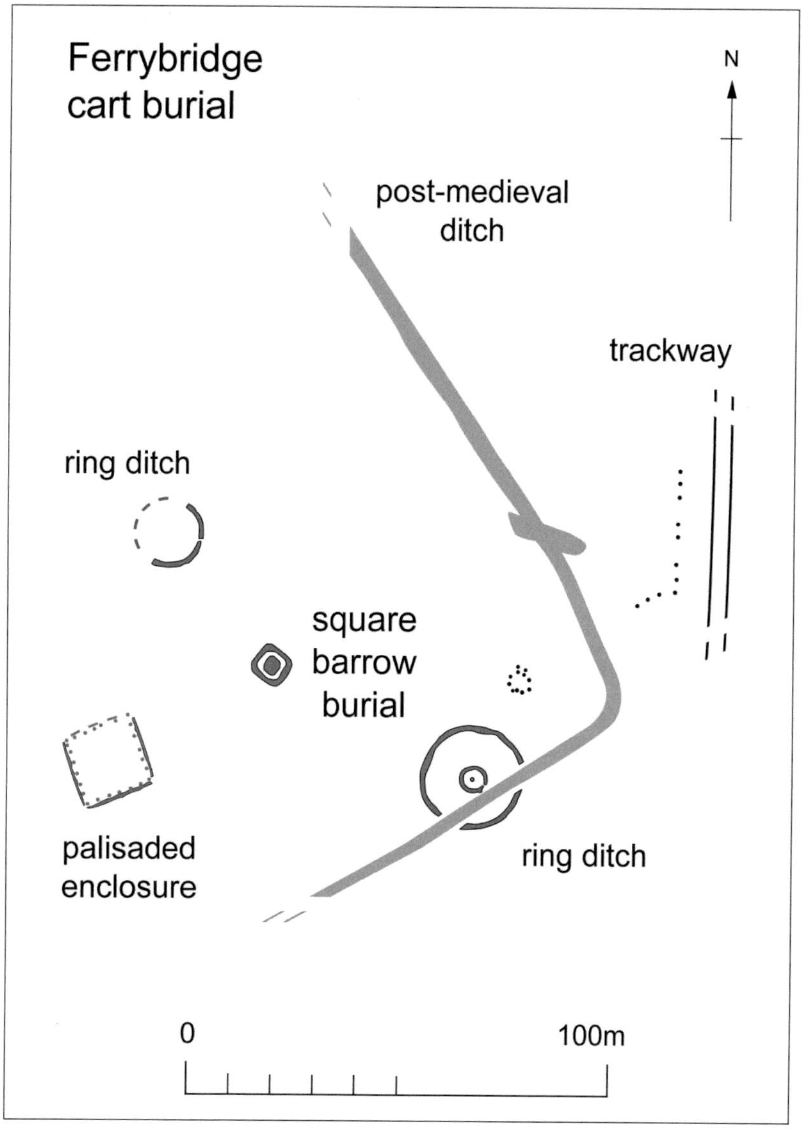

Fig. 13.4. Detail of archaeological features at Ferrybridge Henge (drawing: A. Leaver, after unpublished digital information provided by Oxford Archaeology North, to be published in Brown et al. *forthcoming)*

may have held great political and/or spiritual power and status, and his death may have been perceived as especially unlucky or tragic. But if there was a gap of several generations or even centuries between his death and the feast, then honouring an ancestor in this way and re-establishing a link to the past might have been connected to issues of communal identity, perhaps at a time of crisis or anxiety, as a reaction to the Roman invasion or occupation,[4] or the troubled late Roman period.

The possible sight of the cart as part of a funerary procession along the trackways would have been dramatic, as would, at a later date, the numbers of cattle driven along the track before their killing, butchering and consumption. The smell of the cattle piss and shit, the sound of their death bellows, the smell and sight of their blood and guts, the eating of so much charred flesh – all of this would have been an extraordinary experience for all the people taking part. It has been suggested that Iron Age carts were 'technologies of power', which compressed time and distance for those riding in them (Giles 2002). If so, then trackways could also be conduits for such power. Earlier constructions and significant places in the landscape, and the journeys along trackways, were thus vital to the social relations manifested through such practices.

So, we journey to the place where many trackways open out, near the great works left behind by the ancient ones. Here, the giant ringwork of ditch and bank still lies, like some giant torc discarded on the ground by the gods. Around it are clustered mounds of the dead, deliberately left undisturbed. It is said that these are the graves of the ancient ones, peoples so unimaginably old that no living lineage can now claim descent from them with certainty, though this has not stopped some from trying. The great one was buried near here, where a huge pit had been dug in the earth to receive him and his bier. Having come from the far north, his own track had come to its end, but so suddenly that it had shocked and disconcerted many. And so, in a way never done before, he had been put into the earth, here, near the centre of things, and between two of the older mounds. It seemed fitting.

Adwick-le-Street, South Yorkshire

Most trackways and field systems in the region were abandoned at the end of the Romano-British period, and in most areas there is little evidence for continuity of boundaries into the post-Roman and earlier medieval periods (O'Neill 2001b; Unwin 1983; but see Roberts 2005a). However, near Adwick-le-Street in South Yorkshire, recent excavations discovered a ninth century AD burial of an adult Viking woman, with grave goods including two oval bronze brooches, a bronze bowl, a knife and a latch-lifter (Speed and Rogers 2004). Her grave was cut into the backfill of a trackway ditch containing Romano-British pottery of third and fourth century date, although the trackway possibly had earlier origins. This suggests that this trackway was still partially visible in the landscape, and remained not only a well-known and used routeway, but a socially and perhaps symbolically important feature too.

Movement, trackways and inhabiting the landscape

Earlier interpretations of the field systems noted the poor soils in the region, usually unable to support arable agriculture without intensive use of fertilisers. The large size of many brickwork fields in particular was thought to have excluded ploughing with the equipment available (Riley 1980, 26). Others suggested they were used for extensive grazing of cattle or sheep, to meet the demands of the Roman army for meat, hides and wool (Branigan 1989, 166; Hayes 1981, 117) – this assumed that the field systems and trackways were Romano-British, and also failed to take account of soil degradation and erosion. Furthermore, on Magnesian Limestone areas fertile loess deposits were once present that have largely disappeared (Buckland *pers. comm.*). Furthermore, it assumed a modern, Western 'common-sense' approach to land ownership and agricultural production.

Yet not every field, and not every part of each field, may have been in use at any one time. Fields may have rotated between arable, fallow and pasture, and indeed manure would have probably been needed to maintain soil fertility. Rights of tenure and access may have fluctuated between different lineages and clans, or as land-use passed down through the generations. The evidence for repeated but intermittent recutting of some ditches, and changes of alignment and/or access, supports these ideas (Chadwick 1999, 163–4). Sometimes field patterns were different on one side of a trackway than on the other, as at Edenthorpe in South Yorkshire, and Harworth and Osberton in Nottinghamshire (Riley 1980, 90, 103, 129). These variations may reflect different periods of enclosure, the landholdings or tenure of different communities, or different agricultural and social practices.

Palaeo-environmental evidence has proved mixed farming did take place in the late Iron Age and the Romano-British periods (Bastow and Murray 1990; Berg 2001; Bogaard 1997; Giorgi 2004; Jones 1987; Richardson 2001; Van der Veen 1992). Excavated enclosures have produced quernstones, carbonised grain and sometimes grain ovens, and palaeo-environmental analyses show that some settlements were producers of crops, rather than simply consumers of them. Arable fields must have been significant in some places, but this should also be apparent in the layout of the landscapes. Where crops and livestock needed to be separated, this should produce more complex field patterns, with fields of different sizes, and droveways leading from enclosures and byres, through arable infields to pastures beyond (Ramm 1980: 31). In predominantly pastoral regimes, there should be simpler patterns of more similar-sized fields, with isolated stock enclosures and more droveways.

Fields around Sutton, Lound and Babworth in Nottinghamshire, Dearne and Sprotbrough in South Yorkshire, and Garforth and Methley in West Yorkshire, all show features characteristic of more mixed farming (Chadwick 1998; Deegan 2001b; Riley 1980). This is not so evident around Rossington, Edenthorpe, Armthorpe, Hodsock, Blyth, Torworth, Swillington Common, Barwick in Elmet and other areas where fields were very regular in shape and size. Many areas of brickwork fields also had the greatest frequency of trackways, not just of main axial routeways but also more minor routes too, indicating an increased emphasis on animal movement. So it is thus likely that many of the brickwork fields were indeed used mostly for grazing.

Pryor (1996; 1998) has outlined some of the functional features to be expected with stock handling, including 'funnels' or 'crushes' and 'races', where livestock can be concentrated and separated out for breeding, shearing or culling.[5] Near Welbeck, Babworth, Edenthorpe and Broom Hill, Harworth, there are particularly pronounced funnels (Riley 1980, 90, 103, 129, 144), the size of some indicating the movement of considerable numbers of livestock. Again, these are within what were mainly brickwork areas. However, across the region, not just in areas of brickwork fields, there are many sites whose plans show features likely to have been associated with the handling of stock, such as crushes, races, pens or corrals. These include Dunston's Clump, Wild Goose Cottage and Hoveringham in Nottinghamshire; Billingley Drive, Thurnscoe, Balby Carr, Barnsdale Bar, Norton and West Moor Park, Armthorpe in South Yorkshire; and Upton, Apple Tree Close, Bullerthorpe Lane, Swillington Common North and Parlington Hollins in West Yorkshire (AS WYAS 2001; Deegan 2001a; Elliott and Knight 1998; Garton 1987; Garton and Salisbury 1995; Neal and Fraser 2004; Roberts 1995; Roberts *et al.* 2001; Rose 2003; Wrathmell 2001).

Many trackways seem to have been the earliest components of the field system landscapes, probably in the earlier or middle Iron Age. However, many might themselves have followed pre-existing, traditional paths, as Chris Fenton-Thomas has suggested for middle Iron Age trackways in East Yorkshire (Fenton-Thomas 2003; forthcoming). At Swillington Common for example, the early Iron Age trackway ran close by an even earlier, Bronze Age, 'open' settlement of roundhouses and pits (Howell 2001). This implies that the demarcation or 'formalisation' of routeways by double-ditched trackways was, at least early on, of equal if not more importance than issues of land division. Trackways linked some settlements, and allowed people to visit kin or to trade, and thus aided the spread of goods and ideas. Arguments and feuds would have been played out along them, but lovers and marriage partners would also have travelled them too. Animals from one herd or flock could be taken to mate with those belonging to other groups. For both humans and animals therefore, blood lines and lines on the land merged and mingled with one another.

Trackways often referenced natural topography and watercourses, and earlier human constructions. Notions of memory and history, genealogy and cosmology, were thus implicit in how people moved through the landscape. As with the field systems, the digging of ditches to create the trackways was the result of much time and embodied, socialised community-based labour. In their routine movements, people and animals returned from communal grazing grounds or less well-defined outfields, past more tightly bounded fields and into enclosures, paddocks and corrals that were much more well-defined expressions of kin, tenure and identities (Robbins 1998). Indeed, the appearance of field systems and enclosed, ditched settlements in the later Iron Age may have reflected wider social processes involving changes in kinship relations, tenure and access to land, with increased emphasis on families and immediate kinship ties (Thomas 1997).

In the brickwork field systems, many trackways were arranged at right-angles to rivers and streams, leading towards them (Deegan 1996; 1998; Robbins 1998). During the late Iron Age and until the Roman occupation, and in some cases beyond, these river floodplains do not seem to have been enclosed to the same degree as the rest of the landscape. Interestingly, some of the first land divisions on many of the floodplains were pit alignments, most probably late Bronze Age or early Iron Age in date. Several researchers have suggested that these were deliberately permeable boundaries that reflected group rather than individual or kinship based claims of tenure, and which were therefore not too restrictive (Pollard 1996; Thomas 2003; forthcoming). Some pit alignments may even have been designed to flood, so that their visual or symbolic impact would be heightened by pools of standing water. On the floodplains, individuals or families worked amongst each other and amongst their animal charges, communal affiliations reinforced through work and talk (Robbins 1998), and where bonds between human and animal were strengthened.

Near Cromwell in Nottinghamshire, aerial photographs of the River Trent floodplain revealed two pairs of converging pit alignments, underlying a later Iron Age and Romano-British enclosure complex, which was eventually transformed into a villa estate (Whimster 1989, 79). At Gonalston, there was division of the floodplain terrace and adjacent alluvial areas by an early, middle Iron Age rectilinear boundary system, roughly contemporary with the earliest enclosed settlements (Knight and Elliott forthcoming; Knight and Howard 2004). This also suggests that floodplains had great importance, and could become significant locales within the landscape.

Different livestock would have required different directions and scales of movement around the landscape. In some cases these would have been daily journeys, undertaken with the sunrise and the sunset. At other times people and animals may have been away for days or even weeks. During the summer months, cattle in particular, and perhaps any horses too, would have been grazed in the broad, shallow river valleys, which were often flooded during the winter, but provided lush summer growth. Proximity to water sources would have been necessary for cattle, which need large amounts of water daily. Sheep and goats require much less water, and can also do well on poorer grazing. The upland hills and heath-covered ridges would have been suitable locations for them. Pigs would probably have been kept much closer to settlements, but might have been driven to copses of wood or scrubland for foraging. They may also have been used to strip vegetation, and to break the earth on arable fields that had lain fallow for periods. During spring, pregnant animals would have been confined to infields or to pens, so births could be monitored and assisted. In the autumn and early winter, some animals would have been brought back into infields, folds and byres, and many pigs, fattened since spring, may have been slaughtered so that their meat could be salted or smoked. These daily, seasonal and annual routines of agricultural life were nevertheless fundamental to beliefs concerning identity, cosmology and the landscape (Giles and Parker Pearson 1999).

Longer-distance journeys with sheep, cattle and horses might also have been necessary, particularly for those settlements furthest away from good grazing. There was perhaps sometimes alternation between winter kin-held fields and summer communal grazing. Linked to settlements by trackways, these places would have had access to grazing, and might have been relatively permeable places that allowed herders and their animals to keep close company for weeks or months at a time. Some buildings and settlements may reflect places that were only occupied during the summer months, like lowland versions of shielings or *hafodydd*. At East Carr, Mattersey in Nottinghamshire, around seventy rectangular structures were found on the flood plain of the River Idle (Morris and Garton 1998, 140). Many were probably hay and fodder ricks or turf stacks, but the larger examples may possibly reflect shieling-like, temporary buildings. Their insubstantial nature and lack of hearths and domestic refuse would suggest short-lived, transient occupation during summer.

Certain age-grades or cohorts of people would probably have been associated with these daily and seasonal movements, and some people and animals would thus pass through life stages together. Ethnohistorical accounts from Britain suggest that young women and men often accompanied sheep and cattle to temporary summer settlements (Arensberg and Kimball 1948; Davies 1984–85; Dodgshon 1981; 1992; Fenton 1976; Howell 1977; Ó Danachair 1983–84; O'Dowd 1981; Sayce 1956; 1957), though we should be cautious in using such socially and topographically varied, and historically specific analogies, and some of these accounts over-romanticise such practices (Ward 1997). Nevertheless, in many societies around the world, it is often young men who look after cattle, and young women and children who tend sheep and goats (e.g. Dyson-Hudson 1973; Pavitt 1991). Young men and women may use the opportunities whilst away from the main settlements to flirt or have sexual relationships. Pigs were too difficult to control to have been taken far, and older men and women might have been in charge of them. There were many human experiences of these trackways and journeys, predicated on age, gender, and other social differences, and the animals concerned might also have had close symbolic or metaphorical references to these. Accounts of journeys may have featured in stories and songs of these people. More widely dispersed extended families or small kinship groups might have come together in spring or autumn to retrieve or store seed grain, to breed and exchange livestock, exchange news and goods, trade, flirt and marry, and carry out other social practices.

Many theorists have shown how bodily movements and actions reproduce peoples' identities and memories (e.g. Butler 1993; Connerton 1989; de Certeau 1988; Ingold 2000; 2004; Lefebvre 1991; Mauss 1973; Merleau-Ponty 1962). Identities are also based on the relationships between people and other human and non-human beings, and with the landscape. Different places within the landscape have varied histories and biographies, and differing associations of tenure and access, power and practice. Ingold has stressed how in many small-scale societies the world is 'perceived through the feet' (2004). Walking around a landscape is vital to the construction of people's identities, notions of space and tenure, and their life experiences and memories. To follow a path is to remember the way (Ingold 2000). So when people moved through their landscapes, they were both subconsciously and consciously engaged in a continuous, recursive process of immersing themselves in memories of the past, negotiating paths and practices in the present, and projecting themselves into futures as yet untravelled.

These experiences were not confined to the human realm alone. Animals too would have remembered these same paths and trackways through the landscape, and may often have taken themselves along them with little urging by humans or dogs. But these would not always have been smooth, uninterrupted journeys. Sheep and cattle would have sometimes clustered in confusion, or lingered wilfully to browse on trees or hedges. Some animals would have responded to the directions of people and dogs, but others might have been more obstreperous. Hedges and fences would have been breached, crops trampled or eaten. Animals would have had preferred places for browsing, grazing and drinking, and favoured spots to scratch against rocks or posts, or to lie in shelter and shade. Both animals and people would have accumulated memories of these places. With people, this knowledge was often articulated and inculcated through manual acts, repetitive embodied movements where muscular and cognitive memories were entwined, like the bones and sinews of people and animals themselves. Animals had insightful webs of relations with each other, with humans, and with their landscapes. Animals thus also helped shape the boundaries, trackways, fields, funnels or crushes, gateways, enclosures and pens – all were partially dependant on what people understood that cattle, sheep and goats, pigs and horses would or would not do. Animal agency and human agency, animal memories and human memories, animal movements and human movements – all creating and maintaining features within the landscape, and giving meaning to them.

Journey's end

There were many different trackways, and many differently embodied experiences of them. Some of this knowledge was shared between people and animals, prompted by similar needs, and memories of the same places and paths of movement. We have come to the end of our journey, yet it is but one of many. We have taken short steps in distance, but great strides in time. The centuries have passed, and these animals and people are long dead. It is now up to us to trace their hoofprints and footprints.

Notes

1 The Hasholme logboat contained a 'cargo' of two timbers, and many animal bones from cattle, sheep, horse and deer. The vast majority were derived from fully fleshed joints of cattle meat, probably from two juvenile individuals. There was also a sheep's head (Stallibrass 1987, 141–3). The logboat was found in the River Foulness, close to an Iron Age and Romano-British settlement (Millett and McGrail 1987, 70), and seems to have 'foundered' in what was actually fairly shallow water.

> It simply does not seem likely that such a large boat, probably of some social importance, should have been unintentionally deposited complete with valuable 'cargo' in such a relatively accessible and unlikely backwater...If this boat was indeed deposited deliberately, so were the joints of meats, the animal parts and the timber. Indeed, such a hypothesis moves inextricably towards the conclusion that this may well have been a ritual act (Ransley 2002, 39–40).

At Holme Pierrepont on the River Trent in Nottinghamshire, three logboats were found buried under nearly 4.5m of gravel deposits, tilted at angles, and two caught up with fallen waterlogged oak trees and timber beams (MacCormick 1968, 16–7). One of the boats was associated with a wooden cart or chariot wheel, now dated to the later first millennium BC (Stead 1996, 79). In addition to another Iron Age and Romano-British settlement (Guilbert *et al.* 1994), timber piling has been recognised nearby, and two early Iron Age swords were found in the Trent near the site (Cowen 1967; Scurfield 1997, 35). The context of the three logboats suggested to MacCormick that 'they had been overwhelmed by flooding and came to rest only where further passage downstream was blocked by tree trunks' (MacCormick 1968, 26).

Although their final resting place is strongly suggestive of a flood-created 'log jam', there are still some questions about how the boats got there, and why the one was so closely associated with a wheel. Were they just swept away during a flood, along with some disused timbers and a wheel that were nearby, or were they lost whilst transporting these objects? Or, were they deliberately set adrift carrying these objects? The logboat found with the wheel had a longitudinal split in its stern, and attempts had been made to repair it – perhaps it was being decommissioned. The association of the boat and wheel may be significant – not only are both perhaps metaphors of journeys and travel, but the wheel was also associated with sun or sky gods (Green 1997, 41–7), and miniature metal wheels have been found in some late Iron Age or Romano-British hoards in Britain, as well as portrayed on some antefixes and metal fittings. Interestingly, a lathe-turned wooden disc was part of a series of placed deposits in the large waterhole at the centre of the Hoveringham Romano-British enclosure (Chadwick 2004a, 98; Elliott and Knight 1998, 30). Two logboats have recently been excavated at Fiskerton up against the timber causeway, and may have been placed deposits (J. Rylatt *pers. comm.*).

2 At Sutton Common near Askern in South Yorkshire, two palisaded enclosures were situated on slight rises or 'islands' in what would have been carr and reed swamp, with a marshy watercourse running between them, and standing water surrounding them. A timber causeway linked the two enclosures. Excavations by the South Yorkshire Archaeology Unit and Sheffield University in the 1980s and early 1990s established that it was constructed during 550–200 BC (Parker Pearson and Sydes 1997, 229). More recent excavations of the larger enclosure in 1998–2003 by the Universities of Hull and Exeter demonstrated that that it had impressive entrances to the west and east formed by massive timbers, and numerous 4-post granary structures. Following a period of disuse, in the late Iron Age it was the location of a cremation burial cemetery (Chapman 2003; Chapman and Van de Noort 2001).

The director of this later excavation project seemed puzzled that there were no signs of domestic occupation within the larger enclosure (Van de Noort 2004, 67–8), but there are many reasons to think that the site enjoyed high status and considerable ceremonial significance (q.v. Parker Pearson and Sydes 1997, 255). A very inadequate excavation sample of the ditch terminals by the western entrance into the larger enclosure nonetheless recovered fragments of two human skulls. The eastern entrance was associated with a causeway leading out into the marsh, but bizarrely, this was not excavated, despite the fact that Sutton Common lies within a significant local cluster of Bronze Age metalwork finds (Parker Pearson and Sydes 1997, 234; P. Robinson *pers. comm.*). Had this been investigated, placed deposits might well have been found.

3 In Nottinghamshire, small coarse sherds recovered from Dunston's Clump (Garton 1987, 43–44), Holme Pierrepont (Guilbert *et al.* 1994, 22), South Muskham (Garton 1998), Priest Ings (Knight and Priest 1997) and Hoveringham (Elliott and Knight 1998) are all either Iron Age, or belong to the Iron Age tradition in the immediate post-conquest period. In South Yorkshire, late Iron Age sherds have been recovered at Pickburn Leys (Sydes 1993), Church Field, Rossington (Atkinson 1998), Armthorpe (Cumberpatch and Webster 1998; Evans 2001), Redhouse Farm, Adwick-le-Street (Cumberpatch 2001), Balby Carr (Rose 2003) and Topham Farm, Sykehouse (Cumberpatch *et al.* 2003). In West Yorkshire, enclosures at St. Aidan's Remainder, Methley (Barkle 1995), Willow Grove, Methley (Yarwood and Marriott 1988), Moss Carr, Methley (Roberts and Richardson 2002), South Elmsall (Howell 1998), and Swillington Common South, Manor Farm and Parlington Hollins (Roberts *et al.* 2001), and Ferrybridge (Roberts 2005a) have all produced Iron Age ceramics, and larger assemblages were found at Ledston (Faull and Moorhouse 1981, 120; Roberts 2005b; Runnacles and Buckland 1998) and Dalton Parlours (Wrathmell and Nicholson 1990, 128). Nevertheless, many settlements may have been largely aceramic in the first centuries BC and AD, employing wooden and leather containers instead.

4 I am indebted to Melanie Giles for this interesting suggestion.

5 Pryor believes that insights derived from his knowledge of agricultural practices are pertinent for later British prehistory, as pastoral farmers 'are still essentially conservative in their methods' (Pryor 1996, 313). But although some of his ideas are interesting and informative, his 'common-sense' explanations may not always be valid. He sees these later prehistoric landscapes as essentially familiar to us today, with patterns of fields, hedgerows and small farmsteads (Pryor 1998, 125). But although some of these features appear superficially similar to modern rural landscapes, they were created and perceived by people living between two to four millennia ago. Other archaeologists have noted that in the past people may have had very different ideas about identity, tenure and the land, cosmologies and beliefs, and social organisation and practices, including agriculture (Evans 1997b; Knight 2002a; 2002b).

Acknowledgements

I would like to thank Vicki Cummings and Bob Johnston for inviting me to speak at their TAG session, and for all of their comments and editorial assistance. Fraser Brown of Oxford Archaeology North and Ian Roberts of Archaeological Services (WYAS) have both provided me with much unpublished information, as have Alison Deegan, David Knight, Pete Robinson and Jim Rylatt. I would also like to thank Louisa Matthews, Jim McNeil, Dinah Saich and Roy Sykes of the South Yorkshire Archaeology Service, the staff of the West Yorkshire Archaeology Service, especially Andrea Burgess and Vince Devine (now at Cadw), and the staff of the Bassetlaw Museum in Retford. I am indebted to Tim Allen, Bill Bevan, Andrea Burgess, Chris Cumberpatch, Mark Edmonds, Chris Fenton-Thomas, Melanie Giles, Kate Howell, Mark Knight, Colin Merrony, Richard O'Neill, Mike Parker Pearson, Rachel Pope, Jesse Ransley, Graham Robbins and Helen Wickstead for being such good friends and valued discussants over the years. Anne Leaver kindly produced the publication illustrations, and Melanie Giles, Joshua Pollard, Jesse Ransley and Jeremy Taylor commented on early drafts of this article, but any remaining inaccuracies or wild statements remain the author's own responsibility.

Bibliography

Alexander, B. and Alexander, C. 1996. *The vanishing Arctic.* London: Blandford.

Archaeological Services West Yorkshire Archaeology

Service. 2001. *West Moor Park, Armthorpe, South Yorkshire: archaeological evaluation and excavation.* Unpublished report: Archaeological Services WYAS.

Arensberg, C.M. and Kimball, S.T. 1948. *Family and community in Ireland.* Cambridge, Mass.: Harvard University Press.

Atkinson, S. 1998. Survey and excavation at Church Field, Stripe Road, Rossington, Doncaster. In C. Cumberpatch, J. McNeil and S. Whiteley (eds), *Archaeology in South Yorkshire 1995–1996*, 15–19. Sheffield: SYAS.

Barkle, R.R. 1995. *St. Aidan's remainder: research archive.* Unpublished report: West Yorkshire Archaeology Service.

Basso, K.H. 1996. Wisdom sits in places: notes on a Western Apache landscape. In S. Feld and K.H. Basso (eds), *Senses of place*, 53–90. Washington: University of Washington Press.

Bastow, M. and Murray, M. 1990. Botanical remains. In S. Wrathmell and A. Nicholson (eds), *Dalton parlours: Iron Age settlement and Roman villa*, 259–67. Wakefield: West Yorkshire Archaeology Service.

Battaglia, D. 1990. *On the bones of the serpent: person, memory and mortality in Sabarl Island society.* Chicago: Chicago University Press.

Berg, D. 2001. The physical environment. In I. Roberts, A. Burgess and D. Berg (eds), *A new link to the past: the archaeological landscape of the M1–A1 link road*, 3–9. Leeds: West Yorkshire Archaeology Service.

Bird-David, N. 1990. The giving environment: another perspective on the economic system of hunter-gatherers. *Current Anthropology* 31, 183–96.

Bird-David, N. 1999. 'Animism' revisited: personhood, environment and relational epistemology. *Current Anthropology* 40, S67–S91.

Bogaard, A. 1997. *Report on the charred plant remains from Scrooby Top, Nottinghamshire.* Unpublished draft report: ARCUS.

Bourdieu, P. 1977. *Outline of a theory of practice.* Cambridge: Cambridge University Press.

Boyle, A. 2004a. Riding into history. *British Archaeology* 76, 27.

Boyle, A. 2004b. The Ferrybridge chariot burial. *Current Archaeology* 191, 485.

Boyle, A., Evans, T., O'Connor, S., Spence, A. and Brennand, M. forthcoming. Site D (Ferry Fryston) in the Iron Age and Romano-British periods. In F. Brown, C. Howard-Davis, M. Brennand, A. Boyle, T. Evans, S. O'Connor, A. Spence, R. Heawood and A. Lupton, *The Archaeology of the A1(M) Darringtron toDishforth DBFO Road Scheme.* Lancaster: Oxford Archaeology North.

Branigan, R. 1989. An early landscape revisited. In D. Kennedy (ed.), *Into the sun: essays in air photography in archaeology in honour of Derrick Riley*, 161–6. Sheffield: Department of Prehistory and Archaeology.

Brody, H. 2001. *The other side of Eden: hunter-gatherers, farmers, and the shaping of the world.* London: Faber and Faber.

Brown, F., Heawood, R., Howard-Davis, C.H. and Lupton, A. forthcoming. *Archaeological investigations along the route of the A1(M) Darrington to Dishforth Road Scheme.* Lancaster: Lancaster Imprints.

Buckland, P.C. 1979. *Thorne Moor: a palaeoecological study of a Bronze Age site.* Birmingham: University of Birmingham Department of Geography Occasional Paper 8.

Buckland, P.C. 1986. *Roman South Yorkshire: a source book.* Sheffield: Department of Archaeology and Prehistory.

Burgess, A. 2001a. The earlier prehistoric periods. In I. Roberts, A. Burgess and D. Berg (eds), *A new link to the past: the archaeological landscape of the M1–A1 Link Road*, 254–60. Leeds: West Yorkshire Archaeology Service.

Burgess, A. 2001b. The Iron Age. In I. Roberts, A. Burgess and D. Berg (eds), *A new link to the past: the archaeological landscape of the M1–A1 Link Road*, 260–9. Leeds: West Yorkshire Archaeology Service.

Burton, J.W. 1980. The village and the cattle camp: aspects of Atuot religion. In I. Karp and C.S. Bird (eds), *Explorations in African systems of thought*, 268–97. Bloomington, Ind.: Indiana University Press.

Burton, J.W. 1982. Figurative language and the definition of experience: the role of ox-songs in Atuaot social theory. *Anthropological Linguistics* 24 (3), 263–79.

Butler, J. 1993. *Bodies that matter: on the discursive limits of 'sex'.* London: Routledge.

Carter, S. and Hunter, F. 2003. An Iron Age chariot burial from Scotland. *Antiquity* 77, 531–5.

Chadwick, A.M. 1995. Further work on the Iron Age and Romano-British landscape at Edenthorpe. In C.G. Cumberpatch, J. McNeil and S.P. Whiteley (eds), *Archaeology in South Yorkshire 1994–1995*, 41–9. Sheffield: South Yorkshire Archaeology Service.

Chadwick, A.M. 1997. Towards a social archaeology of later prehistoric and Romano-British field systems in South Yorkshire, West Yorkshire and Nottinghamshire. Assemblage 2. World Wide Web http://www.shef.ac.uk/~assem/2.

Chadwick, A.M. 1998. *A study of possible Iron Age and Romano-British features revealed by aerial photographs of cropmarks on Coal Measures and Magnesian limestone areas of South Yorkshire: rectification and interpretation.* University of Sheffield: unpublished MA report.

Chadwick, A.M. 1999. Digging ditches, but missing riches? Ways into the Iron Age and Romano-British cropmark landscapes of the north midlands. In B. Bevan (ed.), *Northern exposure. Interpretative devolution and the Iron Ages in Britain*, 149–71. Leicester: Leicester Archaeological Monographs.

Chadwick, A.M. 2004a. 'Heavier burdens for willing shoulders'? Writing different histories, humanities and social practices for the Romano-British countryside. In B. Croxford, H. Eckardt, J. Meade and J. Weekes (eds), *TRAC 2003: Proceedings of the Thirteenth Annual Theoretical Roman Archaeology Conference*, 90–110. Oxford: Oxbow Books.

Chadwick, A.M. 2004b. 'Geographies of sentience' – an introduction to space, place and time. In A.M. Chadwick (ed.), *Stories from the landscape: archaeologies of inhabitation*, 1–31. Oxford: Archaeopress.

Chadwick, A.M. 2004c. Rivers, lakes, springs and streams. In A.M. Chadwick (ed.), *Stories from the landscape: archaeologies of inhabitation*, 52–4. Oxford: Archaeopress.

Challis, A. and Harding, D.W. 1975. *Later prehistory from the Trent to the Tyne*. Oxford: British Archaeological Reports.

Chapman, H.P. 2003. *Wetland research in South Yorkshire – recent work at Sutton Common and Thorne and Hatfield Moors*. Paper presented at the South Yorkshire Archaeology Day, University of Sheffield, November 2003.

Chapman, H.P. and Van de Noort, R. 2001. High-resolution wetland prospection, using GPS and GIS: landscape studies at Sutton Common (South Yorkshire), and Meare Village East (Somerset). *Journal of Archaeological Science* 28, 365–75.

Coles, B.J. 1990. Anthropomorphic wooden figurines from Britain and Ireland. *Proceedings of the Prehistoric Society* 56, 315–33.

Connerton, P. 1989. *How societies remember*. Cambridge: Cambridge University Press.

Coote, J. 1992. 'Marvels of everyday vision': the anthropology of aesthetics and the cattle-keeping Nilotes. In J. Coote and A. Shelton (eds), *Anthropology, art and aesthetics*, 245–73. Oxford: Clarendon Press.

Cowen, J.D. 1967. The Hallstatt sword of bronze: on the continent and in Britain. *Proceedings of the Prehistoric Society* 33, 377–464.

Cox, C. 1984. *Cropmarks on the Magnesian limestone north of the river Don in South Yorkshire*. University of Sheffield: unpublished MA dissertation.

Crandall, D.P. 1998. The role of time in Himba valuations of cattle. *Journal of the Royal Anthropological Institute* 4, 101–114.

Cumberpatch, C.G. 2001. Pottery from excavations at Redhouse Farm, Adwick-le-Street, Doncaster, South Yorkshire. Unpublished draft report produced for Northamptonshire Archaeology. Cumberpatch, C.G., Leary, R. and Willis, S. 2003. The pottery. In I. Roberts, *Excavations at Topham Farm, Sykehouse, South Yorkshire: a Late Iron Age and Romano-British Settlement in the Humberhead Levels*, 18–24. Wakefield: West Yorkshire Archaeology Service.

Cumberpatch, C.G., Leary, R. and Willis, R. 2003. The Pottery. In I. Roberts, *Excavations at Topham Farm, Sykehouse, South Yorkshire. A Late Iron Age and Romano-British Settlement in the Humberhead Levels*. 18–24. Leeds: Archaeology Service WYAS.

Cumberpatch, C.G. and Robbins, G. 1995. *The Iron Age in South Yorkshire, with reference to evidence from north Nottinghamshire and West Yorkshire*. Unpublished paper.

Cumberpatch, C.G. and Webster, S. 1998. Preliminary results of an archaeological evaluation at Nutwell Lane, Armthorpe. In C. Cumberpatch, J. McNeil and S. Whiteley (eds), *Archaeology in South Yorkshire 1995–1996*, 19–22. Sheffield: SYAS.

Cunliffe, B. 1991. Iron Age Communities in Britain. London: Routledge.

Davies, E. 1984–85. *Hafod* and *lluest*. The summering of cattle and upland settlement in Wales. *Folk Life* 23, 76–96.

Davies, G., Parker Pearson, M. and Robbins, G. 1997. *Report on the excavation of the enclosure at Scrooby Top, Nottinghamshire*. Unpublished report: ARCUS/University of Sheffield.

de Certeau, M. 1988. *The practice of everyday life*. Berkeley: University of California Press.

Deegan, A. 1996. North Nottinghamshire field systems – a landscape overview. *Aerial Archaeology Research Group* 12, 18–24.

Deegan, A. 1998. *The interpretation of Nottinghamshire field systems*. Paper presented at the Workshop on Iron Age and Romano-British Cropmark Landscapes in the North Midlands, Sheffield University, February 1998.

Deegan, A. 2001a. *Air photo mapping and interpretation of land at Armthorpe, South Yorkshire*. Unpublished report: Air Photo Mapping.

Deegan, A. 2001b. Aerial photographs. In I. Roberts, A. Burgess and D. Berg, *A New link to the past: the archaeological landscape of the M1–A1 Link Road*, 13–35. Leeds: West Yorkshire Archaeology Service.

Descola, P. and Pálsson, G. (eds) 1996. *Nature and society: anthropological perspectives*. London: Routledge.

Dobney, K. 2001. A place at the table: the role of vertebrate zooarchaeology within a Roman research agenda for Britain. In S. James and M. Millett (eds), *Britons and Romans: advancing an archaeological agenda*, 36–45. London: Council for British Archaeology.

Dodgshon, R.A. 1981. *Land and society in early Scotland*. Oxford: Clarendon.

Dodgshon, R.A. 1992. Farming practices in the Western Highlands and islands before crofting: a study in cultural inertia or opportunity costs? *Rural History* 3, 173–89.

Dyson-Hudson, N. 1973. Turkana. In a harsh land: a precarious survival, an arduous civility. In M.B. Grosvenor (ed.), *Primitive worlds: people lost in time*, 84–111. Washington: National Geographic Society.

Eccles, J., Caldwell, P. and Mincher, R. 1988. Salvage excavations at a Romano-British site at Chainbridge Lane, Lound, Nottinghamshire, 1985. *Transactions of the Thoroton Society of Nottinghamshire* 92, 15–21.

Elder, G., Wolch, J. and Emel, J. 1998. Race, place and the bounds of humanity. *Society and Animals* 6 (2), 183–202.

Elliott, L. and Knight, D. 1998. Further excavations of an Iron Age and Romano-British settlement at Hoveringham Quarry, Nottinghamshire. *Tarmac Papers* 2, 29–38.

Elsdon, S.M. 1992. East Midlands Scored Ware. *Transactions of the Leicestershire Archaeological and Historical Society* 66, 83–91.

Evans, C. 1987. Nomads in 'Waterland'? prehistoric transhumance and Fenland archaeology. *Proceedings of the Cambridge Antiquarian Society* 76, 27–39.

Evans, C. 1997a. Hydraulic communities: Iron Age enclosure in the East Anglia fenlands. In A. Gwilt and C. Haselgrove (eds), *Reconstructing Iron Age societies*, 216–27. Oxford: Oxbow.

Evans, C. 1997b. Sentimental prehistories: the construction of the Fenland past. *Journal of European Archaeology* 5 (2), 105–36.

Evans, J. 1995. Later Iron Age and 'native' pottery in the north-east. In B. Vyner (ed.), *Moorland monuments: studies in the archaeology of north-east Yorkshire in honour of Raymond Hines and Don Spratt*, 46–68. York: Council for British Archaeology.

Evans, J. 1998. The Roman pottery: discussion. In J. Evans (ed.), *The West Yorkshire rural Romano-British pottery sites: the pottery*. Unpublished report: West Yorkshire Archaeology Service.

Evans, J. 2001. Pottery. In J. Richardson, *West Moor Park, Armthorpe, South Yorkshire: archaeological evaluation and excavation*. Unpublished report: Archaeological Services WYAS.

Evans-Pritchard, E.E. 1940. *The Nuer: a description of the modes of livelihood and political institutions of a Nilotic people*. Oxford: Clarendon Press.

Faull, M.L. and Moorhouse, S.A. (eds) 1981. *West Yorkshire: an archaeological survey to AD 1500*. Leeds: University of Leeds.

Fenton, A. 1976. *Scottish country life*. Edinburgh: John Donald.

Fenton-Thomas, C. 2003. *Late prehistoric and early historic landscapes on the Yorkshire chalk*. Oxford: Archaeopress.

Fenton-Thomas, C. forthcoming. Mobile and enclosed landscapes on the Yorkshire Wolds. In A.M. Chadwick (ed.), *Recent approaches to the archaeology of land allotment*. Oxford: Archaeopress.

Field, N. and Parker Pearson, M. 2003. *Fiskerton: Iron Age timber causeway with Iron Age and Roman votive offerings*. Oxford: Oxbow.

Fitzpatrick, A.P. 1997. *Archaeological excavations on the route of the A27 Westhampnett Bypass, West Sussex, 1992. Volume 2: the cemeteries*. Salisbury: Wessex Archaeology.

Fowler, C.S. and Turner, N.J. 1999. Ecological/cosmological knowledge and land-management among hunter-gatherers. In R.B. Lee and R. Daly (eds), *The Cambridge encyclopaedia of hunter-gatherers*, 419–25. Cambridge: Cambridge University Press.

Fulford, M. 2001. Links with the past: pervasive 'ritual' behaviour in Roman Britain. *Britannia* 32, 199–218.

Galaty, J.G. 1989. Cattle and cognition: aspects of Maasai practical reasoning. In J. Clutton-Brock (ed.), *The walking larder: patterns of domestication, pastoralism, and predation*, 215–30. London: Unwin Hyman.

Garton, D. 1987. Dunston's Clump and the brickwork plan field systems at Babworth, Nottinghamshire. *Transactions of the Thoroton Society of Nottinghamshire* 111, 16–73.

Garton, D. 1998. *The South Muskham Fieldwalking Project 1992–7*. Nottingham: Trent and Peak Archaeological Trust/University of Nottingham.

Garton, D., Hunt, C.O., Jenkinson, R.D.S. and Leary, R.S. 1988. Excavations at a Romano-British cropmark enclosure near Menagerie Wood, Worksop, Nottinghamshire. *Transactions of the Thoroton Society of Nottinghamshire* 92, 22–3.

Garton, D. and Salisbury, C.R. 1995. A Romano-British wood-lined well at Wild Goose Cottage, Lound, Nottinghamshire. *Transactions of the Thoroton Society of Nottinghamshire* 99, 15–41.

Geertz, C. 1983. *Local knowledge: further essays in interpretative anthropology*. London: Fontana.

Gell, A. 1998. *Art and agency: an anthropological theory*. Oxford: Oxford University Press.

Giles, M. 2000. *'Open-weave, close-knit': archaeologies of identity in the later prehistoric landscape of East Yorkshire*. University of Sheffield: Unpublished PhD thesis.

Giles, M. 2002. *Harnessing histories in later prehistoric East Yorkshire*. Paper presented at the Landscapes of Inhabitation, Taskscapes of Tradition conference, University of Wales Newport, March 2002.

Giles, M. and Parker Pearson, M. 1999. Learning to live in the Iron Age: dwelling and praxis. In B. Bevan (ed.), *Northern exposure: interpretative devolution in the British Iron Ages*, 217–31. Leicester: Leicester Archaeological Monographs.

Gillison, D. 2002. *New Guinea ceremonies*. New York: Abrams.

Giorgi, J.A. 2004. The charred plant remains. In P.G.E. Neal and R. Fraser, A Romano-British enclosed farmstead at Billingley Drive, Thurnscoe, South Yorkshire. *Yorkshire Archaeological Journal* 76, 7–92.

Grant, A. 1984. Survival or sacrifice: a critical reappraisal of animal burials in Britain in the Iron Age. In J. Clutton Brock and C. Grigson (eds), *Animals and archaeology 4: husbandry in Europe*, 221–7. Oxford: British Archaeological Reports.

Grant, A. 1991. Economic or symbolic? Animals and ritual behaviour. In P. Garwood, D. Jennings, R. Skeates and J. Thoms (eds), *Sacred and profane*, 109–14. Oxford: Oxford University.

Green, M. 1997 [1986]. *The Gods of the Celts* (3rd edition). Stroud: Sutton.

Gudeman, S. and Rivera, A. 1990. *Conversations in Colombia: the domestic economy in life and text*. Cambridge: Cambridge University Press.

Guenther, M. 1988. Animals in Bushman thought, myth and art. In T. Ingold, D. Riches and J. Woodburn (eds), *Hunters and gatherers volume two: property, power and ideology*, 192–202. Oxford: Berg.

Guilbert, G., Fearn, K. and Woodhouse, G. 1994. Archaeological evaluation of crop-marks near Holme Pierrepont, Nottinghamshire 1992 – interim report. *Transactions of the Thoroton Society of Nottinghamshire* 98, 19–23.

Hallowell, A.I. 1960. Ojibwa ontology, behaviour and world view. In S. Diamond (ed.), *Culture in history: essays in honour of Paul Radin*, 19–52. New York: Columbia University Press.

Hart, M. and Ingelby, J. 1990. *Life and tradition in the moorlands of north-east Yorkshire*. Otley: J.M. Dent.

Harvey, D. 1996. *Justice, nature and the geography of difference*. Oxford: Blackwell.

Hayes, P. 1981. New approaches to ancient fields. In G. Barker (ed.), *Prehistoric communities in Northern England*, 105–21. Sheffield: Department of Prehistory and Archaeology.

Hill, J.D. 1992. Can we recognise a different European past? A contrastive archaeology of later prehistoric settlements in southern England. *Journal of European Archaeology* 1, 57–75.

Hill, J.D. 1995. *Ritual and rubbish in the Iron Age of Wessex: a study on the formation of a specific archaeological record*. Oxford: British Archaeological Reports.

Howell, D.W. 1977. *Land and people in nineteenth-century Wales*. London: Routledge and Kegan Paul.

Howell, J.K. 1998. *Land to the north of Field Lane (Area D),*

South Elmsall, West Yorkshire. Unpublished assessment report: Archaeological Services (WYAS).

Howell, J.K. 2001. Swillington Common. In I. Roberts, A. Burgess and D. Berg (eds), *A new link to the past: the archaeological landscape of the M1–A1 Link Road*, 47–68. Leeds: West Yorkshire Archaeology Service.

Ingold, T. 1980. *Hunters, pastoralists and ranchers: reindeer economies and their transformations.* Cambridge: Cambridge University Press.

Ingold, T. 1986. *The appropriation of nature: essays on human ecology and social relations.* Manchester: Manchester University Press.

Ingold, T. (ed.) 1988. *What is an animal?* London: Unwin Hyman.

Ingold, T. 1996a. Growing plants and raising animals: an anthropological perspective on domestication. In D. Harris (ed.), *The origins of agriculture and pastoralism in Eurasia*, 12–24. Washington D.C.: Smithsonian Institution Press.

Ingold, T. 1996b. Hunting and gathering as ways of perceiving the environment. In R. Ellen and K. Fukui (eds), *Redefining nature: ecology, culture and domestication*, 117–55. Oxford: Berg.

Ingold, T. 2000. *The perception of the environment: essays in livelihood, dwelling and skill.* London: Routledge.

Ingold, T. 2001. From complementarity to obviation: on dissolving the boundaries between social and biological anthropology, archaeology and psychology. In S. Oyama, P.E. Griffiths and R.D. Gray (eds), *Cycles of contingency: developmental systems and evolution*, 255–79. Cambridge, Ma.: MIT Press.

Ingold, T. 2004. Culture on the ground: the world perceived through the feet. *Journal of Material Culture* 9 (3), 315–40.

Ingold, T. and Jones, A. 2002. From the perception of archaeology to the anthropology of perception: an interview with Tim Ingold. *Journal of Social Archaeology* 3 (1), 5–22.

Jones, G. 1987. The plant remains. In D. Garton, Dunston's Clump and the brickwork plan field systems at Babworth, Nottinghamshire. *Transactions of the Thoroton Society of Nottinghamshire* 111, 58–61.

Jones, O. and Cloke, P. 2002. *Tree cultures: the place of trees and trees in their place.* Oxford: Berg.

Kayano, S. 1994. *Our land was a forest: an Ainu memoir* (trans. K. Selden and L. Selden). Boulder, Colorado: Westview Press.

Knight, D. and Elliott, L. forthcoming. Towards a bounded landscape: the earliest field systems of the Trent Valley. In A.M. Chadwick (ed.), *Recent approaches to the archaeology of land allotment.* Oxford: Archaeopress.

Knight, D. and Howard, A.J. 2004. *Trent Valley landscapes.* King's Lynn: Heritage Marketing and Publications.

Knight, D. and Priest, V. 1997. Excavations of a Romano-British field system at Lamb's Close, Kelham, Nottinghamshire. *Transactions of the Thoroton Society of Nottinghamshire* 102, 27–36.

Knight, M. 2002a. *Working next to Flag Fen and other prehistories.* Paper presented at the Landscapes of Inhabitation, Taskscapes of Tradition conference, University of Wales College Newport, Caerleon, March 2002.

Knight, M. 2002b. *Finding it different.* Paper presented at the session on the Archaeology of Land Allotment, 24th annual Theoretical Archaeology Group conference, Manchester University, December 2002.

Latour, B. 1993. *We have never been modern.* Hemel Hempstead: Harvester/Wheatsheaf.

Law, J. and Hassard, J. (eds) 1999. *Actor network theory and after.* Oxford: Blackwell.

Lefebvre, H. 1991. [1974]. *The production of space* (trans. D. Nicolson-Smith). Oxford: Blackwell.

Lorimer, H. 2004. *Herding memories of humans and animals.* World Wide Web http://web.geog.gla.ac.uk/olpapers/hlorimer001.pdf

MacCormack, C. and Strathern, M. (eds) 1980. *Nature, culture and gender.* Cambridge: Cambridge University Press.

MacCormick, A.G. 1968. Three dug-out canoes and a wheel from Holme Pierrepont, Nottinghamshire. *Transactions of the Thoroton Society of Nottinghamshire* 72, 14–31.

Macnaghten, P. and Urry, J. 1998. *Contested natures.* London: Sage.

Mauss, M. 1973 [1934]. Techniques of the body. *Economy and Society* 2 (1), 70–88.

McGrail, S. 1981. *The Brigg 'Raft' and her prehistoric environment.* Oxford: British Archaeological Reports.

McGrail, S. 1987. *Ancient boats in north-west Europe: the archaeology of water transport to AD 1500.* London: Longman.

McGrail, S. 1990. Early boats in the Humber basin. In S. Ellis and D. Crowther (eds), *Humber perspectives: a region through the ages*, 199–210. Hull: Hull University Press.

Merleau-Ponty, M. 1962 [1945]. *Phenomenology of perception.* London: Routledge.

Millett, M. 1999. New perspectives on the *civitas Parisorum.* In P. Halkon and M. Millett (eds), *Rural settlement and industry: studies in the Iron Age and Roman archaeology of lowland East Yorkshire*, 221–7. Leeds: Yorkshire Archaeology Society.

Millett, M. and McGrail, S. 1987. The archaeology of the Hasholme logboat. *Archaeological Journal* 144, 69–155.

Morris, T. and Garton, D. 1998. Romano-British ditch digging at East Carr, Mattersey, Lound Quarry, Nottinghamshire. *Tarmac Papers* 1, 51–63.

Murdoch, J. 1997. Inhuman/nonhuman/human: actor-network theory and the potential for a non-dualistic and symmetrical perspective on nature and society. *Environment and Planning D* 15, 731–56.

Neal, P.G.E. and Fraser, R. 2004. A Romano-British enclosed farmstead at Billingley Drive, Thurnscoe, South Yorkshire. *Yorkshire Archaeological Journal* 76, 7–92.

Noske, B. 1989. *Humans and other animals: beyond the boundaries of anthropology.* London: Pluto Press.

Ó Danachair, C. 1983–84. Summer pasture in Ireland. *Folk Life* 22, 36–41.

O'Dowd, A. 1981. *Meitheal: a study of co-operative labour in rural Ireland.* Dublin: Comhairle Bhéaloideas Éireann

O'Neill, R. 2001a. Roman Ridge. In I. Roberts, A. Burgess

and D. Berg (eds), *A new link to the past: the archaeological landscape of the M1–A1 Link Road*, 105–117. Leeds: West Yorkshire Archaeology Service.

O'Neill, R. 2001b. The Roman period. In I. Roberts, A. Burgess and D. Berg (eds), *A new link to the past: the archaeological landscape of the M1–A1 Link Road*, 269–80. Leeds: West Yorkshire Archaeology Service.

Parker Pearson, M. 1999. Food, sex and death: cosmologies in the British Iron Age with particular reference to East Yorkshire. *Cambridge Archaeological Journal* 9 (1), 43–69.

Parker Pearson, M. 2000. Eating money: a study in the ethnoarchaeology of food. *Archaeological Dialogues* 7 (2), 217–33.

Parker Pearson, M. and Sydes, R.E. 1997. The Iron Age enclosures and prehistoric landscape of Sutton Common, South Yorkshire. *Proceedings of the Prehistoric Society* 63, 221–59.

Pavitt, N. 1991. *Samburu*. London: Kyle Cathie.

Petts, D. 1998. Landscape and cultural identity in Roman Britain. In R. Laurence and J. Berry (eds), *Cultural identity in the Roman Empire*, 79–124. London: Routledge.

Philo, C. and Wilbert, C. (eds) 2000. *Animal spaces, beastly places: new geographies of human-animal relations*. London: Routledge.

Pollard, J. 1996. Iron Age riverside pit alignments at St. Ives, Cambridgeshire. *Proceedings of the Prehistoric Society* 62, 93–116.

Pryor, F.M.M. 1996. Sheep, stockyards and field systems: Bronze Age livestock populations in the Fenlands of eastern England. *Antiquity* 70, 313–24.

Pryor, F.M.M. 1998. *Farmers in prehistoric Britain*. Stroud: Tempus.

Ramm, H. 1980. Native settlements east of the Pennines. In K. Branigan (ed.), *Rome and the Brigantes: the impact of Rome on northern England*, 28–40. Sheffield: Department of Prehistory and Archaeology.

Ransley, J. 2002. *A contextual analysis of prehistoric logboats: readdressing Northern European examples from later prehistory*. University of Southampton: unpublished MA dissertation.

Rappaport, R.A. 1984 [1968]. *Pigs for the ancestors: ritual in the ecology of a New Guinea People* (2nd edition). New Haven: Yale University Press.

Richardson, J. 2001. Soil, plant and invertebrate evidence: conclusions. In I. Roberts, A. Burgess and D. Berg (eds), *A new link to the past: the archaeological landscape of the M1–A1 Link Road*, 246–8. Leeds: West Yorkshire Archaeology Service.

Richardson, J. 2005. The pit alignment. In I. Roberts (ed.), *Ferrybridge henge: the ritual landscape*, 53–71. Leeds: West Yorkshire Archaeology Service.

Riley, D.N. 1980. *Early landscape from the air*. Sheffield: Department of Prehistory and Archaeology.

Robbins, G. 1998. Cropmark landscapes and domestic space. *Assemblage* 3. World Wide Web http://www.shef.ac.uk/~assem/3.

Roberts, I. 1995. Excavation of a D-shaped enclosure at Upton, West Yorkshire. *Yorkshire Archaeology Journal* 67, 7–22.

Roberts, I. 2003. *Excavations at Topham Farm, Sykehouse, South Yorkshire. A Late Iron Age and Romano-British Settlement in the Humberhead Levels*. Wakefield: West Yorkshire Archaeology Service.

Roberts, I. (ed.) 2005a. The adaptation of the landscape from the later Iron Age. In I. Roberts (ed.), *Ferrybridge henge: the ritual landscape*, 210–18. Leeds: West Yorkshire Archaeology Service.

Roberts, I. (ed.) 2005b. *Excavations at the Iron Age Settlement at Ledston, West Yorkshire, 1976 and 1996*. Wakefield: West Yorkshire Archaeology Service.

Roberts, I., Burgess, A. and Berg, D. (eds) 2001. *A new link to the past: the archaeological landscape of the M1–A1 Link Road*. Leeds: West Yorkshire Archaeology Service.

Roberts, I. and Richardson, J. 2002. *Iron Age and Romano-British settlement enclosures at Moss Carr, Methley, West Yorkshire*. Leeds: West Yorkshire Archaeology Service.

Rose, M. 2003. *Balby Carr, Doncaster, South Yorkshire: archaeological evaluation*. Unpublished report: Archaeological Services (WYAS).

Runnacles, R.B. and Buckland, P.C. 1998. Ledston Iron Age pottery. In J. Evans (ed.), *The West Yorkshire rural Romano-British sites: the pottery*. Unpublished report: West Yorkshire Archaeology Service.

Samuels, J. and Buckland, P.C. 1978. A Romano-British settlement at Sandtoft, South Humberside. *Yorkshire Archaeological Journal* 50, 65–75.

Sayce, R.Y. 1956. The old summer pastures: a comparative study. *Montgomeryshire Collections* 54, 117–45.

Sayce, R.Y. 1957. The old summer pastures part 2: life at the *hafod*. *Montgomeryshire Collections* 55, 7–86.

Scaife, R.G. 1992. Flag Fen: the vegetational environment. *Antiquity* 66, 462–66.

Scurfield, C.J. 1997. Bronze Age metalworking from the river Trent in Nottinghamshire. *Transactions of the Thoroton Society of Nottinghamshire* 101, 29–57.

Serpell, J. 1985. From paragon to pariah: some reflections on human attitudes to dogs. In J. Serpell (ed.), *The domestic dog*, 246–56. Cambridge: Cambridge University Press.

Serpell, J. 1986. *In the company of animals*. Oxford: Blackwell.

Sillitoe, P. 1983. *Roots of the earth: crops in the Highlands of Papua New Guinea*. Manchester: Manchester University Press.

Sökefeld, M. 1999. Debating self, identity and culture in anthropology. *Current Anthropology* 40 (4), 417–47.

Speed, G. and Rogers, P.W. 2004. A burial of a Viking woman at Adwick-le-Street, South Yorkshire. *Medieval Archaeology* 48, 51–90.

Stallibrass, S. 1987. The animal bones. In M. Millett and S. McGrail, The archaeology of the Hasholme logboat. *Archaeological Journal* 144, 69–155.

Stead I.M. 1992. *Iron Age cemeteries in East Yorkshire*. London: English Heritage.

Stead, I.M. 1996. *Celtic Art in Britain before the Roman Conquest* (2nd edition). London: British Museum.

Strathern, M. 1980. No nature, no culture: the Hagen case. In C. MacCormack and M. Strathern (eds), *Nature, culture and gender*, 174–222. Cambridge: Cambridge University Press.

Strathern, M. 1988. *The gender of the gift: problems with women and problems with society in Melanesia*. Berkeley, Ca.: University of California Press.

Sydes, R.E. 1993. Excavations at Pickburn Leys, Adwick-le-Street, Doncaster. In M.J. Francis and C.G. Cumberpatch (eds), *Archaeology in South Yorkshire 1992–1993*, 36–42. Sheffield: SYAS.

Tambiah, S.J. 1969. Animals are good to think with and good to prohibit. *Ethnology* 8, 423–59.

Tanner, A. 1979. *Bringing home animals: religious ideology and mode of production of the Mistassini Cree hunters*. London: Hurst.

Tapper, R. 1988. Animality, humanity, morality, society. In T. Ingold (ed.), *What is an animal?*, 47–62. London: Unwin Hyman.

Taylor, J. 1997. Space and place: some thoughts on Iron Age and Romano-British landscapes. In A. Gwilt and C. Haselgrove (eds), *Reconstructing Iron Age societies*, 192–203. Oxford: Oxbow.

Taylor, J. 2001. Rural society in Roman Britain. In S. James and M. Millett (eds), *Britons and Romans: advancing an archaeological agenda*, 46–59. London: Council for British Archaeology.

Thomas, J. 2003 Prehistoric pit alignments and their significance in the archaeological landscape. In J. Humphrey (ed.), *Re-searching the Iron Age*, 79–86. Leicester: Leicester Archaeology Monographs 11.

Thomas, J. forthcoming. An empty hole, or a meaningful whole? Approaches to the study of pit alignments. In A.M. Chadwick (ed.), *Recent approaches to the archaeology of land allotment*. Oxford: Archaeopress.

Thomas, R. 1997. Land, kinship relations and the rise of enclosed settlement in first millennium B.C. Britain. *Oxford Journal of Archaeology* 16 (2), 211–8.

Thrift, N. 1996. *Spatial formations*. London: Sage.

Unwin, T. 1983. Townships and early fields in north Nottinghamshire. *Journal of Historical Geography* 9 (4), 341–6.

Van de Noort, R. 2004. *The Humber Wetlands: the archaeology of a dynamic landscape*. Macclesfield: Windgather Press.

Van de Noort, R. and S. Ellis (eds) 1997. *Wetland heritage of the Humberhead Levels: an archaeological survey*. Hull: University of Hull.

Van der Veen, M. 1992. *Crop husbandry regimes: an archaeobotanical study of farming in northern England 1000 BC – AD 500*. Sheffield: Department of Archaeology and Prehistory.

Vitebsky, P. 2005. *Reindeer people: living with animals and spirits in Siberia*. London: Harper Collins.

Ward, A.H. 1997. Transhumance and settlement on the Welsh uplands: a view from the Black Mountain. In N. Edwards (ed.), *Landscape and settlement in Medieval Wales*, 97–111. Oxford: Oxbow.

Watanabe, H. 1972. *The Ainu ecosystem. Environment and group structure*. Seattle: University of Washington Press.

Watanabe, H. 1999. The Ainu ecosystem. In W.W. Fitzhugh and C.O. Dubreuil (eds), *Ainu: spirit of a northern people*, 198–201. Washington: University of Washington Press/Smithsonian Institute/Arctic Studies Centre.

Whatmore, S. 2002. *Hybrid geographies: natures, cultures, spaces*. London: Sage.

Wheelhouse, P. 2005. The ritual monuments. In I. Roberts (ed.), *Ferrybridge henge: the ritual landscape*, 21–49. Leeds: West Yorkshire Archaeology Service.

Whimster, R. 1989. *The emerging past: air photography and the buried landscape*. Abingdon: RCHME.

Willis, R. (ed.) 1990. *Signifying animals: human meaning in the natural world*. London: Unwin Hyman.

Willis, S. 1997. Settlement, materiality and landscape in the Iron Age of the East Midlands: evidence, interpretation and wider resonance. In A. Gwilt and C. Haselgrove (eds), *Reconstructing Iron Age societies*, 205–15. Oxford: Oxbow.

Wolch, J. and Emel, J. (eds) 1995. *Animal geographies; place, politics and identity in the nature-culture borderlands*. London: Verso.

Woodward, P. and Woodward, A. 2004. Dedicating the town: urban foundation deposits in Roman Britain. *World Archaeology* 36 (1): 68–86.

Wrathmell, S. and Nicholson, A. (eds) 1990. *Dalton parlours. Iron Age settlement and Roman villa*. Wakefield: West Yorkshire Archaeology Service.

Wrathmell, S. 2001. *Romano-British enclosures at Apple Tree Close, Pontefract, West Yorkshire: excavations, 1987*. Leeds: West Yorkshire Archaeology Service.

Wright, W.M. 1990. *The Ferriby boats: seacraft of the Bronze Age*. London: Routledge.

Wright, W.M., Hedges, R., Bayliss, A. and Van de Noort, R. 2001. New AMS dates for the Ferriby boats: a contribution to the origins of sea-faring. *Antiquity* 75, 726–34.

Yarwood, B. 1981. The environmental background. In M.L. Faull and S.A. Moorhouse (eds), *West Yorkshire: an archaeological survey to AD 1500*, 33–72. Leeds: University of Leeds.

Yarwood, B. and Marriott, J. 1988. Willow Grove, Methley SE411266. *CBA Group 4 Forum 1988*, 27.